Margate before Sea Bathing

MARGATE BEFORE SEA BATHING

(1300 – 1736)

Anthony Lee

Droit House Press

Margate before Sea Bathing

By Anthony Lee

First edition published 2015

Copyright © 2015 Anthony Lee

All rights reserved. No part of this publication may be reproduced, stored in a retrieval system, or transmitted, in any form or by any means, without the prior permission in writing of the publisher, nor be otherwise circulated in any form of binding or cover other than that in which it is published and without a similar condition including this condition being imposed on the subsequent purchaser.

Typeface: Fournier

Printing: CreateSpace

Web site: www.Margatelocalhistory.co.uk.

Contents

Regnal Years	vi
Notes on Dates and Money	vii
Plan of the Town of Margate	ix
Introduction	1
CHAPTER 1: The Town	12
CHAPTER 2: The Pier and the Harbour	71
CHAPTER 3: The People of Margate	123
CHAPTER 4: The Poor	164
CHAPTER 5: Managing Margate	203
CHAPTER 6: Riots and Wars	271
The Future	331
Notes	336
Index	368

Regnal Years

Edward I	20 Nov. 1272-7 July 1307
Edward II	8 July 1307-20 Jan. 1327
Edward III	25 Jan. 1327-21 June 1377
Richard II	22 June 1377-29 Sept. 1399
Henry IV	30 Sept. 1399-20 Mar. 1413
Henry V	21 Mar. 1413-31 Aug. 1422
Henry VI	1 Sept. 1422-4 Mar. 1461 (and 9 Oct. 1470-14 Apr. 1471)
Edward IV	4 Mar. 1461-9 Apr. 1483
Edward V	9 Apr. 1483-25 June 1483
Richard III	26 June 1483-22 Aug. 1485
Henry VII	22 Aug. 1485-21 Apr. 1509
Henry VIII	22 Apr. 1509-28 Jan. 1547
Edward VI	28 Jan. 1547-6 July 1553
Mary	6 July 1553-24 July 1554
Philip and Mary	25 July 1554-17 Nov. 1558
Elizabeth I	17 Nov. 1558-24 Mar. 1603
James I	24 Mar. 1603-27 Mar. 1625
Charles I	27 Mar. 1625-30 Jan. 1649
Interregnum	30 Jan. 1649-29 May 1660
Charles II	29 May 1660-6 Feb. 1685 (but reckoned from 30 Jan. 1649)
James II	6 Feb. 1685-11 Dec. 1688
Interregnum	12 Dec. 1688-12 Feb. 1689
William and Mary	13 Feb. 1689-27 Dec. 1694
William III	28 Dec. 1694-8 Mar. 1702
Anne	8 Mar. 1702-1 Aug. 1714
George I	1 Aug. 1714-11 June 1727
George II	11 June 1727-25 Oct. 1760

From: David Hey, (Ed.), *The Oxford Companion to Family and Local History*, Oxford University Press, 2008.

Notes on Dates and Money

A Note on Dates:

From the 12th century until 1751 there were two ways of counting a year. There was the 'historical' year starting on 1 January and there was also the 'civil year' starting on 25 March (Lady day). This means that, in this period, any day between 1 January and 24 March inclusive would be in different historical and civil years. For example, 7 February 1694 in the historical calendar corresponds to 7 February 1693 in the civil calendar; such a date would often appear in records as 7 February 1693-4, to take account of the two calendars. After 1751 only the historical year was used. Here, all dates are written as historical years.

A Note on Money:

Values were expressed in units of pounds, shillings, and pence: £3 7s 6d is three pounds, seven shillings and six pence.
    1 pound (£1) = 20 shillings (20s)
    1 shilling (1s) = 12 pence (12d)
    1 guinea = 21s
    1 farthing = ¼d

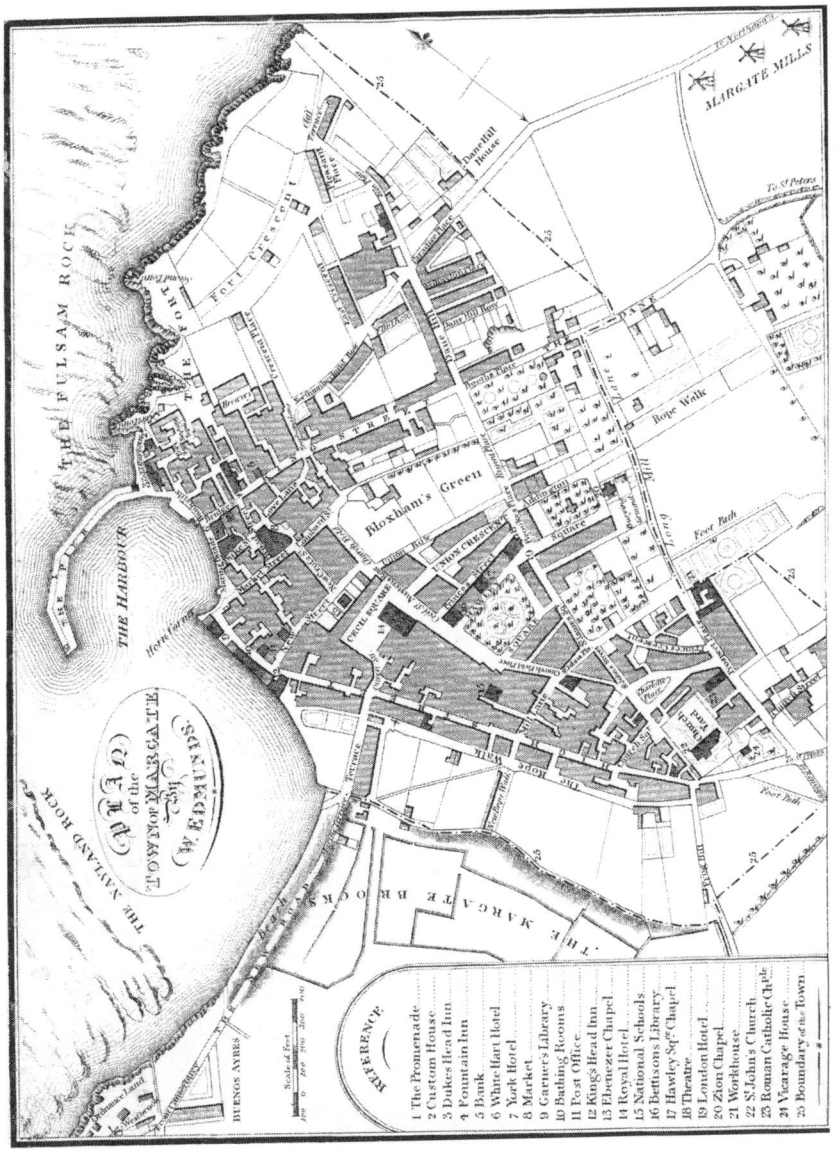

Edmund's map of Margate 1821. A larger scale version is available at www.margatelocalhistory.co.uk

Introduction

Even then Margate received a bad press. John Leland, visiting the town during his famous tour of England in 1535-1543, wrote that 'Margate lyith in St John's paroche, yn Thant, a V myles upward fro Reculver, and there is a village and a peere for shyppes, but now sore decayed'.[1] John Evelyn who visited Margate in 1672 described the town as consisting of 'brewers of a certain heady ale [Northdown Ale]' with a good trade in malt, but 'for the rest is raggedly built; and an ill haven, with a small fort of little concernement'.[2] A member of William III's household reported that, returning from the continent in 1691, the King landed at a 'wretched village called Marguet'.[3] Things were no better in the 1720s when Daniel Defoe visited the town: 'The town of Margate is eminent for nothing that I know of, but for King William's frequently landing here in his returns from Holland, and for shipping a vast quantity of corn for London Market'.[4] Even John Lewis, vicar of the local parish, described Margate in 1723 as 'a small fishing town, irregularly built, and the houses very low'.[5]

Until the early part of the eighteenth century Margate was, then, little more than a village, depending on farming and shipping for its survival. It was known by a variety of names including Marguet, Mergate and Meregate, and lay on the northern coast of the Isle of Thanet, in the parish of St John's, one of the seven parishes in the island, the others being St Peter's, St Lawrence, Minster, Birchington, St Nicholas and Monkton. Although in fact the Isle of Thanet was no longer an island it had once been separated from the rest of Kent by the rivers Stour and Wantsom, and still kept the name. The parish of St John's was about three and a half miles across in each direction and Margate occupied just a small part of the parish.[6]

The first picture we have of Margate is in an oil painting, *The*

Figure 1. A watercolour of 'Marcoaet' by the Dutch artist Michiel van Overbeck, who was in England between 1663 and 1666.
© Trustees of the British Museum.

Embarkation at Margate of Elector Palatine and Princess Eliȝabeth, by the Dutch painter Adam Willaerts, dating from 1623, one of a series illustrating the marriage of the Elector Palatine to Princess Elizabeth, the daughter of James I. After the marriage ceremony, the couple and their retinue travelled to the coast at Margate where they boarded the English flagship, *Prince Royal*, and eventually set sail for the continent on April 25 1613. The painting shows the royal couple about to board the *Prince Royal* with Margate represented by a small cluster of houses in a gap in the cliffs. Houses climb a hill to the left, with a church and two windmills on the horizon; on the sea shore itself is a large cylindrical structure issuing smoke. Although Willaerts lived most of his life in Utrecht he was born in London and it is possible that he actually saw Margate on his travels from London to Holland.[7] If so, his picture of Margate could be more than just a formulaic representation of a typical English scene. The large cylindrical structure on the shore is puzzling and, if not a fort of some kind, could represent a lime kiln or a kiln for burning seaweed to make kelp, a process that was common in Margate at the time.

Luckily there is no ambiguity about the second early picture of Margate, a watercolour by another Dutch artist, Michiel van Overbeck, who was in England between 1663 and 1666 (Figure 1). The drawing, labelled 'Marcoaet', shows high cliffs to the east and low ones to the west, on either side of a large creek; a boat is shown entering the creek. Buildings line the creek and, as in Willaerts' picture, climb up the slopes of the hill leading to the Church; there is a windmill on the horizon. The ramshackle state of the harbour is all too apparent.

The original line of the creek can be traced easily in modern maps of the town. Deposits of sand and sea pebbles have often been uncovered during building work in Margate, showing that the creek used to extend from the sea along the line of the present King Street and Dane Road. As described by Arthur Rowe 'we have to picture to ourselves a Creek which was always tidal to some extent, and when northerly gales and high spring tides prevailed we can well imagine that the sea rushed up what is now King Street almost as far as Addiscombe Road'.[8] Further along Dane Valley, salt water driven inland would have met fresh water issuing from the many springs lining the sides of the valley; at one time the Creek would have drained the whole of the Dane Valley. Again quoting Arthur Rowe, the presence of a sheltered creek and ample spring water made the area suitable for settlement: 'early sea-faring man asked but three things — spring-water to drink, a reasonably safe offing for his fishing, and a secure haven for his little dug-out boats, which he could draw up on the high ground when the sea bore too heavily on him'.[8]

The creek, at its seaward end, was some 150 yards wide, stretching between the bottom end of the High Street and the northern side of King Street at its junction with the Parade at the bottom of Fort Hill. The southern boundary of the creek followed the line of Market Street, Market Place and Lombard Street, and through what was Garden Row and is now the supermarket at the bottom of Hawley Street; the northern boundary of the creek followed the line of King Street and Dane Road.[8,9] Buildings on the Parade and those in Broad Street, Duke Street, Market Place, the bottom of Hawley Street and the lower part of King Street all had to have their foundations strengthened by piles because of the old creek.[8] Excavations in King Street have uncovered timber piles that could have lined the sides of the creek.[9]

With time the main channel of the creek became narrower and, together with several of its branches, came to serve as an open drain for the town. As late as 1799 George Carey provided an unflattering description of the area: 'What the old Parade might have been is no easy matter to tell, but in its present state, and in this improving age, it has little to boast of in respect to elegance, or even cleanliness, and in rainy weather it is a mere swamp. The greater part of it lies between a noisy stable-yard, well furnished with manure, and the common sewer [then an open channel] of the contiguous Market Place as well as all the lower part of the town, which frequently yields up the most ungrateful exhalations and unsavoury smells to those who choose to regale themselves in this delicious neighbourhood'.[10]

Growth of Margate to the west was limited by another stretch of water, a mere or lake, commonly called the *Brooks*. This originally formed a large sheet of water measuring some 300 yards at its outlet, extending inland as far as the site of the Tivoli Gardens and cut off from the sea by a sand-bar.[8] The Brooks gradually silted up to form a marshy area intersected by ditches, making it difficult to enter the town from the west. Because of the Brooks there was no coach road along the coast; the road from Sarre to St Nicholas at Wade, Birchington and Westgate was only a bridle-track ending at the cliff edge near Westbrook Mill, where Royal Crescent now stands. The lack of a road from Westbrook Mill into Margate meant that the few inhabitants of Westbrook would often be cut off from Margate, except at low water; access to the town at high tide could only be obtained by passing through the fields to Salmestone and Frog Hill.[8] The land to the west of Margate was only developed after a massive road embankment was carried along the shore line early in the nineteenth century, although even then Lower Marine Terrace had to be built on exceptionally long piles and the London Chatham and Dover Railway embankment across the Brooks had to be built on thousands of bundles of brushwood sunk into the marsh land.[8]

The best description of Margate in its early days is that provided by John Lewis in his *History and antiquities ecclesiastical and civil, of the Isle of Tenet, in Kent*, published in 1723:[5]

Mergate seems to have had its name from their being in it a gate or way into the Sea which lies just by a little Mere, called by the inhabitants now the *Brooks*. By this gate is situated the vill [*vill* is an old term for a hamlet or village] called Meregate, partly on the side of a hill, and partly in a little valley one end of which goes into the sea. It is a small Fishing Town, irregularly built, and the houses very low, and has formerly been of good repute for the fishing and coasting Trade.

On that part of the town which lies next the Sea, is a Peer of timber, built East and West, in the form of a half moon to defend the bay from the main sea, and make a small harbour ... By the present appearance of the Chalky rocks on each side of this Peer at low water, it should seem as if anciently Nature itself had formed a Creek or harbour there, the mouth of which was just broad enough to let small vessels go in it. But, as the land on each side of this creek was, in the process of time, washed away by the sea, the inhabitants were obliged to build this Peer, to keep their town from being overflown by the ocean; and to defend that part of it which lies next the water by Jettes, or Piles of timber. This Peer was at first, but small, and went but a little way out into the sea; But the land still continuing to wash away, so that the sea lay more heavily on the back of it than usual, it has been, by degrees, enlarged.

On a little Hill, about half a Mile from the lower part of *Mergate* next the Sea, stands the Church, which is dedicated to *St John Baptist*.

The extent of erosion around the creek is obvious in modern maps of the coast line. The most accurate of the early maps of Kent is a half-inch scale map surveyed and drawn by Philip Symonson and published in 1596.[11] This shows the bay as a clear half-circle, very different from what is shown on modern maps, where many of the surrounding cliffs have gone, particularly on the east side.

Lewis described the rest of the parish of St John's as follows:[5]

Besides the vill of Mergate, there are other lesser vills or clusters of houses in this parish, viz. 1. West-brooke, so called for being situate on the west-side of the Mere just by Mergate, commonly called the Brooks. 2. Garlinge, which is a pretty large vill, consisting of about 20 or 30 houses, about midway betwixt Mergate and Birchington. 3. Shonken-dane. 4. Lyden. 5. Flete. 6. Little Nash, partly in this parish and partly in St Peter's. 7. East-North-down, which is likewise part of it in St Peter's. 8. West-North-down. 9. Lucas-dane, almost joining to Mergate East, in the same valley.

Margate probably developed from two small hamlets, one a group of fishermen's cottages nestling around the outlet of the creek, and the other a group of houses clustered around the parish church that had been built in about 1050 on elevated ground about half a mile from the creek. A third hamlet, straggling along the valley marked by the present King Street and Dane Road, was known as Wilds Dane, Lucas Dane, Lucks Dane, Luke Dane, or Luke's Dane, from the Anglo-Saxon 'denu', a valley.[12,13] Lewis, in the quotation just given, referred to it as 'almost joining to Mergate East, in the same valley'. The name persisted locally in the parish rate books until about 1800, with the valley farm being known as Luke Dane Farm, Lukes Dane Farm, or Lucas Dane Farm.[12] The origin of the name is uncertain, but a will from St John's, that of John Safoull in 1474, includes a bequest 'to Simon Grannte a certain messuage called Lukke and six acres of land, to his heirs for ever', and another local will, that of Simon Grannt in 1486, includes a bequest to his wife Isabella of 'my tenement called Lukks, and thirty acres of land until my son comes to the age of 20 years then to John'.[14] Lucas Dane could have taken its name from the house called Lukke or Lukks. The will of John Lucas, a 'shipman', in 1486 leaves land to his wife Alice at 'the Lutt park', which, given the difficulty in distinguishing between the written 't' and 'c' could also be read as 'Luce park'; Lucas Dane could therefore also take its name from the family of Lucas.[14]

Another 'Dane' also appears in early wills, Palmer Dane. The will of Thomas Baseley of St John's in 1479 leaves to his sister Agnes 'three acres of land situated in Palmers Dane, and to her heirs for ever', that of Simon att Berough in 1491 decrees that 'one acre and a half in the Cumbe [a valley] and three rods at Palmerden shall be sold to pay my debts', and that of Roger Johnson in 1498 decrees that 'one acres and half of land at Palmersden to be sold, and the money to my wife Joan to pay debts'.[14] The location of Palmer Dane is not known.

The two main settlements, around the creek and around the church, are still clear in Harris's map of the Isle of Thanet of 1717 (Figure 2). Buildings can be seen around the creek and along the road leading to St John's church, and it seems likely that the name Margate referred initially to just this built up area. The earliest surviving Parish Rate Book dating from 1666 shows that the Parish Overseers for the Poor divided the parish into three parts: the first corresponded to the outlying regions of the parish, *Nash, Fleet and Lidden, Westbrook, Garlinge, Dandelyon*, and *Northdown*; the second, *Church hill*, corresponded to the area around the church, including much farm land; and the third, *Margate*, contained the largest number of rateable properties in the parish, and was concentrated close to the harbour.[15] Precisely which parts of the parish were covered by the name Margate is not totally clear and even at the time could lead to confusion. For example, in the thirteenth century the original

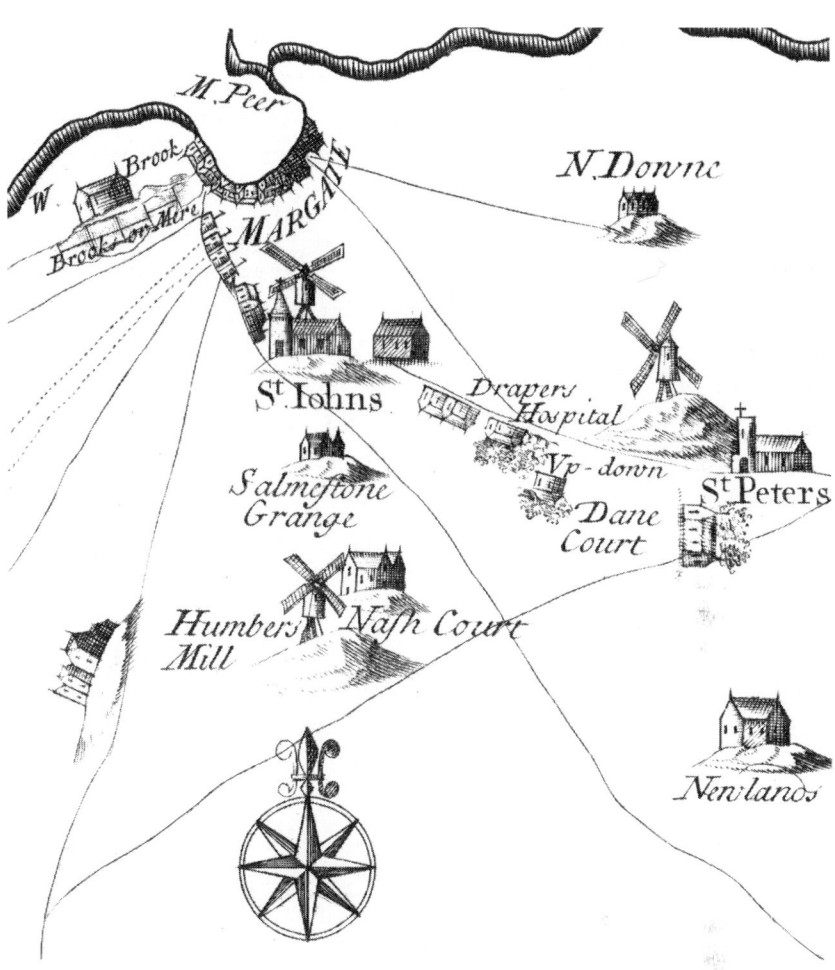

Figure 2. A section from Harris's map of the Isle of Thanet of 1717, showing the parish of St John's. From *John Harris, History of Kent, D. Midwinter, London, 1719.*

Confederation of the Cinque Ports was extended with the addition of new members referred to as 'limbs', one of which was Margate, which became a limb of Dover.[16,17] This meant that Margate shared the privileges of the other members of the Cinque Ports and was answerable to the Justices of the Peace at Dover and not to the Justices of the Peace for Kent (Chapter 5). However, from time to time the Justices of the Peace for Kent tried to claim that the part of the parish of St John's that was not Margate came under their jurisdiction.[18] This situation was clearly untenable and Henry VIII solved the problem by also making St John's a limb of Dover, even though this meant that Margate was effectively included twice in the charter, once under its own name and once as part of St John's parish.[17,18] Dover simply considered Margate and St John's as one for purposes of taxation: in 1521 when the Cinque Ports received a demand for a levy from the King, 'Margate and St John' was ordered to pay 26s 8d,[19] and a list of debts due to Dover in 1530 included 'the contribution and forfeit of Margate and St John's, in Thanet, 53s 4d, unpaid cess money, fines and poundgelt'.[20] The issue of the exact boundary between Margate and the rest of the parish was only to become important much later with the introduction of property rates, different for town and country properties.

The populations of Margate and of the parish of St John's are uncertain before the nineteenth century, but it is possible to make some rough estimates. In the reign of Edward I (1272-1307) a tax, the Romescot, was collected for every hearth, and sent to Rome. The number of inhabitants of St John's paying the tax was 208, compared to 141 at St Lawrence and 163 at St Peter.[21] Assuming an average of five per household, this suggests a total population for the parish of about 1000. In 1377 the first poll tax was introduced, at a flat rate of one groat (four pence), charged on everyone over the age of 16, both male and female, with exceptions that included the clergy and those who could demonstrate that they were genuinely paupers. The number taxed in the parish of St John's was 264, compared to 54 in Birchington.[22] Although widespread evasion of the tax makes it difficult to use this figure to calculate an acurate population, it suggests a minimum population for the parish of about 600. Margaret Bolton used parish registers and probate records to estimate a population for the parish of about 810 in 1558, at the start of the reign of Elizabeth I, and 1020 in 1603, at the end of her reign.[23] A survey taken in 1566 reported that Margate had 108 houses and 8 'persons lacking proper habitation'.[24] At the visitation of Archbishop Parker in 1569 the number of houses in the parish was reported to be 120, with 400 communicants.[25] The muster role of 1599 lists 158 men for the Parish of St John's, a number that probably included all the able-bodied men in the parish;[23] an average of 5 per household would then give a population for the parish of around 800. When the hearth or chimney tax was collected in 1673 there were 552 hearths in the parish, in 174 houses; 100 houses occupied by the poor were excused.[21] In the Isle of Thanet as a whole there were 1142 houses, of which 364 were excused payment of the hearth tax.[21] A total of 274 houses in St John's suggests a total population of about 1,400 for the parish. A census of church goers in 1676 suggests an adult population for the parish of about 750 which, assuming 0.66 children per adult, gives a total population of about 1,300.[26] A similar number can be estimated from the 55 burials in 1680 which, assuming a scaling factor of 31 between population and burials, gives a population of about 1,700.[27,28] Lewis, in his *History of the Isle of Thanet*, estimated that there were about six hundred families in the parish in 1723, giving a population of about 2,400.[5] In 1781 there were 444 inhabited houses in the parish chargeable to window duties.[29]

It has been suggested that for a settlement to be counted as a town it had to have an independent local government, a diverse economic base, and a market; it also had to be a social and religious centre.[30] By these criteria Canterbury, Dover, Maidstone and Rochester were indisputably towns, but Margate was not. Indeed a list of 26 towns in Kent produced by John Norden in 1625 did not include Margate, and Margate was not one of the twelve towns in Kent listed by the early Tudor traveller John Leland.[30] A reading of the local newspaper, the *Kentish Post*, also suggests that Margate had few of the amenities expected of a fully-fledged town. For example, in 1726 the newspaper included advertisements for the sale of goods, properties and services in many local towns including Canterbury, Deal, Dover, Ramsgate and Sandwich, but none for Margate; Margate, it seems, had little to offer the surrounding towns. Nevertheless, even today the distinction between a small town and a large village is often unclear and Mary Dobson has described many of the towns in Kent at this time as being 'little more than overgrown villages, focused on and extending into the surrounding fields. Pigs and people roamed around the towns just as they did in the countryside. Kent in the seventeenth century was essentially a landscape of farming regions studded only with an array of small towns and cities serving, for the most part, the needs of a rural hinterland'.[31] Even in 1800 Edward Hasted in his *History and Topographical Survey of the County of Kent* was uncertain of the status of Margate, referring to it as 'the village or town, now called Margate'. What is certain is that Margate was the largest of the settlements in the Isle of Thanet, the population of Ramsgate in 1671, for example, being estimated to be 701, compared to the estimate of 1,173 for Margate.[32] This, combined with its extensive trade with London by sea, gave Margate at least some of the characteristics of a town, and, for simplicity, in what follows Margate will be referred to as a town.

Here the history of Margate is taken up to 1736, a date less arbitrary than it may at first seem. The fortunes of Margate were to be transformed by the fashion for sea bathing. Bathing and swimming have, of course, very long histories. The first book on swimming to be written in English, Everard Digby's A *Short Introduction for to Learne to Swimme*, was published as early as 1595, and William Shakespeare, in King Henry VIII, had Cardinal Wolsey say of his fall from power:

> I have ventur'd
> Like little wanton boys that swim on bladders,
> These many summers in a sea of glory;
> But far beyond my depth.

Even some Margate sailors knew how to swim, according to a report in the *Newcastle Courant* in 1739:[33]

On Tuesday morning last two young fellows, sailors belonging to Margate, went in a fishing boat to catch whitings and were drowned. They were taken up by the next day, and it was observed one of them had ript his boots, untied his handkerchief, and loosened his shirt buttons, to facilitate his swimming. They have left two young widows, and two children each.

Despite this long history, the commercial potential of sea bathing only became apparent in the eighteenth century, a potential first realised in Margate by Thomas Barber, a local carpenter, who placed the following advertisement in the *Kentish Post* in 1736:[34]

Whereas Bathing in Sea-Water has for several Years, and by great Numbers of People, been found to be of great Service in many Cronical Cases, but for want of a convenient and private Bathing Place, many of both Sexes have not cared to expose themselves to the Open Air: This is to inform all Persons that Thomas Barber, Carpenter, at Margate, in the Isle of Thanett, hath lately made a very convenient Bath, into which the Sea Water runs every tide through a Channel about 15 Foot long; You descend into the Bath from a private Room adjoining to it.

N.B. There are in the same House convenient Lodgings to be Lett.

The advertisement makes it clear that bathing in sea water at Margate for medical reasons was already fairly common by 1736. However, this was the first time that facilities had been provided specifically for visitors to Margate wishing to bathe in the sea, or, at least, in sea water. From these humble beginnings the 'House' referred to in the advertisement, the Black Horse Inn, developed into a major hotel and Margate developed into a town with assembly rooms, subscription balls, theatres, promenades, circulating libraries, and orchestras. Margate was no longer to be 'a small fishing town, irregularly built'.

CHAPTER 1

The Town

We are lucky to have a good description of Margate in 1723 in the first edition of John Lewis's *The history and antiquities ecclesiastical and civil, of the Isle of Tenet, in Kent*,[1] and, in the second edition of 1736,[2] a sketch map of the town (Figure 3) The map shows the harbour protected by a single curved pier designed to exclude winds and waves from the most dangerous direction, the north-east.[3] The Pier was a simple box-like structure consisting of wooden piles, packed with anything available, including chalk, soil, flint, and sand;[4] a stone structure would have been better able to withstand the winter storms, but there was no local source of stone. The harbour was dry at low water, and had to be entered with care at all times, as a long ledge of rock ran out from the West Cliff across the harbour mouth.[3] Lewis described it as 'a small harbor for ships of no great burden, and for fishing craft'.[1] The story of the Pier is told in Chapter 2.

To the north of the harbour, and overlooking it, was the Fort. This was a simple earthwork with platforms for guns, with a watch-house 'in which men watched with the Parish's Arms, provided for that purpose'.[1] The Fort, says John Lewis, was 'not only a safeguard to the town, but a great means of preserving merchants ships, going round the North Foreland into the Downes, from the enemies privateers, which often lurk there about to snap up ships sailing that way, which cannot see them behind the land'.[1] The Fort was later to become a popular place for visitors to meet and promenade, and is remembered in the name of the present Fort Hill. The history of the Fort is described in Chapter 6.

About half a mile from the harbour was the church of St John the Baptist. The church was first a chapel and then a dependency of St Mary's Minster in Thanet.[5] A chronicle compiled by Thorne, a monk of St Augustine's Abbey in about 1380 records that in 1124 St Mary's Minster and its chapels, including that of St John's, were all assigned for the upkeep of St Augustine's. The assignment was confirmed in 1182 and in 1237 St John's acquired a perpetual chaplain. The Archdeacon's visitations to St John's in the sixteenth century record that the church was in a very poor state of repair at that time, the chancel without a proper roof and the vicarage in ruins (Chapter 5).[7] Gradually, though, things improved and in 1769 the Church was described as:[6]

a large building of flints rough-cast, with the quoins, windows and door-cases of hewn stone. It has three isles, three chancels, and in the times of popery, there were three altars dedicated to St Anne, St John, and St George, and over them in niches stood the images of those saints. At the west end of the north isle stands the tower, which is square and low, with only a short spire on the top of it; and within this tower is a ring of five bells, the largest in the Island. Adjoining to the south side of the church yard, anciently stood two houses called the Wax-houses, where were made the wax lights used in the church, and at processions. The wax-houses burnt down in 1641.

In the fifteenth century a treasury was built on the north side of the church, 'a square building of hewn stone with battlements, and a flat roof covered with lead'.[1,5] At first this was used for the safe keeping of the church treasures but then became a general store-house for 'gun-powder, shot, match, &c. for the use of the Fort'.[1] In 1701 it was converted into a vestry, 'and a chimney built', presumably to keep those using the vestry warm in winter;[1] the vestry was used to hold parish meetings and administer poor relief. The west end of the south aisle of the church was partitioned off and used as a schoolroom, probably in the sixteenth century.[5]

Lewis's sketch map of Margate of 1736 shows how the town had developed around the bay (Figure 3). On the left of the map are the pier, the King's Warehouse, and the other warehouses. To the right (marked C on the map) are King George's Stairs, shown close to Horn Corner on Edmunds map of 1821, at the west end of what was to become the Marine Parade. Roughly midway between the landward end of the Pier and King George's Stairs is an inlet corresponding to the remains of the old creek; by the time of Edmund's map this had become Bridge Street, leading into King Street. Immediately to the west of King George's stairs another inlet

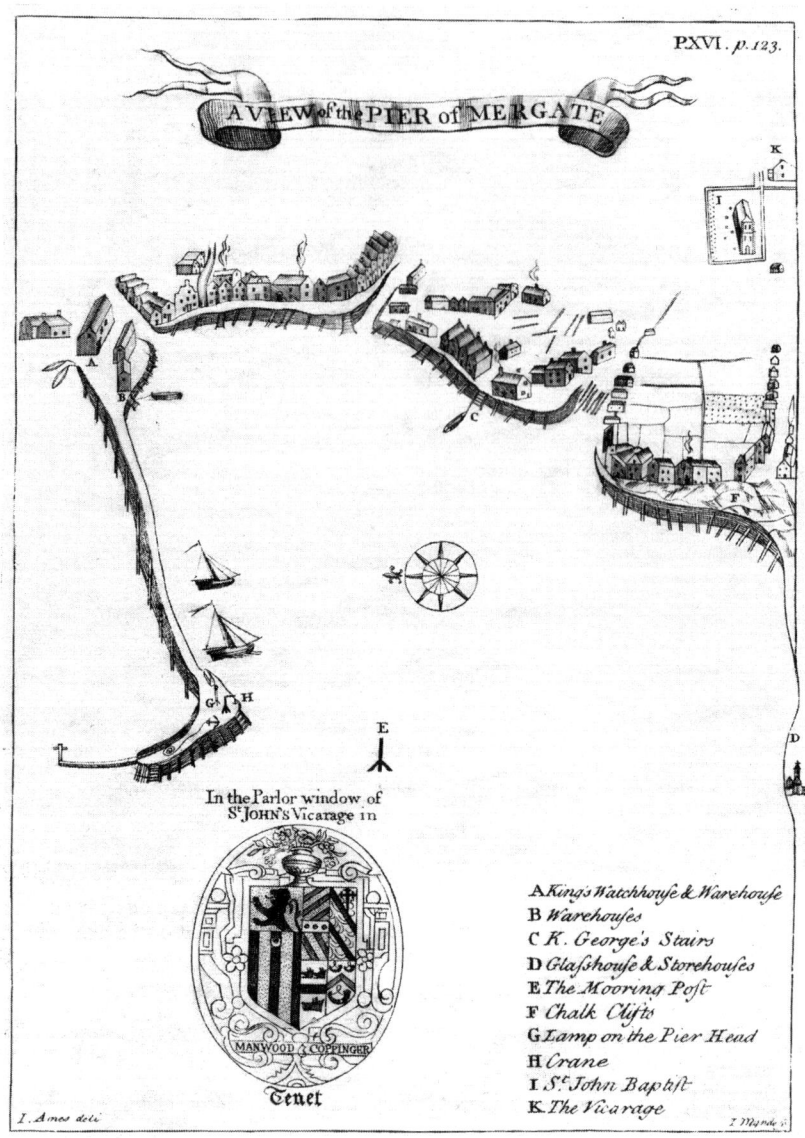

Figure 3. Margate in 1736, from John Lewis *The History and antiquities as well ecclesiastical as civil, of the Isle of Tenet, in Kent*, 2nd ed., 1736.

corresponds to the seaward end of the future Market Street. To the west of the inlet a road runs west a short way along the bay before turning inland and up the hill to the Church, corresponding to the present High Street. On the extreme right of the map, the 'Glasshouse and Storehouses' (D) probably correspond to a location west of the Brooks, around the position of Buenos Ayres in Edmund's map. The Glasshouse is described in an advertisement from 1723: 'There is now erecting in the Isle of Thanet a large Glass-house, with convenient store or warehouses for carrying on the Glass Trade, and the gentlemen concerned, propose, from the situation, to carry it on with less expense than attends those built about this City [London]'.[8] This scant information is all we have about the glasshouse. It is not certain why it was felt that Margate was a suitable place for the glass trade but the key factor could have been the ready availability of kelp ash used in the manufacture of glass and produced by the burning of kelp (sea weed). The production of kelp ash for the glass industry was continued in Margate until the 19th century, in Alkali Row.[9]

The larger of the Margate inns were concentrated close to the harbour, on what was to become the Parade and Bankside and, indeed, the largest of the buildings shown on Lewis's map of the town are in this area. Unfortunately the early Parade was not a very attractive place, as made clear by George Cary in the quotation already given from his guide book of 1799.[10] Lewis's map (Figure 3) shows the simple piles of timber, the jetties, lining the shore and protecting the town from the sea. These jetties were frequently damaged by winter storms. For example, in 1691 the inhabitants of Margate petitioned parliament asking for financial help as 'on the 10th and 13th days of October and the 8th of December last [1690], by the violent blowing of the north-west wind . . . that part of the town which is guarded by the pier and jetties, is so laid open that it is expected to be washed away if the wind should blow fresh at north-west'.[11]

Two of the roads leading towards the harbour were referred to as the King's Highway. One led from the Church to the harbour, and eventually became known as the High Street, a name first used in print in 1766, in an advertisement in a London newspaper for a property 'situated at the upper end of High-street, near the Church in Margate'.[12] The other King's Highway, leading to the east end of the future Parade, was later known as King Street. Traffic going to and from Canterbury entered the Isle of Thanet at Sarre, and then, according to the season of the year, took

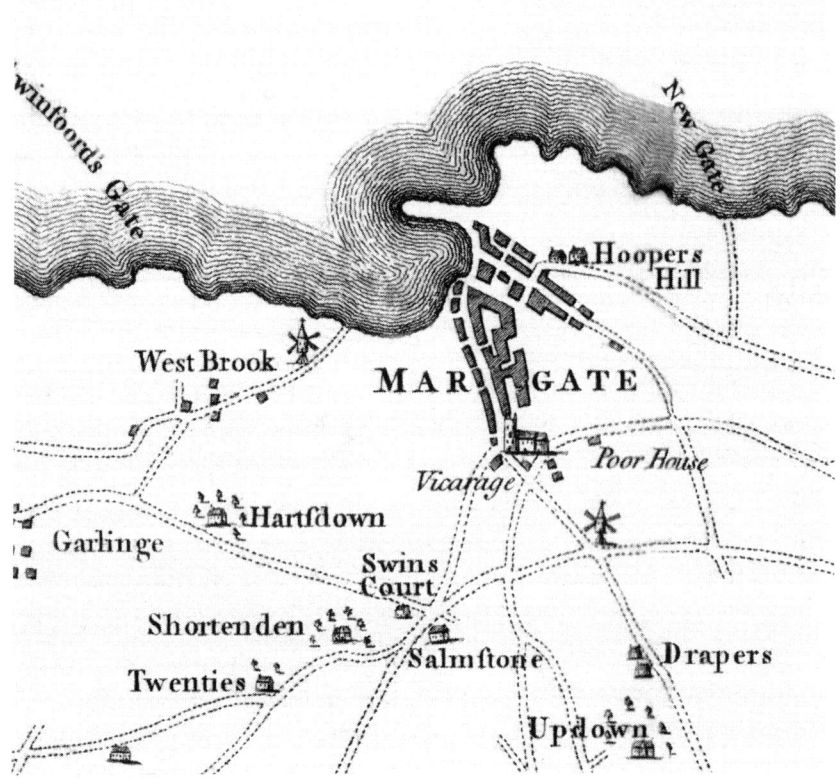

Figure 4. Detail from J. Hall's map of the Isle of Thanet of 1777.

either the summer or the winter road, the latter joining the former above Monkton, then passing through Acol, Hengrove, Twenties, Shottendane and Salmestone to join the first King's Highway. In Harris's map of 1717 (Figure 2) the junction between the road from Canterbury and the King's Highway is at a point roughly half way between the harbour and the Church. However, in Hall's map of 1777 (Figure 4) the road from Canterbury joins the King's Highway at a point opposite the Church. It may be that the local roads were realigned at some period between the publication of these two maps to meet the needs of the holiday trade.

The King's Highway leading from the Church to the harbour was narrow and winding. In *A description of the Isle of Thanet* published in 1765 the 'Principal street', as it was referred to, was described as being 'built on an easy descent, by which means the upper part is clean and dry, but the lower end much otherwise'.[13] Zechariah Cozens, in his *Tour through the Isle of Thanet*, published in 1793, says of the High-street that it was originally 'but a long dirty lane, consisting chiefly of malt-houses, herring-hangs, and the poor little cottages of fishermen'.[14] Malt-houses were buildings in which cereal grain, particularly barley, was converted into malt by soaking the grain in water, allowing it to sprout, and then drying it to stop further growth; the malt was used in brewing, and was either used locally or exported to London by hoy. A herring hang was a shed where the local herring catch was dried and smoked to preserve it. Malthouses and herring-hangs were important for the economy of Margate,[1] but would hardly have added to the attractions of this, the principal road into Margate. As late as 1799 George Seville Carey was reporting in his *The Balnea, an impartial description of all the popular Watering Places in England*, that 'there is no proper inlet to the town of Margate from any direction whatever; and what they call High-street is a close contracted thoroughfare; many parts of it filthy, with scarcely a decent habitation, and only serves in the present instance to show us what their now-flourishing town was in its original state. The street is too narrow for one carriage to pass another in the day, but in the night it is dangerous indeed!'[10]

The early history of the High Street is closely linked to the story of the Norwoods, a local family of prosperous yeomen with a long history described in detail in Peter Hill's book *Dane Court, St Peter's in Thanet*; what follows is taken largely from that book.[15] In the parish of St John's was the manor of Dene which, in the seventeenth century, was owned by the Norwood family; the Norwoods also owned Dane Court, a property in the parish of St Peter's, not to be confused with the manor of Dene. The story of the Norwood family in Thanet starts with Richard Norwood who bought Dane Court in about 1520. On the death of Richard Norwood, Dane Court passed to his son Alexander who died in 1558. Alexander Norwood was described in a document of 1551 as 'Baylif of Margate' and another Norwood, William Norwood, was similarly described as being 'portreeve of Margate' in the sixteenth century.[16,17] The exact meanings of the terms *baylif* and *portreeve* vary with time and place but generally a port-reeve is the bailiff of a port town and a port-reeve is the same as a Port warden,[18] a position known in Margate as a Pier warden, a position of some authority and importance in the town.

In his will dated 1 January 1558 Alexander Norwood specified that at the time of his burial, 'there be dispended and layde out . . . in the service of God, and to poore people' the sum of 40 shillings. There was a further 40 shillings for similar purposes, and within one month of his death £20 was to be distributed to the poor of St John's and St Peter's 'and in other deades of charitie, where moste neade shalbee': in addition, he gave to 'the poor of Margate all that mony that I have bestowed and layde out all redye'. His bequests included one to his son Valentine of 'all such store of come [corn?], cattal and other thinges' at Lucks Dane [Lucas Dane] in St John's 'where I dwell'. The main properties described in the will were the house and lands known as Lucks Dane, the Court House and barn with 20 acres of land also in St John's, leased to his son Alexander II, and Dane Court and a windmill in St Peter's. Lucks Dane went to his wife Joan and, after her death, descended to Alexander II who also inherited Dane Court. The location of the Court House is unknown.

Alexander II married Joan, nee Kempe, the widow of Roger Howlett of Margate, and all their children were baptised at St John's; at the time of his death in 1583 he was living at Lucks Dane. Alexander II and his wife Joan had three daughters and three sons who survived childhood. In his will Alexander II left to his wife Joan two annuities of £10 each, one 'issuinge and goinge out of my mansion house wherein I now inhabite [Lucks Dane] and out of all the landes thereunto belonginge' and the other 'out of my messuage and farme called Dane Court'. His properties included, in addition to Lucks Dane and Dane Court, 'my house at Margate called the Corte House, and my little house in the occupation of Peter Dalient and two parcells of arrable lande conjoyninge, by estimation six acres, lienge and beinge not far from the said little house', and a mill and land at St Peter's. These properties were to be used by his wife for seven years and then to go to his three sons, Lucks Dane to his son Joseph, Dane Court to his son Manasses, and his remaining property to his son Alexander III.

Manasses Norwood was responsible for a considerable expansion of the property owned by the Norwoods in Thanet, purchasing the manor of Dene, together with the Hengrove estate in the parish of St John's; the manor of Dene had passed into the hands of the Crown on the dissolution of the monasteries, and had then been granted by James I to William Salter who sold it to Manasses Norwood. On Manasses Norwood's death in 1637 most of his land went to his son Richard, and Richard, on his death in 1644, left most of his property to his three sons Alexander, the eldest, William, the middle son, and Paul, the youngest, although some land was to be sold for his daughter, this being 'lands lying on the east side of ye way leading from Church-hill to Margate'.[19] His will also included a small bequest of £10 a year to his 'good friend . . . Daniel Gibbons, gent' to be paid for from the windmill and lands in St John's.[15] Harris's map of Thanet (Figure 2) shows three windmills in Margate, one behind the Church, in what later became Mill Lane, one on rising ground S. S. W. of Nash Court and known as Humber's Mill, and one between Dandelion and Birchington, close to Quex. The map of Kent published by Symonson in 1596 shows just two of these three mills, Humber's Mill and the Mill near Quex.[20,21] The earliest known reference to a mill in the parish of St John's is in the report of the annual visitation of the Archdeacon of Canterbury to the parish in 1581, when Thomas Deale was reported 'for being absent from Common Prayer on the Sabbath Day, and for grinding with his wind mill':[7] this presumably corresponds to one of the two mills on Symonson's 1596 map. Humber's Mill burnt down in 1732: 'On Thursday the 16th past between nine and ten o'clock at night a fire broke out by an accident unknown in the windmill of the widow Pannell, commonly call'd Humber's Mill, in the Parish of St John Baptist in the Isle of Thanet, which in less than an hour's time burnt down the said mill, to the great impoverishment of the two poor families who had their dependence on it'.[22] It is likely that the windmill referred to in Richard Norwood's will of 1644 was the Mill Lane Mill.

The break up of the estate put together by Manasses Norwood proved to be the beginning of the end of the Norwoods' influence in Thanet. Alexander Norwood received, amongst other land, the manor of Dene, Nash Court, and other lands in St John's. It seems that Alexander ran up debts; he died before his mother and his mother's will records that he died owing her money. During his life he mortgaged the manor of Dene and part of the demesne lands (demesne land is land, not necessarily contiguous with a manor house, but retained by the owner of the manor for his own use). Alexander's widow was living in Nash Court when she died in 1706, and Nash Court was sold to David Turner, a yeoman of St John's.

The exact location of the demesne land belonging to the manor of

Dene is not known; Lewis reports that it amounted to 203 acres.[2] However, Lewis's description of the Vicarage land and the glebe land belonging to it provides some clues. Lewis says: 'the site of the Vicarage, with the dove-house, garden, containing one acre and three rods more or less, doth lie to the tenement of Edward Toddye and the land of John Goodwin East; to the church-yard and Deanery land in the tenure of Christopher Hayes West; to the common street and Church yard and tenement of the same Edward Toddy North; and to the King's Highway South'. Of the glebe land he says: 'one parcel of land containing four acres and one rod more or less doth lye at a place called the Vicars Cross, to Deanrye land, and the lands of Michael Allen east; to the King's Highway West; to Deanrie lands and the lands of the said John Goodwin North; and to Deanrie lands South'.[2] The Deanery (or Deanrie or Deanrye) land referred to here is land formerly belonging to the Manor of Dene, and Lewis's description shows that this included much land in the vicinity of the Church and the King's Highway.

The district around the Church was referred to as *Cherchedowne* and then as *Church Hill*. The reference to *Cherchedowne* occurs in a deed dating to 1444:[23]

William Crawe of the parish of St John, Isle of Thanet, grants to John Gotle, esq., of the same 5 roods lying at Cherchedowne between the land of the lord vicar of the parish of St John on the E. and the land of the Church of St John on the W. and the common way on the S. and N.

Warranty. Witnesses: John Cowharde, William Sprakelyng, John Lucas, Thomas Lyon, John Crosse and others.

The reference to the 'common way on the S. and N.' probably puts Churchedowne between the roads from Margate to St Peters, to the north, and to Ramsgate, to the south. Later the area around the Church was referred to in deeds and parish records as *Church Hill*. This included the upper end of the present High Street and the whole of the plateau on which the Church stood, including Frog Hill (now Grosvenor Gardens), the church-ward ends of Long Mill Lane (now Victoria Road) and Ramsgate Road and the old Church Field.[24] The King's Highway leading from Church Hill to the harbour ran for most of its length through farm land, and the settlements around the Church and around the harbour were originally quite distinct. This is reflected in the description in Richard

Norwood's will of 1644 quoted above of 'lands lying on the east side of ye way leading from Church-hill to Margate'; at this time Margate was used as a term for just the area around the harbour.[19]

When the Norwoods came to sell their land in St John's, they did so in a piecemeal fashion, selling off small quantities of land to individual purchasers, resulting in an interesting hotchpotch that survives to this day. In 1643 Richard Norwood sold 10 perches of land at Church Hill, adjacent to the King's highway, to Edward Poole, 'butcher of the parish of St John', and in 1647 Alexander Norwood sold him a further 10 perches of land, adjacent to the first.[19] Two years later, in 1649, Edward Poole, now described as a bricklayer, bought from Alexander Norwood 'his two messuages situated at or near a place commonly called by the name of Church-Hill, yielding one shilling a year at feast of St Michael the Archangel'.[19] In his 1661 will Edward Poole left to his son John Poole 'all that messuage, and one piece of land, situated at a place called Church-hill, with the Lyme Killne adjoining'.[19]

In 1647 Robert Todd, a mariner of St John's parish, gave Alexander Norwood £4 for:[25]

one piece or parcel of land containing by estimation 8 perches, lying and being in the said parish of St John Baptist, abutting to the lands of Edward Poole there towards the north, to the demesne land of the Manor of Deane there towards the east and south, and to the King's highway there towards the west. To have and to hold the said piece or parcel of land with the appurtenances unto the said Robert Todd, his executors, administrators and assignes from the day of the date of these presents for and during the full end and term of one thousand years from thence next ensuing fully to be complete and ended, yielding and paying therefore yearly during the said term unto the said Alexander Norwood the sum of twelve pence of lawful English money, at the feast of St Michael the Archangel in every year of the said tenure.

This land was then bought by Matthew Silk, a bricklayer, who, at some time before his death in 1729, built 'a messuage and kitchen' on part of the land, the kitchen presumably being a separate building. The property was advertised for letting in 1733:[26]

Now to be let
A lime kiln and a very good convenient Whiting-House and well supplied with

fresh water. ¼ acre of land adjoining to it, and a very good Dwelling House in Margate in the Isle of Thanet, late in the occupation of Mr Matthew Silk, deceased. Inquire of Mr Robert Wells or of William Simmons, of Margate.
NB. All customers may be supplied with Whiting at the Whiting-house as usual.

In 1769 the site still contained 'one whiting shed and lime kiln' and 'a garden, containing one rod, lying and being on the Wind Mill Green'; Wind Mill Green was a reference to the location of the old Mill Lane Mill located behind the Church in Harris's map (Figure 2), on what was to become Mill Lane.[25] By 1876 the original house had been converted into two, being numbers 123 and 125 High Street; they can be seen on modern maps of Margate on the East side of the High Street just below the junction with Mill Lane, close to the Saracen's Head.[25] The presence of a lime kiln on the land of a bricklayer and builder such as Matthew Silk was not surprising, builders using the kilns to prepare lime for mortar. Arthur Rowe reported that, in 1801, there were three lime-kilns in nearby Church street, all belonging to builders.[24] Such lime kilns were a major source of air pollution in many towns.[27]

Early deeds for properties on the north side of Mill Lane tell us more about this part of Margate.[28] The first, from 1681, records a conveyance from John Smith, a chirurgeon (doctor) of Margate, to John Prince of Margate, a famous local brewer of ale, of two acres of arable land 'abutting to the Church way leading from Margate east to the way leading to the mill there from the street south, to the lands of John Smith north, to the lands of Matthew Smith and Nicholas Laming west'; 'the way leading to the mill' became Mill Lane and the 'street' became the High Street. The land then passed from John Prince to his son Thomas, and then to his son Richard, whose widow Mary sold it to Matthew Smith, a Margate butcher, in 1730, for £100.

It is not known when the Mill behind the church was built. The mill mentioned in Richard Norwood's will of 1644 was probably Mill Lane Mill and an indenture of 1693 records the purchase of 'Margate Mill' by Roger Pannell.[15,29] An analysis of the parish rate books by Arthur Rowe gives a list of the occupiers of the mill from 1716:[30]

1716-1717   Thomas Pannell
1717-1725   Roger Pannell
1724-1725   Mr Cowell (probably Benjamin Cowell the Elder)

1725-1730   John Webb
1730-1733   Mr Dunn
1733-1747   Mr Cramp
1747-1759   Thomas Hollam (Holland)
1759-1772   Thomas Doorn (Down) (pulled down)

In 1772 the mill, owned at the time by Benjamin Cowell the elder, was removed by his son John Cowell to a new site where Thanet House was later built; the mill was eventually demolished in 1789.[30] The reason for moving the mill was given in the *Canterbury Journal*: 'Last week a Windmill belonging to Mr Cowell, at Margate, was obliged to be moved a further distance from the town. The many new houses lately built near it obstructed the wind in such a manner that it could not work.'[31]

Amongst the lime kilns, herring-hangs, and the windmill at the upper end of the High Street were a number of malt houses. In 1766 an advertisement appeared for the sale of the property of the late William Jarvis, a Margate maltster:[32]

A freehold estate, lately the Property of Mr William Jarvis, Maltster, deceased, consisting of a large good Dwelling House containing three Parlours, three Chambers, two Shops two Kitchens, two Cellars, &c. together with a large Malt-house, that wets 20 Quarter per Week, also a Brewhouse, Stables, and other Out-houses, Yards, Gardens, &c. situated at the upper End of Highstreet, near the Church in Margate, very commodious, and capable of great Improvement.

A malthouse and a brewhouse at Church Hill, owned by Henry Petken and then by his son William Petken, brewers and maltsters, are also mentioned in mortgages of 1719 and 1737.[33] These talk of 'outhouses, malthouse, yard, garden etc. and two pieces of arable land about 8 acres, at or near St John's Church hill, in tenure of Henry Petken' and also of 'copper tuns, barks, float, brewing vessels, great and small casks, utensils, implements of brewing, horses, carts, and dray.' It is not known whether or not this was the property later owned by William Jarvis. Henry and William Petken were major figures in Margate, both, at one time, being Deputies of the town;[34] they also had the original brewery on King's Street, that was later to become Cobb's Brewery. An indenture of 1743

Figure 5. (Top): Buller's Court, 1939. (Bottom): Old houses between the Six Bells and the west gate of the Church, ca 1910.

refers to a tenement owned by William Petken 'commonly known by the name or sign of the Five Bells, late in occupation of Abraham Mummery, victualler, at yearly rent of £4 5s'.[33] The Five Bells was a popular inn, used for entertaining by the Parish Overseers, first appearing in the Parish rate books in 1698.[35] It seems likely that the Five Bells was the inn that later became the Six Bells, the public house that once stood at the top end of the High Street, facing the Church.

Little is known about the houses at Church Hill and none of the old buildings now survive. An indenture of 1671 refers to 'all that messuage in Church hill and commonly called Jumble House, now or later in occupation of Edward Cobb',[36] an intriguing reference given the fact that a group of old houses in this area were later referred to as 'Jumble Joss Island'. Opposite the Six Bells was Buller's court; photographs of Buller's Court show that it bore a stone plaque above the archway leading into the Court, with the words 'Bullers Court, 1673' (Figure 5). John Lewis describes how, in 1673, Francis Buller gave to the Parish 'several tenements, and half an acre of land, lying at Church-hill, the rents of which are to be laid out . . . in binding poor boys apprentices to some sea-faring employment'.[1] Buller's Court came to be used to house the poor, as described in Chapter 4. Further down the High Street, on the corner of High Street and Church Square, was another old courtyard, called Dixon's Row on Edmunds map of 1821, but Dixon's Place in a street directory of 1883.[37] Rowe reports that this also bore an inscription, this time in the form of a brick insert 'E.B. 1676'. Close by was Dixon's Court; a sale of the estate of the late James Dixon in 1831 included a house at the entrance to Dixon's Court, No. 69 High Street, containing nine 'large airy rooms'.[38] Edmunds 1821 map shows the One Bell public house in the northern corner of Dixon's Court. An entry in the records of the Overseers of the Poor for 1733 shows a payment to 'Mr [William] Simmons for half years rent for the house at the Signe of the Bell'; Rowe suggests that the overseers probably paid Simmons, a local brewer and maltster, for the use of one or more rooms in the inn as a parochial office.[39] An indenture of 1777 for James Dixon speaks of 'the shop formerly a smith's forge and now a wheelwrights shop' and an indenture of 1664 between John Parker and Josiah Simmons speaks of 'a small piece of land with smiths forge'; it is not known whether the forge was in Dixon's Row or in Dixon's Court.[38,40] The deeds of the old houses between the Six Bells and the west gates of the Church (Figure 5) show that they date from before 1696.[24]

Land on the opposite, west, side of the High Street, between the modern Grosvenor Hill and Marine Gardens, was also sold off in the middle years of the seventeenth century. In 1650 Alexander Norwood sold 11 perches of land to John Hodges, yeoman; by 1781 Isaac Covell had built four messuages on this land, later referred to as Covells Row and found between Nos. 132 and 134 High Street.[41] Three years earlier, in 1647, Alexander Norwood had sold 8 perches of land for £4 to John Spratling, 'mariner of St John's'; this was adjacent to the 11 perches of land sold by Norwood to John Hodges, land on which Hodges 'soon after built a messuage, still standing [in 1680]'.[42] These properties were to become No. 122 High Street; Nos. 122A and 124 were later additions built in the yard attached to No. 122.[42] Further down we come to Nos. 106A and 106B High Street, in Prince of Wales' Yard. These properties were built on some of the 40 perches of land sold by Alexander Norwood in 1647 to Henry Samways, a gentleman of the Parish of St John's, for £5.[43] The land already contained 'two old thatched cottages and a draw well'. That the cottages were referred to as old in 1647 suggests that they could have dated back to the sixteenth century, and the selling price of £5 for the land and two cottages suggests that they must have been pretty ramshackle. On a further portion of Samways' 40 perches of land were built what later became Nos. 98, 100 and 102 High Street.[44]

The picture we are left with is of a highway from the church to the harbour that, before Norwood's great sell off of land, ran through open fields with just an occasional thatched cottage. Even after the selloff, plots of land were slow to be developed, and the many herring hangs and malt houses, not to mention the local lime kilns, scattered along its length well justified the judgment of future generations that it was 'but a long dirty lane.' It is not certain that much better can be said about the other King's highway, the one that was to become King Street.

The second King's highway ran from the Pier to Lucas Dane; to the north of the highway, running up to the Fort and the cliffs, was arable land. Lining the highway were a number of the more prestigious houses in Margate, together with malt houses and at least one brew house, later to develop into Cobb's brewery. At the corner of the future King Street and Fort Road (previously Fountain Lane) was the Fountain Inn, later the site of Cobb's Bank. The Fountain Inn extended almost a hundred feet along Fountain Lane, its odd shape reflecting its complex history.[45] Part of the site, containing a house, shop and garden, belonged in 1688 to Jeremiah Fanting, described as a yeoman. The property passed to his granddaughter Mary, who was married to John Covell, who sold it to William Armstrong, described in his will as a Tavern Keeper. The neighbouring property, also a house, shop and garden, was sold by John Glover to Thomas Grinder in 1681, who then sold it to Ralph Constant in 1685; John Glover becomes important later in relation to the Mansion House. Ralph Constant's wife Mary passed the property in her will to her three daughters, Mary Tomlin, Ann Laming and Elizabeth Pamflett. In turn they sold the property in 1731 to William Armstrong and it seems likely that it was Armstrong who was responsible for the development of the inn. In 1756 the Fountain was sold to George Friend and, in 1772, to Francis Cobb.[46,47]

Further along King Street was the site of what was to become Cobb's Brewery. The site was large, extending from the highway up to the Fort. In November 1615 Richard Lee, a maltster of St John's, acquired premises in Margate from William Parker, including a malthouse or brewhouse together with buildings and land, amounting to about 3 acres in all.[48] His son, Daniel Lee, sold the property to Dame Mabel Finch, a widow of Canterbury, in 1663, at which time it consisted of land and a brewhouse, occupied by Richard May, a brewer, and a malthouse, occupied by Rowntree Cockaine.[48,49] The property then seems to have returned to the Lee family as an indenture dated 1681 records the sale of the property by John Lee, a tailor of Canterbury, to William Petken, a brewer of Margate: it was described as 'one malthouse and brew house, one millhouse, one stable, in or near a place commonly called or known by the name of Lucas Dane'. The location of the property was described as abutting 'the King's Highway towards the south, to the lands of Mary Wright widow towards the west, to the land of the heirs of James Trapham and to the Kings Highway towards the East, and to the Lands of John Jewell towards the North.' An early name for Trinity Hill was Trapham's Lane and, assuming that 'the land of the heirs of James Trapham' was located close to Trapham's Lane, this locates the site of Petken's brewery as the site of the later Cobb's brewery. Ownership of the site becomes confused for a few years but evidently remained in the Petken family, passing from William Petken, on his death, to his wife Mary and to their two sons Henry and Thomas; on

Henry's death, the property moved to his son William Petken jun. and then, on his death, to his brother Henry Petken jun., who was now living in Dover. An indenture of July 1763 passed the property from Henry Petken jun. to George Rainer of Ramsgate and in August 1763 George Rainer sold it to Francis Cobb. The indenture of August 1763 described the property as:

all those 3 messuages, one counting house, two cellars, one washhouse, one brewhouse, and all the brewing vessels, copper implements and utensils of and belonging to the said Brewhouse, two large vaults, one stable, one malthouse, 2 dry lofts, one millhouse, two herring houses or storehouse, one summer house, two cowhouses, one coalhouse, one large Tiled lodge, three yards, 2 gardens, and a parcel of pasture land commonly called the Green which is walled in and contains ca 3 acres, and 2 small pieces of land with a carriage-way and gutter or watercourse heretofore part of a Great Backyard. All lying and together adjoining; some parts do abut bound or lye to or upon the Kings Highway or Street there leading from a certain place commonly called Lucas and otherwise Luke's Dane to Margate pier towards the south and heretofore in the several tenancies or occupations of William Petken, John Pearse, Thomas Row jun. and Robert Brooke

The original Brewhouse was on the north side of the highway, probably on the site of the garden behind the house later built by Francis Cobb on King Street.[50] Close to the brewery site were three large houses, two of which can be identified with some certainty thanks to a sketch map produced, probably in 1796, to help settle an argument about access to the houses (Figure 6). The map shows the passageway giving access to the brewery site from the King's Highway; the passageway was referred to in later street directories as Brewery Hill and is now Cobb Court. On the east side of the passageway were the house and lands of Captain Brooke (probably Captain Robert Brooke), previously belonging to Richard Lister. On the west side was land belonging to the Petkens, leading up to a house probably built by Benjamin Doncaster [or Donkester] in the 1680s; in 1682 Benjamin Doncaster, a mariner, bought 6 perches of land from William Petken, together with the use of a 'carriageway leading from the Street or Kings highway south by the lands of Richard Lister up to the Gate or doors now late built upon some of the above bargained land'.[46] In 1729 Benjamin Doncaster, now residing in Petersburg, sold the

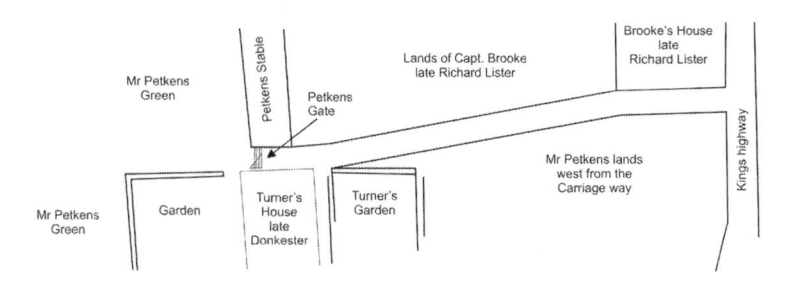

Figure 6. Sketch showing the location of properties on the Brewery Site, produced to settle an argument about rights of way, probably in 1796. Based on the original in the Kent Archives [U1453/T8, Foley House Deeds].

property to Richard Foley, and the house took the name of Foley House. In 1688 Captain Turner (probably Captain David Turner) purchased the land adjacent to the house as a garden (Figure 6) so that it is likely that Turner occupied the house at that time.[46] In 1732 both Captain Robert Brookes and Captain David Turner were Pier Wardens.[51] By about 1796 Foley House was in the occupation of Charles Boncey, a local builder.[46] His advertisement for its sale in 1807 gives a description of the house:[53]

A large genteel Family House, called FOLEY HOUSE, situated near King-street, Margate; consists of two good parlours, two drawing rooms, hall, kitchen, counting-house, extensive cellars, large and airy bedrooms, makes fourteen beds; coach house, stable for six horses a good flower and kitchen garden; large storehouses, pump with fresh water, and every requisite for a genteel family, or trade.

In 1811 Foley House was bought by Francis Cobb.[46] The location of the third large house off the King's highesy, the *Mansion House*, is less certain and its interest, together with that of its builder, John Glover, is sufficient to warrant a separate section.

Further along King Street we come to Lucas Dane proper which was, at this time, largely agricultural. Just beyond the future site of

Cobb's brewery, on the north side of the King's highway, was a cart road leading to Northdown, shown on Edmunds map of 1821 as Trapham's Lane and now known as Trinity Hill. A map of 1774 showing the land owned by Charles James Fox in this area shows a house with a malt house and garden on the east side of the junction of the cart road and the King's highway, with land extending up to the cliffs; the house was later to be known as the Tudor House.[54] The Tudor House has a complex history dating back to the sixteenth century or before.[55] Abstracts of deeds date the house back to 1681 when it was sold to Thomas Grant, a mariner, by John Savage, another mariner; at the time the house and land was rented by John Laming, a member of a wealthy family of Margate ship owners. John Savage was probably the son of William Savage who died in 1662;[56] William Savage was a wealthy mercer, a mercer being a merchant, especially one involved in the export of wool and the import of luxurious fabrics such as velvet and silk.

The indenture of 1681 between John Savage and Thomas Grant suggests that by then the house was used as a farmhouse. The indenture describes a cart way 8 feet in breadth through the land to allow 'horses, carts and carriages to pass up and down from the messuage lands ... unto the King's highway adjoining to the lands of the said Savage', it being this cart way that eventually become Trapham's Lane.[56] The land and buildings were sold by Thomas Grant in 1687 to Stephen Higgins, a London victualler, who leased them in 1714 to Valentine Denne, a yeoman of Reculver; at this time the 'tenement, garden, malthouse, barns, stables, Podwarehouse [the meaning of 'Podwarehouse' is now lost], storehouse, cellars, court yards, backsides, orchard, garden, well house, outhouses, edifices . . . and parcels of arable and pasture land' occupied about 23 acres and were in the tenure of John Castle. A sale of the farm in 1741 refers to 'the farmhouse wherein John Castle then or lately did dwell', the first time that the house was explicitly referred to as farmhouse; a sale of the property in 1770 to Henry Lord Holland also refers to 'all that farmhouse where John Castle did dwell'.[56] A document of 1790 again refers to 'all that messuage or farmhouse where John Castle [used to] dwell' but then adds that it had been 'converted into dwellings'.[56] Finally, in the early 1800s Fort Crescent, East Crescent Place, and West Crescent Place were built by Claude Benezet on the 20 acres of land originally belonging to the farmhouse.[56]

Another large farm in Lucas Dane was owned by James Taddy, a Margate mariner. In 1705 James Taddy married Susannah Laming, the daughter of Peter Sackett, a yeoman also of Margate, and Taddy, on his marriage, settled the farm on himself and his new wife.[57] The farm was described as 'all that Mansion House ... with kitchens, barns, stables, gardens, orchard, backsides, court, yards, and appurtenances ... also nine several pieces of arable land to the said messuage belonging, containing ca 40 acres ... at or near a place called Wilds Dane or Lucas Dane and now in the occupation of John Cowell.' In an indenture of 1733, the house was described as a farmhouse rather than as a Mansion House, and included a malthouse along with all the other buildings.[57] The property remained in the Taddy family until 1795 when it was sold to Francis Cobb the younger.[57] Unfortunately, the exact location of the farm is not known.

Behind the buildings facing the harbour was what is now referred to as the 'Old Town' (Figure 3). Unfortunately it is difficult to identify particular streets and buildings at this time as the requirement to name streets and number houses was only introduced in 1787 with the Margate Improvement Act. However, comparing Lewis's drawing and Harris's Map with modern maps of the town shows that as well as the buildings facing the harbour and those along what were to become High Street and King Street, houses had been built along another street running inland, later to be named Market Street. The site of the present Market Place was originally an open space called the Bowling Green. Lewis reported that 'in 1631 I find a Market was kept [in Margate], of which a return was made to Dover every month, but this seems not to have continued long, nor does it appear by what authority it was kept at all'.[1] The early market referred to by Lewis would have been just a series of market stalls for produce such as fruit, vegetables and meat, lining a street or an open space such as the Bowling Green, much like a modern street-market. The principal public and official buildings in many country towns came to be built around the market place, and a covered space would often be provided for the market stalls; often a hall or court room would be built above the market.[58] This was the pattern of development at Margate, although the town had to wait until 1777 for its permanent market building, which was built on the site of the Bowling Green. A legal document of 1789 refers to buildings 'near the place there formerly called the Pier Green since called the Bowling Green and then called Market Place',[59] but this sequence of names seems likely to be wrong. An indenture of 1641 refers to a messuage 'called the Queens Arms [abutting] a place called the Bowling Green',[60] and, since the present Queens Arms abuts the Market Place, this seems to confirm that the site occupied by the Market building was originally called the Bowling Green. Pier Green was the name used for a piece of land near the Pier and the papers in a legal case of 1755 describe how some time before the 1750s a storehouse had been built on a part of the Pier Green that had been used previously as a sawpit, and that the sawpit was then moved to the spot 'where the Market now stands'.[61] It is possible that the original name of Bowling Green was changed to Pier Green when the sawpit was moved to the Bowling Green site, but, if so, the name did not stick, as deeds of 1705, 1729, 1765, 1768, and 1789 all refer to the Bowling Green.[62,63]

Buildings around the Bowling Green were likely to have been mostly commercial premises. Rowe describes the deeds of an old butcher's shop in the Market Place, Dale and Son, that was originally a herring-house, but was bought in 1707 by John Barnett, a butcher; Rowe established that the premises were certainly a butcher's shop by 1752.[24] An indenture of 1632 between John Bunson and Nicholas Woolman records the sale for £300 of the Old Kings Arms, 'close to the green called the bowling green', and, on the back of the indenture, someone has written 'the Queen's Armes'.[64] The indenture of 1641 already referred to describes the Queen's Arms as abutting on the Bowling Green, so that we can be fairly certain that the Old Kings Arms was an earlier name for the Queen's Arms.

Leading into the Market Place was Puddle Dock, now called Love Lane, a lane lined by herring hangs and stables.[24] At the corner of Love Lane and the Market Place was the Old Crown, mentioned in deeds of 1776.[63] In neighbouring Lombard Street a brick building, still there, is decorated with small brick arches and pilasters and dates to the late 17th century, and must have been a prestigious house when it was built.[65] The will of Edward Diggs in 1725 refers to five messuages 'at or near Pier Green' and a legal document of 1811 makes clear that these properties were in Lombard Street.[59] In 1730 Jeremiah Jewell, of East London and John Jewell a Margate mariner sold 5 messuages on the south side of Lombard Street, 'of yearly value 22 pounds ten shillings, now or late in the occupations of Thomas Slayton, Richard Laming, John Culmer, Thomas Burnell and Wm. Pain', including a herring hang, to Stephen Swinford, another Margate mariner.[66] Lombard Street was one of the earliest streets in Margate to bear a name, as indentures of 1738 and 1750 refer to 'a certain street in Margate there called or known by the name of Lombard Street'.[67]

The Mansion House and John Glover

The location of the third of the large houses off King Street, the Mansion House, is uncertain because the house was demolished before the publication of the first detailed map of Margate, Edmund's map of 1821. The most likely site for the house was on the east side of Fountain Lane at the point where Fountain Lane became a footway, as shown on Edmund's map of Margate. The strongest evidence for this being the location is contained in an indenture for the sale of the house in 1768.[47] This describes the sale of:

all that messuage or Mansion House heretofore erected and built by John Glover, together with the outhouses, etc. securing and reserving the several rights of the respective owners of several messuages situate at or near a certain passage belonging to the said messuage or Mansion House, and then in the occupation of Anthony Walton, John Price, Richard Goadson, Joseph Griggs, Abraham Hedgecock, and Thos. White to the use of a way to go into and out of and from the back doors, of the six several messuages or tenements, by and through the aforesaid passage leading from the Street between the messuages there of John Gore, and a messuage there of Geo. Friend, known by the name of the Sign of the Fountain, up by the said messuage or Mansion House, and also from thence towards and up to the Fort Green there. . . . And also reserving to such persons who should be owners of the new-built messuages, standing in the aforesaid passage, in the occupations of Daniel Rose and Edw. Goatham, the right to the use of a way by and through the said passage (that is to say) a carriage and footway to and from the street, to and from the houses, and to and from the same houses to and from the Fort Green aforesaid only a footway.

The six messuages referred to here are the six houses shown in Edmunds map of 1821 making up the row of houses between Pump Lane and

Fountain Lane. The passageway, later called Fountain Lane, ran from the King's Highway or Street, later called King Street, along the side of the Fountain Inn. Edmunds map and the Ordnance Survey Map of 1852 shows that, just beyond the six messuages, Fountain Lane changed into a footway leading to the Fort. The indenture of 1768 continues:[47]

And also reserving to Francis Cobb, owner of a certain storehouse standing also in the said passage, to use of the passage, with liberty to turn any carriage in that part of the passage leading from the street to the entrance of the courtyard of the said Mansion House. And also reserving the use of the Pump standing near the said two new-built houses and the water thereof, and also the privilege of going in and out of the Great Gate standing in the same passage near to the said Pump, leading to a Lane called Pump Lane for the use and benefit of the said two new-built houses, the owners of the said two houses paying a proportionate part of the repairs of the said Pump and Gate.

The Pump, after which Pump Land was named, was located in a recess on the west side of Pump Lane opposite the Fountain Inn, where the old Ambulance Station building of 1896 was erected in what by then had become Fort Road.[47]

The story of the Mansion House starts in 1672 with the sale by John Crispe to John Glover, gentleman, for £150 of 'all that messuage with the shop, outhouse, buildings and gardens, in Margate, towards the street there south, towards the Highway leading from the said street west and towards the messuage of Robert Brooke east'.[48] The 'street there south' was the King's Highway, later King Street. A second indenture, dated 1677, records a grant and demise [lease] by John Glover to Henry Yeates of 'all that capital messuage then lately erected with all and every the outhouses buildings Court yards gardens and green spot of Grounds thereunto belonging, whereof part was then lately purchased by Jeffrey Tomlin gentleman.' The indenture goes on to detail 'one large capital messuage or tenement then lately erected and built by him and wherein the said John Glover then dwelt...' and a 'garden and orchard, together with the dove house, brewhouse and other outhouses'.[48] All this suggests that John Glover over-extended himself financially in building the Mansion House and, indeed, in his will of 1681 he suggests that his wife Susannah should, if necessary, sell 'the messuage and premises' to pay his debts.[47,68] During a court case of 1716 it was reported that about three years before the death of Susannah Glover, to whom the house had passed, Nicholas Constant 'did hire from her half of the said house for which he gave the yearly rent of £8'.

The land referred to above as 'lately purchased by Jeffrey Tomlin gentleman' was probably at the north end of the site, close to the cliffs. A document of 1697 records the gift by Jeffrey Tomlin, of St Peter's, to William Goatham, brewer, in 1697 of 'my chalk wall containing fourteen roods be there more or less with the ground whereon the wall standing . . . at or near a place there called the Fort Green' separating the land of William Goatham from Fort Green.[48] A rood, or rod, was a measure of length equal to about 16 feet,[70] so that the length of this wall was about 224 feet. This matches the length of the wall shown on Edmunds map of 1821 separating the top end of the Brewery site from the Fort.

John Glover died in 1685 and his wife Susannah died in 1713.[71] In the court case of 1716 that followed Susannah Glover's death, the Glover's house, 'commonly called the great house in Margate' was described as 'the largest and most capacious house in Margate'.[69] The house had often been used by 'persons of quality' on their journeys from England to Holland or France.[69] John Evelyn records in his diary on March 27 1672 that on a visit to Kent he stayed at Margate and 'was handsomely entertained and lay at my deputy's Captain Glover'.[72] In a letter of November 1677 to Sir Joseph Williamson, John Glover reported that 'last night, the wind being S., the Prince and Princess of Orange went on board *Sir John Holmes* and stood off to sea, but, the wind coming N.E. in the night, they came back again into this road, and about 11 this morning came ashore to my house, where at present they are in very good health'.[73] In her evidence to the court case of 1716 Martha Harman, Susannah Glover's servant, reported that 'his late Majesty King William, his Grace the Duke of Marlborough, his Grace the Duke Shrewsbury and diverse other persons of quality and distinction in journey or passage from England to Holland or France . . . did frequently take up the said house and sometimes lodge there at other times . . . for which they used to make presents or other gratifications to the said Susannah Glover'.[69] Following Susannah Glover's death in 1713 the house stood empty while the arguments over her will were fought through the courts. Martha Harman reported that after Susannah's death, although people of quality had been at Margate, 'they did not stay in the House but went to the house of Mr Jewell and lodged there'.[69] Confusingly, one of the London papers, *Applebee's Original Weekly Journal*, reported in November 1720 that: 'Yesterday Morning, between One and Two, his Majesty landed at Margate in Kent, and lay at the House of Mrs Glover in that Town, and came to St. James's last Night'.[74] Since this was seven years after Susannah Glover's death either her old house was again being used by 'persons of quality' or the paper had got it wrong.

Even before Susannah Glover's death the house 'was very much out of repair' and it was reported that 'the stable belonging to the said great house was blown down several years before the death of the said Susannah Glover'.[69] Vincent Barber, a 'house carpenter' reported that the house 'was unfit for any Gentleman's use without repairing' and that 'the said house standing out of the way of trade and business' was 'only fit for a Gentleman's use.' Edward Constant, the Margate postmaster in 1716, reported that at the time of Susannah Glover's death 'the said great house, outhouses and garden were in tolerable repair sufficient for any common tradesman but not for a Gentleman.'

Following the end of the court case in 1717 the house was advertised for sale in the *London Gazette*:[75]

A good brick messuage, four rooms on a floor, situate in Margate in the Isle of Thanet in the County of Kent, with good gardens, brewhouse, stables, and other conveniences, late the estate of John Glover, Gent. deceased, is to be sold by decree of the High Court of Chancery, before John Bennett, Esq, one of the Masters of the said Court. Inquire for a particular at the said Master's House, at the upper end of Chancery lane.

The house was finally purchased in 1721 from James Glover, son and heir of John Glover, by John Wheatley of Margate, acting on behalf of Stephen Baker, a gentleman and mariner of Margate.[47] Stephen Baker died in 1751, and, in his will proved 'on oath of Elizabeth Baker spinster', he left money and 'my fishing boat' to John Baker, and money to his son Stephen and to his daughter Elizabeth.[76] Although there was no specific mention of the Mansion House in his will, the house was clearly passed on to his daughter as her will of 1764 declares:[77]

First I give and devise all that my messuage or Mansion House with all and singular the outhouses buildings yards gardens land hereditaments ... situate in Margate ... now in my own occupation and also all those two messuages or tenements and all that Brewhouse of building with the outhouses buildings ground ... together adjoining near to my said Messuage or Mansion House and now or late in the several occupations of Daniel Rose, Edward Goatham and George Friend ... and also all that Messuage or Tenement with the outhouses buildings ground ... at or near a place now called Puddle Dock and now or late in the occupation of John Palmer together with all other my messuages lands tenements ... real estate ... unto Richard Ward of Woolwich in the said county of Kent, Shipwright and John Baker of the parish of St John.

Richard Ward and John Baker were to sell the property, including 'my said Mansion House' and to use the money for a variety of bequests specified in the will. The house was duly advertised for sale in a London paper in 1766:[78]

To be sold to the highest Bidder, on Tuesday the 6th day of May ... at the New Inn

The several messuages and tenements after-mentioned, situate and together being in the said town of Margate in several lots, viz.

Lot 1. A large Mansion-house, with four rooms on a floor, late in the occupation of Mrs Elizabeth Baker, deceased, standing upon a rising ground, so as to command from some of the upper rooms a prospect of the sea and land: the size of each room as follows, viz,

	Length		Breadth		Height	
	Ft.	Ins.	Ft.	Ins.	Ft.	Ins.
The Ground Floor						
One large kitchen	20	6	20	1		
One scullery with pump	21	1	9	6		
One cellar	17	6	14	6	8	0
One cellar with pantry	11	3	7	6		
A place for coals	11	3	7	6		
The First Floor						
One large parlour with two closets	21	4	16	8		
One parlour with ditto	14	7	12	0	9	8
One servants hall	17	10	13	0		
One back parlour	17	10	11	8		
A fine open stair-case with two others close						
The passage leading from the fore door			6	8		

The Second Floor

One large dining-room hung with painted cloth	21	9	21	6		
One chamber	21	6	15	9	10	10
One back chamber with closet	17	8	12	0		
One back chamber with ditto	18	3	17	8		

The Third Floor

One large laundry	25	0	16	0		
One chamber	15	8	14	6		
One chamber	18	0	14	7	8	3
One chamber	16	0	14	6		
Two small store rooms, each	14	6	7	0		

The garden before the house	50	6	41	6
The back yard	42	0	12	0
The garden behind the house	97	6	42	0

N.B. The gardens and yard are walled in.

Lot 2. One new built messuage, in the occupation of Mr Daniel Rose.

Lot 3. One new built messuage, in the occupation of Mr Edward Goatham.

Lot 4. One store-house with a vault thereunder, in the occupation of Mr George Friend, or his under tenant, the size thereof being 54 feet 9 inches by 20 feet.

N.B. The premises are all freehold.

Enquire in the mean time of Mr Richard Ward, at Woolwich, in the county of Kent; Mr John Baker, at North Down, near Margate; or Mr Daniel Marsh, attorney at law, in Margate.

The property did not sell and in 1767 Francis Cobb took the opportunity to purchase just the 'brewhouse and storehouse and vaults', but not the house.[48] The Indenture of sale, as usual, describes the location of the brewhouse property and also clarified the rights of access to it:

abuting and bounding to a building or ground of Stephen Sackett towards the East, to a building or grounds of George Friend towards the south, to a passage belonging to and leading from the Street up to the Mansion house late the said Elizabeth Baker's and from thence to the Fort Green there towards the West, and to a messuage or tenement also late the said Elizabeth Baker's now in the occupation of Edward Goatham towards the North, or howsoever otherwise the said premises do or doth abut bound or lye late in the tenure or occupation of George Friend or his assigns or under-tenants and now or late in the tenure or occupation of the said Francis Cobb his assigns or under-tenants which said Brewhouse, Storehouse or building and premises hereby granted and released being part and parcel of the said messuages, lands, tenements and hereditaments before mentioned to be devised by the said Elizabeth Baker to be sold as aforesaid and were heretofore the estate and inheritance of the said Stephen Baker deceased and are part of the estate purchased by John Wheatley of James Glover and others by indentures of lease and release in trust for the said Stephen Baker – and also the free use liberty privilege and benefit from time to time and at all times hereafter of a way in over and through the passage aforesaid belonging to the said Mansion house from the street to and from the said Brewhouse, Storehouse or building and premises for the said Francis Cobb, his heirs and assigns and his and their tenants servants and workmen to pass and repass in over and through the said way with horses, cattle, carts and other carriages . . . and liberty at all times to turn any carriage in that part of the said passage leading from the street to the entrance of the Court yard of the said Mansion house. And also the free use . . . of a footway from the said Brewhouse Storehouse or buildings and premises in over and through the said passage up by the said Mansion House to and from the Fort Green aforesaid for the said Frances Cobb.

The Mansion House itself was advertised again in 1768, this time in the *Kentish Gazette*, and with less detail:[79]

TO BE SOLD; By Public AUCTION, to the Highest-Bidder, at the Mansion-house after mentioned, on Monday the Twenty-second Day of August Inst. between the Hours of Four and Five o'clock in the Afternoon,

The said MANSION-HOUSE (being Freehold) having four Rooms on a Floor, Closets, and other Conveniences, Two Gardens walled in, viz. a fore Garden and a back Garden, and all other Appurtenances to the same belonging, situate in Margate, upon a rising Ground, so as to Command, from some of the upper Rooms, a prospect of the Sea and Land, late in the Occupation of Mrs Elizabeth Baker, deceased.

And in two separate Lots, Two New-built MESSUAGES or TENEMENTS (being likewise Freehold) situate also in Margate, near to the said Mansion-house; now in the several Occupations of Daniel Rose and Edward Goatham. For further Particulars enquire of Mr John Baker, at North Down, near Margate, or Mr Daniel Marsh, Attorney, at Margate.

The house was bought at the auction by Thomas Smith for £400, on behalf of Holles Henry Bull of Strand in the Green, Chiswick.[47] It remained in the ownership of the Bull family until 1792 but toward the end was occupied by Francis Sackett who ran a boarding house there. Sackett advertised the attractions of the 'Royal Mansion' in 1788:[80]

Royal Mansion,
At Margate in Kent, near the Play-house
Francis Sackett begs leave respectfully to inform the Noblemen, Ladies, and Gentlemen, that he keeps a good table, and other accommodation at the following terms, viz;

	£	s	d
For the first floor per week	1	8	0
Second floor ditto	1	6	0
For boarding, without Lodging	1	1	0
For boarding, without Lodging		4	0

The reference to 'near the Play-house' refers to the location of the original Margate playhouse, at the Fountain Inn.[81]

Following Bull's death the house was advertised for sale in *The Times*, in 1791, by which time it was known as Sacket's Boarding House;[82]

For sale at Bensons Hotel... Large freehold mansion house with four rooms on a floor, known by the name of Sacket's Boarding House; situated near the Fort, standing on a rising ground, so has a command from some of the rooms of a prospect of the sea and land, the busy picture of the London Commerce passing in Review, capable of great improvements. A garden behind the house 97 feet 6 inches by 42 feet, with a door that opens into the Fort. Back yard 42 feet by 12. The approach from the Street is a Coach road to the House, inclosed with iron gates. A flower garden in front, walled round, 50 feet 6 inches by 41 feet 6, with a flight of stone steps. Coach house with stabling for two horses, and loft over.

The above premises are fit for the reception of a genteel family.

The corresponding advertisement in the *Kentish Chronicle* of June 14 1791 is the same as that in *The Times*, but incudes full room dimensions, exactly matching those in the advertisement of 1766 quoted above.[83]

The house was bought in 1792 by John Mitchener, of the New Inn, and

John Drayton Sawkins.[47] It is possible that the House was then occupied by a school teacher, Mrs Peacock, who advertised in 1796 that 'Mrs and Miss Peacocks – Mansion House – school recommences on 25th'.[84] However, in 1803 it was sold by Mitchener and Sawkins to Matthias Mummery, a Margate coachmaster, and Stephen Mummery, a Margate farmer.[47] An indenture of 1809 reported that 'Matthew and Stephen Mummery had pulled down the Mansion House, and on the site and grounds thereof had built . . . coach-houses, stables, and buildings' referred to as being 'in or near Pump lane and Fountain Lane', and that they had used the property as a security for a loan of £2500 from Francis Cobb and Francis William Cobb; in 1816 the Mummerys were declared bankrupt on a petition of the Cobbs.[47]

A little is known about John Glover, who built the Mansion House and was a man of some standing in Margate. In the parish church was a memorial to 'John Glover, Gentleman, who died at London in 1685, aged 56 years, born in 1629'; an inscription underneath recorded the death of his wife, 'Mrs Susanna Glover, his wife, Obiciit in 1713, aged 75 years'.[71] At the time of his death he left an estate worth some £2000, with shares in a number of 'good ships and vessels'.[69] In 1656 John Glover had been made master of one of Oliver Cromwell's ships:[85]

To Commissioners of Admiralty and Navy. Our will and please is that you forthwith make and direct your warrant to John Glover of our Isle of Thenet in our Countie of Kent gent authorizing him to bee Master and Commander of our shallop called *The Welcome* of our Port of Margate in the said Isle, for our special and ymediate service at sea. Given at Whitehall the Nineteenth day of February 1656.

This was a position of no little importance because of the extensive naval activity off the coast of Margate at the time, resulting from the three wars fought with the Dutch during the years 1652 to 1674 (Chapter 6). At one time he was also postmaster at Margate, but a petition to the Privy Council in 1658 shows that, about this time, he was in some trouble:[86]

April 22 1658. Petition of John Cockaine, John Hill, and Hen. Giles, to Privy Council.
    Being ordered to appear before you, to give evidence on a charge against

John Glover, officer of Margate, Kent, we have attended 12 days. Being very poor, and having large families, we beg speedy hearing or dismissal till required, and an order that Rich. Bartlet, surveyor of Customs at Gravesend, may then appear.

The nature of the charge is unknown, but a letter of 1660 from the Council of State to the Commissioners of Customs describes John Glover as 'late postmaster' at Margate and suggests that the Commissioners of Customs might like to think about dismissing him from his job with them as searcher and waiter with the Customs at Margate:[87]

January 28, 1660. Council of State to the Commissioners of Customs. Being informed that Jno. Glover, customer and searcher at Margate, and late postmaster there, is very intimate and holds correspondence with disaffected persons, — whereby, if he be continued in that employment, danger may ensue, — we have removed him from the office of postmaster there, and appointed Nich. Hooke in his stead. We recommend you to remove Glover from being customer and searcher of that port, and to put Hooke into the employment, if you hold him qualified.

There is no record of whether or not Glover was in fact dismissed from his post with the Customs at Margate, but there is a record in 1672 of his appointment as commander of a Customs smack at Margate:[88]

The Treasury Lords to the Customs Commissioners to employ Capt. Glover as commander of a Customs smack to be settled about Margets and Ramsgate: with an establishment of £306 per an. for himself, one mate, 6 men and a boy for said smack.

This appointment was short lived as in 1675 it was decided to remove the smack at Margate and instead for the 'smack at Quinborough [Queenborough] to have the inspection of the Isle of Thanet insead of . . . Mr Glover'; Glover was then dismissed 'as an unnecessary officer'.[89]

Glover's period as commander of a Customs smack coincided with the third of the Anglo-Dutch wars, from 1672 to 1674 (Chapter 6). During this period Sir Joseph Williamson, Under Secretary to the Secretary of State, headed the government's intelligence network of informants. He had correspondents in almost all the ports along the east and south coasts of England, many of whom were customs officers, and one of them was Glover.[91,92] Williamson's informants were not paid for their work but often received a copy of his manuscript newsletter, an important source of news at a time when the only licensed news sheet, the *London Gazette*, carried no domestic news worth reading. Informants were instructed to write to Williamson by every post, as acknowledged in the first of the letters sent by Glover to Williamson on May 10 1672:[93]

May 10, 1672. Margate.
John Glover to Williamson. According to the directions of yours of the 8th I will give you an account daily. Just now came about the Foreland two Holland men-of-war, and a great flyboat, which I conceive is a fireship. They all lie loose with their sails baled up, and have stopped two billanders that were coming in upon the Foreland. The whole fleet are at the back of the Goodwin. If the ships you spoke of come over the flats, it will be very dangerous if these Dutch ships continue on the Foreland; but if it be resolved they shall come, I will have lights kept on the two buoys, that they may come through by night as well as by day. I am just going to the Foreland.

He then wrote again the same day:

May 10, 1672, 2 pm. Margate.
John Glover to Williamson. Since my last by Mr Langley's express [the postmaster at Margate] I have been at the North Foreland and on the lighthouse, which is the best prospect we have, and while there another ship came in upon the Foreland, and spoke to the three I mentioned in my last, and after they had lain by about half an hour they made all sail, and stood off the Foreland again, carrying with them the billanders they stopped, and, I presume, they will go off to their grand fleet, which lies off the flats of the Foreland, and at the back of the Goodwin. These are all the ships that were in sight, only one great ship was between the Northsand head and the Foreland, but she stood off when she saw the others stand off too. It is very hazy, with wind N.N.E., so that we cannot see far to sea, but about sunrise this morning the whole Holland fleet was seen at the back of the Goodwin, and about 30 nearer in upon the Foreland than the rest. If the ships yet in the river are ready to come down, my boat shall ply off the Foreland and inform me of all ships there, and I will contrive, by boats placed from the Redsand to the two buoys of the Narrow with lights in them, and by lights at the two buoys, that the ships shall come down as well in the night as in the day, and then those ready may be at the Foreland before daylight,

and if any of the Holland fleet be there, it will not be above four or eight sail, for they never come in with more. If you will tell his Majesty he will doubtless understand the management of the affair, and if it be concluded pray send me orders what I shall do, and I will consult the commanders about it, and doubt not to bring them down safe. I will send you an account every night by express of what happens here in the day, so pray write to the postmasters to forward them. I guess the biggest ship here not to have above 50 guns, and the rest 20 or 30 apiece.

In his next letter, of May 11, John Glover explained that he had to send his letter via Sandwich, as mail from Margate was only sent out on Tuesdays and Fridays.[93] Despite these problems Glover managed to keep up a regular stream of letters to Williamson, although most contained little of interest.

In November 1672 John Glover wrote to Williamson asking for a job, either as postmaster again, as Richard Langley had just died, or as a customs officer: 'Mr Langley is dead, and the post place here not yet settled, but let me receive your commands, and I will serve you what I am able, but the Commissioners of the Customs have deprived me of my employment in the smack, which I hope you will be a means to restore me to, when you hear my case'.[94] In 1675 he asked for a reward of £52 for having seized a load of wool and a small boat: 'John Glover of Margate. Petition for a gift of about £52, the King's moiety of a seizure of wool, now in the petitioner's hands, and of a small boat forfeited for importing fish. Was often employed during the late Dutch war to go on board his Royal Highness with letters and messages as he and Sir J. Williamson can testify, his charges being above £60'.[95]

With the end of the third Dutch war in 1674 the regular correspondence between Glover and Williamson came to an end, but there is one final letter of interest, concerning religious dissenters at Margate, whose meeting houses were referred to as conventicles (Chapter 5):[96]

February 12 1675. John Glover to Williamson
The fanatic party are building a conventicle house here where we never had any before, and I know not why they go about it now unless it be in spite of the proclamation against them. They make great haste to get it up, and I tell them it may be it will be pulled down as fast ere long.

This was probably a reference to the Baptists. There was a Baptist church in Dover in 1654, and the Baptists met in the Isle of Thanet in a chalk pit at St Peters; the first Baptist chapel was built in Thanet in 1690 by Stephen Shallows, at a site known by his name.[97,98]

Inns and Innkeepers

Margate in the seventeenth and eighteenth centuries enjoyed some renown as a port of embarkation and disembarkation for the Low Countries (Chapter 2). Travellers using the harbour would sometimes need overnight accommodation and somewhere to eat and drink, facilities provided by the local inns. Inns also served as staging-points for carriers and coaches and, in the absence of other public buildings, as places where traders, farmers and ship's masters could meet to discuss business; they also provided rooms where public events such as meetings and auctions could be held. In fact, in the years before the middle of the eighteenth century, Margate seems to have been rather poorly served with inns. A list of 'tavernes in tenne shires about London' published in 1636 included just two in Margate, those of 'Averie Ienkinson and Henry [..]ulmer'.[99] The second of these is probably Henry Culmer, Culmer being a common Margate name at the time; a Henry Culmer was buried at St John's in 1661. A national survey of the accommodation available at inns and alehouses in England in 1686 found that Margate had just 27 guest beds and stabling for just 40 horses, compared for example, to 236 guest beds and stabling for 467 horses in Canterbury, and 132 guest beds and stabling for 189 horses in Dover; Ramsgate had 17 available guest beds and stabling for 19 horses.[100] These numbers had, however, increased considerably by the time of a second survey in 1756, the report of which provides more information about how the survey was carried out.[101] In 1693 the country had been divided into 39 areas for Excise purposes, the areas being called *Collections*, loosely based on County boundaries. Each *Collection*, under the control of a *Collector*, was divided into a number of districts under the control of *Supervisors*. Districts were usually centered in local towns, and were referred to as *Divisions*; the countryside outside a town was called an *Out-Ride*. Margate was in the Sandwich Collection, and the town of Margate made up the Margate Division, with the surrounding countryside, probably corresponding to the rest of the parish of St John's, making up the Margate Out-Ride. In 1756 the Margate Division contained 16 inns and public houses, with 46 beds and stabling for 29 horses, and the Margate Out-Ride contained 12 inns and public houses, with 19 beds and stabling for 33 horses, giving a total of 28 inns and public houses, 65 beds, and stabling for 62 horses.[101] This is somewhat more than the provision at Ramsgate, which had 21 inns and public houses, 34 beds and stabling for 56 horses, but considerable less than the 69 inns and public houses with 182 beds and stabling for 193 horses available at Dover. These numbers emphasize that the number of travellers passing through Margate at the time was still very small compared to the number passing through Canterbury or Dover, and that Margate's few inns were rather small.

The larger of the inns were likely to have been located close to the harbour, on what was to become the Parade and Bankside. Edmund's map of 1821 and the Ordnance Survey map of Margate of 1852 show six inns there, starting at the west end with the York Hotel at the junction of Duke Street with the Parade and, next to it, the White Hart Hotel at the junction of the Parade with Bridge Street. Further to the east were the Hoy Inn, at the junction of Bankside with Pump Lane, and the Ship Inn, the Dukes Head Hotel, and the Pier Hotel, originally the Foy Boat, opposite the Pier. The most important of these inns for the history of Margate was the York Hotel, originally called the Black Horse Inn, and renamed the New Inn from 1761 and the York Hotel from 1793. It was here that Thomas Barber erected the first salt-water bath in Margate in 1736 and where, in 1753, his widow built the first assembly room in Margate.[102,103] The early history of the Black Horse is unknown. We know more about the early history of the White Hart, although much of that is confusing. The first deed for the White Hart identified by Arthur Rowe was dated 1701: 'John Savage, victualler, of the White Hart, leaves to Mary Savage, his wife, the White Hart, and all stables, buildings, and outhouses, and gardens. Also all those two messuages adjoining, in the occupation of John Turner and Arthur Geerson'.[24] In 1711 Mary Savage married Edward Constant, a mariner, both of whom died in 1729.[24] An advertisement in 1729 in the *Kentish Post* announced that 'Valentine Jewell, junior, who married Mr Abraham Hudson's Daughter of Deal, having taken the sign of the White-Hart Inn in Margate, Mr Constant and his wife being deceased; this is to give notice, that all Gentlemen and others will there find good entertainment; and may be furnished with good Horses, at reasonable Rates'.[104]

A clue to the earlier history of the White Hart is provided by references to an inn known as the Posthouse. A post-house or posting-house was a house or inn where stage coaches stopped, horses were fed and watered, teams changed, and post-chaises could be hired for short journeys off the main coach-routes. Although posthouses were not necessarily connected to the postal service, local postmasters were often innkeepers who took the position of postmaster to bring custom to their houses.[105] The advertisement referred to above shows that Valentine Jewell purchased the White Hart after the death of the previous owners, Edward Constant and his wife. However, witness statements in the legal case of 1716 concerning the will of John Glover were taken 'at the dwelling house of Edward Constant commonly called by the name of the Posthouse in the village of Margate'.[69] The obvious conclusion is that the White Hart and the Posthouse were one and the same. The witness statements also describe Edward Constant, a witness in the case, as 'postmaster'.

There are several other early references to the Margate Posthouse. One is in *A new journey to France*, a book published by J. Baker in 1715, describing incidents on his journey:[106]

Margate is a small village in the Isle of Thanet, just on this side of the point call'd the North Foreland . . . we arrived safe at Margate . . . I lay there at the Post-house . . . and next day I set out in a wherry for Gravesend

A more intriguing reference occurs in an account of the role of Captain William Ricards in foiling a plot against the life of William III in 1695. Ricards at the time was living in London:[107]

[and] he became intimate with one *Bourne*, who in conversation . . . confessed that he had come to the knowledge of a traitorous conspiracy against the King. After which, Mr Ricards never left him till he went with him to Sir William Trumbal, one of his Majesty's Principal Secretaries of State, about the 20th of September, 1695, at what time his Majesty was expected to return to England [from Holland] . . . Bourne gave sufficient information to satisfy Mr Secretary there was a secret enterprise resolved upon; to execute which several persons lay concealed at Margate, where it was expected his Majesty would land [and] that these men were provided with firearms, and had a vessel for their service, which lay off of Margate . . . The Secretary of State, and Lords of the Council, thought it prudent to look farther into the matter, and see whether any such persons

could be found at that place. To this end, they proposed to Capt. Ricards to go himself thither, having understood by him that he was a native of that place, and very well acquainted with it; they offered him whatever assistance and support he desired. Their Lordships had no difficulty to prevail with a gentleman so well affected to King William, to undertake that service; and the Earl of Romney, Lord Warden of the Cinque Ports, signed the following warrant.

> To all whom these Presents may concern.
> Know ye, that the Bearer hereof, Capt. William Ricards, by command from me, is commissioned hereby to seize and apprehend several dangerous persons, of which you shall receive notice by him. I therefore hereby require and command all officers both military and civil, to be aiding and assisting to the said Capt. William Ricards, in effecting the same. Given under my hand and seal this 25th day of September, 1695.
> ROMNEY

Capt. Ricards took two yachts, and a company of soldiers from the tower [of London], and without communicating his departure to any one person whatsoever, made down to Margate; pretending to spend a few days with his friends and acquaintance there, whom he had not seen in many year: and that none of them might take it ill in particular, that he did not lodge at his house, he took lodgings at *Paul Hart's*, the Posthouse, yet the most suspected place in the town for the conspirators to be conceal'd in. Major *Gregory*, Tower-Armourer, was the only man who came ashore with him, and tho' he made as diligent search as could be done, without giving the alarm to those that were concealed there, he at first made no discovery, those persons keeping close all day. The wind was contrary, and kept the King back a fortnight, and in that length of time, Capt. Ricards found out that there were persons concealed in the house, with some circumstances that were very suspicious. Five lodg'd in one room, where was good store of fire-arms, and that room very convenient for any sudden attempt upon landing; He often heard them drink mysterious healths in their midnight revellings, 'twas plain by their discourse that there were others concerned, by whom they expected to be joined, as soon as they were ready for it; which fully convinced Capt. Ricards that he could not use too many precautions, to prevent their executing their hellish design.

The wind coming fair for his Majesty, he ordered the officers of the yachts ashore, and invited several of his friends in the town, which he could trust, to an entertainment, under pretence of paying his foy [a farewell feast or drink] upon his return to London the next day: and after he had entertained them till near midnight, he fasten'd the door, and made known to the company the business he came for, and what he had done in it; that he had discovered several suspicious fellows, who were concealed in that House, and he then shewed the necessity of securing their persons before the King landed. He called in *Paul Hart* the innkeeper, and clapping a pistol to his breast, threatened immediately to shoot him, if he did not discover who were the persons concealed in such a room in his inn, and what was their intent. Paul Hart presently owned their being there, and that they had been thus shut up in a room for some time, but he knew not their Intent, nor anything more of them, than that they ordered him to keep their being there a secret; and that as soon as the fleet which was to bring over the King appeared in sight, he was to knock at their chamber-door, and say *Twynam is come*. Capt. Ricards obliged Hart to go with him and his friends directly to the room these fellows were in, to knock at the door, and cry *Twynam is come*; upon which, it was immediately opened by an Irishman, who seemed to be the head of them; he had a pistol in his hand, which Capt. Ricards laid hold on, and obliged him to drop it; and the company breaking in at the same time, secured the rest in their beds. He found a great many fire-arms, as Bourne had informed him, which were all loaden; and lay on the table. The King landed in a few hours after, and Capt. Ricards brought away the five ruffians to London, where they were committed to Newgate, and having lain there some weeks, they were let go; Bourne's evidence being single, and not sufficient to convict them of treason.

Paul Hart, as well as being the innkeeper of the Posthouse, was also the Margate postmaster but was dismissed in 1697 for 'assisting in the running a parcel of lace'.[108]

The White Hart remained in the hands of Valentine Jewell until at least February 1747. An advertisement for an auction of smuggled drinks held in 1737 in the White Hart announced:[109]

To be sold to the highest and best bidder, by publick sale, On Tuesday the 12th of July, 1737, by one o'clock in the afternoon, At the House of Valentine Jewell, call'd or known by the name of the White Hart in Margate in the Isle of Thanet,
70 Hogsheads of French white wines in good condition
16 ditto, but indifferent
1 ditto and half French claret in good condition
670 Gallons of good old French brandy,
In several lots, clear of all duties.

Again, ten years later, in February 1747, the auction of a ship, the *Success*, was advertised 'at Mr Valentine Jewell's at the White Hart in Margate'.[110]

However, later in 1747 the situation becomes confused. An advertisement of May 1747 reported that the master of the Posthouse was Michael Trapp:[111]

WHEREAS Bathing in the SALT-WATER, hath been found by Experience to have very great Effect on various Diseases, incident to Human Nature, as well Chronick as Acute, I take this Opportunity to acquaint the Publick, that there is at the Post-House in Margate, in the Isle of Thanet, a new, very large and convenient Salt-Water Bath, much larger than any of its Kind hereabout, where the Morning Sun reflects it's Rays on the Surface of the Water, in a most agreeable Manner, and yet free from any Inclemency of the Air; with all necessary Accommodations for Gentlemen and Ladies.
N.B. Very good Private Lodgings, Stabling and Coach-Rooms, and the best of Usage,
By their most Obedient
Humble Servant,
MICHAEL TRAPP.

Valentine Jewell appears now to be master of another inn, the White Hart and Star. An advertisement of December 1747 for the auction of the ship, the *Posbroke*, described the auction as being held at 'the sign of the White Hart and Star, in Margate' and reported that 'an inventory [can] be seen at Mr Jewell's, the Place of Sale'.[112] Similar advertisements in 1760 refer to an auction of a farm house held at 'the House of Mr Valentine Jewell, known by the name or sign of the White Hart and Star, in Margate' and to an auction of spirits at 'the Excise-Office at the White Hart and Star at Margate.'[113,114] Then an advertisement appeared in 1761 referring to both the White Hart and Star and to another inn, The Old White Hart:[115]

A coach, or a post-chaise sets out every Monday, Wednesday, Thursday and Saturday, during the Bathing Season, from the Old White Hart, The White Hart and Star, or the Fountain, alternately, to the King's Head and George in Canterbury. – wait the coming in of the machines from London, and returns to Margate the same evening – 5s each passenger.

One possibility is that in late 1747 a new inn had appeared, the *White Hart and Star*, under Jewell, with the original *White Hart* now being referred to as the *Old White Hart*. Indeed, the first mention of the Old White Hart is in advertisement of December 1747, the year in which the first mention of the White Hart and Star appeared:[116]

Whereas it hath been insinuated since the Death of my Husband John Pannell, that I Martha Pannell intend to quit the Old White Hart Inn in the Town of Margate in the Isle of Thanet; this is therefore to inform all my Friends, Customers, and all others that will be so kind as to become so, that I never had an Intention to leave the said Inn, but to follow the said Business, and that whoever will be so kind as to make use of my House shall meet with good Entertainment. From their most obliged humble servant,
Martha Pannell,
    Horses and chaise to be Lett. Likewise, a Milch Ass and Foal to be Lett or Sold, at the same Place.

Despite Martha Pannell's wish to continue running the Old White Hart, by 1750 it had been taken over by John Watson; by 1759 John Watson was dead and his wife was probably running the inn, as an advertisement of March 1759 speaks of the auction of some houses 'at Mrs Watson's the Old White Hart'.[117,118] References to auctions at the Old White Hart appear in 1770 and 1774.[119,120] However, by then references to the White Hart and Star had ceased and, for example, sales of spirit that had previously been advertised as taking place in the Excise Office at the White Hart and Star[121] were now advertised at the Excise office at the White Hart.[122-124] It seems likely that the White Hart and Star either changed its name or closed down, and that the Old White Hart reverted back to its old name of the White Hart. In 1786 the announcement of the death of John Pain, the eldest son of Martin Pain, included the information that Martin Pain was 'master of the White Hart, Margate. and then in 1789 it was announced that 'William Mitchener from the New Inn Tap . . . informs his friends . . . he has taken the White Hart, on the Parade, near the Bridge (late Martin Paine's)'.[125,126]

    Of the other inns on the Parade, the Ship was probably the oldest: an indenture of 1699 refers to 'all that messuage or tenement called or known by the name or sign of the Shipp, with the backside, cellar, house of office and the lower end of the garden, now in occupation of John Wells'.[127] An indenture of 1761 gives some of its later history, describing how the Ship, 'at or near the Pier' was 'formerly in occupation of Edward Tibb and Elizabeth Laming, and late in occupation of Ann Ladd, widow, deceased, and now of Robert Ladd, son of Ann Ladd, and lately purchased by Francis Cobb from William and George Brooke'.[128] In contrast, the Hoy inn was not a particularly old inn; in 1713 the site of the Hoy was two houses in the occupation of William Brasford and John Freeman, and the first reference to the Hoy inn found by Arthur Rowe dates to 1753.[24] The Duke's Head was, however, old, being referred to in the Parish Burial Register for 1683: '2 Sept., 1683. Phillipe du Marius of the island of Gersey, master of the Shipp called the Guift of God, who died at the house of Roger Laming, known by the name of the Signe of the Dukes head in Margate'.[24] It is not known when the inn was first established. The old Foy Boat Inn adjoined the Duke's Head, on the east side, and, although its date is not known, Rowe identified it in the Poor Rate Assessments from 1726:[30]

    1726-1729   William Kerby
    1730-1738   Henry Amess (or Ames or Amos)
    1739   Thomas Ladd
    1739-1778   William Boorn (Bourn).

An assignment of lease of 1761 between William Friend and Francis Cobb refers to 'that messuage . . . known by the name of the Dolphin and then of the King William at or near the pier and late in the tenure of William Ladd', but its exact location is unknown.[129]

Edmunds map of 1821 shows a number of other inns and public houses in the streets leading from the sea, including the Queens Arms in Queen's Arms Yard, off Market Street, the Bulls Head opposite the Market, the Old Crown on Love Lane, the Fountain Inn and the George Inn on King street, the King's Head at the lower end of High Street and the Jolly Sailor, later the Prince of Wales, further along High Street. The indenture of 1632 already described records the sale of The Old Kings Arms and associated yards, stable and outhouses, 'close to the green called the bowling green' for £300 to Nicholas Woolman with, written on the back, 'the Queen's Armes'.[64] An indenture of 1641 then records the sale by Jasper Woolman to Jarvis Herniker of the Queens Arms, abutting 'a place called the Bowling Green'.[60] It seems certain therefore that sometime between 1632 and 1641 the inn changed its name from the Old Kings Arms to the Queens Arms. The inn can be traced back to 1616 when the head tapster of the inn was named and shamed at the annual visitation of the Archdeacon of Canterbury to the parish: 'William Saunders, the head tapster at the "King's Arms" for refusing to pay his cess to the poor, being twelve pence'.[7] Roadways led to the Queens Arm's yard from Market Street and Duke Street and early maps show a third roadway leading to the yard from Broad Street, via a break in the houses on Broad Street where the Wellington public house was later built. The Queen's Arms with its large yard and three roads leading to it must have been a place of some importance. The Accounts of the Overseers of the Poor show that the Queen's Arms was much used by the Overseers and that the inn was kept by Stephen Pamflett from at least 1679 and that in 1697 it was taken over by his widow.[35]

The Bull's Head dates back to at least 1732 when an advertisement appeared in the *Kentish Post* for the auction of a boat there; before 1800 it was always called the Bull Head. The George inn in King Street, although old, is of unknown date.[24] The early history of the Fountain Inn has already been touched on in the discussion of King Street. It was offered for sale in 1761 in the local and London papers:[130]

To be sold, either separate or together,
All that Messuage or Tenement, consisting of four Rooms on a Floor, commonly called or known by the Name or Sign of the FOUNTAIN and COFFEE HOUSE (being a good-accustomed Public House, free from Brewer) together with the Storehouses, Outhouses, Edifices, Buildings, Yards, Backsides, Ground, and Appurtenances thereunto belonging, with a good Lead Pump in the Kitchen, and exceeding fine Water, situate in the Center of the Town of Margate in the Isle of Thanet, in the County of Kent and now in the occupation of Mrs Elizabeth Pollen.

Also, two large Stables, with Stalls sufficient for 16 Horses, and a Hay-loft over the same, together with a Coach-house and Yard thereunto belonging, with a Pump with good Water, and a Tallow Chandler's Workshop, also situate at Margate aforesaid, and now in the Occupation of Jeremiah Salter and George Petter.

For further particulars inquire of Mess. Benn, Attorneys at Law, in Pudding lane, near the Monument, London; or of Mr George Friend, of Margate, aforesaid; or of Mr Samuel Simmons, Attorney at Law, at Sandwich in Kent.

The Fountain Inn had an important connection with the theatre at Margate, with a stable at the back of the inn being used as a theatre in the 1770s.[81]

The age of the King's Head in the High Street is unknown, but it was old enough to have received a bad press in 1724:[131]

We hear that some gentlemen coming from France, and stopping at a certain noted Inn, not seven miles off the King's Head in Margate, their landlord had the civility to demand of them 16s for a gallon of brandy, 2s 6d for only boiling a leg of mutton and cabbage, and 6d for a tea-kettle of water; and insisted so very strenuously on his demands, that rather than abate anything, he saw fit to follow the gentlemen three miles who were so well pleased with their treatment, that they were resolved to have their landlord's company so far before they would discharge him, and now publish it that all persons who are desirous of the same kind of usage, may know where to find it.

The Jolly Sailor, later the Prince of Wales, on the High Street is also of unknown vintage, its first mention being in an advertisement in the *Kentish Post* for 1765:[132]

Abraham Cottew and Francis Wood, having opened a shoe-warehouse, near the sign of the Jolly Sailor, in the Town of Margate, where they intend to sell all sorts of means and womens shoes and pumps, mens channel pumps, with all sorts of childrens shoes and pumps, clogs and womens stuff shoes and pumps, at the lowest prices, for ready money.

A lease of 1765 refers to 'the messuage or tenement known by the sign of the Old Crown ... formerly in occupation of Joseph Miller and now of Charles Cricket'; the Old Crown was in Love Lane.[63]

Early newspaper advertisements mention a number of other inns in Margate whose locations are unknown. In 1729 an advertisement for 'Dr Daffey's Original and Famous Cordial Elixir Salutis, the Great Preserver of Mankind' listed one supplier as Mr Armstrong at the Rose and Crown, Margate.[133] An advertisement in the same paper in 1733 reported that 'William Armstrong is removed from the Rose and Crown in Margate to the Wheat-Sheaf in the said Place, a fine commodious new built house, with a pleasant prospect of the sea, from the top of it, and a good Summer House. There is also very good stabling, and good entertainment for Man and Horse'.[134] The location of the Rose and Crown is unknown but given William Armstrong's connection with the Fountain Inn in King Street, it is possible that this is an earlier name for the Fountain. The Wheatsheaf could be the inn of that name still to be found in Northdown Road. The Crown and Thistle is mentioned in the *Kentish Post* in 1759 and a robbery is reported there in 1795; Arthur Rowe locates it on the east side of Bridge Street.[24,135] The Rose was a very old inn; in 1662 the Governor of Dover Castle called a meeting of the Pier Wardens 'at the signe of the Rose, being the house of John Bushell in Margate', and several payments to John Bushell for refreshments appear in the accounts of the Overseers of the Poor in the period 1680-1699, but the location of the Rose is also unknown.[2,35]

Entertainment

The only places of public entertainment in Margate were the inns where the entertainment on offer was unlikely to have been much more than wine, women, and song. Valentine Jewell junior, when he took over the White-Hart Inn in 1729, advertised that 'all Gentlemen and others will there find good entertainment'.[104] Similarly, William Armstrong on moving to the Wheat-Sheaf advertised that the inn provided 'very good stabling, and good entertainment for Man and Horse'.[134] Sports and games, of course, were popular, often organized around the inns. In 1600 a group of men were reported to the Archdeacon of Canterbury during his visit to the parish 'for playing at Bowles in time of Divine Service, forenoon and afternoon', possibly on Bowling Green, the former name for the Market Place. In 1615 two men were found in an inn 'in the time of Divine service in the afternoon' playing at tables, a popular game similar to backgammon.[7,136]

Although there was no permanent theatre in the town at this time, strolling bands of players were common. Mr Dymer's Company of Comedians, during their tour of Kent in 1730, travelled from Canterbury to Margate, with a 'diverting comedy called The Busie Body'.[137] This was apparently a great success: 'We hear from Margate, that Mr Dymer meets with so great encouragement that notwithstanding the Play-house is very large it will not contain the Company that Resort there'.[138] It is not known where the playhouse referred to was, but it could have been a building specially adapted for the occasion or, more likely, a barn attached to one of the inns in the town.[81] There are no further records of professional players in Margate until 1752, but, as strolling bands of players were common everywhere, it is quite likely that Margate enjoyed its share of such visits.[81] The only other organized entertainment of which we have record is horse racing. An advertisement appeared in the *Kentish Post* in September 1732 for a race to be held at Hartsdown:[139]

To be run for, on Hartsdown at Margate in the Isle of Thanet, on Wednesday the 20th of this instant September, a Saddle and Bridle of a guinea and a half value, and a whip of half a guinea, by any horse, mare, or gelding, of the said Isle that has been in the possession of the owner one month past, or any horse, mare, or gelding elsewhere, that never started for the value of five pounds, carrying ten stone, the best of three heats, two miles each heat. To pay half a crown entrance, and to be shewn and enter'd at 12 o'clock on the day of running, at the White Hart in Margate. To start by three, and the second best horse to have the whip.

Communications

Roads

The most important road in Kent was the Dover Road, formerly known as Watling Street, running from London, through Dartford, Rochester and Canterbury, to Dover, the usual port for crossing to France or Flanders. Travellers to London by road from the Isle of Thanet would first have travelled to Canterbury and then continued to London by the Dover Road. The Dover Road was described by Ogilby in his *Britannia* in 1675 as being 'in general a very good and well beaten way, chiefly chalky and gravelly', running over solid, gravel-based ground from London to Rochester and then over chalk to Canterbury and Dover.[140,141]

An act of 1555 had made it the duty of every parish to look after the roads in the parish.[142] On four days of the year those occupying land in the parish had to provide carts and men, two per cart, to work on the highway and every other householder in the parish had to labour themselves on the road, or send a substitute. This system of statute labour was deeply unpopular, and largely failed to keep the roads in good condition; it was replaced in the middle 1600s by a parish rate to be used to hire labourers to do any necessary work on the roads.[143] The work deemed necessary would have been simple tasks such as clearing ditches, cutting back overhanging trees and hedges and filling in the worst of the ruts and potholes with a bit of gravel. On rural roads with only light traffic this would have kept the roads passable but for busy main routes more was required and that would have cost money, money that the parishes did not have. The problem was overcome by the introduction of turnpikes, roads which travellers paid to use, the money raised being used to pay for the upkeep of the road. Much of the road from London to Dover was turnpiked in the first half of the eighteenth century, with one of the busiest parts, between Northfleet and Rochester being completed in 1711, and that between Rochester and Canterbury soon after, in 1730; turnpikes were not built in Thanet until the early 1800s.[141,144]

Traffic on the roads was a mixture of those walking, those riding, and those using horse-drawn vehicles. The fastest of the horse-drawn vehicles was the coach, a mode of transport originally only available to the wealthy who owned their own, but becoming more widely available after the introduction of long-distance coach services in the seventeenth century. Transport along the Dover road was well organized from at least the seventeenth century.[141] Wagons provided a regular carrier service, leaving at advertised times from specified inns and calling at others along the route. By 1681 there was a regular postal service between London and Canterbury with post boys leaving Canterbury every Saturday and Wednesday for The Dark Horse in Billingsgate, returning every Monday and Thursday. As early as 1647 regular coach services ran between Rochester and Gravesend, from where it was usual to proceed to London by ferry, thus avoiding the bad roads in London and the robbers waiting for coaches at Shooter's Hill and Blackheath.[145]

Travel by coach could be surprisingly fast. The system of changing horses at regular stages along the route, introduced in the middle of the seventeenth century, had increased the speed of coach travel from about 10-15 miles per day to 50 miles a day.[146] The Dutch painter William Schellinks described his coach journey from Canterbury to London in 1661; he caught the 6 am coach from Canterbury, reaching Sittingbourne at 9 am 'where we refreshed ourselves with few oysters and a cup of sack', and Chatham at 12 noon, which it took them 'almost an hour to get through', it being market day, finally reaching Gravesend at 2 pm.[147] Their plan was then to continue to London by river, but they missed the tide and had to stay the night. The following day they left Gravesend at 10 am and reached Tower Wharf in London at about noon. The details of their return journey emphasize the speeds that could be achieved – they left London at 2.30 in the afternoon, stayed overnight at Gravesend, set off by coach at 8 am next morning, getting to Sittingbourne by noon in time for a midday meal, continuing to Canterbury where they took lodgings for the night.

In 1681 a regular coach travelled between Canterbury and The George in Southwark leaving Canterbury on Monday, Wednesday and Friday, returning on Tuesday, Thursday and Saturday.[148] In 1692 the Canterbury Flying-Stage Coach also did the journey in a day:[149]

Canterbury Flying-Stage Coach
These are to acquaint all gentlemen and others, that the old stage-coach sets out from the Crown Inn in Canterbury, every Monday, Wednesday and Friday and returns to Canterbury from the Starr Inn on Fish-street-Hill next the Monument every Tuesday, Thursday and Saturday. And if you have occasion for a coach to Deal, Dover, or any other place on that road, you may be faithfully furnished at the same place. Performed if God permit, by William Powell, and William Varnam.

Advertisements for two competing Canterbury Flying Stage Coach services appeared regularly from 1729, one run by John Bolver from the Red Lyon in Canterbury to the Cross Keys in Grace Church Street, London, and the other by Thomas Hartup from the King's Head Canterbury to the Spread Eagle, also in Grace Church Street, both leaving Canterbury on Monday, Wednesday and Friday, and returning on Tuesday, Thursday and Saturday.[150] By 1736 the services had combined and were advertised as being run by 'John Bolver and Thomas Hartcup'.[151] These fast timings required large numbers of horses. In 1701 the establishment kept by William Vernon at Rochester was advertised for sale, following his death: 'A hearse, 4 stage coaches and 26 Coach horses with their harness, lately kept by Mr Vernon of Rochester, deceased, for the stages of Canterbury, Dover, Deale, Maidstone, Rochester, Gravesend and London, and a stock of hay and oats. Are to be sold'.[152]

Those who could afford it travelled inside the coach, sitting two or three to a side; the less affluent would travel on the roof, with little protection from the elements. For those who could not afford even the roof, there were the regular waggon services where passengers could pay to sit on top of the freight.[153] Waggons were large and cumbersome, sometimes pulled by horses and sometimes by trains of packhorses, which had the advantage of being smaller and eating less than the horses used to pull waggons. The waggons could be large; as early as 1604 Canterbury Quarter Sessions heard that waggons were carrying 'above 50 hundredweight' (2½ tons) along the road between Canterbury and Sittingbourne 'to the great annoyance of all travaylers'.[143]

Early travellers have left us reports of their experiences on the Dover road. In about 1600 Paul Hentzner, a German lawyer, became tutor to a young Silesian nobleman, and embarked on a three year tour of England, France, Switzerland, and Italy. He described their journey by post-horse from Canterbury to Dover:[154]

We came to it [Canterbury] on foot . . . Being tired with walking, we refreshed ourselves here with a mouthful of bread and some ale, and immediately mounted post-horses, and arrived about two or three o'clock in the morning at Dover. In our way to it, which was rough and dangerous enough, the following accident happened to us: our guide, or postillion, a youth, was before with two of our company, about the distance of a musketshot; we, by not following quick enough, had lost sight of our friends; we came afterwards to where the road divided; on the right it was downhill and marshy, on the left was a small hill: whilst we stopped here in doubt, and consulted which of the roads we should take, we saw all on a sudden on our right hand some horsemen, their stature, dress, and horses exactly resembling those of our friends; glad of having found them again, we determined to set on after them; but it happened, through God's mercy, that though we called to them, they did not answer us, but kept on down the marshy road at such a rate, that their horses' feet struck fire at every stretch, which made us, with reason, begin to suspect they were thieves, having had warning of such; or rather, that they were nocturnal spectres, who, as we were afterwards told, are frequently seen in those places: there were likewise a great many Jack-a-lanterns, so that we were quite seized with horror and amazement! But, fortunately for us, our guide soon after sounded his horn, and we, following the noise, turned down the left-hand road, and arrived safe to our companions; who, when we had asked them if they had not seen the horsemen who had gone by us, answered, not a soul. Our opinions, according to custom, were various upon this matter; but whatever the thing was, we were, without doubt, in imminent danger, from which that we escaped, the glory is to be ascribed to God alone.

In about 1663 Samuel Sorbiere, a French physician, described how, having landed at Dover, he journeyed on to London:[155]

I travelled by the way of Canterbury and Rochester to Gravesend, where, for the greater expedition, I took the boat, and the opportunity of the tide, to go to that city [London]; its fifty miles from Dover to London, from the first of which Canterbury is distant twelve miles; and a good horseman, well mounted, may gallop it in an hour's time... That I might not take Post, or be obliged to make use of the Stage Coach, I went from Dover to London in a waggon, it was drawn by six horses, one before another, and drove by a waggoner, who walked by the side of it; he was clothed in black . . . he had a brave Mounteero on his head, and was a merry fellow, fancy's he made a figure, and seemed mightly pleased with himself.

In 1670 another French traveller, Monsieur Jouvin De Rochefort, Treasurer of France, went from Canterbury to Gravesend by stage coach:[156]

Here [at Canterbury] we took the Ordinary coach for Gravesine (Gravesend) in order to embark there for London, and we passed by Arbertoon (Harbledown); from thence we found some woods near Baton (Boughton) and Asbery (Ospringe). We passed through Grinsrit (Greenstreet), Sitingborn, Nieuvetoon (Newington) and Renem (Rainham) which has a fine tower to its church. We observed all along this road high poles, on the tops of which were small kettles, in which fires were lighted to give notice when there is any danger in the country, and robbers on the way. The towns and neighbouring villages are obliged to send guards to drive them away or take them, and to keep the highways always safe and secure for passengers; these likewise serve as I imagine in time of war to give notice to the neighbouring towns of the march of the enemy and of his designs: these poles are about a mile distant from each other, and to every one there is a small hut for those persons whose business it is to light the fires.

Finally, yet another Frenchman, M. Grosley, provides a description of a journey along the Dover road in 1765, by which time the road had been turnpiked:[157]

The great multitude of travellers with which Dover was crowded afforded a reason for dispensing with a law of the police, by which public carriages are in England forbid to travel on Sundays. I myself set out on a Sunday with seven more passengers in two carriages called flying machines. These vehicles which are drawn by six horses, go twenty-eight leagues in a day from Dover to London for a single guinea. Servants are entitled to a place for half that money, either behind the coach, or upon the coach-box, which has three places. A vast repository under this seat, which is very lofty, holds the passengers luggage, which is paid separately. The coachmen, whom we changed every time with our horses, were lusty well-made men, dressed in good cloth. When they set off, or were for animating their horses, I heard a sort of periodical noise, resembling that of a stick striking against the nave of the fore-wheel. I have since discovered, that it is customary with the English coachmen, to give their horses the signal for setting off by making this noise, and by beating their stools with their feet in cadence; they likewise use the same signal to make them mend their pace. The coach-whip, which is nothing else but a long piece of whalebone covered with hair, and with a small cord at the end of it, is no more in their hands than the fan is in winter in the hand of a lady; it only serves then to make a shew with, as their horses scare ever feel it.

Grosley explained that an advantage of traveling on a Sunday was that 'we met with no custom-house officers in the places where they are usually posted; this saved us a great deal of searching and visiting' although time was lost as 'on account of the absence of the custom-house officers, care had been taken to fill the boxes of our carriages with kegs of brandy, which we left at the inns upon the road'. Another advantage of travelling on a Sunday was that highwaymen did not work on Sundays and the only highwaymen that he saw 'were hanging upon gibbets at the road-side; there they dangle, dressed from head to foot, and with wigs upon their heads'.

He also reported on the state of the road:

The high roads, which, like all those of England, had been ruined during the civil wars, and entirely neglected till the reign of George the second, were then taken into consideration by the parliament. Being covered with powdered flint stones, they are kept in perfect repair, though in England, neither the duty of average nor the proper art of raising causeways are known.

It must be acknowledged, that the expense for keeping them in repair is not so considerable as elsewhere; in England the sea supplies the principal means of transporting goods of all sorts. The repairing of the high roads is at the expense of those who use them; the turnpikes or barriers are shut, against the carriages; where they pay the price settled by a tariff fixed up, according to the number of horses which draw them. Neither rank nor dignity is exempt from these payments: the king himself is subject to them.

The high roads have all along them a little bank raised above them, and two or three feet broad, with a row of posts on each side, whose tops are whitened that they may be seen during the night by the drivers of carriages. This is for the conveniency of those that walk afoot. In places where the narrowness of the ground is unfavourable to this arrangement, the proprietors of adjoining lands are obliged to give a passage through their fields, which are all inclosed with strong hedges. The communications of these passages, as well as of those around villages, are formed by hurdles of about four feet high; passengers must partly leap and partly climb over them.

The high roads are very far from being exactly rectilineal; not but that there are engineers in England skilful enough to draw a right line across a field; but, besides that the dearness of land requires some caution, property is in England a thing sacred, which the laws protect from all encroachment, not only from engineers, inspectors, and other people of that stamp, but even from the king himself.

Finally he reported on the carts seen on the road:

We met a considerable number of carriages loaded with corn and hay, which were going to the ports. Each of the drivers (who were all either labourers or husbandmen) dressed in good cloth, a warm great coat upon his back, and good boots on his legs, rode upon a little nag; he had a long whip in his hand to drive his team; the horses were vigorous and in good plight, and drew with strong chains instead of traces.

Those heading to Margate from Canterbury would have had to travel over the local roads. A sketch map of the Isle of Thanet by Thomas of Elmham dating to about 1414 shows a trackway leading from Sarre to the church of St John's and then to Mergate on the coast. The crossing at Sarre was originally by ferry but an Act passed in 1485 allowed for the ferry to be replaced by a bridge.[158] It is worth quoting the preamble to the bill as it gives the reasons for building the bridge:

Forasmuch as the Isle of Tenet, in the county of Kent, lying upon the high sea on the east and north parts thereof, and to the river of salt water leading from a place called Northmouth, joining the sea, to a place within the shire called Sarre, and from thence to the town and haven of Sandwich, and so forth to the sea on the west and south parts of the isle, out of time of mind, hath been enclosed and environed with the sea and river; at which place, called Sarre, by all this time, hath been had and used a passage, and a ferry, called Sarre ferry, over the said river, by a ferry boat, out of the isle into the country of the shire of

Kent, for all manner of persons, beasts, corn, and other things, to pass and be conveyed at all seasons, to and from the same isle and country; by which same ferry also, when enemies afore this time have arrived, and purposed to have arrived in the isle, the people of the same country lightly have been conveyed and might be conveyed into the isle to resist all such enemies for defence and tuition [protection] of the isle. It is so now that, by change of the course of the sea, which hath fortuned in years late passed, the river at the place called Sarre, where the ferry and passage was had and used, is so swared, [sluggish] grown, and highed with wose, [silted up with ooze, etc.] mud, and sand, that now no ferry or other passage may be there, nor in any other place nigh adjoining and convenient, to or from the isle, by boat or otherwise, but only at high spring floods, and that not passing an hour at a tide, to the great hurt and impoverishing of the possessioners, landholders, owners, and inhabitants of the isle and country, and by likelihood in time of war great jeopardy and fear of loss of the isle, if enemies should fortune to arrive in the same.

The bill allowed the inhabitants of Thanet to build a bridge at Sarre Ferry, 'of such reasonable length, height, and large space between the arches thereof, that boats and lighters may pass to and fro under the same, at any time hereafter when the water may happen to increase and be sufficient' for their passage. After completion of the bridge Commissioners were to be appointed who would make provision for repairs and maintenance of the bridge and approaches, paid for by the inhabitants of Thanet. Major repairs were indeed needed by 1729 and the bridge had to be closed while the work was being done; forewarning of the expected disruption was given in an advertisement in the local paper:[160]

Whereas the bridge at Saar that doth lead the way into the Island of Thanet being out of repair, is by the Honourable the Commissioners of Sewers ordered to be immediately repaired and sufficiently amended, for the safe passage of cattle, carriages, horses, and passengers over the same, and that in order to the repair of the said bridge, the same will on Monday the 19th day of May instant be uncovered, laid open, and be uncapable to be passed on and over until Friday the 23rd day of this said month of May. This is to give notice thereof to all whom it may concern. And it is desired of those who meet with and read this Advertisement, that they will help to perfect it, by giving notice of the same to others it may concern, that they know or see, and who they think may not happen to see or read this Advertisement.

The bridge is shown on the earliest detailed map of Kent, that of Symonson of 1596. This shows the main road from Canterbury to the Isle of Thanet crossing over the bridge at Sarre, and then following a fairly straight inland route through Monkton and Acol, bypassing Birchington, to reach Margate at the west end of the bay. Symonson's map shows none of the minor roads, most of which would have been just bridle paths; the first map to include such roads was that of John Harris published in 1717 (Figure 2). Harris's map shows the main road from Canterbury following the same route as that shown by Symonson, except that the road reaches Margate not at the bay but at a junction with the King's Highway leading to the church, later to become the High Street. A minor road is also shown, branching off from the main road from Canterbury just beyond the crossing at Sarre, and running through St Nicholas to Birchington and Garlinge to join the King's Highway at its northern end, close to Margate bay. Other minor roads link Margate to Minster in the west, to Sandwich, to Broadstairs and to Ramsgate. Later maps, such as John Hall's map of 1777 (Figure 4) show the Canterbury road taking a more inland route beyond Acol to pass by Hengrove and Shotendane to reach Salmstone, where the road turns north to reach the King's Highway at its southern end near the church. The minor road from Birchington also now takes a more inland course beyond Garlinge to pass through Hartsdown to reach Salmestone where it joins the main Canterbury Road. This realignment of the roads was probably required to improve access to the town and cope with the increased levels of traffic experienced once Margate had become established as a sea-side resort. Arthur Rowe suggested that the main road from Canterbury was the 'winter road' whereas in the summer coaches followed the minor road via Birchington.[161] There was no road to Margate from the west along the coast because of the barrier provided by the Brooks. The road shown on Hall's map of 1777 from Birchington to Westgate was only a bridle-track ending at the cliff edge near Westbrook Mill, where Royal Crescent now stands; there was no road from Westbrook Mill into Margate.[161]

The roads in Thanet would have been something of a disappointment to a traveller after the Dover road. *A Description of the Isle of Thanet and particularly of the Town of Margate*, published in 1763, described what a traveller could expect: 'The Roads about the islands are rendered so intricate, by means of many short turnings, as to be extremely disagreeable to those who are not well acquainted with them. The inhabitants of Ramsgate from a just sense of the respect due to Strangers, have lately erected Guide-posts in all places of difficulty within their precinct; and I hope the adjacent parishes will not hesitate to follow so truly laudable an example. Nor is this the only inconvenience; for the Bye-roads are by no means fit for quartering carriages. It is but a short time since they have been much used by any others, than those employed in husbandry; but the Land-holders, now finding themselves every where under a necessity of rendering the ways passable, or of having their corn trampled down, are beginning to make improvements of this sort'.[162] A description of the roads in 1796 gives a picture of what they must have been like earlier in the century: 'The roads about this island being originally intended only for carts and waggons, were formerly much neglected, and scarcely passable by the more delicate carriages of convenience or pleasure, but, to the credit of the inhabitants, they have been lately much improved, and are now made so commodious, that although there are no turnpikes, the traveller in Thanet will, without expence, experience all the advantages of that useful institution'.[163]

There are no records of regular coach services from Thanet to Canterbury until after the holiday trade developed later in the eighteenth century, or of regular waggon or cart services, although there is an advertisement for a regular tilt wagon service from Canterbury to Deal, run by Thomas Beale in 1735:[164]

Thomas Beale sets out with a Tilt Cart and two horses from his House in Deale to the Bell in Sandwich, and from thence to the Vine in the Fish Market, Canterbury, every Monday and returns on Tuesdays, and will continue to carry passengers or Goods at reasonable rates.

Few, if any, of the inhabitants of Margate were wealthy enough to own their own carriage; whilst documents of the time contain many references to horses, stables, and farmer's carts there are no references to carriages and carriage houses. An inventory of 1732 of the goods of Edward Jarvis, one of the local doctors, included a stable containing one horse, but no mention of a carriage.[166] The great and the good arriving by sea in Margate ensured that their own coaches would be waiting there for them (Chapter 2). In 1718 'A Coach and Six Horses are gone to Margate to meet the Earl Cardogan, who is hourly expected there from Holland'

and in October 1720 'Tuesday Morning several of the King's Coaches and Carriages set out for Margate, to wait his Arrival from Holland'.[167,168]

Most journeys, if not on foot or in a farmer's cart, were on horseback. The national survey of inns undertaken in 1686 found that there was stabling for 40 traveller's horses in the town's inns, the number increasing to 62 in 1756.[100,101] An advertisement for the White Hart Inn in 1729 assured 'all Gentlemen and others' that they 'may be furnished with good Horses, at reasonable Rates'.[169] Carriages are not mentioned until 1747 when an advertisement for the Posthouse at Margate mentions 'very good . . . stabling and coach-rooms'.[111] Pier Accounts and the Accounts of the Overseers of the Poor include many charges for the hire of horses but none for the hire of carriages.[39,51] In 1686 the Deputy and one of the Pier Wardens travelled to London and charged £4 1s 'for 11 days for our horses and our selves' and a Pier Warden charged £1 4s for '2 horses hire to London and Maidstone'. There are occasional references in the overseers' accounts to the hire of carts, as in 1733 when they moved a woman and her child out of the parish and paid 1s 3d 'for a cart to carry the woman and child aboard of the hoy, and other help'.

Someone wishing to send a small package would have been able to make use of the newsmen who distributed the local Canterbury paper, the *Kentish Post and Canterbury Newsletter.* The paper had been established in 1717 and its agents, the newsmen, each had a route, radiating out from Canterbury which they followed to distribute the paper, together with parcels and patent medicines, which were much in demand at the time. The routes of two of these newsmen are known, one going from Canterbury to Barham, Elham, Folkestone, Hythe, Dymchurch, Romney and Lydd, and the other from Canterbury to Faversham, Sittingbourne, Milton, Chatham and Rochester.[165] We also know that there was another route including Dover and Margate as in 1733 the Overseers of the Poor at Margate paid 5s 2d 'for a warrant from Dover by the News-man'.[39] Paying a newsman was a cheaper way of getting a warrant from Dover to Margate than sending a man especially to Dover to collect it, and the service was reasonably frequent, as the *Kentish Post and Canterbury Newsletter* was published twice weekly.

The Hoys

The importance of the harbour at Margate for the import and export of goods will be described in the following chapter. The speed and low cost of moving things by sea made the hoy a popular mode of transport for small items as well as for bulk cargos such as corn and coal. Hoymen would often carry parcels from Margate to London, acting as a 'common carrier'. The parcels would be put onto the hoy without any proper inspection, convenient for anyone trying to move smuggled goods landed at Margate up to London, as found to his cost by Roger Laming, a local hoyman, in 1798 (Chapter 5). Hoys were also much used for passenger traffic; by the early eighteenth century the open holds of the old hoys had been 'decked-in', increasing the comfort of the journey.[170] In 1637 John Taylor provided a list of ships sailing from London 'to carry passegers and goods to the towns of England' and reported that 'a Hoigh from Rochester Margate in Kent, or Feversham and Maydston doth come to St Katherines Dock'.[171] By 1710 there was a weekly hoy service between Margate and London.[2,172] The hoys were used by the 'middling-sort' as well as by the poor; in 1635 Peter Criche, the vicar of St John's, and his parish clerk were drowned on a voyage to London in a hoy.[1] In 1731 a hoy with 30 passengers was reported lost: 'On Tuesday last a Hoy, bound to Margate in Kent, turning to windward under a hard gale of wind, was unhappily overset between Eriff and Woolwich, by which accident about 30 passengers were all lost'.[173] Hoys were also used by the Overseers of the Poor to transport seriously ill people for treatment in one of the London hospitals (Chapter 4).

The Post Office

The history of the post office in Kent has been told by Brian Austen in his *English Provincial Posts* and much of what follows is based on his book.[105] The beginnings of the postal system can be dated to Henry VIII's appointment of Sir Brian Tuke as the first Master of the Post. Tuke established a permanent post route along the Dover Road, dividing the road into stages with postmasters at each stage to provide horses for the King's messengers. Merchants and others were encouraged to take advantage of these royal mails, the recipient paying for the service at a fixed sum per sheet of paper, charged according to the distance travelled. In 1632 Thomas Witherings, a London merchant, took over responsibility for the foreign mails, increasing their speed and frequency. Under his management it was intended that letters leaving London by 6 pm should reach Dover early next day 'that ther may be sufficient day light for passage over sea the same day'. The postmasters along the road, mostly innkeepers, agreed that they would have 'sufficient horses and messingers alwaies in redinesse, to go forth with the pacquets with out aine delay and to deliver them from stage to stage within the compass of an hour & half for ene stage'.[105]

Speeds increased from about sixteen miles a day, achieved by foot post, to about 120 miles a day. In 1635 Withering also took over the inland posts, converting them to the system in operation on the Dover road. Rates for a letter consisting of a single sheet of paper were 2d up to 80 miles, 4d up to 140 miles, 6d over a 140 miles, and 8d to Scotland. Between London and Dover there were postmasters at Dartford, Gravesend, Rochester, Sittingbourne and Canterbury; there were also postmasters at Deal and Sandwich, probably to sends orders to and from any ships sheltering in the anchorage of the Downs. Postmasters were not directly employed by the Post Office but received a shilling a day for their services, except for the postmaster at Gravesend who received only sixpence, and 2½d per mile for the hire of horses. Postmasters were also granted sole right to provide horses for travellers wishing to travel post along the road.

It is not known when a postmaster was first appointed at Margate but it must have been before 1660 as in that year John Glover was sacked as postmaster because of his close contacts with 'disaffected persons', as described earlier in this Chapter.[87] A list of stages on the Dover Road dating from 1667 includes Deal, Sandwich and Margate, the mail between Canterbury and Deal going via Sandwich, with letters for Margate being left at Sandwich to be taken on by a separate post boy.[105] The service was not very good, as is clear from a letter from John Glover to Sir Joseph Williamson in London in 1672:[93]

May 11, 2 pm 1672. About sunrise this morning the whole Dutch fleet came in upon the Foreland, and lay off and on Margate, there most of the forenoon with their sails haled up. They were so near in that we could see their hulks very plain, but now they are beating off to sea again. I must send this to the post house at Sandwich, for no post goes from us, except Tuesdays and Fridays.

The postmaster at Deal appears to have been in charge of the post offices at Sandwich and Margate; in October 1674 he was asked to settle the Sandwich and Margate offices;[105]

I heare from Sandwich, that Mr Finch is gone into ye Contrey quits his Imployment soe doth his agents in ye Isle of Thanet, and without giveing me the least notice ... I must desire your assistance ernestly desiring you to go imediately to Sandwich and Thanet, and settle ye office in both places.

The postmaster at Margate in 1667 was Richard Langley, and Langley continued in post until 1672 when he died. In October 1674 'Mr Laming' was appointed postmaster at Margate, showing once again the importance of this family in the early history of the town.[105]

However good the postal service at Margate, many would ask a local sailor to carry their letters to London for them on one of the hoys, at a cost considerably less than that charged by the post office. On his appointment, Mr Laming was instructed 'to hinder the Hoys, wch Carry abundance of Letters from that Place'.[105] Another problem was that a significant part of the income of a postmaster came from his monopoly on providing horses for those travelling post, an income threatened when others also provided post horses. In February 1678 Mr Laming was advised to take legal action against those illegally hiring out post horses.[105]

Payments in the accounts of the Overseers of the Poor suggest that Paul Hart, the postmaster from 1691-1709, was an innkeeper who, sadly, at the end of his life fell on hard times, for in 1715 the Overseers paid 2s 'to Paul Hart in need'.[35] The next postmaster was Henry Savage, probably related to Mary Savage, wife of John Savage, the owner of the White Hart Inn in 1701.[35] Following the death of John Savage in 1710, Mary Savage married Edward Constant, who became Margate postmaster in 1719.

The Town Crier

In a small town like Margate, gossip and rumour would keep people informed about their neighbours' business, but for more formal matters there was the town crier, or bellman. As described in Chapter 5 the bellman would help in raising a hue and cry to catch a criminal, would let people know when something had been stolen, and so help in its recovery, and would let people know about articles that had been lost. The bellman would also broadcast the news of local events such as entertainments and auctions. A particularly important task was to announce when goods such as coal, wood, salt, butter or cheese had arrived in the harbour, as these had to be offered for sale to the inhabitants of the town according to the orders governing the Pier and Harbour (Chapter 2). The first town crier of whom we have any information is Abraham Pond who, in 1666, was paid an unknown sum 'for going to Lidden to fetch the Barley wee destrained and crying of it', that is, letting the inhabitants know that some barley was available for purchase.[35] Pond later became an innkeeper and was replaced as town crier by Thomas Bishop who, in 1702, was paid 4d 'for crying Widd Baylyes Goods'.[35] A later town crier was William Birch, who died in 1744, aged 77; Birch was also the Parish Beadle.[39] In 1735 the parish paid £2 2s 6d for a coat and a hat for William Birch, so that he must have been a resplendent figure in the town.[39]

CHAPTER 2

The Pier and the Harbour

Chalk cliffs on either side of the creek at Margate formed a small natural harbour with a mouth just wide enough to allow in small vessels. The harbour was used to ship corn and barley grown in the fertile lands of the Isle of Thanet to London; as far back as 1225 a licence had been given to Ricardus (Richard) of Margate and Sandwich to transport corn in his ship along the coast.[1] Unfortunately the cliffs were vulnerable to erosion by the sea and the gradual loss of the cliffs and the protection they provided meant that steps had to be taken to defend the harbour and prevent flooding of low lying land close to the shore. From the later thirteenth century it had been possible to compel local landowners to work together to tackle threats of flooding by issuing a Commissions *de walliis et fossatis* (of walls and ditches). In December 1331 a Commission *de walliis et fossatis* was issued to 'Master John de Rodeswell, Thomas de Faversham, Nigel de Wheteacre, and William de Reculvre' to protect 'the coast between the towns of Sere and Mergate in Thanet Island, co. Kent'.[2] In 1369 another Commission was issued, this time specifically to protect the harbours of the Isle of Thanet:[3]

Commission to John de Cobeham, Robert Bealknap, William de Horne, Simon de Kegworth and Thomas de Garwynton to survey the coasts of the isle of Thanet and to have all places in which ships or boats can put in defended by walls and dykes where possible, and all other necessary measures taken for defence of the island.

In 1377 steps were taken to protect a sea wall near Sarre:[4]

Appointment of William Tidecombe and John Fraunceys to take in the county of Kent labourers and workmen for the repair of a wall standing by the sea-shore in the isle of Thanet, called Saint Nicholas by Sarre, by the breaking and ruin of which great damage to the people of the adjacent country is feared, and to put them to the works at the king's wages.

In 1380 the problem was a more general one with all the 'walls of earth and the dykes' protecting the Isle of Thanet:[5]

Appointment of Robert Bealknap, Stephen de Valoynz, Thomas Fog, William Septvauntz, Nicholas atte Crouche, William Makenade, Thomas Garwynton of Well, Thomas Chiche of Balnerle and William Tytecombe, as the king's justices, to survey the condition of the isle of Thanet, the king being informed that divers inhabitants daily withdraw therefrom, that the walls of earth and the dykes formerly constructed for defence against hostile invasions are weak and in ruins, and that divers persons of that island, bound to find and maintain boats and other vessels for the passage and carriage of men and animals to and fro, have neglected to do so. They are to enquire who are so bound and to compel them thereto, as well as to repair the walls and cleanse the dykes, and those who are withdrawing to remain or find others in their place, with power to hear and determine the premises.

The reference to 'hostile invasions' suggests that the walls of earth were there to protect against foreign forces as well as against the sea.

Eventually the inhabitants of Margate were forced to construct a pier to provide protection for shipping and to construct walls or jetties of timber along the shore line to prevent the buildings around the creek from being flooded. These precautions were of limited success; John Leyland in the famous quotation already given said of Margate when he saw it in 1535-43 that 'there is a village and a peere for shyppes, but now sore decayed'.[6] From the time of Elizabeth I, if not before, the costs of maintaining the pier and the other sea defences were met by dues, or Droits, levied on corn and other merchandise shipped and landed at the pier.[7] In charge of collecting the Droits were two Pier Wardens and overseeing the whole process was the Lord Warden of the Cinque Ports because Margate was a 'member,' or administrative part, of the Cinque Port of Dover (Chapter 5). As described by Lewis in 1723:[7]

These rates were confirmed by the Lord Wardens of the Cinque Ports, who from time to time renewed and altered the Decrees made for Ordering and Management of this little harbour. The oldest we now have, are dated September 1615,

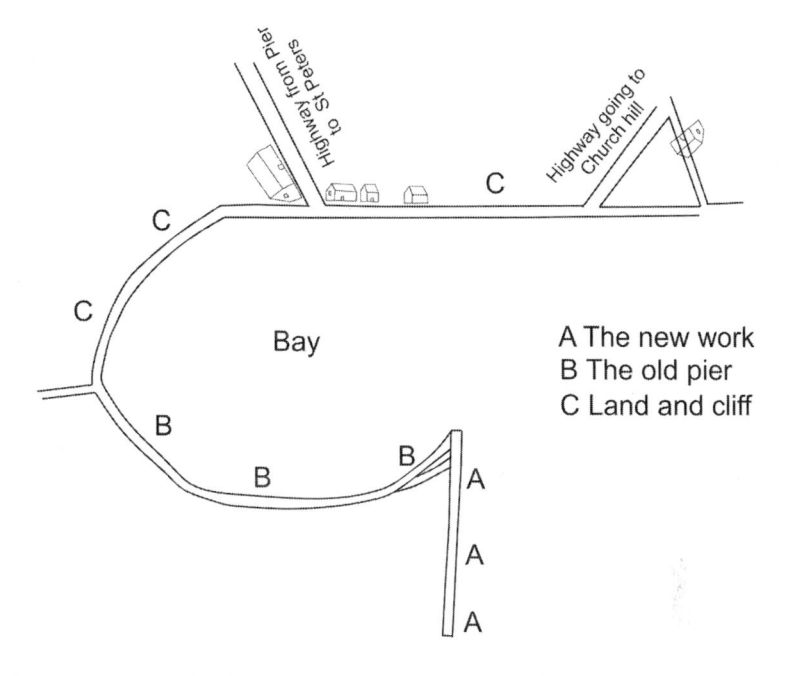

Figure 7. A sketch of the Pier in 1646 based on the Harleian manuscript in the British Library.

and confirmed by Edward Lord Zouch, St. Mauer, and Cantelpe, Lord Warden, Chancellor and Admiral of the Cinque Ports. In these orders &c it is said that they have been *usually confirmed* by the Lord Warden for the time being, and *Time out of Mind*, used by the inhabitants of Margate and St John's in the Isle of Thanet.

Membership of the Cinque Port system had many advantages for Margate, the principal one being that the town was exempt from many of the taxes and regulations governing the rest of Britain. Sometimes, though, exemption from regulation proved to be a disadvantage, as was the case with exemption from the regulations governing sea defences. Sea defences were normally the responsibility of the Commissioners of Sewers, a body concerned with land drainage and the prevention of flooding, not with the removal of sewage in the modern sense. The authority of the Commissioners dated back to the Statute of Sewers 1531, passed in the reign of Henry VIII. This gave the Commissioners, appointees of the Crown, the power to levy drainage rates on the occupiers of land benefiting from any drainage or sea defence works carried out on behalf of the Commissioners. The problem was that it was uncertain whether or not the Commissioners were responsible for flood defence work in the Cinque Ports.

In August 1621 the Commissioners of Sewers for Kent wrote to Lord Zouch, the Lord Warden of the Cinque Ports, enclosing a report on 'the loss of eighteen houses at Margate, and the peril of seventy-four more, and of 350 acres of land, by the building of the pier and jetty'.[8] Here, 'jetty' is used as a term for simple breakwaters and, more commonly, for retaining walls, or revetments, built along the shore line. As to the 'pier', this at the time was a simple wooden structure following a semi-circular course from south-east to north-west, with a breakwater called the New Work running northwards from the pier head (Figure 7).[9] It seems that this breakwater, although protecting the pier, caused considerable damage along the shore line around the creek. The Commissioners suggested that this damage could be prevented 'by erecting two jetties to preserve the houses; the expense to be met by a tax on the pier, which is the cause of the mischief and on the houses and land.' Although the Commissioners felt that 'the business of Margate Pier admits of no delay' they were not sure if their powers as Commissioners of Sewers for Kent actually extended to Margate as it was part of the Cinque Port system.[10] Whatever the exact legal position, Lord Zouch agreed to impose a tax on the Pier to pay for the necessary changes and repairs at Margate, but later in August he received a petition from some of the parishioners of St John's arguing 'against his decision that part of the profits of the pier at Margate should be employed to defend the houses against the encroachments of the sea, the pier being poor, and its funds needed for its own repairs or rebuilding, if swept away'.[8] The petition bore 21 signatures, including those of Paul Claybrook, William Claybrook, Daniel Pamphlett, John Laming, Valentine Pettit, Edward Taddye, and Henry Sandford, some of the wealthiest of the local landowners and merchants. It seems that those living in safety up the hill did not see why they should contribute, through a tax on the profits earned at the pier, to the safety of those living around the creek at the bottom of the hill. Lord Zouch arranged for an inspection of the pier and, in September 1621, Sir Henry Mainwaring, the Member of Parliament for Dover, and Robert Garrett, the Mayor of Dover, wrote to Lord Zouch saying that they had 'viewed the ruins made by the sea at Margate' and had concluded that 'the jetty [the New Work] built adjoining the pier is the cause of the danger'. They thought that 'the pier wardens, though unwilling, should bear the charge of repairs laid on them by the Commissioners of Sewers' and that 'the commission should be renewed and strengthened, that the work may be well furthered before winter'.[10] They also suggested that the jurisdiction of the Commissioners should be extended 'and the whole of the Isle of Thanet inserted' so that it would be clear that they had jurisdiction over the work at Margate.[10]

It seems that a compromise was reached in which some of the costs of the repairs were to fall on the users of the pier but some were to be bourn by those whose properties would be protected by the new defences. The Commissioners raised a tax of £223 0s 6d 'levied on the pier of Margate, and on the houses and lands endangered by the sea' but this proved to be insufficient and in April 1622 the Commissioners announced that 'a second tax, but less in amount, is to be raised, to pay the remainder'.[11] A letter of January 1623 from Valentine Pettit confirms that this second tax was imposed: 'The Commissioners of Sewers have imposed another scot on Margate, for the works against the sea'.[12] In 1629 the then Admiral of the Cinque Ports, Theophilus Earl of Suffolk, made some 'new additions' to the decrees under which the pier was managed, but it is not known what these changes were.[13]

The sea-works, paid for by a tax, or scot, of two shillings in the pound on the houses and land at Margate that benefited from the work, together with £36 a year from the profits of the Pier, all overseen by the Commissioners of Sewers, continued to protect Margate until about 1640 when the argument about who should pay for repairs to the sea defences flared up again: 'divers persons whose estates lies more backward from the Sea, and in lesse danger; aiming more at their private ends, than the publicke good, questioned the power of the Commissioners, alledging the said Seaworks were not in compasse of the Statute, on which their Commission was granted' and pressed the Commissioners to end the scot.[14] The objectors suggested that as an alternative 'every man might defend himself against the sea'. These arguments caused the Commissioners to doubt their authority in Margate and, as a consequence, they then 'wholly rejected the said works'. The result was disastrous, and by 1645, 'the Sea hath done about four thousand pounds worth of hurt [at Margate]; and threatens the destruction of the Town'.[14] At this time the

'Expenditor of Sea-works of the Town of Margate,' an expenditor being an officer appointed to expend [spend] the money collected by taxes for the repair of flood defences, was John Smith, a wealthy draper at Sandwich with property in Margate worth some £1000. He borrowed £200 to pay for temporary repairs to protect his property in Margate, but the cost of a permanent repair of all the sea defences was 'insupportable for himself alone'. It seemed to Smith that any long-term solution would require help from the appropriate authority, the Committee of Lords and Commons for the Admiralty and Cinque Ports, a committee newly established in April 1645 to oversee the navy and the cinque ports.[15] This was, however, a bad time to approach parliament for money. War with the Scots, confrontations between parliament and Charles I, and religious arguments led to the first civil war, lasting from 1642 to 1646, and in the following years parliament was penniless and in disarray. Nevertheless, the condition of the sea defences at Margate were such that Smith went ahead and petitioned the Earl of Warwick, the Commander of the Fleet, for help in July 1646.[14]

In December 1645 Smith had obtained a report from the Mayor and Jurats of Dover confirming the dangers facing Margate:[14]

TO all Christian people to whom these Presents shall come: JOHN GOLDER Gent. Mayor of the Town and Port of Dover in the County of Kent, and the JURATS of the same, send greeting in our Lord God everlasting.

Forasmuch as we hold it the office of Magistrates, and the duty of all other persons, to certifie and declare the truth, in all matters and things doubtfull or suspitious, whereby wrongs and injuries may be avoyded, and truth take place and be manifested, especially being thereunto requested: Know ye therefore, that a great part of the Village of Margate in the Isle of Thanet in the said County, a Limb of this Town and Port, is in danger to be overflowed and ruined by the Sea, (the Works and Jetties about 25 years past made at the great charge of the then Inhabitants there by Scots granted and allowed by the then Commissioners of Sewers for those parts having been of late, for want of repair, subverted and ruined by the rage and violence of the Sea) and thereby divers houses overwhelmed, foot and horse-wayes diverted, and other houses likely to be carried to sea, to the impoverishing of divers persons, and decay of the said Village, if some speedy course be not taken for the repaire and making of other Jetties there. In witnesse whereof, We the said Mayor and Jurats of the said Town and Port, the Seale of Office of Majority of the same Town and Port have caused to be set and put, the four and twentieth day of December,

Then in January 1646 he had organized a petition signed by 'near threescore hands' requesting 'an Order from the Parliament for some Tymber out of some Delinquents lands ['delinquent' was a term used for royalists during the English Civil war], to make up the sea-works, and to have the accustomed Scot continued for the preservation of the Town of Margate'. Smith submitted the petition to the Committee of Lords and Commons for the Admiralty and Cinque Ports and, Smith reported, the petition 'upon reading, was very well approved of'. However, the Committee thought that the '200 Tuns of Tymber' that Smith had requested would be insufficient and they decided that a survey of the jetties at Margate should be prepared. Given the nature of the times it is not surprising to hear that the inspection was not well organized: in Smith's words[14]

The Gentlemen appointed for [the survey], promising to come to Margate, I provided a dinner of my own charge for them, but two only came, who told me they could do nothing of themselves without another: Thereupon I intreated them, though they wanted one of their number, they would give way to some Workmen to measure the works, whereupon workmen were sent for, so I procured three Carpenters, who measured 55 rods of work, which they cast up, and they conceived every rod of work would take up five tun and a half of tymber for single work, and double work would ask as much more; It was two moneths before I could get them together, after I was forced to make severall journies to Dover-castle to procure Major Boys Governour thereof to Margate, and going often thither for that purpose, I hapned to meet with Sir Henry Heyman a Parliament man, with whom I made bold to lay open our grievance to him; whereupon he was perswaded to go to Margate with me, and at my request he desired and gained Major Bois to go with him: Upon view of the works, they found the same was gone to ruine, and that the Peer of Margate was the cause of the destruction of a great part of the Town, and this Peere was accustomed to pay scot to the said works, but for these four years and upwards hath not paid one penny, yet some particular men make a benefit of the Peer mony, which can be proved by very able witnesse.

The sketch of the harbour at Margate shown in Figure 7 was produced at this time.[16]

In his petition to the Earl of Warwick in July 1646 Smith explained all this past history and the great trouble to which he had been put.[14] He complained of 'what trouble and charge I have been at, and how wearied and discouraged with attendance, often waiting on your Honour and the Committee, with Councel; but hitherto all I could do, ineffectuall, my travel lost, and the fees and monies given my Councel, hath served to no purpose. By which doings and slow proceedings (if your Lordship afford not help) I shall be utterly disabled further to prosecute this good work, and every one affected will be discouraged either to ingage or undertake the same for the future; and what mischief may ensue thereupon, and how Malignants and disaffected will be imboldned who have opposed us herein, I leave to your Lordships consideration.' He gave an example of the problems he had with 'Malignants at Margate': 'When Major Boys gave me his warrant for 24 Tuns of tymber, which came to £36, being the arreare for one yeare due by the Peere of Margate, the same was slighted: when afterwards your Honour issued another warrant to the same purpose (you being then at Weymouth castle) confirming the Majors warrant, the same was likewise disregarded and disobeyed by the Peer wardens of Margate, who would neither give us the tymber, nor mony in lieu thereof, but disposed the same as they thought good themselves, some to their private use, and selling some for signe posts, yea though we would have given them ready mony of our own for it, we could not have it, such is the malignancy and disaffection of these to this good and publike work.' He concluded: 'All which I hope your Honour will see timely remedied and redressed, and will not suffer us to be longer exposed to contempt, and such apparent destruction, nor further wearied and wasted with a long and fruitlesse attendance. Therefore my humble request unto your Lordship and the rest of the honourable Committee of the Admiralty, is, that you will be pleased to give your order and present direction for what you intend, and conceive fit to be done touching the whole business.'

In early 1647 the Commissioners of Lords and Commons for the Admiralty and Cinque Ports considered the reports on Margate pier produced by Sir Henry Heyman and by another parliamentarian, Sir James Oxenden:[17]

Whereas the Jetty-works of *Mar'att*, in the Isle of *Thannett*, according to Order of the Right Honourable Committee of the Admiralty and Cinque Ports, being surveyed by us, Sir *James Oxenden* and Sir *Henry Heyman* Knights, and others; and we calling Three sufficient Carpenters to measure the Works, it was found to be in Decay as followeth:

1. That there was Fifty-five Rods of Work measured, and found in Decay, each of which Rods was conceived would take up Five Tons and Half of Timber for Single Works, and for Double Works so much more; and the same requiring all Double Work, it will take up in the Whole Six Hundred and Five Tons of Oaken Timber.

2. That the Workmanship, for Carpenters, Sawyers, and other Workmen, will amount to as much or more Charges than the Timber to compleat the said Works.

3. That it will require a constant and continual Charge, in repairing, upholding, and keeping, the same Works.

4. That if the now Expenditor *John Smith* may be Yearly allowed Twelve Pence in the Pound upon all Houses and Lands, which for Twenty-five Years past paid Two Shillings in the Pound, as appears by Scot; and also if he may receive according to the Rates of and upon the particular Commodities set down and expressed in a Schedule hereunto annexed, and as this Honourable House shall think fit, and as is used in other Maritime Towns; he is willing to undertake to perform the said Work, being furnished with Timber sufficient as aforesaid; and will engage One Thousand Pounds, Lands and Houses in the said Island, for Performance and Keeping of the said Work for ever; he being the fittest Man for the same, as being already intrusted for by the said Town, and the said Town being now in most imminent Danger to be lost if not speedily helped as aforesaid.

Ja. Oxinden.

Having about Eight Months past, with the Lieutenant of *Dover Castle* and Mr *Henry Crispe*, surveyed the dangerous Condition of *Margatt*; I did find that there is Fifty-five Rods, or thereabouts, which of Necessity must be maintained against the Rage of the Sea; and did also find, by the Judgement of able Workmen then present, that the Premises will require the Timber here above-mentioned.

H. Heyman.

An additional report was provided by Major Boys, Governor of Dover Castle, Henry Crisp of Quex, and, again, Sir James Oxenden:[14]

Right Honourable,
IN pursuance of your Lordships command, The Peere at Margate, and the defence made by the Works at the Shore for the defence of the Town have been surveyed by Sir James Oxenden Knight, Major Boys Governour of Dover castle, and Henry Crisp of Queeks Esq

And we find,

That about 25 or 26 years since, there was a peece of work added to the said Peer of Margate, which had proved very advantagious for the Peer, but desperately ruinous for part of the said Town.

That before the making of the aforesaid new peece of Peerwork, it is not known to any man living that ever there was any work at the shore for the defence of any of the houses of Margate, or that there was any need of any such work; but since the making of that new peece of Peerwork, there hath been as much Tymber-work set down by the Inhabitants at the shore for the defence of the houses there, as by credible relation hath cost them fifteen hundred pounds and upwards, the which is now wholly ruined by violence of the sea.

Whereupon we conceive, that if the Peer be continued as now it is, the Town must suffer; and if the Peer do not continue as now it is, the Peer will quickly fail, and the Publique suffer for want of trade.

The houses at Margate now in danger, are conceived to be near the fourth part of the Town, and will require fifty five rods of new work, which wil take up five tun and a half to every Rod of single work (by the judgement of the best experienced workmen) For which, they are humble suitors to your Lordships.

James Oxenden, Kt., Major Boys, Esq., Henry Crisp, Esq.

Based on these surveys and the petition from John Smith, the Committee of Lords and Commons for the Admiralty and Cinque Ports produced their report, on 27 February 1647:[17]

On Consideration of a Petition presented to the Committee, by *John Smith*, Expenditor for *Margett*, in the Isle of *Thanett*, in the County of *Kent*, in Behalf of himself and the rest of the Inhabitants and Owners of Houses and Lands lying against the Sea at *Margett* aforesaid, the same setting forth the great Danger the said Town is in of being carried to Sea, and the great Losses already befallen the Estates of many of the Inhabitants, by the carrying of many of their Houses already to Sea, through the Decay of certain Jetty-works heretofore made for Defence thereof; and praying that Timber may be appointed for repairing of the same, as also that Money may be raised for the perfecting thereof out of the Arrears of a Scot of Two Shillings *per* Pound, heretofore charged upon the Houses and Lands there, and of another Scot of Thirty-six Pounds *per Annum* laid upon the Pier of *Margett* by the Commissioners of Sewers for the East of *Kent*, about Twenty-five Years ago, the Payment thereof having been for some Years discontinued; and that, for the future maintaining thereof, the said Scots may be confirmed; or that, in Lieu of a Moiety of the said Two Shillings *per* Pound, a reasonable Poundage may be set upon certain Commodities going into and out of the said Island, a List of which Commodities, and of a Rate proposed to be set upon them respectively, was now presented; and upon reading of a Certificate from some Gentlemen of the County of *Kent* (to whom the State thereof was referred by this Committee to be viewed and certified), they thereby setting forth that, the said Jetty-works being by them surveyed, and Workmen consulted, they found that Fifty-five Rods of Work is in Decay, which, requiring Double Work, will take up Six Hundred and Five Tons of Oaken Timber; that the Workmanship will amount to as much or more Charge than the Timber; and that there will need a continual Charge to keep it for the future: And for that this Committee is informed, by some Members of both Houses, that they have viewed the same, and find the Defects and Danger of the said Town to be very great; and forasmuch as the same is within the Jurisdiction of the Cinque Ports: This Committee doth therefore conceive it their Duty to represent it to both Houses of Parliament; and doth recommend it to them, That the present Defects may be repaired, and sufficient Timber for that End allowed; and that the Town may in Time to come be secured by a Scot upon the said Houses and Lands, or by a Poundage upon Commodities exported and imported from and to the said Island, or otherwise as they shall in their Wisdom think fit; as also that Consideration may be had of the Petitioner *John Smith's* Disbursements for upholding of the said Works (which, by his Petition, is alledged to amount unto Four Hundred and Twenty Pounds), in such a Way as they shall think meet, he having offered (as by the said Certificate is mentioned), upon Allowance of a Moiety of the said Scot, and of a Poundage upon the said Commodities, to perform the said Work (being first furnished with Timber as aforesaid) and to engage an Estate of One Thousand Pounds Value to keep the same for ever: And it is lastly Ordered, That a Copy of the said Certificate, and of the Schedule of Rates upon the said Commodities, be annexed to this Report.

W. Jessop, Secr.

The Committee produced a detailed financial plan of 'Monies to levy, to maintain the Jetty-works at *Margate*, in the Isle of *Thannett*, in *Kent*, against the Sea, for ever'.[17] Some of the required money would come from the Pier Wardens: 'That the Pier Wardens at *Margate* may pass over the Accompts to the Mayor of *Sandwich* and *Dover*; and, as they shall think fit, that Half the Overplus may be paid to the Expenditor, towards the Maintaining of the Sea-works at *Margate* for ever, the Pier having for Twenty-five Years and more paid Thirty-six Pounds *per Annum*, as by the Scot appears.' The rest of the money would come from the houses and lands that would gain from the sea-works but, rather than the two shillings in the pound that had been charged on such properties for the last twenty-five years, only one shilling in the pound would be charged, the difference being made up by charges imposed on goods landed at the Pier, such as 7d for each quarter of wheat, malt and salt, 8d for every pack of wool transported to London, 5d for every hundred North Sea cod-fish, 2d for every hundred mackerel, 2d for every hundred weight of 'Holland Cheese, Cheshire and Thin Cheese', and so on, in great detail.

Meanwhile, the Committee had received an alternative proposal for the repair and upkeep of the sea-works at Margate, in the form of a petition denying Smith's claim that the town was in danger and suggesting that no new taxes were required:[18]

Petition of gentlemen, freeholders, and yeomen, inhabitants in the Isle of Thanet, to the Committee for the Admiralty and Cinque Ports.

Petitioners and their predecessors have, time out of mind, shipped their corn at Margate, and have always been and still are ready to pay all ancient and accustomed duties for the maintenance of the pier and harbour. These duties hitherto have been, and still are, sufficient for the purpose, and the town is not in that danger which is falsely suggested in the petition of John Smith. The inhabitants will undertake to maintain the works now standing against the sea, with a moiety of the timber desired by Smith, and without any new imposition laid upon the country, which would compel petitioners and their successors to ship their corn elsewhere, to the utter ruin of the inhabitants. Pray that the old duties may be maintained, and that they may be collected and disposed of by pier wardens chosen as they have been accustomed to be chosen time out of mind.

Sir Henry Crispe and his son Henry Crispe wrote to the Earl of Warwick supporting the petition:[18]

Letter from Henry Crispe, sen., and Henry Crispe, jun., at Queakes [Quex], to the Earl of Warwick.

Having been directed by the Committee to survey the decays of the jetty works at Margate, they have made their report. They have seen both the petition presented by Smith, and also that from the inhabitants of Margate, who, for the real performance of the works and safety of the town, faithfully promise to give six times the security proffered by Smith. This the writers desire may be taken into consideration.

27 Mar. 1647.

The Committee were evidently convinced by these arguments and accepted the proposal, coming to an agreement with what Smith referred to as the 'Island-men':[14]

A true Copie of the Agreement which the Island-men, before the Committee of the Admiralty agreed on . . . Here followeth,
Upon debate before the Honourable Committee of Lords and Commons, for the Admiralty and Cinque-ports, of the matter in difference touching the repairing, sustaining, and keeping of Jetty-workes against the Sea at Margate, in the Isle of Thanet, for preventing the destruction and swallowing up of the said Town of Margate, by the violence of the Sea breaking in upon it. And upon hearing of John Smith, Expenditor for the said Town, and his councell on the one side. And of Sir Henry Crisp, Henry Crisp Esq., Richard Hartie, Jeffery Sandwell, John Broxland, Marke Ambrose, Tho. Smith Senior, George Somner, John Tomblin, Wil. Coppin, John Pannell, James Hannaker, and Richard Jenvey, and their Councell on the other side. Upon the whole businesse there arose two Questions. The first, How the said Jetty-works might for the present be repaired, and for the future maintained, so that the Sea might be kept from breaking in, and the said Town might be preserved? The second, How the said Smith, the Expenditor might be satisfied and reimbursed the monies and charges he had laid out, and been at in this publique and common businesse, for the time past? And as to the first, the said Sir Henry Crisp, Henry Crisp Esq., Richard Hartie, Jeffery Sandwell, John Broxland, Marke Ambrose, Tho. Smith, Senior, George Somner, John Tomblin, Wil. Coppin, John Parnell, James Hannaker, Richard Jenvey, and their Councell did offer, That if the repairing of the said Jetty-workes and the keeping thereof, might be entrusted to them, they would with 200 Tunne of Timber, to be allowed unto them for the said worke for the present sufficiently repair the said Jetty-works, and make them defensive against the Sea, and safe guard and preserve the said Town of Margate, and every part thereof, and of the Lands thereto belonging, against the violence and breaking in of the Sea, as well for the present as for the future for ever hereafter, without any further tax, allowance or charge, to be yeilded, made, paid or imposed therefore, but only a scot, or tax of 12 pence in the pound, to be levied and paid out of the Houses erected against the said workes, and to be paid but once in the year and no oftner. And for the performance thereof in every particular, viz. as well for the present repairing, as future sufficient keeping the same for ever, upon the rate aforesaid, and without any further demand. The said parties before mentioned did by themselves and their Councell, make offer, to put in sufficient Security, as this Committee or the Honourable Houses should approve and like of; which being accepted and yielded unto by the said

Smith the Expenditor; the Committee thought fit that the same should be subscribed by the said parties, to remain with this Committee, or be presented to the Honourable Houses, as should be requisite.

And as to the second Question, touching the charge and disbursments of the said Smith, for that the parties could not agree upon the same, nor how and in what manner they had been laid out. It was humbly praied, That a Commission might be ordered to issue out of the Court of Admiralty of the Cinque-ports, to examine witnesses upon such matters, interrogations, and questions, as the said Smith for his part might see cause for the better ascertaining of the said disbursments, and charges by him expended; And wherein the said other parties might joyn and counter examine likewise if they thought meet. That so examinations being duly taken, they might be returned to this Committee, whereupon this Committee might be truly informed of the true state of the matter; and so give such order for relief of the said Smith, as they should hold just and equitable.

While all these discussion were going on, a storm on 12 March 1647 made a breach in the sea defences at Margate, which, according to Smith 'might have been prevented had the island men stood to the forementioned Agreement.' A description of the damage caused by the storm was sent to the Committee by 'the inhabitants of Margate' on 13 March.[14]

To the Right Honorable the Committee for the Admiralty and the Cinque-Ports.

These are further to informe your Honors, That whereas the Jetties of Margate, in the Isle of Thanet, and County of Kent; and the great danger of the said Town, have many times and late been discussed before your Honors, and whereupon your Honors out of a commisseration, and due consideration, of the danger of the said Town and Inhabitants there; have been favourably pleased to grant some convenient quantity of Timber, for the better defence of the said Town and Inhabitants there, against that raging and mercilesse Element, the Sea. And whereas it hath pleased God on Sunday last past, (being the 12 day of this instant March,) to send a most tempestuous tyde, against the said Town, (as at other places) by reason whereof, a great part of the said workes is broken down, and some part of a House of this bearer John Smith, is demollished; and whereas not only the estate there of the said John Smith, but of many other the Inhabitants of the said Town, are (if not very speedily secured) like to come to utter ruine and decay.

The premises considered, May it yet again please your Honors, to take the deplorable condition of the said Town and Inhabitants, into your speedy and mature consideration, and to afford such a quantity of Timber for the defence of the said Town and Inhabitants; and also to appoint and ordain some able man (whom your Honors shall thinke fit) to take care of the said workes, as in an exigence of so much concernment and danger is required.

In witnesse whereof, we your Honours humble petitioners have subscribed our hands (Inhabitants of the said Town) the 13 day of March, Non salutis, 1647.

Subscribed by the Inhabitants of Margate.

The Committee's report was finally accepted by the House of Lords on 26 March 1647, who then passed it on to the House of Commons with the comment 'that this house thinks fit that the Barons of the Cinque Ports do present to the Parliament an Ordinance for the repairing and preserving of the Jetty Works and Pier at Margett . . . and that it be speedily done, because of the danger which will else ensue to the Town of Margett'. Although not explicitly stated, it seems that the proposal passed on to the House of Commons was that of the 'island-men'. Unfortunately, nothing was 'speedily done' and John Smith petitioned the Committee once again later in 1647 'on behalf of himself and the inhabitants of Margate'.[14] He complained that 'by reason of the Kingdomes more weighty businesse, your Petitioner as yet hath had no further order or redresse heerin, although the Sea hath done above five thousand punds worth of hurt within four years past, though in the interim, and for these six years past, your Petitioner hath defended a great part of the Town at his own charge, and expended the summe of four hundred eighty pounds eighteen shillings and eight pence, as by a particular accompt under the workmens hands appears; besides his charges in soliciting of the businesse, amounting to above three hundred pounds, and in the neglect, losse and hinderance of his trade, to at least six hundred and fifty pounds, without any peny recompence; which will be to his sudden ruine and destruction, if not relieved by your Honours.' He stressed how important it was that something should be done: 'that a place of such consequence where Embassadors and persons of great quality take shiping, and are landed, may not be quite overwhelmed, and the estate of your Petitioner, and many others quite destroyed, and their wives, children and families ruined' and he requested 'that sufficient Timber may be allowed, so as the present breaches may be timely repaired, and for time to come upheld, by Scots on the houses and lands there, and by a poundage upon commodities exported and imported from and to the said Island; That the Peer Wardens may be yearly accomptable to the Maior and Jurats of Dover, for the money by them received and expended about the same, a moiety of the overplus to be allowed yearly towards the said Works; and that your Petitioner may be speedily satisfied his said disbursments about the said Works. And Your Petitioner shall ever pray, &c.'

The Committee of Lords and Commons for the Admiralty and Cinque Ports considered Smith's petition on 18 November 1647:[14]

18 November 1647. At the Committee of Lords and Commons for the Admiralty and Cinque-Ports

IN reading the Petition of John Smith Expenditor for the Works against Margate, concerning the deficiency of the said Works, his charg[...]s in attending that businesse of the Isle of Thanet, the delaies used by some that have addressed their Petition to this Committee in opposition of his; by their not standing to what had been mutually agreed before some of this Committee, and proposing away for repaire of the said Works, and keeping of them for the future.

Ordered that Henry Crisp Esquire, George Summer, William Coppin, Thomas Wheatley, Edward Brooks, and Stephen Bishop, doe attend this Committee on this day three weeks, by themselves or some of them, or some other on their behalf, sufficiently instructed to answer the said Petition, and failing thereof, this Committee will proceed to settle such resolution upon John Smith's said Petition, as shall appear most meet, without further delay.

It seems that the 'island-men' had not delivered on their promises, but the outcome of any meeting with Henry Crisp and his colleagues is not known. The Admiralty Committee again reported to the House of Lords in February 1648 on the state of Margate and the House of Lords concluded that the report 'be speedily taken into Consideration, and . . . be sent to the House of Commons'.[19] The House of Commons duly considered the report in March 1648 and ordered 'That the Commissioners of the Great Seal do forthwith issue a Commission, under the Great Seal; to able Persons in the County of Kent, to view and survey the Decays of certain jettie Works belonging to the Town and Port of Margate; and to take the usual Course for Remedies therein as by Law is provided'.[20] Once again little seems to have been achieved. In June 1649 a new Admiralty Committee meeting in Whitehall considered 'the great decay of the jetty works by the ravages of the sea at Margate'; they found 'that the matter was often debated at the Admiralty Committee then sitting at Sir Abraham Williams' house, and that several orders made for repairs, but nothing as yet done, so that the greatest part of the works are like to be carried away by the violence of the sea, and the town is likewise in danger of being swallowed up'. They wrote to 'Rich. Jenvey, Jno. Smith and ten others': 'As the enclosed order is the last made by that Committee, and was consented to by counsel on both sides, we confirm it, unless you, who are concerned therein, attend and show to the contrary. You are therefore either to attend here, or authorize some able men to inform us of the whole matter by Thursday next, at Admiralty Committee Chamber at Whitehall'.[21]

On 23 July 1649 the Council of State again considered the 'petition of John Smyth and other inhabitants of Margate, Isle of Thanet, that by reason of the rage and violence of the sea, the jetty made there for defence of the pier and town, and the pier, are in danger to be swallowed up without sudden reparation.' As a result they requested the Lords Commissioners of the Great Seal to pass 'a commission of sewers to the mayors of Dover and Sandwich, Sir John Williams, Bart., and other gentlemen, to see whether there be any defects in the said works, and if so, take speedy course for repair, as the statute for sewers provides, and appoint one or more able men to oversee the work, and give a yearly account thereof to the Commissioners of Sewers'.[22] Three days later the Admiralty Committee reported to the Council of State that they also thought that the Lords Commissioners of the Great Seal should issue a Commission of Sewers 'for inquiring into and repairing the breaches in the jetty works at Margate, so as to make the town defensible against the sea'.[23] They also suggested that, before the commission was actually issued, a letter should be written to the commissioners of sewers on behalf of John Smith, 'to reimburse him for his charges and expenses beyond his receipts; also to receive his informations and proposals for finding out which way the money may be lawfully raised for his satisfaction'.[23] On 22 November 1649 yet another petition from John Smith 'on behalf of himself and the inhabitants' was referred by the Counsel of State to the Admiralty Committee, 'to consider what may be done for the safety of the harbour, and relief of the petitioners'.[24] The following day the Admiralty Committee considered the petition, John Smith now being referred to as 'late expenditor for the Jetty Works at Margate'.[24] Having considered the petition 'and upon conference with him [John Smith] touching the same' they ordered that:[24]

the Commission of Sewers be desired to take the . . . charges and expenses he hath been at about the said Jetty Works beyond his receipts, into their Consideration and afford him all lawful manner and assistance for reimbursing his said moneys as by the law and their said Commission they may be enabled to do. And that the said Commissioners are further desired to hear and review such information and other fit proposals as the said Smith shall offer unto them for the finding out which way the said moneys may be lawfully gotten up for his satisfaction. And to certify their opinions thereon to this Committee.

On 28 November the Council of State themselves wrote to the Commissioners of Sewers:[25]

The Council (having taken into consideration the enclosed petition of John Smith) have thought fit to desire you to take the petitioners case with the charges and expenses he hath been at about the Jetty works at Margate in Kent beyond his receipts into your consideration, and afford him all lawful means [of] assistance for reimbursing his said moneys as by the Law of Sewers you are enabled to do; And you are further desired to hear and examine such witnesses and receive such informations and other fit proposals as the said Smith shall offer unto you for the finding out which way the said money may be lawfully levied for his satisfaction and to certify your opinions to us what you have done.

It is clear that there was considerable sympathy for Smith in the Counsel of State and at the Admiralty Committee, but it is unlikely that this resulted in any action, as in May 1650 it was recorded by the Council of State that 'the order formerly given to the Commissioners of Sewers for the Isle of Thanet, upon the petition of John Smith, late expenditor of the works against the sea at Margate, be now renewed, upon the petition of Sarah, widow of John Smith'.[26] The unfortunate John Smith had died still waiting for recompense, the Pier Wardens remained a law unto themselves, and the pier remained in a state of decay.

More than ten years later, in 1662, John Stroode, Governor of Dover Castle, wrote to the Pier Wardens about a complaint made to the Duke of York, then Lord Warden of the Cinque Ports, that 'the Peere and Harbour of Margate is much ruinated and decayed, and that the monies formerly collected and received for the repair thereof, have not been duely improved for that end, and that for a long time past there hath been noe due Accounts given nor elections made of successive Peere-Wardens yearly, as by ancient customes and orders of former said Wardens ought to be; and his Royal Highness is very sensible of the great inconvenience that may ensue, if some effectual course be not taken to repair and settle the affairs of that Peree'.[13] Rather than simply 'punish the offenders' Stroode decided 'to summon the parties to appear and to produce the Writings and Orders touching the said Peere, and to give up their accountes concerning the same . . . at the signe of the Rose, being the house of John Bushell in Margate'. The late pier wardens, Edward Taddie, Thomas Wheately, John Franklyn, Jeffery Tomlin, and the Widow Bishop, were duly summoned but, as Lewis reported in 1736 'what was the Effect of this I don't find; I suppose the Persons summoned obeyed . . . and did as they were required'.[13] Meanwhile, the Pier continued to be damaged by storms. In January, 1668, a correspondent wrote that 'the great storm carried away two small houses at Margate, broke into the chief waggon way adjoining to the pier, and made it impassable for wagons or horses; fear the destruction of the pier'.[27] Following another storm in September 1671 'there is about £100 worth of damage done to Margate pier'.[28]

The first surviving book of Pier Accounts dates to 1678, suggesting that some reform of the management of the pier might have taken place at this time.[29] The Pier Wardens in 1678 were Thomas Grant and Joseph Mackwith and their accounts show that in the year 1678-1679 the Pier had receipts of £145 11s and spent £90 19s 11½d mostly on small items, but including £1 4s 8d 'for digging 148 loads of chalk' and £3 14s for carriage of these loads of chalk 'to fill up the new work', showing that some work on the Pier was underway. The accounts were kept in the simplest manner and the profit (or loss) at the end of one year was simply carried over to the following year and added into that years accounts which, unfortunately, makes it difficult to compare the financial positions in each year.

The accounts record that in January 1680 'the pier-wardens and other inhabitants of the parish of St Johns petitioned Lord Sydney, Constable of Dover castle and Lord Warden of the Cinque Ports' with a proposal for meeting the cost of repairing the pier:[29]

The petition of the pier wardens and other inhabitants of the parish of St Johns in the County of Kent whose names are here under subscribed

Humbly showeth that whereas the pier of Margate is very much beaten down and ruined by the general rages of the sea and the stock of the said pier is all expended towards the Maintenance of the same we therefore the said pier wardens for the time being with the assent and consent of the other inhabitants of the said parish for the better maintenance of the said pier for the future have thought fit to propose some additions and alterations to be inparted in the dues of the said pier which we humbly desire your hand would be pleased to allow and confirm.

A memorandum of agreement in the Pier Accounts book gives more detail, although it is still not clear exactly what was being agreed to. It seems that a proposal for a new cess (tax) to pay for Pier repairs would be dropped and that those that had been petitioning for the new cess, together with a group of other parishioners, would, respectively, contribute sums of £20 and £10 each, and if that was not sufficient, they would split the extra contribution required in an equal proportion. It was proposed that work would start by Michaelmas 1681, and that six out of the 32 persons involved in the agreement would be chosen to monitor expenditure, and that two of these six would be chosen as the two Pier Wardens appointed each year.

Unfortunately, the pier accounts for the year 1680-1681 are not sufficiently clear to identify what was spent on maintenance that year. However, it is clear that expenditure in the following year, 1681-1682, was relatively high, with total receipts of £128 2s 4d, including carryover from the previous year, and a total expenditure of £126 17s 10½d. The accounts for the year 1682-1683 included £14 for 'expenditure on Iron Works' and £23 for 'expenditure for plank and timber', suggesting some significant rebuilding of the Pier. The following year, 1683-1684 was worse, with total receipts including carryover of £109 14s 9d which, with a total expenditure of £168 8s 7d, meant that the following year the Pier wardens started with a debt of £58 8s 10d; the accounts for the year included large sums spent on the purchase of timber. Luckily this debt was paid off the following year as in 1684-1685 the total expenditure was only £49 0s 9d, with a positive balance of £21 3s 2d at the end of the year. The balances at the ends of the years 1685-1686 and 1686-1687 were £12 17s 11d and £15 15s 9d, respectively. However, a statement at the end of the accounts for 1686-1687 confusingly states: 'It appears . . . that the pier was in debt by £64 4s 1d less £15 15s 9d gives £48 8s 4d debt' suggesting that the Pier at some stage had taken on a significant level of debt, possibly from the arrangement of January 1680 described above.

The year 1687-1688 was not a good one as it was necessary to 'repair the breach at the Pier' made by a bad storm. In January 1688 the 'poor inhabitants of the parish of St John the Baptist in the Isle of Thanet' petitioned the King 'showing that by a storm and tempest a great part of the pier of Margate was beaten down, the repairing thereof will amount to £250, for raising which they have made an assessment, and praying his Majesty to confirm it and empower the collectors to collect it'.[30] The King apparently was 'willing to give all fitting encouragement and assistance' but there is no report of anything actually being done.[30] The accounts for that year show total receipts of £107 9s 3d but a total expenditure of £284 4s 8d, leading to a debt of £176 15s 5d at the end of the year. The total cost of repairing the breach in the Pier was £176 17s 4d, a noticeably smaller sum than the initial estimate of £250. The accounts confirm the picture of the pier as a rickety structure, taking the form of a box of wood, packed with chalk. No payments are recorded for any survey of the damage, or for anyone to oversee the work. For long periods of the year there are payments for nine or ten labourers to work on the pier, with large numbers of payments 'for bread and beer' for them. Old timbers and planks were saved, presumably to be reused in the repairs; 'old plank' was bought at Chatham, '1164 foot of ships plank' was bought for £12 3s, and 'new plank' was bought from Maidstone, but there is no mention of the purchase of any stone. Twenty two pounds fifteen shillings and one penny were spent on 'spikes and nayles' to hold the planks together. Payment was made for 154 loads of chalk and for baskets, probably to be filled with the chalk and used to pack the pier; 7 labourers were paid 16s 6d for '1 day and a half work to fill the pier with baskets' and 3s 11d was spent 'for ropes to draw up the baskets'. The accounts also include a charge of £4 1s for the costs incurred in January 1688 when 'the Deputy and I [one of the Pier-wardens] went to London, our charges for 11 days for our selves'; this was to present the petition to the King described above.

In 1691 Margate again suffered storm damage and again petitioned the King:[31]

On the 10th and 13th days of October and the 8th of December last, by the violent blowing of the north-west wind, part of the pier called the "New Pier" was carried away, and that part of the town which is guarded by the pier and jetties, is so laid open that it is expected to be washed away if the wind should blow fresh at north-west. The repairing of this will cost £2,500 as appears by oaths taken before the Mayor and Jurats of Dover, and by the opinion of Sir Christopher Wren, who viewed the same in January last; and the townsmen, being already so much in debt, are not able to do these repairs without some help from their Majesties, and without such repairs, their town will be entirely destroyed by the storms which usually happen in winter.

The petition was passed on to the Lord Committee of the Admiralty but the outcome is not known. However, the Pier wardens Thomas Underdowne and Roger Laming actually spent just £13 6s 10d in the year 1691-1692 on repairing the pier, including 5s spent in June 1691 'for Vincent Barber, John Smith, James Yeoman for taking their oath's before the Mayor and Jurats of Dover what the repair of the pier would cost and a certificate upon the same.'[29]

In March 1693 twelve inhabitants agreed to lend the money required to rebuild the pier:[29]

Know all men by these accounts that we who are undertakers for rebuilding the pier of Margate did on the 12 day of March 1693 assemble ourselves together and made and equall proportionally [. . .] out in paying the pier debts and for the timber and it is agreed between us who are undertakers that any of the persons which the parishioners shall choose pier wardens shall pay each man or his heirs or assignees their equal and proportionable share of what money the pier shall [. . .] at any time and of them being pier wardens if anything other be cleared until the principal and interest is paid of all such sums or sum of [. . .] of money which shall be laid out by us in witness whereof we have set our hands

Francis Diggs	Thomas Grant	Roger Laming
Valentine Jewell	Roger Omer	Thomas Baker
Dudly Diggs	Vincent Barber	Richard Lister
John Brooman	Stephen Goldfinch	Daniel Basdon

The gist of the agreement is clear even though some of it is now illegible. Fortunately, a covenant entered into with 55 of 'the inhabitants of St John Thanet' fills in some of the missing detail.[32] The covenant makes clear that the 'undertakers' had agreed to rebuild the pier and pay off its debts, on the understanding that they would receive 5 % interest on their loan until the loan had been paid off, the money coming out of the profits of the pier, and that the two pier wardens chosen annually by the inhabitants would be chosen from among the twelve 'undertakers'.

In June 1693 the inhabitants of Margate once again petitioned the government, complaining that 'Margate Pier has been broken down, and pray an allowance of £20 per annum towards the repair of it, now paid to a gunner of that place, and that a deputy of their own may supply the place of gunner'.[33] The Queen was 'graciously pleased to refer the [petition] to the Rt. Hon. Sir Henry Goodrick, Lieutenant General [of the Ordnance] and the rest of the officers of the Board of Ordnance, to consider thereof, and report their opinions what may be fit for Her Majesty to do in it'. It seems likely that this request was turned down as there is a report that the Government only ceased to pay for a Gunner at Margate sometime after 1697.[34]

Dissent continued in the town over pier charges, and Henry Lord Viscount Sydney, the Admiral of the Cinque Ports, felt it necessary on 7 February 1694 to confirm the decrees under which the pier was managed, publishing his 'Orders, decrees, and rates, time out of mind used by the inhabitants of Margate and St John's in Thanet . . . for and towards the perpetual maintenance and preservation of the pier and harbour of Margate . . . newly revised, ratified, confirmed and allowed, by his Excellency the Right Honourable Henry Lord Viscount Sydney'.[35]

The regulations start with a clear statement of what was expected from users of the pier:

THAT all and every person and persons which do dwell or at any time hereafter shall dwell in *Margate* and the parish of *St John's* aforesaid, or any other person or persons whatsoever which shall have occasion to use or harbour in the said Pier at *Margate* with their boats or vessels either lading or unlading of any kind of victual, goods, or any other kind of merchandize whatsoever, or in any other sort or manner do use or have any trade, traffick or dealing in the said Pier, shall well and truly stand to, pay, obey, discharge, observe, fulfil and keep, all and singular the ancient customs, orders, decrees, payments and agreements, whatsoever there used, and all other hereafter in these presents contained, upon the pains and forfeitures hereafter mentioned.

The eleventh paragraph explains that the inhabitants were expected to be able to buy 'durable commodities' such as salt, butter, cheese, coal and wood directly from the ships in the harbour. Any ship coming into the harbour with such commodities for sale had to get the town crier to announce in the town that a ship had arrived with goods for sale, and for the first three days after the arrival of the ship only private individuals could buy the goods for their own, private use. After three days the goods could be sold to shopkeepers and others, to be put on sale:

Item 11. That every person or persons whatever, that shall bring into the said Pier or Harbour any quantity of salt, salt-fish, butter, cheese, coals, wood, or any other durable commodities, to the intent to sell the same there, shall first give public notice thereof to the country by the common cryer there appointed, and shall lie the space of three days after such public notice given, to the intent that the country may buy for their needful provisions, upon pain to forfeit 10s and that no inhabitant of *Margate* and *St John's*, or any other person or persons whatsoever, shall buy, forestall, or ingross the same commodities, or any part thereof, to sell out by retail again, until the said three days be expired, upon pain to forfeit the commodity or commodities, so bought contrary to this article, or the value thereof; after which time it shall be lawful for any towns-man, or other, to buy the same commodities. And that no inhabitant or ports-man shall take upon him to own the goods or merchandizes belonging to any foreigner or stranger, to the prejudice of the Pier or Harbour, upon the pain above specified in this article.

The thirtieth paragraph made it clear that all money raised by the Pier could only be spent for the 'benefit and maintenance' of the Pier and Harbour, preventing Pier money from being used, for example, for work designed to protect the town:

Item 30. It is further ordered, decreed and appointed, that all the sum and sums of money before mentioned, either to be levied, paid or forfeited, shall wholly be used, employed and bestowed, to the use, benefit and maintenance of the Pier or Harbour aforesaid, as need shall require, by the direction of the Pier-Wardens for the time being.

Paragraph 32 makes it clear that in the case of damage to the pier, for example by a storm, the Pier Wardens and inhabitants should either use a tax (cess) to raise the money required to pay for the repair of the pier, or do the repair work themselves:

Item 32 . . . And if it should chance (as God forbid it should) that either, by tempestuousness or rage of weather, or any other casual means whatsoever, the said Pier or any part thereof be overthrown and beaten down to the ground, then the Inhabitants and Pier-Wardens aforesaid shall within twenty days next after the beating down of the same, assemble themselves, and make a cess, either to discharge the Pier-Wardens of all such sum and sums of money as they stand bound for, to any person or persons, for and towards the use and behoof of the said Pier and Harbour, or else shall build and make up the said hurts with as much speed as maybe.

Fortunately, the 'undertakers' stood by their agreement to provide funds for rebuilding the Pier, and the Pier accounts for 1693-1694 include receipt of a sum of £20 from each of the 12 undertakers named in the agreement, 'towards rebuilding the new pier head and paying debt.' The reference to 'rebuilding the new pier head' is obscure, but at least it is clear that the Pier wardens had it in mind to improve the pier, and not simply patch it up one again. With a sum of £9 16s 8d 'left in our hands of the last years accounts' the Pier-wardens were able to pass on £249 16s 8d to Roger Omer, 'Gent', and Valentine Jewell, Pier-wardens for the following year. Expenditure in the year 1694-1695 was high, £312 5s, including large amounts for workers' wages and loads of chalk, leaving a deficit at the end of the year of £8 15s 2d. The Pier Wardens for the following year, Valentine Jewell and John Brooman were, however, able to turn this into a small positive balance of £21 5s 8d, and receipts and expenditure seem to have remained pretty much in balance for the rest of the century. Up until the year1701-2 the two Pier wardens were chosen from the list of the 'undertakers', in accordance with the agreement made with them, but in 1702-3 Walter Tomlin and William Norwood were chosen, possibly because the loan from the 'undertakers' had by then been paid off.

In May 1696 the Pier Wardens took the opportunity of William III's passing through Margate on his way to Holland, to present him with a petition asking for payment of a grant of £100 that had been awarded some time earlier for the repair of the pier. The King was sympathetic and, it is recorded, 'recommends the payment of the hundred pounds . . . formerly granted for the repair of the said pier, which has been already laid out on that service'.[36] It is unclear whether or not the £100 was forthcoming.

Unfortunately, with the start of the new century problems reappeared in the town. In November 1700 the two Pier-wardens, Roger Omer and

John Turner, had to obtain a bond of indemnity from the inhabitants of Margate, to allow them to proceed against two hoymen, William Payne [Paine] and Valentine Hogbin, who refused to pay their dues:[37]

Whereas William Payne, gent, and Valentine Hogbin, mariner, do refuse to pay towards the maintenance of the pier of Margate . . . according to the decrees of the said pier – Now know you that if the said William Payne or Valentine Hogbin or either of them of any other person do or shall bring a cause to be brought any action against Roger Omer or John Turner present Pier wardens for executing the office according to the decrees of the pier . . . That we the parishioners of the parish whose names are hereunder written do hereby promise in the behalf of the parish that we will . . . indemnify Roger Omer and John Turner in defending the suit if it commenced by William Payne and Valentine Hogbin.

The petition was signed by 40 of the inhabitants.

In the year 1702 the argument with William Paine and Valentine Hogbin came to a head when, with others, they objected to the way in which the annual election of the Pier Wardens had been carried out.[38] The system for electing Pier wardens was laid down in Viscount Sydney's orders of 1694:[35]

That the Deputy of *St John's* for the time being shall yearly, the *Sunday* before *May-day* cause public notice to be given in the parish church of *St John's*, immediately after divine service in the forenoon, to the inhabitants that shall be there present, that they shall assemble themselves together upon *May-day* next following, at some convenient place and hour, to be appointed by the Deputy: And there the Deputy with the greater number of them which shall be there present shall make choice by voices (and the Deputy to have a double voice) of two Wardens, commonly called Pier-Wardens, and also two Deputy Pier Wardens, chosen to execute the said office when and so often as the said Pier Wardens shall be absent, or otherwise not able to execute the office of Pier Wardenship; upon pain the Deputy neglecting his warning of the inhabitants of *Margate* and *St John's* shall forfeit 10s.

In 1702 the Deputy had duly announced that the inhabitants should meet in the church vestry on May day at nine o'clock in the morning to elect the Pier Wardens and deputy-Wardens.[38] It appears that one group of inhabitants met in the vestry on that day, at some time before nine 'and for that reason because they were not willing to proceed to an election before the hour they stated, it was agreed by all those present that it was past nine, and then proceeded to an election – as the first company were going out of the church they met another company going in to the election who pretended the first election was before the hour and so was not legal, and so they went into the vestry and made an election by themselves and chose other men to be Pier wardens'. Both groups immediately appealed to the Mayor of Dover to sort out the mess, and on May 7 he made an order in the Court of Chancery at Dover that both parties should appear before him at Margate on May 8. This they did and the Mayor having heard 'the several allegations of both sides and the matters alleged for and against the several elections' decided that both elections were 'null and void', because it appeared to him that there had been 'artifice and trick on both sides, at their last pretended elections'. He asked both sides to get the opinion of legal counsel on their cases and he told them that he would consider these opinions and make a final decision. Much to his annoyance, however, the group that included the current Pier Wardens, Walter Tomlyn [Tomlin] and William Norwood, and the current deputy Pier Wardens, Daniel Baseon and Valentine Jewell, together with Roger Lamming, Roger Omer and Thomas Grant 'on behalf of the inhabitants of Margate' sent a petition to the Lord Warden of the Cinque Ports, his Royal Highness Prince George, setting out their case. Presumably Prince George simply passed this on to the Mayor of Dover to deal with. In a letter the mayor complained that 'my only aim was to compose matters between them, and not to favour any side, being equally a stranger to them all' and he was worried that now the Prince had been 'troubled' over the matter. In the letter he went on, 'I fear preferring a private interest, before the good of their harbour', and he explained that those who had sent the petition to the Prince 'told me themselves, they would not insist on the validity of their first election, provided the contending party would agree with them, in choosing the same person to gather the Harbour Droits as they had before, and desired me to recommend him for them, which I did, but the Right of Naming him by Ancient Custom, is in the Pier wardens. This I understand is a place of profit to the person that has it, and the fear of losing it, is the cause of all this contention'. The Pier Wardens finally appointed for the year 1703-4 were Richard Stoakes [or Stookes] and John Jarves.[29,39]

To add to all the town's woes the pier was damaged in a storm on 26 November 1703. The storm actually damaged much of the town:[40]

The following account is what I can give you, of what damage is done in this Island in the late great storm; in this town [Margate] hardly a house escaped without damage, and for the most part of them the tiles blown totally off from the Roof, and several Chimneys blown down, that broke through part of the Houses to the Ground, and several Families very narrowly escaped being kill'd in their Beds, being by Providence just got up, so that they escaped, and none was kill'd; the like Damages being done in most little Towns and Villages upon this Island [Thanet], as likewise Barns, Stables and Out-housing blown down to the Ground in a great many Farm-houses and Villages within the Island, part of the Leads of our Church blown clear off, and a great deal of Damage to the Church is felt.

As to the pier:[41]

At Margate the Sea made a free passage over the new pier-head, beat down the light that guided vessels into port, threw down the gun-battery, and forced the cannon into the sea; some shops and warehouses on the shore were washed away, and a great number of small craft were dashed to pieces.

Unfortunately, the problem of non-payment of pier dues continued. In 1705 Ralph Constant and Robert Smith called a meeting of the parishioners to consider what steps should be taken:[29]

Memorandum: That whereas the parishioners being met together 13 November 1705 to consider what measures to take to collect some arrears due to the harbour from refusing to pay the same, we whose names are under written, do hereby empower the present pier wardens Peter Sackett and John Turner to go to Counsel and have advice and take such measures as the law shall direct in that case for to recover the same.

The memorandum was signed by 10 people. Immediately following the memorandum in the Accounts Book was a further memorandum showing that the threat had worked:

Memorandum that at the same time as above that Mr Tho. Grant did affirm that he had but thirty six tun of Kelp in arrears for which said Kelp he then paid eighteen shillings, and forty three quarters of barley and ½ for which he paid four shillings, in all one pound and five shillings in full for poundage to May day last past.

    Paid at the same time of Val. Jewell — 6s
    Received of Jn. Pegdon — 4s
    Received of Paul Hart — 2s
    Received of Higgins — 6d
    Received of Mrs Sarah [. . .] that was left in arrears in the year 1705 — 10s

The accounts of the pier remained positive until 1707-8 and, at the end of that year, had reached £40 17s 4d.[29] This tempted John Brook [Brooke] and Roger Whitehead, the pier-wardens for the year 1708-9 to carry out some necessary improvements to the roadway leading to the Pier:

Memorandum: that on the 11th day of August 1708 at a public vestry being lawfully called it was then and there concluded and agreed by us whose names are under written (being the majority of voters) to build and set up a Jetty and make a sufficient way for the use of the pier where the sea hath washed away the same being near the pier and joining to the land and premises of Joseph Jewells heirs and David Austins heirs which Jetty and way so to be built and made. We do hereby authorize and appoint Mr John Brook and Roger Whitehead present pier wardens to so make such a Jetty and convenient way to the pier at the discretion of the said pier wardens as shall be for the best advantage and conveniency for the use of the pier. Witness our hands dated the day and year first above written.

In that year the expenditure was £165 16s 1d against receipts of £173 2s 9d so that John Brook and Roger Whitehead were able to pass on only £7 6s 8d to the following year's pier wardens.

    In 1717 a petition was presented to the House of Commons asking for Margate to be exempt from the Dover Harbour Bill then going through parliament. In 1698 a bill had been passed whose aim was to raise money for the repair of the harbour at Dover.[42] The bill decreed that 'there shall be paid by the Master Owner or Skipper of every English Ship Vessell or Crayer of the Burthen of Twenty Tons or upwards and not exceeding the Burthen of Three hundred Tons for every loading and dischargeing within this Realme for from to or by Dover or comeing into the Harbour there not haveing a Cocquet testifying his Payment before that Voyage towards the Repaire of Dover Harbour the Summe of Three

Pence for every Ton'. What this meant was that every vessel of over 20 tons passing by Dover had to pay towards the repair of Dover harbour, a reflection of the important role played by the harbour in protecting shipping in the Channel. There were, however, a few exemptions, including one for fishermen allowing them to make payments only once a year, and one exempting ships belonging to the ports of Weymouth and Ramsgate from having to pay, because of the poverty of these towns. The exclusion clause for Ramsgate reads: 'That all Ships and Vessells belonging to the Port of Ramsgate in the Isle of Thanet and County aforesaid having a Pier of their owne (which by reason of their Poverty at present they are not able to maintain) shall be exempted from contributing and paying any thing towards Dover Harbour aforesaid'.[42] The fact that Ramsgate was exempt and Margate was not might have been because Ramsgate was in a worse financial state than Margate, but was more likely to have been because Ramsgate had thought to petition parliament for an exemption whereas Margate had not. The 1698 act was due to run out in 1709, but in 1703 an extension was obtained until 1718, and in 1717 Dover applied for a further extension of the bill until 1727 since it had become obvious that there was still much work to be done at Dover.[43] It was now that Margate, belatedly, applied for an exclusion in the new bill, along the lines of that enjoyed by Ramsgate, on the grounds of the poor state of the Pier at Margate:[44]

A Petition of the Pier-Wardens, Masters of Ships and Vessels, and other Inhabitants, belonging to Margate, in the Isle of Thanet, in the County of Kent, was presented to the House and read; setting forth, That, there being a Bill depending for continuing a further Term for repairing Dover Harbour; That the Petitioners, by way of Contribution, have expended very great Sums of Money for repairing the Pier and Harbour of Margate, over and above the Income thereof; and must, every Year, on account of the Sea's lying harder on it than usual, lay out more than the Revenue therefore will amount unto; without which the said Pier or Harbour of Margate must fall to decay; to the great Prejudice of the Estates and Inhabitants of that Island; And praying, That the Ships and Vessels belonging to Margate may be exempted from Payment of any Duties towards the Repair of Dover Harbour.

In the event the new Dover Harbour Bill was passed with no exclusion terms for Margate.[45]

The year 1720-21 was another bad year for the Pier with a large expenditure on chalk and timber, presumably used for necessary repairs. Problems with the hoy-men also continued. In 1736 Lewis wrote: 'the Hoy-men having agreed with the Farmers to carry their Corn at a certain Rate, and they, the Hoymen, to pay the Pierage &c some of them pretended to pay even what they pleased, on a Supposition that the Pier Wardens had no legal Power to compel them to pay the Droits assigned by the Pier Decrees'.[13] In Lewis's words 'this obliged the Pier Wardens and Inhabitants to petition parliament', complaining:[46]

That there has been built, time immemorial, a Pier of Timber, for the Defence of the Town *of Margate* from the Sea, and a Harbour for Merchant Ships and Boats, and for Corn Hoys, to carry the Produce of the Isle of *Thanet* to *London* Market: That on the Preservation of the said Pier depends not only the Safety of the said Town, but the Interests of the several Estates in the Isle of *Thanet*: That the said Pier has hitherto been supported by certain Droits or Duties, paid for several Commodities landed, or put on board, in the said Pier; the Payment of which Droits or Duties have been confirmed by Orders and Decrees of the Lord Wardens of the Cinque Ports, under whose Jurisdiction the Town of *Margate* is; but that, of late, the Payment of the said Duties has been disputed by several ill-minded and contentious Persons: And praying, That the Petitioners may be enabled more effectually to recover the said several Duties, for the keeping up, and preserving, the said Pier.

On December 1 1724 the petition was considered by the House of Commons and it was agreed to refer the matter to a Committee with the power 'to send for Persons, Papers, and Records' who would consider the petition and report back to the House. The report of the committee was duly considered on December 14:[47]

Sir *Edward Knatchbull* reported from the Committee, to whom the Petition of the Inhabitants of *St John Baptist,* and Town of *Margate,* and of the neighbouring Parishes of *St Peter the Apostle, St Laurence* Minster, *Monckton, Birchington,* and *St. Nicholas,* at *Wade,* in the Isle of *Thanet,* and County of *Kent* was referred, the Matter, as it appeared to them; and which they had directed him to report to the House; and he read the Report in his Place; and afterwards delivered it in at the Clerk's Table: Where the same was read; and is as follows: *viz.*

That the said Committee, pursuant to an Order of the House have examined the Matter of the said Petition; and do find, upon the Examination of several Witnesses, the same to be as follows; *viz.*

John Laming said, that the Timber Pier of *Margate* had been erected and built, Time out of Mind, for the Defence of the said Town from the Sea: That he has known the said Pier upwards of Sixty years; That he is Master of a Vessel; and always paid certain Droits or Duties on landing or putting on board, within the said Pier, several Commodities; which Droits have constantly been applied to the Support and Repair of the said Pier; and which Droits or Duties have been, Time immemorial, paid once a Year to the Pier-wardens of the Town of *Margate*, who are yearly elected to that Office;

That the Pier of *Margate* is the most commodious Place to ship off the Corn, and other Produce of the Isle of *Thanet*, to *London* Market, and that the several Estates in the said Isle would be much less in their Value, and the Town drowned, should the said Pier be let go to ruin;

That several Inhabitants of *Margate*, who are Hoy-men, have lately disputed, and refused to pay, the said accustomed Duties, which have been confirmed by several Orders and Decrees of the Lord Warden of the Cinque Ports; One whereof was produced to the Committee, bearing Date in 1613; under whose Jurisdiction the said Town of *Margate* is, although the said Duties are paid them by the Farmer;

That about 34 Years ago, the said Pier was almost lost, and it cost about £500 to repair the same;

That they do not collect the said Duties of any Vessels, but such as lade and unlade at the said Pier; and that if the old accustomed Duties were paid, as usual, they would be sufficient to support and keep the said Pier in Repair;

That he never knew any Suits commenced for any of the Duties that are in Arrear;

That the said Pier is a great Preservation and Safeguard to Merchant Ships, in time of War, from the Enemy's Privateers lurking about the *North Foreland;* who take them as they sail from the River to the *Downs.*

Valentine Jewell produced the Book of Account of the said Pier; whereby it appeared that, one Year with another, for seven Years last past, the Duties amounted to about £140 or £150 a Year.

Mr *Brooke* said, That several of the Inhabitants, which are Hoymen, have refused to pay the said Duties, alleging there is no Law to compel them to it.

And the Petitioners produced many other Witnesses to prove the Matter of the said Petition; but the Committee did not think fit to trouble the House with the Report of any further Examinations.

Ordered, That Leave be given to bring in a Bill, to enable the Pier wardens of the Town of *Margate*, in the Isle of *Thanet*, more effectually to recover the ancient and customary Droits for the Support and Maintenance of the said Pier: And that Sir *Edward Knatchbull*, Sir *Robert Furnese*, Sir *George Oxenden*, Mr

Attorney General, Mr *Milles*, and Mr *Onslow*, do prepare, and bring in, the same.

The bill went through quickly. It was read in the House of Commons for the first time on 16 January 1725, had a second reading on 20 January, and, after some minor modifications, a third reading on 5 February; it was then passed to the House of Lords and received the Royal assent on 17 February.[48] The bill was entitled *An Act to enable the Pier-wardens of the Town of Margate, in the County of Kent, more effectually to recover the ancient and customary Droits, for the Support and Maintenance of the said Pier.*[49] The preamble to the act summarised the reasons why the act was needed: that the ancient town of Margate 'time out of mind, had a pier and harbour very commodious, and of great benefit and advantage to the trade and navigation of this kingdom, in the preservation of ships and mariners in storms and stress of weather, and from enemies in times of wars; and also very convenient for the exporting and importing many sorts of commodities', that 'the safety of the town of Margate, and of all the neighbouring country depended on the preservation of this pier and harbour', and that the maintenance of the pier had depended on 'certain droits, commonly called poundage, and lastage, and other rates or duties' paid to the Pier Wardens. The preamble ended with a warning that without payment of these droits the pier would inevitable fall into decay, 'to the utter ruin of the inhabitants of the said town, and of all the neighbouring country, and to the great prejudice of the trade and navigation of this kingdom.' To prevent this it was necessary 'to make more effectual provision, as well for the recovery of the said droits and rates, or duties aforesaid, and for enforcing due payment thereof, in case of refusal or non-payment.'

The Act then stated that the ancient droits should continue to be paid, and that to this end the pier-wardens should choose men to act as collectors of the droits, who would be allowed 'for their pains in the collecting of them' a sum not exceeding one shilling and sixpence in the pound. These collectors were required to provide 'good and sufficient security' in case they were tempted to abscond with any of the pier's money, and to keep accounts in writing of all the money they received and spent. The accounts of the collectors were to be audited each year by the Pier Wardens, and the accounts of the Pier Wardens were, in turn, each year to be laid 'before the Lord Warden of the Cinque Ports, for the time being, or his Deputy'. Anyone suspecting a Pier Warden of 'concealment, imbezzlement or misapplication of any monies collected or received' was free to complain in writing to the Court of Admiralty of the Cinque-Ports, and the Judge of the Court would then issue a summons for the Pier Warden to appear before the Court to answer the complaint. If found guilty, the Court would issue a fine 'not exceeding treble the sum so concealed, imbezzled or misapplied' and the Pier Warden, if unable to pay, would be committed to prison 'there to remain without bail or mainprize [effectively another way of being bailed for an offence], until payment of such sum as aforesaid.'

To carry out the task of collecting the droits the Pier Wardens and Collectors were authorized to go on board any ship 'belonging to the said town and port of Margate, making use of, or being within the said pier or harbour of Margate', calculate what was due 'in respect of any goods, wares, or merchandise then on board', and then collect this money. If payment was not forthcoming, they could seize goods and 'guns, tackle, furniture and apparel' belonging to the ship, and then, if payment was not received within ten days, sell them.

Finally, the Act stated that all sums of money collected should be paid to the Pier Wardens, to be 'laid out and employed in and towards the repairing, improving and continually keeping in good repair, the said pier and harbour of Margate, and shall not be applied or disposed to any other use, intent or purpose whatsoever.' This final requirement confirmed the previous restrictions on using the droits to maintain the jetties along the shore line. The Pier rates established in 1693 were still in use in 1784, and the Pier and Harbour at Margate were maintained under this Act until 1787 when Margate's first Improvement Bill was passed.

The receipts of the Pier for the year 1733-34 were £253 5s 2d, to be added to the sum of £224 15s 10d carried over from the last year. The total expenditure for the year was relatively modest, £98 8s 10d. This included a number of minor items such as 'work upon the crane', 'a new crane rope', and 'paint and work upon the new crane.' There were payments for 'painting the lamp' and 'looking after the lamp'; £1 11s 3d was spent upon five and a half dozen candles, but it is not clear if these candles were for 'the lamp' or not. A number of loads of chalk and flint were purchased, together with 12 shovels costing 10s, presumably for running repairs on the pier. A sum of £5 5s was spent 'at the choice of Pier Wardens at May Day 1733', which sounds rather like a celebration. A sum of £1 11s 6d was paid 'for the journey of the Pier Wardens and one of the Deputy Pier Wardens to Sir Basil Dixwell's for passing the accounts'; Sir Basil Dixwell was the Governor of Dover Castle and had, once a year, to pass the accounts of the Pier Wardens. The accounts for 1732-33 explain that this sum covered 'horse hire and expenses.' A sum of £12 12s 3d was paid to the Droit Collector for collecting the Pier Droits, at a rate of 1d in the pound. The Pier continued to be damaged by storms: In January 1737 'so wide a breach is made in Margate pier that a first rate man of war may enter therein; but the damage cannot be easily guessed at'.[50]

The Harbour

The harbour at Margate played a vital role in the economy of the Isle of Thanet. Local produce, particularly corn, was exported from the harbour to London and a wide range of goods were imported, mostly from London, although large amounts of coal came from Newcastle. The harbour was also used by passengers travelling to and from London and the continent. Nevertheless, the harbour was small; in 1723 Lewis described it as 'a small harbor for ships of no great burden, and for fishing craft', and in 1769 it was described as 'pleasant, but not much frequented, for want of depth of water sufficient for ships of heavy burden'.[7,51] Making things worse, the pier, as we have seen, had been much damaged by storms and, as a consequence, 'the harbor of Margate has gone very much to decay, and the masters of ships which used to live there are almost all removed to London for the sake of their business'.[7]

Most of the corn shipped from Margate to London was carried in hoys, ships of cutter-rigged design that had been developed at the estuary port of Faversham (Figure 8).[52,53] The hoys had to be sturdy enough to weather rough seas, shallow enough to enter an estuary, and fast enough to make regular passages.[52] They originally had open holds but by the early eighteenth century these had been 'decked-in', and their tonnage had inceased from between 20 and 30 tons to sixty tons burthen.[54] Other ships such as the slower brigs and other square-riggers were used on the coal trade to the north and for the Baltic timber trades.

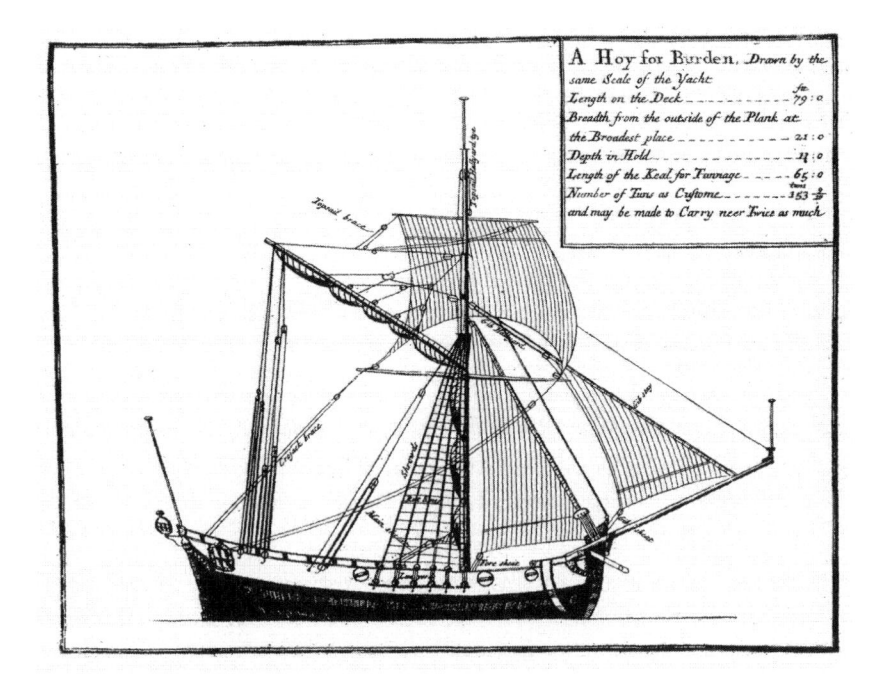

Figure 8. An early eighteenth-century English hoy, from William Sutherland, *Britain's Glory or ship-building unvail'd*, London, 1717.

One measure of the importance of a port was the number of ships 'belonging' to it, although it has to be remembered that a ship might trade anywhere but 'belonged' to the place of residence of its owner.[55] In 1366 Edward III raised a fleet of 'eleven hundred sail' to transport 100,000 men to France, and of these ships 15, with 160 mariners, came from Margate. This compares with Dover which provided 16 ships and 504 mariners, so that the vessels from Margate were obviously relatively small.[56] In 1544 Layton [probably Richard Layton] was requested by the Privy Council to 'prest 200 hoys' and reported that he had managed to press '18 for Dover, 18 for Sandwich, 6 for Ramsgate, 10 for Margate, 8 for Rye, 6 for Winchilsee, 5 for Hythe, 10 for Folston, 43 for Ipsewhich'.[57]

In 1564-5 the French and Spanish ambassadors had cause to complain about the actions of English pirates in the Channel, and it was decided to undertake a survey of 'all portes crekes and landing places' along the coast (Chapter 6). The survey, dated 18 March 1566, showed that at the time Margate had 108 houses and 8 'persons lacking proper habitation' and 15 'boats and other vessels' involved in carrying grain and fishing, four of 18 tons, one of 16 tons, one of 5 tons, one of 4 tons, and eight of 1 ton, employing 60 men.[58] In 1584 a survey was made of all 'barques and vessels belonging to the peere or harbour at Margate', probably as part of the preparation for the abortive expedition sent to Flanders to oppose the Spanish forces under Parma. Margate was credited with 14 ships: one barke (70 tons), one crayer (a small sailing cargo ship, 28 tons), five fishing vessels (10-25 tons) and seven hoys (25-60 tons). There were 32 'common sailors and fishermen' and 8 pilots at Margate, and the ships were owned by 2 joint owners and two sole owners. In 1623 a list of Margate mariners aged between 18 and 60 included 67 names.[59] By 1665-66 there were nine hoys registered at Margate and eleven by 1699-1700.[60]

In 1701 the total numbers of vessels belonging to Margate and other Kentish ports were as follows:[9]

	Ships	Tonnage	Men
Margate	37	2,909	138
Ramsgate	45	4,100	388
Broadstairs	17	731	90
Dover	7	415	44
Sandwich	21	1,146	104

Andrews has estimated the extent of the coastal trade of the Thanet ports in the period 1676-86 as follows:[9]

Number of Coastwise Cargoes per year, 1676-86

	Outwards	Inwards	Total
Margate	93	21	114
Broadstairs	2	6	8
Ramsgate	2	11	13
Sandwich	108	81	189

The outward coastwise trade of Thanet was largely in corn and, at the end of the seventeenth century, Thanet exported, per year, 7,000 quarters of malt, 3,500 quarters of wheat and 500 quarters of barley, shipped in small cargoes of two to three hundred quarters each.[9] Most of the corn grown in Thanet was handled by the harbour at Margate because it was closer to London than any of the other harbours on the Island; Harris reported in his *History of Kent* of 1719 that 20,000 quarters of barley were shipped each year to London.[61] Although the major market for Thanet corn was London, Margate was also an important port for the export trade to Calais, especially before 1558 when Calais was still an English outpost. A letter of 1391 reports on a contract to supply Calais with 'wheat, barley, malt, beans, pease or other victuals' from the Isle of Thanet, a contract which, from some confusion at Calais, was never actually issued:[62]

To the treasurer and the barons of the exchequer. Writ of *supersedeas* in respect of their demand against Peter Popr and John Jory of the isle of Tanet or either of them to render account of wheat, barley, malt, beans, pease or other victuals needful for furnishing the town of Calais which, by Letters patent of 20 April II Richard II, they were appointed to buy and purvey from time to time for the king's moneys wheresoever within the realm within liberties and without, the fee of the church excepted, and order to discharge them, releasing any distress made for that cause; as Roger de Walden the king's clerk, treasurer of Calais, has borne true witness in chancery that the commission was not delivered to them, neither did they meddle in aught therein contained, having no knowledge thereof.

Providing provisions for Calais was particularly important at times of war with France. In May 1449 an order was issued that no food should be exported from the Isle of Thanet except to Calais and to Dover castle:

Grant, pursuant to the ordinance of the king's progenitors that no purveyor should take victuals or grain from Canterbury to the sea-shore to wit, from the shore extending 12 miles inland in breadth and in length from Sandwich to Apuldore, but that those parts should be reserved for the victualling of Calais and the marches there and Dover castle and the officers and ministers there, — that no purveyor take oxen, sheep, calves, swine, capons, hens, chickens, corn or other victuals of any person within the said precinct, nor in the Isle of Thanet, the hundreds of Maydeston, Hayhorn and Twyford, save the victualler and purveyor of Calais and the marches there and Dover Castle, Calais and the marches being now in great need.

In January 1582 French troops marched into Bruges, and Francis, Duke of Anjou, supported by the English, was installed as Duke of Brabant. Margate and Sandwich then became important suppliers of food to Bruges: in February 1581 it was reported from Bruges that from 'Sandwich and from the Isle of Thanet and from Margate comes daily great store of wheat and malt to these parts. Within these four days there is come to Sluys from those places eight ships laden with wheat and malt, some to this town, and more are coming'; the worry was expressed that 'if this be suffered, it will occasion some great dearth in England'.[64] This worry was not new. London had a constant demand for grain from the southern-eastern counties but these same counties also had a ready market for their grain in Calais and Flanders. To prevent the creation of local shortages, Commissioners for Restraint of Grain and Victuals had been appointed to monitor the stocks of grain in England and, by regulating grain exports, avert the risk of famine.[65] At the end of February 1581 the Commissioners were asked to investigate the export of grain from the Isle of Thanet:[66]

A letter to the Commissioners for the Restrainte of Graine and Victualls within the countie of Kent signifieing unto their Lordships that notwithstanding the Generall Restrainte made as well within that countie as in other counties of the Realme againste the transportacion of graine beyonde the seas, there are of late viij[t] [eight] shippes with wheate and maulte laden within the Isle of Tennette and at Sandwich arrived at Sluce in Flaunders, and that sundry other shippes to be laden with graine in Kent are expected to come unto the place aforesaid and other parties in that cuntrye, they are therfor required fourthwith not onlie to examyn what shipps have departed from those places laden with anie kynde of graine, what quantities have ben shipped by them, by whom and by what licence, and theruppon to certifie the personnes and their doinges accordingly that order maie be taken for the meeting with their offence, and hereafter to have a more vigilant regard to the execution of her Majesties Commission addressed unto them in that behaulf.

A report from Bruges in 1582 suggests that the investigation had little effect: 'The Dutchmen of Sandwich and London send daily into these parts great store of wheat out of the Isle of Tennett, and from Margate, laden in English ships . . . Bruges, 17 February, 1582'.[67]

In 1588 the worry returned to the trade with Calais:[68]

There are certain here [Calais] who have obtained licence to transport beefs, muttons, wheat, oats, malt, beer and other victuals, "under a colour for the Lords [Commissioners] provision," which are being passed over for the Prince of Parma, and there are now great provisions of such things shipped from Margate, Ramsgate, Sandwich and Dover, "whither to be transported God knoweth . . . The enemy will be glad of victual, and will stand in as great need as before, if they were not so plentifully every day resorted unto. — Calles, the last of March, 1588."

❋ ❋ ❋

Unfortunately there is rather little information available about the inward foreign trade at Margate, because this trade was recorded in the Sandwich Port books and no attempt was made to distinguish between the foreign trade of Sandwich itself and that of Margate and the other Thanet ports.[9] The Sandwich Port books show a variety of imported goods including wine, timber, and general cargos from Rotterdam and Ostend, with exported goods including corn and herrings. Margate itself counted only as a 'creek', with no legal quay (see Chapter 5) and so its trade was usually limited to corn, fish and timber although, in fact, some wine, linen and fruit were also imported at Margate.[9] Ships arrived in Margate from Venice and from the Low Countries, but in small numbers. In the year 1513-1514 there were just 6 recorded arrivals of 'alien' ships at Margate.[69] In 1555 the Venetian Ambassador in England reported on the arrival of two Venetian ships at Margate: 'The ships *Barbara* and *Vianuola* have arrived safe at Margate, so that there will be much business to transact on account of these vessels, besides the many disputes of daily occurrence with the crews'.[70] In 1563 the arrival of another two Venetian ships at Margate was recorded, one carrying a load of currants from Zante; in 1566 there are records of a ship that, having sailed from Venice via Malta, Majorca, Cadiz, and Lisbon, finally reached Margate where its cargo of raisins was unloaded to be sent to London.[71,72] In 1587 a Venetian ship carrying wine for London was unloaded at Margate but ran into problems with the Customs:[73]

A letter to Customer Smith that whereas of the number of two hundred and fouretene buttes of swete wines lately brought by an Argosie [a type of large Venetian merchant ship] lieng presently at Margett, and sent by one Lewes Erizzo, a Venetian, there was by order from our verie good Lord the Erle of Leicester unladen threscore and thre buttes and fower carettalles (*sic*), the rest of the same wines, being afterward for verie good reasons stayed from being landed, remayning at this presente on boarde or in divers hoyes upon the ryver of the Thames, amounting togither, with the quantitie yet remaining in the Argousie, to one hundred and fifty buttes or thereaboutes; forasmuche as it hath bene declared unto their Lordships that the furder contynuance of the said wines on boarde the hoyes and Argousie might bringe greate hurte and daunger of spoile unto them upon peticion made in that behalf, their Lordships have thought good to requier [him] to take order that the same wines maie be landed, and to take the same into his custody and so to remaine unsolde and well looked unto without any diminishing thereof (at the charges of the said Erizzo), untill their Lordships shall have taken furder order for the same.

Other imports into Margate included silks and cloth. In July 1628 a parcel of silk was imported from Dunkirk on a Shallop carrying prisoners, but was detained by 'Customer Smith':[74]

An order concerning a fatt [a fatt was a measure of capacity; one fatt held 9 bushels, and one bushel held about 9 gallons] of Silks brought from Dunkirke belonging to Robert Cudenor of London, Marchant.

Whereas there was this day presented to the Boarde a Peticion of Robert Cudenor of London, Marchaunt, wherein he doth remonstrate that there was landed at Margat in Kent one small fatt of silke, which came in a Shallop that brought English Prysoners from Dunkerke, which saide Fat of silke doth belong to the Petitioner, and were sent over lande from Italy, and now is at Margat and there deteined by one Smith, upon no other pretence then because it came from Dunkerke, the same having beene deteined in his Custodie about twoe monethes alreadie, to the Petitioners greate hinderance for which Cause he doth humbly sue that in paying all due charges of Custome he may have his goods delivered unto him: Their Lordships having taken this his humble Sute into consideration doe thinke fit to graunt the same, the rather in regarde that Phillip Burlemachy, Marchaunt, doth undertake for the truth of that which is alleagcd in the said Petition. Hereof the Lorde Treasurer is prayed and required to take notice, and to give presente and effectuall order to the Officers of the Porte of Margat for the delivery of the aforesaid Fat of silke to the Petitioner or his Assigne without dilay.

On the same day there was another complaint about the Customs at Margate impounding some silks and lined cloth imported from Dunkirk, possibly brought in on the same ship:[74]

An order concerning foure bailes of Silke, Lined Cloth belonging to Samuel Alderson, John Bowater and others.

Whereas a peticion was this day presented to the Board by Samuell Alderson, John Bowater, John Parker and William Burley, all Natives and Subjects to his Majestie, in which they remonstrate, that they have foure bailes and twoe trunkes of Silke, linin Cloth, and other commodities not prohibited landed at Margat, which goods doe belong unto them, as may appear by oth and otherwise, some of the said goods being come out of Italie over lande, and others having bene taken for debts long forborne; all which goods being landed are stayed by his Majesties Officers, because thay came from Dunkerke; whereas the peticioners had no other meanes to have them brought, seing they cannot come through France without danger of confiscation, whereupon the said petitioners doe humblie sue that the said goods may be delivered unto them, paying his Majesties Customes. Their Lordships having taken this their humble suite into consideration, doe thinke and order that if they can make sufficient proofe of this which they alledge, before the Judge of his Majesties High Court of Admiralty, all the aforesaid goods shalbe delivered unto them. Whereof the Lorde Treasurer is hereby prayed and required to take notice and upon the said proofes being sufficient to give order accordingly.

From an early date the Margate hoys carried passengers as well as goods. John Taylor's *The carriers cosmographie* of 1637 listed 'where the ships, hoighs, barkes, tiltboats, barges and wherries, do usually attend to carry passengers and goods to the towns of England' and reported that 'a Hoigh from Rochester Margate in Kent, or Feversham and Maydston doth come to St Katherines Dock'.[75] In the eighteenth century there was a weekly hoy service between Margate and London.[13,76] Even before Margate's development as a resort for sea bathing the numbers of passengers carried by hoy could by quite large, as is clear from the report of the overturning of a hoy in 1731:[77]

On Tuesday last a Hoy, bound to Margate in Kent, turning to windward under a hard gale of wind, was unhappily overset between Erith and Woolwich, by which accident about 30 passengers were all lost.

A useful source of information about shipping at Margate is the collection of Pier Wardens Accounts that have been preserved for 1678-1724 and 1732-1749.[29,78] For the year 1678-9 the Pier receipts totalled £145 11s 0d, including £59 2s 5d for shipments of corn, £23 9s 6d for shipments of coal, £7 5s 7½d for 'small duties', including items such as butter, cheese, tombstones, iron, faggots, tiles, and anchors, and 'overseas voyages' that included voyages to Norway and France. For the year 1679-1680 we have more details about the payments for corn voyages, giving the numbers of voyages and those involved:

Booorman 14 voyages to London	£5 0s 6d
Stevens 40 voyages to London	£5 2s 6d
Roger Laming 22 voyages to London	£11 19s 6d
John Laming 13 voyages to London	£7 15s 0d
Valentine Hogbin 22 voyages to London	£12 6s 0d
Adrian Moys 13 voyages to London	£9 16s 6d
Adrian Moys and Son 8 voyages to London	£4 17s 6d

Particularly informative are the payments received for 'succor', which was defined in item 15 of the Orders of Viscount Sydney:

That every other ship, crayer, hoy, or any other vessel that doth come into the said Pier or Harbour only for succour, and not to lade or unlade, shall pay according to their burthens, *viz.* of ten tons and under 4d, of twenty tons and under 6d, of thirty tons and under 8d, of forty tons and under 12d, and those of greater burthen to pay accordingly; and for aliens double the rate.

The accounts for 1679-1680 list 96 payments for succour, of which four are for ships from foreign ports, with payments of 1s and 2s 'from a Spaniard', a payment of 2s from 'John Lumas of Ostend', and one payment of 1s for a ship from a port whose name is illegible. The total number of ships using the Pier for succor and their sizes were as follows:

Size of ship	Number of ships
10 tons and under	12
10 to 20 tons	45
20 to 30 tons	3
30 to 40 tons	33
Over 40 tons	3

These numbers agree with Lewis's description of the harbour in 1723 as a harbour used by ships 'of no great burthen'.[7]

The Pier Accounts for the years following 1732 give a lot more detail and clarify how the finances were handled. On 1 May each year the old pier wardens handed over any cash remaining from the previous year to the two new Pier Wardens. The new Pier wardens were allowed to keep up to £100 of this cash as a 'stock of running cash' to fund repairs and improvements to the Pier, and, it seems, were allowed to keep for themselves any interest they might receive on this money; this would be some recompense for the time they devoted to the job, which was unpaid except for a sum 5s a year paid to them 'according to custom.' The first item of income listed for the year 1733-34 was the sum of £224 16s 10d received from the Pier wardens for the previous year. The next item, and the largest source of income for the Pier, was for shipment of 'corn' from the pier. The shipments were divided into 'heavy grain' and 'malt'. Wheat and corn were classed as 'heavy grains' when transported by sea as they stowed more closely than barley or oats, which were termed 'light grains'; the rate charged for transporting light grain was higher than for heavy grain because the rate was calculated on weight rather than on volume. The total shipments of wheat and corn were 19,040 quarters with 8013 quarters of malt. The grain was shipped by eleven men, the greatest quantities by Stephen Baker, John Simson, John Stoacks, Stephen Swinford, Richard Laming, and Daniel Pamflett.

Receipts for colliers for the year 1733-34 show 19 shipments of coal in the year, totalling 1087 chaldrons. Nine men were responsible for this trade, eight of whom were probably from Margate. Fish landed at Margate were mackerel, herring, whiting, and red herrings, mostly by Margate boats, with red herrings bringing in the largest income for the pier, £10 6s 10d. Small items included wine, butter, timber, salt, sugar, hemp and kelp, although there is no way of knowing from the accounts whether these were imports or exports. The number of 'town ships' going on longer voyages were small. In 1733-34, Capt. Brooks paid £1 for 'four voyages' and Mr Bowman 10s for 'two voyages'. The accounts for 1732-33 give more detail, with Mr John Tibb paying 15s for three voyages 'to the East Country' and Richard Bowman paying 15s for three voyages to Portugal.

Item 21 of the Orders of 1693 established that half the value of any wrecked goods saved by a vessel coming into the harbour, or half the value of any saved anchors, would be taken by the Pier Wardens. In 1733-34 fourteen anchors were saved, adding £1 3s to the Pier accounts. For wrecked ships the pier received 2s 6d in this year from John Randall 'for getting the sugar out of the ship upon Girdle sand', 6s from 'William Ladd and others for getting the sugar ship off the said sand' and 19s from 'William Ladd and others for ½ a share of their saving sugar out of the said ship'. In 1732-33 Capt. Brooks paid £7 12s 6d to the pier 'for 166 bales out of a Turkey ship', and Stephen Swinford, John Staner and John Harison paid 10s 6d, 5s and 2s 6d respectively 'for an half share [of their] earnings out of the Turks ship upon the Woolpack Sand'.

Saving goods from wrecked ships was part of the trade called *foying* which included several maritime functions, including servicing and provisioning passing ships, helping vessels in distress, and rescuing crews.[79] Boats involved in foying were generally referred to as hovellers or luggers, and were kept in readiness all along the coast, at Ramsgate, Broadstairs, Deal and Dover, as well as at Margate. As described by William Camden in 1586: 'when there happen any shipwrecks, as there do now and then, for those shallows and shelves so much dreaded by seamen, lie over and against it; namely the Godwin, etc. . . . they [the seamen] are extremely anxious to save the Lading'.[80] Of course, the line between saving and pilfering would not always be clear and this worried Lewis: 'it's a thousand pities that they [the seamen] are so apt to pilfer stranded Ships, and abuse those who have already suffered so much'.[7]

The accounts for 1733-34 include amongst the receipts from tenants of the Pier, £8 from 'the Collector of Sandwich for a year's rent'; the Collector of Sandwich was head of the Customs establishment at Sandwich, which covered the harbour at Margate (see Chapter 5), and the accounts for 1744-45 show that the rent of £8 paid by the Collector was for 'the storehouse and Watch house.' The next highest rents received were rents of £3 10s received from H. Swinford and John Stoacks. Just three years later, in 1737, we hear that John Stoacks 'late of Margate . . . Mariner or Hoyman' was in prison in Dover Castle for debt.[81] Also imprisoned in Dover Castle for debt in 1737 was John Simson, 'late of Margate . . . a Hoyman';[82] it is not known if the problems faced by Stoacks and Simson were linked or not.

The receipts for the year 1733-34 show that considerable quantities of coal were landed at the harbour. The import of coal had long been an important part of the trade of the harbour. Over the period 1676-86 the average annual import of coal at Margate was 579 chaldrons, compared to 427 chaldrons at Ramsgate and, in the years 1702-4, 24 vessels were involved in the import of coal from Newcastle, importing 1,001 chaldrons.[9] The import of coal was particularly important because of the lack of timber on the island. A correspondent from Deal wrote to Joseph Williamson, Under Secretary to the Secretary of State, in July 1672 about the dangers posed to the supply of coal by enemy privateers during the Dutch wars:[83]

Richard Watts to Williamson. We heard last night from Margate that a Dutch fleet of capers appeared in sight of the North Foreland, and had both English and French colours. They took within these four days four Margate vessels, one brand new that had not been twelve hours out of Margate pier. Another from Bradster (Broadstairs), in the Isle of Thanet, reports that this morning the Dutch capers took the boldness to fetch three ketches from Broadstairs pier mouth. So that several vessels that yesterday and to-night resolved to go to Newcastle, have laid up in the several piers of Thanet and Sandwich, and if speedy care be not taken our people will starve for want of fuel in the winter.

As already described, the accounts show that significant amounts of fish were landed at the harbour, predominantly red herring with lesser amounts of mackerel, herring and whiting. There was also an active trade in salt fish at Margate, sufficient to require an officer to deal with the salt duties.[84] Duty was charged on salt as a way of raising money for the Government, but the duty paid on any salt used on board ship to cure fish caught in the North Seas or around Iceland could be reclaimed when the fish were landed in England. The duties were collected by a Salt officer, one of whose duties was to cut off part of the tail of any salted fish on which the salt duty had been repaid, to prevent the duty being reclaimed more than once.[85] There was, in particular, an active trade in exporting fish to Italy, where there was a great demand for it. In 1720 an Act of Parliament was proposed to protect the clothes trade in England, 'An Act for prohibiting the importation of raw silk and mohair yarn, of the product or manufacture of Asia, from any ports or places in The Straights or Levant Seas'.[86] Unfortunately, this had a knock on effect on the fish trade with Italy, as the fishing boats, after unloading their fish in Italy, would often return with a cargo of Asian produce. Petitions against the bill were presented from London, Exeter, Totnes, Great Yarmouth, Falmouth, Penryn and Plymouth, with a joint petition from 'the merchants, owners and commanders of ships of the towns of Ramsgate and Margate in the Isle of Thanet', signed by forty seven petitioners from Margate and fifty two from Ramsgate:[87]

the inhabitants of the towns of Ramsgate and Margate are become owners and proprietors in a great number of ships using the Levant Seas and are considerably concerned in the fishery of these Kingdoms, which fish is for the most part consumed in Italy, and your petitioners observe with great grief that there is now depending in your Lordships House a Bill to repeal so much of the Act of Navigation as permits the importation of goods of the growth of Asia into Great Britain, by which restraint your Petitioners will lose a part of the freight of their ships in their return to England and the burthen will lye wholly on the outward bound cargo, which will render the same delivered at market very dear and hinder the consumption of fish and other manufactures of these Kingdoms. Wherefore your petitioners humbly hope that the said Act will not pass which in its consequences must be very detrimental to your Petitioners and the navigation of these Kingdoms.

Unfortunately, for Margate, the Bill received strong support from the West Country clothiers and received the Royal Assent on June 11 1720.[88]

According to Lewis a lack of fish in the local waters was causing problems for the fishermen by the 1720s:[7]

The Fish generally caught here are *Whitings*, (which are often no bigger than *Smelts*) *Wraiths*, *Wilks*, Red and White, *Lobsters*, *Pungers*, *Oysters*, and *Eeles*. Of these last (I have been told by the old Fisher-men) such Plenty has been caught here formerly, that they used to measure them by the Bushel; but for these many Years past they have been very scarce.

Fishing in the North Sea was also in decline and 'the little success they [the fishermen] have met with of late Years, has very much discouraged them from following that Employment'.[7] The result was that the fishermen 'were forced to sell their large Boats, or let them run out. So that now the Boats in which they fish are so small that they dare not go far off to Sea in them, nor venture out of the Peer in a fresh gale of Wind'.[7] Nevertheless Margate was still known for its fishing; in the *New General Atlas of Mr Senex* of 1721 Margate was said to be 'chiefly inhabited by Mariners and Fishermen' and even in 1754 Richard Pococke described Margate as 'a fishing town'.[89,90]

In the seventeenth and eighteenth centuries Margate enjoyed some renown as a port of embarkation and disembarkation for the Low Countries. In 1721 Senex noted how passengers from Holland frequently disembarked in Margate, 'when the wind does not serve to carry them up the Thames'.[89] Lewis made a similar point in 1723:[7]

as the passage from *England* to *Holland* is reckoned the shortest from this place, it has had the Honour of being often visited, of late Years, by great Personages who have gone over thither. Thus, in particular, that Noble Asserter and Defender of the Rights and Liberties of Mankind, and particularly of those of *Great Britain*, K. *William III* of glorious memory often came hither in his way to and from *Holland*. His present most excellent Majesty has twice landed here. Her Royal Highness the Princess of *Wales* came first on shore at this place, and that successful and victorious General the late Duke of *Marlborough* used to choose this for his place of going abroad and landing when he went and came to and from the several Campaigns he made.

In 1636 the Earl of Arundel sailed from Margate to the continent to visit the emperor in Prague, as recorded in the diary of one of his servants:[91]

The seventh of April being Thursday, 1636. His Excellency departed from Greenwich for Germanie, tooke Barge about three of the clocke in the morning, and landed at Gravesend, from thence by Coach to Canterbury to bed, the next day to Margate where wee dined, and about three of the clocke in the atternoone, hee tooke shipping in one of the Kings Ships called the Happy Entrance, and landed the tenth day being Sunday at Helver-sluce.

William III's return from Holland in 1691, when he landed at a 'wretched village called Marguet', was something of a disaster:[92,93]

Oct. 20. Last night King William came to town from Margate, having had a mighty favourable wind to bring him from Holland thither in 24 hours and so home that day. He took shipping upon Sunday in the morning, about 7 o'clock, all his guards and retinue who went to bring him home were disappointed, thinking he would have come by Harwich; but coming the other way he was forced to send to the country gentlemen, and the people to conduct and guard him home on his journey. A gentleman's coachman turned over the coach wherein was himself, Lord Churchill, Lord Portland, and Mons. Overkirk, or the Duke of Ormond, I am not certain which, but I do not hear that any great damage was done, only Churchill complained of his neck being broken; the King told him there was little danger [of that] by his speaking.

Details of William III's journey from Margate to Holland in April 1697 show the level of protection provided for the King: 'The King designs to set out tomorrow if the wind is fair, and in the meantime a Detachment of the Marcuis *de Fuizar's* Regiment is ordered to Margate to keep Guard at Mr Ball's House in case his Majesty tarry there for a wind.[94] Mr Ball's house was, in fact, Quex Mansion at Birchington, then the property of the heirs of Thomas Crispe, but in the occupation of John Ball.[95] On his return to Margate on 14 November 1697 'this evening the Towne guns, etc., fired and bells rang for news of the King's Landing'.[96] The King again travelled to Holland via Margate on 20 July 1698 and also on 3 June 1699.[97,98] A description of the latter journey makes clear the size of the royal party: 'His Majesty left Kensington about 10 last night, in order to embark at Margate, in which road the yachts and men-of-war, which attend His Majesty, are ordered to be: The Earl of Romney, Lord Albemarle, Monsr. d'Auerquerke, Lord Raby, Lord Selkirk and Mr Blathwayt, and other persons of quality, accompany his Majesty'.[99]

Often the King, having landed at Margate, would leave immediately for London. This required a good deal of organization, and expense, as teams of fresh horses need to be supplied along the route to London. In July 1701 William III had embarked at Margate for Holland, expecting to return to England in October, but ill-health delayed his journey and he did not get back to Margate until 4 November.[100,101] This delay meant that the horses that had been sent to towns along the route on October 13 to be ready for the King's expected return journey had to be kept there until November. Details exist in a document, 'Hackney coachmens bills that lay on Margate Roads to waite for his Majesty October 1701'.[102] A total of 37 horses had been sent to Margate for the King's body coach, which needed a team of 7 horses, for three other coaches each needing a team of 6 horses, and for 2 sashmares, also needing six horses each; a sashmare was clearly a type of coach, but the exact meaning of the name has been lost. On 4 November these horses took William III and his party to Canterbury, where a further 37 horses took them to Sittingbourne, where yet another 37 horses were waiting. The King stayed at Sittingbourne overnight, and then travelled on to Northfleet where another 37 horses took the party to Blackheath; at Blackheath all the coaches except that of the King returned to London but the King went to Hampton Court.[102,103] The total cost for the horses was £1026 10s, of which the bill for the horses held at Margate was £265 5s, made up as follows:

Stapler with seven horses for the Body Coach to Margate went out October the 13th returned Nov 6th both inclusive being 25 days at 40s per diem — £50
Whitehart with 6 horses for the Leading Coach the said journey at 35s per day — £43 15s
Long with 6 horses for the following Coach the said journey at 35s per day — £43 15s
Browne with 6 horses for one of the Sashmarees at 35s per day — £43 15s
Haslome with 6 horses for the other Sashmare at 35s per day — £43 15s
Bulmer with six horses for another Coach to Margate went out October the 15th returned November 6th being 23 days at 35s per diem — £40 5s

The hackney coachmen who provided the horses were most probably all from London; of the men named in the account, one, Richard Ketchlove, is known to have been a licensed hackney coachman and two, Searin [John Searing] and Blunt [Thomas Blunt] are likely to have been two of the London hackney coachmen named in a pamphlet of 1716, *The case of Thomas Blunt, John Searing, Charles Sewell, Thomas Holland, Thomas Storey, Cornelius Rose, and the rest of the eight hundred licensed Hackney Coachmen*.[104,105] Others of the gentry landing at Margate would also ensure that they had onward transportation. In November 1718 'A Coach and Six Horses are gone to Margate to meet the Earl Cardogan, who is hourly expected there from Holland'.[106]

The arrangements were particularly complex when it was uncertain where the King would land. In December 1736 it was reported that 'Tomorrow the Horse and Grenadier Guards march to the Margate and Harwich Roads, to escorte his Majesty, from which of those Places he shall land at, to Town. Mr Ashburnham and Mr Lee, two of his Majesty's Pages of Honour, are gone, the one to Margate, and the other to Harwich, to wait for their Royal Master'.[107] Of course, the arrangements would sometimes go wrong. In October 1740 the King again landed in Margate:[108]

Monday October 13, his Majesty landed at Margate in his return to his British Dominions; and as there were none of his own coaches there waiting for him, he was received from the Boat, which brought him to the shore, into a chaise belonging to Mr Carr, Collector of the Customs at Deal, which carried him to Capt. Hercules Baker's, and in his Chariot his Majesty was carried to Canterbury, where he was taken up by his own Coaches, and about nine at night arrived safe and in good health at St James's.

In September 1729 George II had a bad passage from Holland: 'the king landed from the *William and Mary* Yacht, after a Passage of eighteen Hours, by which his Majesty was greatly fatigued, having been very Seasick'.[109] This time the decision was made to stay a while at Margate: 'he went to the Mayor's House, and walk's to it from the Sea-side, refusing the Use of a Chariot which was offered his Majesty, and continued there about an Hour, and then with the Marquess Le Foret set out for Kensington'.[110] A further report tells us that the King 'refresh'd himself at the House of Capt. Brooke'.[111] These reports are confusing in that Margate did not have a Mayor, and, although it had a Deputy, the Deputy in 1729 was Henry Petken and not Capt. Brooke.[112] All that we can be fairly certain of is that the King visited the house of Capt. Brooke who was a major figure in the town. To celebrate the King's landing at Margate 'the Guns fired there, and from thence all the Forts and Ships in the River to the Tower took the Signal from one another'.[113] However, all did not go well: 'We hear from Margate, that the Day the King landed there, a poor Man who was a Guide to one of the Chaise Marines [a single-horse carriage with one pair of wheels, seating one or two passengers], was hurt by its being overturn'd, has received ten Guineas by his Majesty's Order'.[114] Finally, 'his Majesty finding the Roads to be well furnish'd with Sets of Horses, set out from Margate about noon, and arrived at Kensington between ten and Eleven at Noon in good Health'.[115]

The story of this event recalls the legend of George II's visit in 1745. According to the *London Magazine* the journey was uneventful: 'On Saturday, August 31, about four in the morning his Majesty landed at Margate from his German dominations, and having passed thro' the City [of London] at one in the afternoon, amidst the repeated acclamations of his people, arrived at Kensington Palace in good health'. The local version, as reported in a letter to *Notes and Queries* in 1881 is more colourful: 'His Majesty once landed here in the middle of the night, on some crazy steps — which have lately disappeared — and was taken to a house, still standing, in King Street, to sleep. Local tradition further states that an old lady preceded him with a tallow candle in a lantern, and said at the corner "Oh, please, Mr King, mind the puddle"'.[117] Some doubt the veracity of this tale.

Sometimes the King and other members of the aristocracy would choose to stay the night at Margate. 'Persons of quality' including William III, the Duke of Marlborough and the Duke of Shrewsbury stayed at the Mansion House in Margate (see Chapter 1), the Glover's house, 'for which they used to make presents or other gratifications to the said Susannah Glover'.[118] For example, in May 1709: 'London, May 6. On Tuesday last, at 7 of the Clock in the Evening, the Duke and Duchess of Marlborough arriv'd at Margate, and lodg'd at the Widow's House, where the late K. William us'd to do'.[119] Following Susannah Glover's death in 1713 the Mansion House stood empty and people of quality no longer stayed there 'but went to the house of Mr Jewell [the White Hart] and lodged there'.[118]

CHAPTER 3

The People of Margate

William Harrison, writing at the end of the sixteenth century, was very clear about how society was structured: 'We, in England, divide our people commonly into four sorts, as gentlemen, citizens or burgesses, yeomen, and artificers or labourers'.[1] Of gentlemen he said 'the first and chief (next the king) be the prince, dukes, marquesses, earls, viscounts, and barons; and these are called gentlemen of the greater sort, or (as our common usage of speech is) lords and noblemen: and next unto them be knights, esquires, and, last of all, they that are simply called gentlemen'. There were few men in Thanet that Harrison would have classed as gentlemen. Topping Thanet society in the fifteenth century were the Manston and Daundelion families, both of whom were armiger esquires, gentleman just below the rank of knight but entitled to bear arms and wear armour; the Queyk and Parker families at Birchington were of a slightly lower status.[2] The Conyngham family, important in the history of Thanet because of their land holdings, were finally ennobled to Earl in 1780, but seem never to have lived in Thanet. Thanet men who became High Sheriffs of Kent all came from one family of the squirearchy, the Crispes of Quekes.[2]

At the next level of society were the 'citizens or burgesses'. Since there were no cities or large towns in Thanet, there were no burgesses. However, Harrison classed merchants amongst the citizens, noting that 'they often change estate with gentlemen, as gentlemen do with them, by a mutual conversion of the one into the other'. These merchants exported goods such as 'broad clothes . . . of all colours, likewise cottons, friezes, rugs, tin, wool, our best beer, baize, bustian, mockadoes (tufted and plain), rash, lead, fells, etc.' which would be taken 'into all quarters of the world, and there either exchanged for other wares or ready money, to the great gain and commodity of our merchants'. Harrison might have included in this category the 'Masters of Ships', the wealthy owners of hoys, living in Margate.

The third of Harrison's classes were the yeomen:

> This sort of people have a certain pre-eminence, and more estimation than labourers and the common sort of artificers, and these commonly live wealthily, keep good houses, and travel to get riches. They are also for the most part farmers to gentlemen ... or at the leastwise artificers, and with grazing, frequenting of markets, and keeping of servants (not idle servants, as the gentlemen do, but such as get both their own and part of their masters' living), do come to great wealth, insomuch that many of them are able and do buy the lands of unthrifty gentlemen, and often setting their sons to the schools, to the universities, and to the Inns of the Court, or, otherwise leaving them sufficient lands whereupon they may live without labour, do make them by those means to become gentlemen. These were they that in times past made all France afraid. And albeit they be not called "Master," as gentlemen are, or "Sir," as to knights appertaineth, but only "John" and "Thomas," etc., yet have they been found to have done very good service.

The chief families of Margate probably fell into this category, including the Norwoods discussed in Chapter 2, and the Lamings, Omars, Claybrookes and other families to be discussed later in this chapter.

Finally, 'the fourth and last sort of people in England are day-labourers, poor husbandmen, and some retailers (which have no free land), copyholders, and all artificers, as tailors, shoemakers, carpenters, brick makers, masons, etc.' Margate was not a wealthy town and had few wealthy inhabitants, and so most of its inhabitant's would have fallen into this fourth group. Harris wrote of the Isle of Thanet in 1719 that 'there is not one Gentleman that now lives on this Island' and that the former gentry had left and their estates were 'sold off from the Mansion Seats, and the houses converted into farm houses', although he did concede that the local yeomanry and farmers were 'many of them men of good estates ... and accordingly live in a very handsome and gentleman-like manner'.[3] Lewis wrote in 1723 about a decline in the fortunes of Margate: '*Mergate* was on account of its harbour, and trade to *London*, the only place of business [in the Isle of Thanet], and whose inhabitants were wealthy and lived in plenty. But time has made a very great alteration in these places.

By the Sea's falling so heavy on the North part of the island, the harbour of *Mergate* is gone very much to decay, and the Masters of Ships which used to live there are almost all removed to *London* for the sake of their business. So that the place is in a manner deserted by them. Whereas the Town of *Ramsgate* has all this while been growing and encreasing, being almost half of it new built, and their Peer being considerably enlarged; so that there are many wealthy persons among them'.[4]

One of the chief Margate families, the Norwoods, has already been described in Chapter 1. The Parish Church contains two brasses for members of the Norwood family, one for William Norwood who died in 1605 and one for Alexander Norwood who died in 1557, Alexander his son who died in 1583, and Joanna his wife who died in 1605.[5] The prominence of the family in the sixteenth century is clear in the Parish registers where on several occasions the baptism of a Norwood child is recorded in a large embossed hand so that it is the most conspicuous entry on the page.[6] Members of the Norwood family and of another important family, the Claybrookes, enjoyed privileges not extended to others, such as eating meat at Lent:[6]

Mrs Mary Claybrooke licensed according to the statute to eat flesh the 1 of March, entred this 8 day. And likewise Rich. Norwood both licensed and entred upon the same first and 8th of March 1619.

Another local family of note is the Laming family, notable not least because of the network of marriages linking the Lamings to other families of significance in the development of Margate. Roger Laming junior, who died in 1743, was the 'owner of several hoys' and 'reputed to be worth £30,000'.[7,8] His father, Roger Laming senior, was the son of John Laming, the Margate Deputy in 1651,[9] and Joyce Grant, and was born in Margate in 1612; in 1633 Roger Laming senior marred Joan Omer of Minster and the couple had eight children, of whom the last was Roger Laming junior, born in 1653.[10,11] Roger Laming junior's wife was named Mary but, unfortunately, we know nothing about her; it is likely that Roger Laming junior married late in life as their only child was baptised in August 1721, when Roger Laming was 68. The child, also named Roger Laming, died in February 1739, at the age of 18. At the time of his death Roger Laming junior therefore had no surviving children, and his will leaves all his considerable wealth to his wife, to his various nephews and nieces and their children, and to other relatives and friends.[12] One niece, Joanna Culmer, received £700 in the will, with her son Roger and her three daughters each receiving £500. The Culmer's were an established family of Margate mariners, owning property on what was to become the Parade at Margate, including the Ship Inn.[13] Rowe reports that Roger Culmer was a cooper who died a rich man and owner of Hartsdown.[14]

A kinswoman of Roger Laming junior was Rachell, the wife of Captain Daniel Pamflett; Rachell received £500 in the will and Daniel Pamflett £200. Daniel Pamflett was a hoyman and at one time an Overseer of the Poor for the parish.[14] A kinsman was Valentine Jewell junior who received £500, a number of other Jewells receiving a total of over £1500. Valentine Jewell senior, born in 1659 and dying in 1730, was the son of Joseph Jewell and Elizabeth Laming, Elizabeth Laming being one of the sisters of Roger Laming junior. Valentine Jewell senior and his son Valentine Jewell junior were important figures in the development of Margate. In 1693 the list of Margate inhabitants who contributed to the repair of the Pier included, as well as Roger Laming, Valentine Jewell senior, Roger Omer and Thomas Grant. Valentine Jewell senior was married twice, first to Martha Grant who died in 1698 and then, in 1699, to Anne Prince, the first child of that marriage being Valentine Jewell, junior. Joseph Jewell issued a halfpenny trade token in 1669 showing a cheese-knife on the reverse, showing that he was a grocer, and Valentine Jewell senior was a witness in a court case in 1716 concerning the sale of the Mansion House in Margate, in which he also was described as a grocer, aged 58.[15] Valentine Jewell senior must have been a man of some wealth as he was able to lend money for the rebuilding of Margate Pier; at various times he was a Pier Warden, an Overseer of the Poor, and a Churchwarden. His son, Valentine Jewell, junior, married the daughter of Abraham Hudson, the Mayor of Deal, and, in 1729, purchased the White Hart Inn which was to become one of the town's most important hotels.[16,17]

Roger Laming senior had, in 1633, married Joan Omer who was the daughter of Roger Omer and Elizabeth Sayer, a Minster family, one of whose brothers, Richard Omer, married Sarah Henneker.[11] Richard and Sarah's son, Roger Omer senior, born in 1657, married Mary Tomlin in 1680 and one of their children, James Omer, married Anne Jewell in 1717. Ann Jewell was one of the daughters of Valentine Jewell senior and Martha Grant. Roger Laming junior left £150 each to three of the children of James Omer and Anne Jewell, Roger Omer, James Omer and Ann Omer. Roger Omer senior was one of those contributing to the cost of rebuilding Margate Pier in 1693 and served as an Overseer of the Poor, as Churchwarden, and as the town Deputy on two occasions.[18,19] The Poor Accounts for 1716 show a Captain Omer at Northdown paying £1 0s 7½d towards the poor rates, suggesting that Roger Omer senior was both a mariner and a farmer.[14] The children of James Omer and Anne Jewell born after 1720 were all baptised at St Dunstan, Stepney, suggesting that James Omer could have been one of the 'masters of ships' referred to by Lewis in 1723 who used to live in Margate but are now 'almost all removed to London for the sake of their business'.[4] The 1789 will of Richard Sackett of East Northdown speaks of a house and farm at West Northdown 'lately purchased from heirs of Roger Omer', so that Roger Omer junior was a farmer and landowner.[20]

Roger Laming junior also left money to two other relations who were part of the maritime community at Margate. Mary, the wife of Edward Robson, and her children were left a total of £1000; Edward Robson appears in the Pier Wardens accounts for 1732 and 1733, Robson paying 10s for 2,500 fish caught in the North Sea and £1 10s for six voyages delivering 180 chaldron of coal to Margate.[21] The other relation with maritime connections was Peter Swinford, left £100 in Roger Laming junior's will. Poor House Accounts suggest that Peter Swinford was a coal merchant, but this probably included the shipping of coal from Newcastle. He was a Churchwarden in 1685 and signed the Poor House accounts for that year with his mark, a simple P; this was unusual since the great majority of the Churchwardens were sufficiently literate to be able at least to sign their own names.[18] Swinford was a relatively common name in Margate, many of the Swinfords being mariners, and Stephen Swinford, for example, was one of the major owners of hoys, shipping large quantities of grain from Margate to London.

A number of properties are mentioned in Roger Laming's will. These include the Bull Head inn, in the occupation of William Brown, a Windmill with outhouses, buildings and yard, presumably Mill Lane Mill, his farm and lands at Harts Down and his land at North Down.[12] Roger Laming's involvement in the farming as well as the maritime worlds was not unusual in Thanet, both the wealthy and the poor often being involved in both, as described by William Camden in 1586:[22]

Neither must I passe over heere in silence that which maketh for the singular praise of the inhabitants of Tenet, those especially which dwell by the roads or harboroughs of Margat, Ramsgat and Broadstear. For they are passing industrious, and as if they were *amphibii*, that is, both land-creatures and sea-creatures, get their living both by sea and land, as one would say, with both these elements: they be fisher-men and plough men, as well husband-men as mariners, and they that hold the plough-taile in earing [tilling] the ground, the same hold the helme in steering the ship. According to the season of the yeare, they knit nets, they fish for cods, herrings, mackarels, &c, they saile, and carry foorth merchandise. The same againe dung and mannure their grounds, plough, sow, harrow, reape their corne, and they inne [store] it, men most ready and well apointed both for sea and land, and thus goe they round and keepe a circle in these their labours. Furthermore, whereas that otherwhiles there happen shipwrackes here (for they lie full against the shore those most dangerous flats, shallowes, shelves, and sands so much feared of sailers, which they use to call The Goodwin Sands, The Brakes, The Four-Foots, The Whitdick &c, these men are wont to bestir themselves lustily in recovering both ships, men, and marchandise endangered.

This same pattern of working still existed at the start of the eighteenth century:[4]

They who live by the sea side are generally fishermen, or those who go voyages to foreign parts, or such as depend on what they call *foying*, i.e. going off to ships with provisions, and to help them in distress &c. . . . When they are boys they go to catch whitings and herrings, and to the North Seas whither they make two voyages a year, and come home the latter one soon enough for the men to go to wheat season, and take a winters thresh; which last they have done time enough to go to sea in the Spring. Besides this, there are here two seasons for the Home-Fishery . . . The first of these is the macarel season, which commonly is about the beginning of May when the sowing of barley is ended. The other is the season for catching herrings which begins about the end of harvest, and ends soon enough for the wheat season, the time of sowing which here is about November.

This dual employment probably resulted in what, for the time, was a more than averagely comfortable life for the farm labourer and, indeed, farmers would sometimes have problems getting men to work on their farms because of the rival attractions of working on a fishing boat.[4]

Other examples of land owners in Margate with an interest in the sea include William Lucas, described in a Patent Roll of 1442 as the master of a ship, the *Nicholas,*:[23]

Grant to the king' servants Henry Rosyngton, yeoman of the crown, John Trevelyn, yeoman of the chamber, and Henry Wareyn, groom of the chamber, of the goods and merchandise of John Daundelion of the Isle of Tenet late in a ship called the *Nicholas* of Mergate, whereof William Lucas was master, within the port of Mergate, and carried and placed in a house uncustomed and without licence and so forfeit to the king.

His land holdings were described in a deed of 1440:[24]

Richard Raven of Northdowne, in the par. of St John, Isle of Thanet, grants to John Basele and Thomas Cosyn of the same 3 acres of land with appurtenances lying separately in the said par. in the tenure of the Lord of Menstre, of which half an acre and half a rood lie at Seler' between the land of John Daundelyon on the S., the land of Edward Ropkyn on the N., another half acre and half rood at Hor'downe between the land of William Lucas on the N. and the land of John Cowpere on the S., another half acre at Steuene Steyr' between the land of John Noyl on the W. and E., another half acre at Steuene Steyr' between the land of Nicholas Lucas on the E. and the land of the heirs of John Curlyng on the W. and another half acre and half rood at Helmnesse between the land of William Lucas on the E. and W. and another 1½ roods at Westdowne between the land of Richard Lederer' on the N. and the land of William Crowe on the S.
    Warranty. Witnesses: Richard Lederer', William Lucas, Nicholas Lucas, Stephen Kempe, John Crosse and others.

Unfortunately the locations of most of the places mentioned, such as Hor'downe and Steuene Steyr', are now lost (the apostrophes in these names are referred to as 'scribal suspensions' and correspond to one or more letters left out by the scribe; the missing letters are unknowable unless the equivalent modern place name is obvious), but William Lucas was clearly the owner of significant amounts of farm land. It is possible that the area of Margate formerly known as Lucas Dane was named after a member of the Lucas family (see Introduction).

A later example of a farmer-mariner is Daniel Faireman who was described in 1685 as both a seaman of St John's parish and as a labourer who had worked regularly for William Payne, a local farmer, 'in harvest time about two or three yeares since for the space of five years'.[25] Indentures also confirm that many farmers had interests in the sea, owning shares in fishing vessels and considerable amounts of fishing tackle.[25] An inventory of the goods of Robert Bennett, a husbandman who farmed near Margate, taken in 1692, shows this combination of farming and fishing: 'In the outhouse and loft. - Item one woollen wheell, one bushell [measure], one skrye, one fan, five and twenty sax, certaine herring netts and shott [mackerel] netts, certaine harvest tooles, stake, ropes, one grindstone, fower bushells of wheat, two bushells of beans and other things there'.[25]

Farms in Thanet were described by Lewis in 1723 as being 'generally large' and 'the occupiers of these farms, especially of the larger ones' as being 'generally . . . men of good substance'.[4] The farms were productive and profitable, the soil of Thanet being renowned during the eighteenth and nineteenth centuries for its thin, light, and chalky texture, fertilized by an inexhaustible supply of seaweed manure.[26] The farmers also benefited from being close to the expanding London food market, supplied from Margate by the hoys passing up and down the Thames, as described in Chapter 2. John Evelyn was particularly impressed with the farms in Thanet. During his journey from Margate to Rochester in 1672 he reported: 'I came back through a Country the best cultivated of any that in my life I had any where seene, every field lying as even as a bowling greene, & the fences, plantations, & husbandrie in such admirable order, as infinitely delighted me . . . observing almost every tall tree to have a Weather-cock on the top bough'.[27] During another visit to Margate in 1672 he reported how 'I was carried to see a gallant Widow, a Farmoresse [ie a female farmer], & I think of *Gygantic* race, rich, comely, & exceedingly Industrious . . . her house was so plentifully stored with all manner of Countrie provisions, all of her own groth, & all her conveniences so substantiall, neate & well understood: She herselfe so jolly & hospitable, & her land, so trim, & rarely husbanded, that it struck me with a kind of admiration at her Oeconomie'.

An inventory of the belongings of Nicholas Sayer, a farmer in the parish of St John's, in 1548 gives a clear picture of the life of a local farmer. As described by Edward White:[28]

There is no great difficulty in realizing the personal appearance of the man himself. His doublet, a close fitting garment with skirts reaching a very little below the girdle, was either of worsted or canvas. The jerkin was usually worn over the doublet, either of them with or without sleeves as the wearer pleased. There was but very little, if any distinction between the jerkin and jacket. He possessed two petticoats; this garment being during the reign of Henry VIII and Edward VI an article of male attire, and is still worn by the boys of Christ's Hospital, who retain the precise costume of lads of the time of Edward VI. Nicholas Sayer was probably, however, too homespun to have adopted the fashionable yellow stockings of the period, and his hose were, no doubt, of white or grey yarn. His ordinary garments were of frieze; his best apparel of violet cloth; and over all, in rough weather, he wore a long loose gabardine. This name is still given in some parts of Kent to the "smock frock". A flat cap or bonnet upon his head completed his costume. His weapons, whether of offence or for sport, were a bow and sheaf of arrows, which, like most English yeomen, he probably knew how to make right good use of.

In the hall he and his farm servants ate in common. The table was a board laid upon trestles. Quite as late as the 15th century the halls of the gentry were furnished with similar tables, which were only adjusted preparatory to meals; hence is derived our modern phrase to "spread the board", which once had a more practical signification. But Nicholas Sayer had also a counter, table, and chairs. His dinner service consisted of wooden platter and pewter dishes. The culinary utensils were of brass or latten; and these durable vessels were usually bequeathed by will from generation to generation.

His "occupation" was rather small, inasmuch as it required only four horses, one plough, two harrows, and a roller. The more interesting items are the prices of stock and grain. The horses were worth rather less than 15s each; cows and heifers rather more than 26s; a weaning calf could be bought for 2s 4d; a ewe for 3s 4d and a young sheep was worth less than 1s. Wheat was worth 6s a quarter — one parcel rather more — and barley 4s. Considering the relative value of money the sum total of Nicholas Sayer's property would be about equivalent to £350 of modern currency [written in ca. 1920].

An analysis of inventories produced for probate suggest that barley made up about half of the crops grown in Thanet at the end of the 17th and beginning of the 18th centuries, that wheat made up about a third of the crop, and that oats, beans, peas, tares [a kind of legume], and dredge [usually a mixture of oats and barley] made up the rest.[25] Barley was grown largely to make malt and, by the early seventeenth century, malt had become an important export from Margate. A group of prosperous Thanet barley farmers sent their annual crop to London to be sold for them by city factors, at a fee of 2d in the pound; not only were these farmers related, but the factors were their nephews and cousins.[29] With time these close family connections weakened, and Lewis reported in 1723 that farmers were 'obliged to trust to the [corn] factors and others in selling their corn, who, if they are not honest men, have great opportunities of defrauding them'.[4]

The actual process of selling malt through factors was described in some detail by Daniel Defoe in his *The Complete English Tradesman*, published in 1732:[30] Defoe complained that 'maltsters . . . are now no longer farmers, and, as might be said, working labouring people, as was formerly the case, when the public expense of beer and ale, and the number of alehouses, was not so great'. Whereas in the past farmers had malted their own barley, the demand for malt had grown so much that the larger farmers had started to purchase barley from local, smaller farmers, until eventually the malt trade 'came out of the hands of the farmers; for either the farmers found so much business, and to so much advantage, in the malting-trade, that they left off ploughing, and put off their farms, sticking wholly to the malt; or other men, encouraged by the apparent advantage of the malting-trade, set it up by itself, and bought their barley . . . of the farmers . . . and thus malting became a trade by itself.' In turn, this led to the growth of corn-factors, 'many of [whom] sell no other grain than malt', who acted as 'agents for the maltsters who stay in the country, and only send up their goods [to London].' Defoe than reported that the factors 'developed a new way of buying and selling corn, as well as malt', which was the 'buying of corn by samples only':

The farmer, who has perhaps twenty load of wheat in his barn, rubs out only a few handfuls of it with his hand, and puts it into a little money bag; and with this sample, as it is called, in his pocket, away he goes to market. When he comes thither, he stands with his little bag in his hand, at a particular place where such business is done, and thither the factors or buyers come also; the factor looks on the sample, asks his price, bids, and then buys; and that not a sack or a load, but the whole quantity; and away they go together to the next Inn to adjust the bargain . . .

The farmer inquires where he must deliver it, which is generally agreed to be either to such or such Hoys or Barges, or Vessels, as the nearest navigation to the place; or at such and such Mills, if it be wheat, as are nearest to be ground at ... The next demand is the payment, and that is adjusted to be at the delivery, or perhaps the factor will be so kind to the farmer as to bring it to his house, if not far off; upon this the factor gives earnest, and so the whole barn, or stack, or mow of corn is sold at once; and not only so, but 'tis odds but the factor deals with him ever after by coming to his house, and so the farmer troubles the Market no more.

This kind of trade is chiefly carried on in those Market Towns which are at a small distance from London ... such as Rochester, Maidstone ... and particularly at Margate and Whitstable. At these Markets you may see, that besides the Market house where a small quantity of corn perhaps is seen, the place mentioned above, where the farmers and factors meet is like a little exchange, where all the rest of the business is transacted, and where an hundred times the quantity of corn is bought and sold, as appears in sacks in the Market house ... Towns and Inns are throng'd with farmers, and samples on one hand, and with meal-men, London-bakers, millers, and corn-factors, and other buyers on the other; the rest of the week you see the wagons and carts continually coming all night, and all day, laden with corn of all sorts to be deliver'd on board the Hoys, where the Hoy-men stand ready to receive it, and generally to pay for it also.

Pier accounts and the report by Daniel Defoe just quoted suggest that the barley trade was very active in the early eighteenth century, although Lewis in 1723 suggests that by then malting, the conversion of barley into malt in malt-houses, was in decline:[4]

Malting is another Branch of the Trade of this Place [Margate], which was formerly so large, that there were about 40 Malt-houses in this Parish. But this trade is now gone much to decay; tho' certainly here might be made the best Malt in *England*, the Barley which grows here being so very good, and the land naturally so kind for it. The Malt, it seems, here made having formerly been very coarse for the Use of the Distillers, it has so much lost its credit, that the present Maltsters find little encouragement to make their Malt fine for a London Market, where they are almost sure to be out-sold by the *Hertfordshire* and *North Country* Malt-men, whose Malt bears a better Name.

The ale brewed in and around Margate, especially at Northdown had once been very popular. In 1636 John Taylor reported 'there is a Towne neere Margate in Kent, (in the Isle of Thanett) called Northdowne, which Towne hath ingrost much Fame, Wealth, and Reputation from the prevalent potencie of their Attractive Ale'.[31] Northdown Ale had even been praised by Robert Herrick in a poem published in 1646, of which the relevant part reads:[32]

> For gladding so my hearth here,
> With inoffensive mirth here;
> That while the Wassaile Bowle here
> With North-down Ale doth troule here,
> No sillable doth fall here,
> To marre the mirth at all here.

During the second Dutch war Sir Joseph Williamson, Under Secretary to the Secretary of State, was sent quantities of Northdown ale by several of his contacts in Margate. In December 1666 John Smith, a Margate doctor, sent Williamson 'some country ale, good to drink this cold weather, which if bottled, will be the better the longer it is kept'.[33] In 1668 Richard Watts wrote to Williamson from Margate saying 'I intended to send you a barrel of ale which has since been staved, but understand Mayto of Margate has brought or sent you a 10 gallon runlet [a small barrel]'.[34] Northdown ale was praised by John Evelyn, who visited Margate on March 27 1672 to make arrangements for the treatment of the wounded from the second Dutch war; at Margate he 'was handsomely entertained', probably with the local ale, and then 'lay at my deputy's Captain Glover'.[27] He visited Margate again in May 1672, and his diary entry for 21 May reads: 'This towne much consists of Brewers of a certain heady Ale, and deale much in mault etc'.[27] Samuel Pepys was also a fan of Northdown ale; in his diary for 1660 there are four entries mentioning the ale, three of which describe its effects:[35]

May 7 1660: This morning Captain Cuttance sent me 12 bottles of Margate ale. Three of them I drank presently with some friends in the Coach.... After I was in bed Mr Sheply and W. Howe came and sat in my cabin, where I gave them three bottles of Margate ale, and sat laughing and very merry, till almost one o'clock in the morning, and so good night.

August 27 1660: This morning comes one with a vessel of Northdown ale from Mr Pierce, the purser, to me.

September 13, 1660: Old East [a porter] comes to me in the morning with letters, and I did give him a bottle of Northdown ale, which made the poor man almost drunk.

October 26 1660: My father and Dr Thomas Pepys dined at my house, the last of whom I did almost fox with Margate ale.

In 1678 Henry Teonge, a naval chaplain, wrote in his diary about a dinner he had enjoyed on board ship: 'we are fain to make shift with an excellent salad and eggs, a fillett of veal roasted, a grand dish of maccarell, and a large lobster; so hard is our fare at sea; and all washed down with good Marget ale, March beer, and, last of all, a good bowl of punch'.[36]

Unfortunately by the 1720s the trade in Northdown ale was one of the many trades in Margate in decline:[4]

About 40 Years ago, one ---- *Prince* of this place drove a great Trade here in brewing a particular Sort of Ale, which, from its being first brewed at a Place called *North-down* in this Parish, went by the name of *North-down* Ale, and afterwards was called *Mergate* Ale. But whether it is owing to the Art of brewing this liquor dying with the Inventor of it, or the humour of the Gentry and People altering to the liking the Pale North Country Ale better, the present brewers vend little or none of what they call by the Name of *Mergate*-Ale, which is a great disadvantage to their Trade.

The Mr Prince referred to by Lewis was probably John Prince, who is listed in the Parish Burial register as 'brewer'. He died in 1687 and his probate inventory included 'a hopp house' with two bags of 'hopps'.[37]

Although ale and beer were both brewed from malted barley, ale originally contained no hops and so was sweeter and fruitier than beer to which hops was added to balance out the sweetness of the malt, and to extend its life. Herbs or some other additive were frequently added to ale instead of hops to reduce its sweetness, but gradually hops came to be added even to ale, so that by 1773 the *Encyclopaedia Britannica* defined ale as 'a fermented liquor obtained from an infusion of malt and differing only from beer in having a less proportion of hops'.[38] The presence of hops in John Prince's inventory suggests that Northdown Ale had at least some hops in it.

Despite the problems reported by Lewis, maltsters and brewers were amongst the wealthiest inhabitants of the town. An announcement in 1755 describes the advantageous marriage made by one brewer, Thomas Boreman:[39]

On Thursday, last, Mr Thomas Boreman, brewer at Margate (who succeeded the late Mr William Simmons, an eminent Brewer of that place) was married to Miss Ann Matson, daughter of Mr Robert Matson, farmer and grasier, a gentleman of known probity in East Kent, a very agreeable young lady, indow'd with the most valuable qualities for making them happy in that honourable state, with a fortune of £2000.

An advertisement of 1766 records the sale of the estate of a maltster, William Jarvis:[40]

To be sold . . . at the New Inn.
A freehold estate, lately the Property of Mr William Jarvis, Maltster, deceased, consisting of a large good Dwelling House containing three Parlours, three Chambers, two Shops, two Kitchens, two Cellars, &c. together with a large Malt-house, that [illegible] 20 Quarter per Week, also a Brewhouse, Stables, and other Out-houses, Yards, Gardens, &c. situated at the upper End of High-street, near the Church in Margate, very commodious, and capable of great Improvement.

As described in Chapter 1, many of Margate's malthouses were located at Church hill, at the upper end of the High Street, where the Petken's also had a brewhouse, and along King Street. The brewhouse in King Street owned by the Petkens was of particular significance as the purchase of this brewhouse by Francis Cobb in 1763 was the start of the family brewery which played such an important part in the rise of the Cobbs to wealth and power in Margate.

The development of Margate in the 1750s led to the gradual selloff of many of the malthouses located in prime positions in the town:[41]

For sale – a malthouse (with a cellar under it) and land of ca 14 perches, situated with a good prospect of the sea, being very convenient for a gentleman or tradesman to build on.
Particulars from Richard Henneker, at Margate.

The memory of these malt-houses survived for a long time; in 1793 Zechariah Cozens described how the High Street was originally 'but a long dirty lane, consisting chiefly of malt-houses, herring-hangs, and the poor cottages of fishermen'.[42] The reference to herring-hangs points to another industry which, together with fishing, was in decline in Margate in the 1720s: 'As to the North-Sea Fishery, it has formerly been much used by the inhabitants of this island; but the little success they have met with of late Years, has very much discouraged them from following that Employment'.[4] The shortage of fish, in turn, hit the trade in curing herrings:[4]

The Hanging and Drying of Herrings is of great Use to the Poor of this Town, a great many of whom are employed, in the season for them, to wash, salt, spit, and hang them. But this is a trade that would be still more beneficial to the Place, were these Herrings caught by the Inhabitants. Because there would then be more imployment for the Poor, many of which have little to do but in spinning and twisting of twine to make nets with, and knitting the Nets, &c. But about 40 Years ago, the fishery here went so much to decay, that they who depended on it, were forced to sell their large Boats, or let them run out. So that now the boats in which they fish are so small, that they dare not go far off to Sea in them, nor venture out of the Peer in a fresh gale of Wind.

Unfortunately, the alternative jobs of spinning, twisting and knitting the fishing nets were poorly paid; in 1736 the rates of pay for spinning and twisting were, by the pound, 2d and 1d respectively, and knitting a herring net earned 1d per awine, a unit corresponding to 5 feet and 7 inches.[43] Mending the nets earned 1s per day with victuals or 1s 3d per day with breakfast only.

Arthur Rowe estimated that there were about two dozen herring houses surviving in Margate at the end of the nineteenth century.[44] Many of these herring houses were probably small as even in the seventeenth century only a few appeared in the Parish rate books, suggesting that many were private hangs, belonging to individuals, not in the trade. For the period 1716-1721 lists of herring hangs charged to the Poor Rates were kept in the Rate Books, as follows:[44]

[House = herring-hang]

1716 Thomas Huffam — for a house
R. Prince — for a house

1717 Thomas Huffam — for a house
Brooman and Jewell — for six houses
Richard Prince — for a house

1718 Thomas Huffman — for Digge's house
Brooman and Jewell — for six houses
Jarvis — for Richardson's house
Roger Whitehead — for ditto

1719 John Salter — for Mrs Digge's house
Thomas Huffam — for Digge's house
Thomas Huffam — for Norwood's house
Brooman and Jewell — for six houses
Jarvis — for Richardson's house
Roger Whitehead — for Richardson's house
Thomas Sprackling — for Mrs Grant's house
Thomas Barker — for Mrs Jewell's house
John Stanner — for Grant's house

1720 Thomas Huffam — for Skinner's house
Henry Sprackling — for Robert Smith's house
Thomas Sprackling — for Grant's house
Robert Gore — for Digge's house
Roger Whitehead — for Richardson's house
John Stanner — for Richardson's house
Valentine Jewell — for Mrs Jewell's house

1721 Thomas Huffam — for Skinner's house
Thomas Huffam — for Digge's house
Henry Sprackling — for Robert Smith's house
John Stanner — for Digge's house
John Stanner — for Richardson's house
Valentine Jewell — for Mrs Jewell's house

Lewis attributed the decline in fishing at Margate to the large amounts of sea weed (sea waur) taken from the sea for use on the land and for burning to make kelp, used in the glass making trade and for dyeing cloth.[4] Collecting and burning sea waur had, in fact, been prohibited in May 1594 by the Lord Warden of the Cinque Ports, because the inhabitants 'are thereby much annoyed in their health and greatly hindered in their fishing'.[4,45] However, it is clear that there were problems in enforcing the ban. In June 1616 John Thurloe of Margate petitioned Lord Zouch, Lord Warden of the Cinque Ports, 'that whereas his Lordship has prohibited the sale of a certain weed called kelkes (kelp) he may have licence to dispose of some which he has on hand, under certificate from the clothiers that it is good for dyeing cloth'.[46] The same month Lord Zouch received an order from the Privy Council 'for Sir Art. Ingram and others, contractors for the alum works, to have permission to burn and carry away the ashes of kelp or sea oare, anywhere within the Cinque Ports'.[46] The following year Lord Zouch also received a petition from the inhabitants of St John's requesting that 'the burning of sea oare into kelp be continued among their poor neighbours, and beg permission for them [the poor neighbours] to sell the same, without limitation of price, and without the intermeddling of strangers'.[47] The petition bore 23 signatures including those of the Deputy, William Fanting, and other local men of standing, including William Coppin, Paul Claybrook and Valentine Pettit. Whether or not the ban was ever formerly removed, it is clear that the collection of sea weed and its burning continued. Hasted reported in 1800 that 'the same custom of taking it away at the free will of those who have a right so to do, has continued (and indeed there can be no reason why it should not) to the present time. The first Lord Conyngham, as Lord of Minster manor, brought an action against the inhabitants of the part of the island within that manor, for taking away this sea-woose from the shore without his licence; which claim was tried at the county assizes, but his lordship failed in the establishment of it'.[45]

Lewis described the process of burning the sea weed as it was practised in 1723:[4]

The poor Men, who get their Summer's Livelihood by it, make several large Holes in the Ground either on the Sea Beach, or the Top of the Cliffs in which they burn the *Waur*, after having thoroughly dried it for that Purpose in the Sun, and made it fit for the Fire. In burning, it becomes a liquid Substance, which the Burners stir well together in the Holes wherein they burn it, and when they have done, they let it stand, cover'd over with dry *Waur*, till it is quite cold, when it looks very much like the Tallow-Chandlers Cakes of Greaves. By the Smoke of this burning *Waur*, which is very nauseous and offensive, is this Island rendered less pleasant than it would otherwise be in the Summer-time.

The ash produced by burning the sea weed, kelp ash, was used in the manufacture of glass; the availability of a local source of kelp ash could explain why a building for carrying on the glass trade was constructed in 1723.[48] The production of kelp ash for the glass industry was continued in Margate until the 19th century, in Alkali Row.[49]

The main source of employment for seamen at Margate, other than in fishing, was on the hoys. The owners of the hoys were amongst the wealthiest of the Margate residents. The ownership of a hoy was frequently shared, as a form of insurance, limiting loss if a hoy was lost at sea. For example, in 1689 Thomas Bax left a 'messuage, herring house, outhouse and garden' in King Street to his nephew Thomas Bax together with 'my sixteenth part of the Hoy or vessel whereof he is now master', to his nephew John Bax 'my sixteenth part of the Pinke or vessel whereof George Garling of Romansgate is master' and 'my sixteenth part of the Ketch or vessel whereof the said John Bax is now master', to his nephew George Bax 'my sixteenth part of the Pinke or vessel of which Ralph Constant is master', to John Hawkes 'my sixteenth part of the Pinke or vessel whereof John Brook is master', and to John Lister, son of John Lister, 'my sixteenth part of the Fisher Boat of which John Lister is master'.[50] A *Pinke*, or Pink (derived from the Dutch word *pincke*), was a small ship with a narrow stern, square rigging, and a large cargo capacity. Their flat bottoms resulted in a shallow draught making them ideal for short-range voyages in protected channels. In 1743 George Bax left to Jeremiah Simmons 'his eighth part of the yawl whereof John Calmer of Margate is now master together with my half part of the rowing boat whereof John Alderstone of Margate is now Master', and to Henry Simmons, the son of Jeremiah Simmons, 'my twenty fourth part of the Ireland fishing vessel whereof Nathaniel Bayly of Broadstairs is now master'.[50]

Seamen were also employed in foying, the 'going off to ships with provisions, and to help them in distress &c' and, for the less scrupulous, there were, of course, the opportunities presented by shipwrecks and smuggling.[4] Shipwrecks were a significant source of income for the poor of Margate. *The Margate Guide* of 1770 described 'the Acquisitions arising to the Common People, from what they consider as the greatest Blessing of Providence - a Shipwreck'.[51] The Guide continued:

They call it a God-send, and, as such, make the most of it, and are thankful. Misfortunes of this kind happen so frequently, that they become a good Revenue to the Fishermen and Peasants who live along the Coast, and who seldom fail to improve them to the utmost advantage. This, however, must be owned in justice to them, that, whenever there is a bare possibility of preserving a Ship-wrecked Crew, they act in Contempt of Danger, and do readily often save the lives of Others, at the most imminent hazard of their own.

Smuggling was also a popular activity, and *The Margate Guide* described the importance of the many gapways along the Thanet coast:[51]

which bear the Name of the Gates or Stairs . . . it may be necessary to say, that they are no other than sloping wagon-ways, which are cut through the high perpendicular Cliff, to the level of the water's edge. Through these are brought up Sea-waur [sea weed] for Manure of Land, Flint, Gravel, Chalk, Pebbles, not to mention now and then a few Articles in the Way of private Trade.

Smuggling and the efforts of the government to suppress it are described in Chapter 5.

All in all, by the 1720s, with the old trades of malting, brewing and fishing in decline, the fortunes of Margate were at a very low ebb. Lewis tells us that the pier had been washed away by the sea and that merchant vessels were being constructed of a tonnage too large to lay up in the harbour:[4]

The Trade of this poor Town is now very small, and would be considerably less, was it not for its being the Market of the whole Island, where the Inhabitants bring their Corn to send it to London by Hoys which go from hence every Week. By this Trade the Pier and Harbour are chiefly maintained . . . The Shipping Trade, (which once was pretty considerable, before the Harbour was so much washed away by the Sea, and the Ships built too large to lay up here) is now all removed to London, where the few Masters who live here lay up, victual, and refit their Vessels.

Lewis attributed the depressed state of the town and the high level of destitution largely to the loss of fishing: 'It seems owing a good deal to this decay of the Fishing here, with the falling off of the foreign trade, and the removal of so many of the substantial Inhabitants on that Account, from this place to London, that the charge of the Poor is so much increased within these 80 Years past'.[4]

A clearer idea of the state of the town can be obtained from the records of the Overseers of the Poor as these show both the numbers of the poor and numbers of those wealthy enough to contribute to the parish poor rate. The poor rate was generally levied on property within a parish 'from which a profit is derived', including houses, land, and commercial properties such as herring hangs and malthouses, the rate being assessed on the basis of the rental income that would be obtained from a property if it were to be rented out (known as *pound rates*).[52] Rates were also charged on 'stock in trade' owned by an inhabitant of the parish, since this was property from which a profit could be made.[52] In their accounts the overseers distinguished between the area around the church, Church hill, that around the harbour, referred to as Margate, and the outlying parts of the parish, Nash, Fleet and Lidden, Westbrook, Garlinge, Dandelyon, and Northdown. In 1717 the accounts list 49 people subject to the poor rate in Church hill and 118 in Margate, with 40 in the outlying parts, making 207 in total for the parish; the accounts also include 4 'out dwellers', who did not reside in the parish but who were charged rates for property they owned in the parish.[53] Lewis estimated that there were about 600 hundred families in the parish in 1723,[4] suggesting that only about a third of the families were wealthy enough to pay the poor rate. A discussion of those receiving poor relief from the parish is provided in Chapter 4.

It is not possible from the surviving records to estimate the number of pauper families in the parish, but national figures suggest that this is unlikely to have been more than about 20 % and was probably significantly less.[54] What this means is that about half of the families in the parish occupied a kind of middle ground, too poor to pay the poor rates, but not poor enough to be in receipt of poor relief. Exactly how the overseers decided where to draw the line is not known, but it was obviously in no one's interest to make a poor family pay the poor rate if this pushed them into penury so that they became a charge on the parish. A clearer picture is available for 1801 where a full list of rateable values for properties in the parish is available.[55] Properties were listed as either 'not rated' or 'rated', corresponding, respectively, to properties not charged a poor rate and those paying a poor rate; typically the annual poor rate was about 1s per pound of the rateable value. Generally, those in houses with a rateable value of less than £3 were not charged poor rates, but there was considerable flexibility. For example, widow Malpus in a house rated at £7 10s paid no rates, whereas John Stranack, in a house rated at £5, did pay rates. In 1801 rates were paid on 9141 properties in the parish (including commercial properties) and 1563 were exempt, corresponding to a total level of exemption of 15%; the number of families exempt from paying the poor rate in 1801 would have been higher than 15% as almost all commercial properties had to pay a poor rate, and would have been considerably higher in the early eighteenth century as the proportion of families paying rates in all parishes increased markedly between the beginning and end of the century.[52]

The relative wealth of Margate, Church hill and the outlying parts of the parish becomes clear from the poor rate payments.[53] For the quarter year starting October 1716 the total poor rate collection for the parish was £59 16s 3d, of which the contribution from Margate was £14 17s 6d, from Church hill £5 19s 2d and from the outlying parts £38 19s 7½d. Clearly, the wealthiest families in the parish lived in the country parts, including Mr Covell who paid £8 2s for 'Parsonage and Glebe Land', Mr Taddy at Garlinge, who paid £1 8s 1½d, Mr Mockett at Dandelyon, who paid £2 3s 1½d, and Captain Omer at Northdown, who paid £1 11s 10½d. At Church hill the payments ranged from 9s for both Mr Lewis, the Vicar of St John's, and Thomas Sprackling, a carpenter, to the 4½d paid by Mr Prince and by Robert Smith for two clover fields. At Margate individual payments were equally modest, one of the largest being the 9s 4½d paid by Roger Laming, a hoyman. The three chirurgeons [doctors] listed, Nicholas Churney, George Hammond and Edward Jarvis, paid 1s 10½d, 2s 3d and 3s, respectively. Henry Petkin, maltster and brewer, paid 6s, the same as paid by Thomas Lansell at Mill Lane Mill, Richard Prince paid 9d for his herring house and Thomas Huffam paid 4½d for his, but John Sackett had to pay 3s 9d for his malthouse. Rather surprising are the small sums paid by the local innkeepers, Mr Constant paying 1s 5d at the White Hart and Mr Wheatley 5s 3d at the Five Bells, with Mr Jarvis paying 4s at the King's Head in 1719.

Helpfully the Overseers' rate books have been annotated at some later date, possibly by Arthur Rowe, giving the occupations of about half of the inhabitants listed in the accounts.[53] As an example, in 1717 the occupations listed for Church hill and Margate combined are as follows:

Occupation	Number
Attorney	1
Barber	1
Blacksmith	2
Bricklayer	2
Butcher	3
Carpenter	6
Carter and Carrier	3
Cheesemonger	1
Chirurgeon	3
Coal Merchant	5
Cooper	2
Gentry	4
Glazier	1
Grocer	1
Herring House Keeper	2
Hoyman	4
Inn Keeper	4
Labourer	1
Malster and/or Brewer	9
Mariner	19
Mason	1
Miller	1
Minister	1
Rope Maker	1
Sail Maker	1
Shoemaker	4
Shopkeeper	1
Tailor and Draper	5
Yeoman or farmer	6

Although only about a quarter of the families in Margate at the time are covered by this list, a number of points are clear. The first is the importance of brewing and malting, the hanging of herrings, and the trade of mariner and hoyman, with a total of 34 employed in these trades. It is noticeable how few are involved with food, with no baker and only one grocer, a reflection of the fact that most families baked at home and most houses had a garden attached where vegetables could be grown; the presence of three butchers in the list shows that most families bought their meat but the absence of a fishmonger suggests that fish were bought directly off the boats. Other foods not produced in the average house would include cheese, hence the presence of a cheesemonger in the town; the absence of dairymen suggests that milk would be bought directly from local farmers. Those in the clothing trade include four shoemakers and five tailors and drapers; those offering more specialist services such as dress-making or wig-making only appeared in the town when holidaymakers started to arrive. The building trade is small, with just two bricklayers, one glazier and one mason; the presence of six carpenters suggests that many of the buildings in the town were of wood, but some of the carpenters were likely to have been involved in boat building and, indeed, the presence of one rope maker and one sail maker suggests that some boat building or repair went on in the town. The two blacksmiths would have been busy keeping the local horses shod, but could also have been involved in producing ironwork for the Pier and for the local ships. The presence of only one barber suggests that few in the town were obsessed with their hair. Professional people in the list include one attorney, three chirurgeons [doctors], and the vicar of St John's, together with six yeomen and farmers and four 'gentlemen'.

Of the early attorneys in Margate we know a little about one, Daniel Butler.[56,57] He was the son of Daniel Butler senior, also an attorney, and was born in the city of Worcester, from where he moved to Rye in Sussex and married, on March 12 1723, Mrs Mary Morris, believed to be of Worcester. Three years later, in 1726, he moved again, this time to Margate, and, in November 1726 placed an advertisement in the *Kentish Post* announcing his arrival:[58]

This is to give notice: That Mr Daniel Butler, who is an Attorney and serv'd his Clerkship at Rye, and has since Practised for himself, is now settled at Margate: Where all persons may have all manner of Business, within the Practise of an Attorney, Diligently, Carefully and Effectually done.

He keeps a day at Mr John Holman's, being the Sign of the Red Lion in Ramsgate; where he may be spoke with every Tuesday, from Ten till Four in the afternoon.

He lived in the High Street in Margate, became the father of nine children, and died on March 22, 1756, at the age of fifty-nine.

Margate Doctors

Members of the medical profession were an important part of any town. The medical profession at this time has been described as 'the physicians (those who advised and prescribed), the surgeons (those who cut into the body and attended to the outer skin), and the apothecaries (those who supplied medicines)'.[59] A true, consultant-like physician would have a medical degree (an MD) from the Universities of Oxford or Cambridge or from one of the many European Universities offering medical degrees. He would only prescribe a treatment; the treatment would actually be carried out by the surgeons and apothecaries. Gradually, however, a new type of physician emerged, more like our general practitioner, who had trained as a surgeon or apothecary but then obtained a licence to practice and 'kept his surgeon's or apothecary's shop, run by apprentices, and did all the treatment himself'.[60] Licenses to practice could be obtained from one of the Royal Colleges in London or from a bishop or archbishop; the Archbishop of Canterbury issued licences to practice medicine and surgery within his diocese of Canterbury, which included Margate.[61] An episcopal license, as it was known, gave permission to practice without the benefit of a university education, for anyone judged by the diocesan authorities to be 'of sober life and conversation', 'conformable to the law and doctrine of the Church of England' and 'well-skilled in the art [of medicine]'.[62] Although it sounds strange to us that the church was able to award licenses to practise medicine, in practice decisions were usually taken on the basis of recommendations from medical practitioners or by examination before a panel of surgeons.[62]

Although a medical practitioner was legally required to hold a licence or a medical degree before they could charge for performing medical services, it has been estimated that at least forty per cent of Kentish practitioners had no such qualification.[59] One of the duties of the parish Churchwardens was to report unlicensed practitioners to the local Archdeacon on one of his visitations to the parish. There are only two records of such reports being made at St John's, both Simon Fuller and Francis Carpenter being reported in 1609 'for practising surgery without licence', the Churchwardens adding that Francis Carpenter was 'a smith by trade'.[63] Of course, questions about paper qualifications would have been of little importance to the average patient; what really mattered was whether or not a practitioner did well for his patients. Of even less importance would have been the distinction between a man licensed to practice surgery and a physician with a medical degree; both would be described by their patients as 'doctor' as, indeed, would the many apothecaries who supplied both physic and advice. For simplicity, in what follows all medical practitioners will be referred to simply as doctors.

At the start of the 17th century in Kent few except the rich sought the help of trained medical practitioners, even when seriously ill; most had to rely on family or local help, but, by the 18th century trained medical practitioners were accessible to all but the destitute.[64] Ian Mortimer has identified doctors practicing in the parish of St John's in the 17th and beginning of the 18th centuries from probate accounts showing the purchase of medical assistance, usually on behalf of the seriously ill and dying.[59] These probate accounts were typically drawn up about a year after someone's death, and so the exact date of the medical treatment is not known.

In the earliest of these probate records the ill who could afford medical help often received it from a doctor living outside the parish. The first record, in 1579, is for William Norwood, one of the rich Norwood family living in the parish of St John's, whose estate had a gross value of £217.[59] His probate account shows that Edward Anderson, a surgeon of Sandwich, had been paid 'for the healinge of William Norwood one of the saide Wm Norwood's sonnes lagges [legs]' and 'for the heling [healing] of Mary Norwood's leg one of the said Wm's children'; one is left wondering why both children should need treatment on their legs at the same time. Stephen Tomlyn, whose estate was worth £33, was treated in about 1616 by John Jacob, a physician of Sandwich, and at about the same time John Cranbrooke, a maltster of St John's with an estate worth £125, was charged by Jasper Wolman of the Cranbrooke region for 'physick administered . . . in the time of his sickness'. In about 1674 Richard Langley, a tailor with an estate of £221, was treated by Richard Pistall, a physician of Sandwich; in about 1688 Anne Coppin/Davis, who had an estate worth £516, was treated by John Peters an MD and physician of Canterbury; and in about 1692 Edward Bilting, a cordwainer with an estate of £32, was treated by William Carder of Sandwich.

There were, however, medical practitioners in St John's parish itself. Thomas Smith, a surgeon of St John's received his diocesan licentiate in

1620 and in about 1636 charged Richard Mills, with an estate worth £32, 'for physic given him in sickness'; Thomas Smith was buried in 1668.[10] John Smith, another surgeon of St John's received his diocesan licentiate in 1638 and in about 1668 charged William Philpott, a yeoman of St John's with an estate worth £178, 'for physick when the said deceased lay upon his death bed'. In 1667-9 John Smith was one of the correspondents of Sir Joseph Williamson, Under Secretary to the Secretary of State, and was 'Deputy Clerk of the Passage, Margate' (Chapter 6).[65] The role of 'deputy clerk of the passage' was to collect customs and other charges on passengers, as made clear in an account of a voyage from Dover to Calais in April 1663:[66]

Before we entered the packet-boat, we pay'd to the clerk of the passage fourpence custom for a trunk, and two-pence a portmanteau, four shillings and ten-pence for transcribing a pass for four persons, and three shillings and six-pence for transcribing a pass for two persons. To the water-bailiff one shilling; to the master of the ferry one shilling and six-pence a man; *i.e.* one shilling town-custom, and six-pence for himself. To the searcher, six-pence a man for writing down our names, and we gave him two shillings and six-pence because he did not search us.

John Smith was active during the second Dutch war, treating the sick and injured landed at Margate but complained in October 1666 to Sir Joseph Williamson that he had not been paid for his work:[67]

Statement by John Smith that in September 1665, and since, many sick and wounded men were set ashore at Margate, and no provision made for their reception; the commissioners' agents at Deal and Dover refused to meddle with them, so he took charge of them, and was paid therefore when the Deal accounts were settled six months ago, and desired to continue his care, but Mr Talbor, agent, and Mr Bullock, surgeon of Dover, now forbid this; desires continuance in the employment, as during the last thirteen months; has no pay unless there be sick and wounded men there, Margate not being in the list for a surgeon; only three have died under his charge; has been vigilant and careful; thinks Talbor and Bullock raise false reports about him, because they have no benefit from him, he having little for himself.

John Smith also provided Williamson with snippets of information and local gossip, and, as we have seen, with Northdown Ale. Unfortunately, the gift of ale was not enough to get Smith the money he thought was due to him:[68]

Dec. 13. Margate.
John Smith to Williamson. Still put off from one to another about his charge in looking after the sick and wounded seamen. Esquire Evelyn says that Mr Bullock and Mr Talbor have received the money to pay him, but such clerks do mischief in slighting their betters, and giving trouble in waiting on them so often.

'Esquire Evelyn' (John Evelyn), writer of the famous diary, was, during the second Anglo-Dutch war, one of the four Commissioners 'for taking care of sick and wounded seamen and for the care and protection of prisoners of war'.

In May 1667 John Smith again complained to Williamson: 'Will be obliged to come to London again to see Squire Evelyn, as neither Mr Bullock nor Mr Talbor will take the writer's accounts for curing the sick and wounded, and he can get no satisfaction'.[69] In July 1667 he wrote again that he wanted 'satisfaction from Squire Evelyn for caring for sick and wounded seamen' and yet again in December 1667: 'I beg you to write a few lines in my behalf to Squire Evelyn, for satisfaction for curing the sick and wounded from the King's ships, landed at Margate, in the Isle of Thanet, for 15 months'.[70,71] This time he also asked for a job: 'I want an order to the farmers of customs for a surveyor or waiter's place at Margate'.[71] Finally, a letter from John Evelyn to Williamson explains why Smith was not getting what he wanted:[72]

J. Evelyn to Williamson. I have promised you 40 times to do Mr Smith all the right in my power, but Smith is never satisfied unless he can be his own carver, which cannot be without injury to the other officer. Smith was employed by a surgeon at Margate, and was to receive his recompense from him, and not from the Commissioners, who could not constitute a new and independent officer, being bound up to certain numbers and places by their instructions. Smith, not being satisfied with what the surgeon allowed him, appealed to the Commissioners; as they could not satisfy him, they advised him to submit it to arbitration, which was consented to; on the determination being sent, the

Commissioners gave his former antagonist two orders on the Exchequer, with an injunction to allow Smith to the full of his agreement. I cannot make out how he now comes to trouble you or clamour against me, who am only one of the Commissioners, after the great pains that have been taken, and the lapse of time that has occurred; the only thing I can do is to stop the orders in the Exchequer, until our surgeon at Dover has given him new satisfaction. This is really hard, after arbitration and a silence of many months about it till now; but as I said, this I will do: *si violandum in jus, violandum est amici causâ*, or if you please *imperii; for qui amicum habet, habet imperatorem.*

In 1672 Smith was again causing problems. On March 18 Williamson received two letters, one from John Smith, and another from J. Knight, Chirurgeon General of the Forces, giving two very different views of the same occasion:[73]

John Smith to Williamson. Yesterday came ashore here about seventy wounded by order from Mr Knight and Mr Peirse, who are committed to my care and cure, from the St Michael, Resolution, and Gloucester.

Surgeon J. Knight to Williamson. Having set on shore the wounded at Deal, I returned to Margate, where I got the wounded on shore from the Resolution and Gloucester. I have employed here your friend Mr Smith, but find him so weak in the affair that I dare not leave this till I have put these miserable wretches in so good a condition that scarce his ignorance can injure them. The number of wounded in all are few more than a hundred, whom I hope five or six days may put in the condition I mention.

Knight wrote again to Williamson on March 20:[74]

J. Knight to Williamson. I am here on the hardest duty I was ever engaged in, making brick without straw, not imagining to have found this place so ill provided with medicaments and those capable of applying them, your friend Smith having valued himself formerly so much to us both. He is a very dog in the manger, full of litigation and strife, and has, on account of not being approved of, put this whole place into a mutiny, and this under pretensions of non payment formerly, which, if wholly true, ought not at this time to have been revived upon the Commissioner being absent and assured to be here within a week. I have been obliged to hear all to comply with the necessity of his Majesty's affairs, and hope all their complaints will prove rather the effect of passion than well grounded. However, Mr Evelyn being absent, I have offered them moneys that have most doubted, which has for the present somewhat pacified the entertainers of the wounded, though not with the same alacrity as on the two first days. I have supplied what was wanting from adjacent places, and hope in a few days to be at liberty for London, when or soon after many here may be in a condition to be moved to the hospitals there, though, in my opinion, his Majesty had better continue the charge here than expose them to the sight of London in the very infancy of the war — the main reason, indeed, why I hazarded this present trouble here, when with almost as little I might have sent them to Chatham and Rochester, where I was certain of their very good entertainment and accommodation.

That is the final report on John Smith as a doctor, but, as described in Chapter 5, John Smith, presumably the same man, was waiter and searcher with the Customs at Margate in 1676.

Hopefully the other doctors in Margate were more capable than John Smith. Ludovic Leese, a physician of St John's, son of Arnold Lees of Faversham, was admitted to Cambridge in 1650, aged 18, and obtained his diocesan licentiate in 1661.[59] He administered to a number of the wealthy of St John's, including Thomas May, a brewer (estate of £140) in about 1665, John Poole, a bricklayer (estate of £84) in about 1668, Henry Pettit, a gentleman (estate of £1,536) in about 1669, and Frances Brooke (estate of £390) in about 1673, although Henry Pettit took the precaution of also being seen by William Jacob, a physician of Canterbury. Nicholas Chewney, the vicar of St John's (estate of £187) also took the precaution of being seen by two doctors when he was dying in 1685, William Jacob again and another doctor, George Chambers. (Nicholas Chewney's probate is dated 1686, but the parish registers show that he actually died in 1685.) George Chambers, originally a surgeon of Canterbury could have moved to Thanet given the number of his Thanet patients; he was awarded a diocesan licentiate in 1662. George Chambers treated, as well as Nicholas Chewney, Samuel Stevens, a mariner (estate of £353) in about 1674, John Wilkins, a blacksmith (estate of £815) in about 1679, James Samwayes, a salesman (estate of £100) in about 1681, James Fasham, a fisherman (estate of £17) in about 1683, and Mary Culmer, a widow (estate of £122) in about 1691. John Watts, a surgeon of St John's who received his diocesan licentiate in 1670, was also active; he treated James Fasham, a fisherman (estate of £17) in about 1683, Anne Wood, a widow (estate £1) in about 1685, Thomas Foster, a cordwainer (estate of £78) in about 1691, and John Philpot (estate of £69) in about 1704.

Edward Jarvis, probably from Guestling, Sussex, became a diocesan licentiate in 1704, and practised in Margate as a surgeon and apothecary.[59] He was paid by Elizabeth Read (estate of £129) in about 1716 'for physick by him administered to the said deceased and for curing the deceased's lame leg' and by Elizabeth Sackett (estate of £194) in about 1720 for 'a debt due and owing unto him by the said deceased at her death for physick'. Also practicing in St John's, although his qualifications are unknown, was John Violett who, in about 1635, was paid by Hester West, a widow of Birchington, 'for phisick ministred to the said deceased in the tyme of her sicknes'. Similarly the qualifications of Nicholas Chewney, probably the son of Nicholas Chewney, vicar of St John's, are unknown; in about 1691 he was paid by Mary Culmer who was also treated by George Chambers, and in about 1692 he was paid by John Wyatt a butcher (estate of £122) and John Baker.

Most of these doctors' names also appear in the overseers' accounts for the poor between 1666 and 1716.[18] John Smith has a single entry in 1666, when he received 19s 1d for 'cureing John Fassam ye last yeare'. A Dr Lees also appears in 1666, and could be the Ludovic Leese referred to above; he was paid 12s 'for his paines and for Phisick he gave to Widdow Beard and others' and 8s 'for looking to some poore people in sickness'. From 1680 the most active of the doctors in treating the poor was George Chambers who appears in the overseers' accounts some 14 times up to 1694, just a year before his death in 1695.[18] Like most doctors he was paid both for 'physick' as well as for treating patients, as in 1681 when he was paid 2s 'for physic for Markett and his wife' and in 1687 when he received 11s for 'medicines for Joh Beard', so that he probably produced his own medicines. His charges seem to have been rather modest; in 1687 he received just 6d for bleeding William Hall's wife. John Watts first appears in 1687 when he was paid 9s 3d 'for medicines for Widdow Beane and John Beard', and appears 17 times in the accounts, largely taking over from George Chambers after about 1690. In 1689 he seems to have been the main supplier of medicine to the poor, receiving £2 17s 6d 'for medicaments for the poore'; he appears in the overseer's accounts until 1705 and died in 1706.[10] Nicholas Chewney also appeared frequently in the overseers' accounts from 1689 to 1718 for attending the poor; he died in 1718. Edward Jarvis first appears in the accounts in 1700 but only makes about five appearances up to 1714. A Dr Checoney makes a single appearance in 1688, receiving 8s 'for Phisick for the poore'.

Four doctors' names appear in the overseers' accounts for the poor between 1716 and 1727, Mr Checoney, Nicholas Chewney, George Hammond and Edward Jarvis.[14] Two of these, Nicholas Chewney and Edward Jarvis have already been mentioned. Mr Checoney is probably the Dr Checoney who received a single payment in 1688; he appears in the account books between 1717 and 1718, and nothing more is known about him. Nicholas Chewney was practising in the parish in 1691 and died in July 1718 and was buried at St John's.[59] George Hammond, originally from Whitstable, became a diocesan licentiate in 1704 and was known to have treated patients in Whitstable, St Lawrence, Thanet, and St John's.[59] In 1726 George Hammond first appears in the accounts as 'Dr Hammond', suggesting that he had obtained an MD, but it is not known from where. Finally, Edward Jarvis died in 1732, aged 64 and was buried at St John's. His house and shop in Margate were advertised for sale in August 1732:[75]

To be let
A very convenient dwelling house, four rooms on a floor, a good shop, and cellars, with a useful garden, large stable and hay loft thereunto belonging, and well supplied with fresh water, situate in the best part of Margate town, where Mr Edward Jarvis, surgeon and practicer of physick, lately deceas'd, dwelt and succeeded in that business for many years. Also the furniture of the shop, drugs, medicines, distill'd waters, and instruments in surgery, to be disposed of. Inquire of Mr David Turner of Margate aforesaid, or Mr Richard Chilton of Ramsgate.

An inventory of Jarvis's possessions shows that he had significant money (£164) invested in South Sea bonds, with other bonds and money lent on mortgage, totalling £813 5s 8d.[76] In comparison, his household possessions were rather modest, with six silver tea spoons, and two large silver spoons, but with plates and dishes of pewter; in his stable he had a horse, but no carriage. He had his own herring house, containing two pickle herring barrels and one hundred and sixty one red herring barrels. His final send-off was, though, rather expensive; his funeral charges were listed as follows:

To Elizabeth Adrions as per bill — 9s
To Matthias Mummery as per bill — 14s 10s
To William Norwood as per bill — £2 2s
To John Brooman as per bill — £27 8s 6d
To George Phillpott as per bill — £1 13s
To Samuel Marks as per bill — £1 6s 6d
To Henry Petkin as per bill — 2s 8d
To laying the deceased forth and to several persons watching the corpse and attending the funeral — 11s
To Mr How for preaching the funeral sermon — £1 1s
To a messenger to invite Mr How to the funeral — 1s

In the overseers' accounts book running from 1728 to 1738 there are the names of six doctors, Dr George Hammond who appeared in the earlier accounts, Dr Watts (probably Dr John Watts), who appears in 1729, Henry Wallis, appearing in 1730, Dr George Slater, appearing in 1733, and Walter Plummer and Thomas Wheatley both first appearing in the accounts in 1735.[14] The last payment to George Hammond occurred in 1728, suggesting that he either died or left Margate at about this time. The last entry for Henry Wallis appeared in 1733 and a payment of 9s 8d in 1734 'To Wid. Wallis as per bill for Tho. Wheatley looking after the Poor' suggests that Henry Wallis had died in 1733-4 and that his practice had been taken over by Thomas Wheatley. Thomas Wheatley died in 1745, at the age of 35.[62] Nothing is known about the medical backgrounds of Henry Wallis, Walter Plummer and Thomas Wheatley. John Watts was awarded his diocesan licentiate in 1670 and was known to be practising in Margate in 1683.[62] George Slater was the first in a long line of Margate surgeons. Many of these doctors sold medicines as part of their job. The overseers' accounts in 1732 record that 1s was paid to Dr Watts 'for salve and balsom' and that Mr Wallis was paid £2 8s 8d 'for physic and looking after the poor'. In 1737 Thomas Wheatley was paid 11s 'as per bill for physick for the poor.'

Ian Mortimer has estimated that there was on average about 1 doctor for every 400 inhabitants in the Canterbury diocese in this period so that it is probable that most, if not all, of the surgeons identified in the overseers' accounts for the parish of St John's worked both with the poor and with patients able to pay for their own treatments.[62] Death rates in the parish suggest that they did a good job. In 1731 the following report appeared in the *Kentish Post*:[77]

It having been reported that at Margate the inhabitants are very sickly and abundance of them die, it's thought proper to give the following account of the burials there this last year, which according to the Parish register, have been as follows:

Strangers	3
Aged from 80 to 90	4
Aged from 70 to 80	8
Aged from 60 to 70	3
Aged from 50 to 60	9
Children under 8 years old	34
Died of consumption	2
Died of the small pox	5
In all	68

Margate Schoolteachers

Most of the Churchwardens at St John's were able to sign their own names in the Churchwarden's account books, suggesting that at least the more affluent members of the parish were literate. Lewis recorded in 1723 that there was a schoolroom in the parish church created by partitioning off the west end of the south aisle, with the implication that this was done before Lewis moved to the parish in 1706.[4] By an Act of Parliament in 1563 schoolmasters were required to acknowledge on oath the royal supremacy, and in 1571 it was laid down that 'it shall not be lawful for any to teach the Latin tongue or to instruct children, neither openly in the schools neither privately in any man's house, but whom the bishop of that diocese hath allowed and to whom he hath given licence to teach under the seal of his office'.[78] The licensing of schoolmasters is recorded in the archiepiscopal registers from 1568 to 1640. The first name in the list of schoolmasters licensed to teach at St John's Parish School is that of James 'Valensis or Duvale', in 1589.[79] The next to appear in the register is Robert Jenkinson, who had been vicar at St John's for 22 years by the time he received his licence to teach in 1599. There were probably a number of teachers covering the period 1589-1599; in 1591 John Alsoppe was reported to the Archdeacon on his visitation 'for teaching [school] without licence in the Church of St John's', and in 1598 the Churchwardens reported Margaret Cates to the Archdeacon 'for a railer and scolder, coming into the Church and misusing the schoolmaster in evil words, and throwing a stone at him in the Church, among the children'.[63] Robert Jenkinson died in 1601 and, after a gap of two years, John Ellfreth received a license to teach in Margate. It is not known when he left but in 1619 he is recorded as teaching in the parish school of St James at Dover. Three men were licensed to teach at St John's between 1604 and 1607, all three going on to become curates in other parishes. The Canterbury licensing books for schoolmasters end in 1640.

Other teachers in the parish were private teachers. In 1580 the Churchwardens complained to the Archdeacon that 'Thomas Deal keepeth in his house a schoolmaster to teach, and also being a victualler suffereth him to remain in his house and not frequent Divine Service on the Sabbath Day.' When Thomas Deal appeared before the Archdeacon's Court he explained 'that one Thomas Sandu came out of Flanders and was at Mr Henry Crispe's house [Quex], and came from there to the defendant with whom he remained, and taught his sons from twelfth time [6 January, the Epiphany] until middle Lent, and during that time he came to the Church about two or three times, and where he is now he ca'not tell, for when he went away he never took leave'.[63] In 1594 complaint was made 'that one Mr Johnson teacheth children and keepeth school in the said parish, having no licence in that behalf', in 1608 the complaint was that 'there is one teacheth in the parish upon request made to him, but not meaning to continue his teaching unless he obtain licence from the Ordinary', and in 1662 John Hiddens was reported 'for teaching school without licence'. Some private teachers did go through proper channels: in 1672 there is a record of a 'request by Peter Johnson, Presbyterian, for a licence to teach at the houses of Robert Smith at Romonsgate (Ramsgate), in the Isle of Thanet, and of William Petkin at Margate'.[80]

It is not known which children attended the schoolroom in the Church and if any charge was made for schooling. In 1731 the Parish Overseers started to pay for schooling for poor children in the Poorhouse, although this seems to have been by unqualified teachers (Chapter 4).[14] In 1731 payment was made for schooling just one poor boy, although the overseers did buy a primer for him, at a cost of 1s 3d. In 1732 and 1733 a series of widows were paid 'for schooling for the poor children'. Since schooling was provided for the poorhouse children, it seems likely that some schooling was also provided for other children in the parish, although children from wealthier families would presumably have received private tutoring or would have attended one of the public schools such as King's School, Canterbury, re-founded with a Royal Charter in 1541.

Shops and shopkeepers

Margate had few shops before the middle of the eighteenth century. The regulations governing the Pier and Harbour at Margate laid down that any 'durable commodity' such as salt, butter or cheese arriving by ship at Margate had to be offered for sale to private individuals for three days before being offered to any trader (Chapter 2). For luxury goods people would have had to travel to Canterbury or London. As late as 1763 John Lyon, in his *Short description of the Isle of Thanet, and particularly of the town of Margate*, said:[81]

As Margate is only a large village, you cannot expect that it should be so regularly supplied with shops, as a market-town; not but that there are several good ones, and many very respectable tradesmen. This deficiency is, in great measure, supplied by the numerous articles to be found in most of them, and by their ready and quick communication with London by the hoys.

Of course, not all makers and retailers of goods would have needed shops to sell their products. For example, many tailors and their female equivalent, mantua-makers or dressmakers, could have worked from home, visiting their customers' houses for fittings. The shops that there were would generally have contained little more than a counter and a few shelves, although in London things were starting to change; Daniel Defoe reported in 1726 that in London the 'modern custom' was for tradesmen to 'lay out two-thirds of their fortune in fitting up their shops' with 'painting and gilding, fine shelves, shutters, boxes, glass doors, sashes, and the like',[30] but the level of trade in Margate would not have supported such sumptuous premises until wealthy visitors started to appear in the town in the middle of the eighteenth century.

Some information about early shop keepers in Margate is provided by 17th century trade tokens. The upheaval of the civil war had led to a dire shortage of coins of small denomination and shopkeepers throughout the country responded by issuing trade tokens. These were usually made of lead, tin or copper, about the size of a modern 1p or 5p piece, and most had a value of a farthing or a halfpenny. If a customer bought something to the value of half a penny and offered a penny in payment, the shopkeeper would give them a token for the other half penny, which could be exchanged for goods at a later date. The tokens were banned after 1672 when the Royal Mint finally produced enough coins to meet the demand. Eight men and one woman are known to have issued tokens in Margate; George Friend, Stephen Greedier, Christian Hogben, Joseph Jewel, Richard Langley, Joseph Mackrith, Sarah Read, William Savage, and John Skinner.[82] Of these Stephen Greedier's token displayed the Fishmongers' arms, so that he was a fishmonger, Joseph Jewell's token showed a cheese-knife so that he was a cheesemonger or grocer, Richard Langley's token showed the Tallow Chandler's arms, Joseph Mackrith's token showed a loaf of sugar, so that he was probably a grocer, and William Savage's token showed the Grocers' arms. Compared to the nine examples of trade tokens known for Margate there are just three for Ramsgate and one for Minster,[82] showing the importance of Margate as a trading centre for the Isle of Thanet.

The list of occupations already given shows that most of the retailers in the town were retailers of food and clothing. Early butchers in Margate included Matthew Smith in the future Mill Lane and John Barnett in the future Market Place.[83] These early butchers did much more than just serve their customers in a shop; the butcher was responsible for slaughtering, cutting up and dressing a carcase, and for selecting animals from the local farmers or at market. Most butchers shops would have been next to a slaughter house and yard where animals could be kept until they were slaughtered. The presence of slaughter houses in the middle of a town resulted in a not insignificant nuisance, which was not solved until slaughter houses were removed to the outside of the town following the implementation of the Health Acts of the middle nineteenth century.[84]

Arthur Rowe identified two grocers in Margate at the end of the seventeenth century from the goods they supplied to the poor house but there might well have been others not supplying the Poor House.[18] One, Stephen Greedier, issued a token with a fisherman's arms (see above), but supplied 'soape and other Commodities' to the Poorhouse in 1680, and so was likely to have been a grocer as well as a fishmonger. The second grocer identified by Arthur Rowe was Valentine Jewell; in a court case in 1716 concerning the sale of the Mansion House he was described as a grocer, aged 58.[15] He was a man of some standing and wealth in Margate. In 1693 he lent money for the rebuilding of Margate Pier and he was at various times a Pier Warden, an Overseer of the Poor, and a Churchwarden; his son, Valentine Jewell junior, was to buy the White Hart Inn in 1729.

At this time grocers sold most of the raw materials needed by a household. According to *The London Tradesman* in 1747, grocers traded in 'Tea, Sugar, Coffee, Chocolate, Raisins, Currants, Prunes, Figs, Almonds, Soap, Starch, Blues of all Sorts, etc. Some of them deal in Rums and Brandy, Oils, Pickles and several other Articles fit for a Kitchen and the Tea Table'.[85] Another commentator, describing country grocers in the seventeenth century, said:[82]

> In country places a grocer comprehended a most extensive dealer in hardware, gingerbread, bobbins, laces, haberdashery, mouse traps, curling tongs, candles, soap, bacon, pickles and every variety of grocery; besides which they sold small coins for money changing. Tea, the staple by which grocers now make good fortunes [i.e. in the 1850s], had not then obtained its footing, for this ... must then have been beyond the means of most sippers, seeing that in 1666 a pound of tea cost sixty shillings, and money was then at a far higher value than in the present century. The multifarious ramifications of these traders justified the application of the term grocers ... because they sold by the gross. Their more ancient name was Pepperers, from the drugs and spices they sold, a branch which was mostly abstracted from them ... by a seceding party who were incorporated by James I under the designation of Apothecaries.

The term *mercer-grocer* is sometimes found. A mercer was a merchant or trader in cloth, often fine cloth not produced locally, but many mercers also sold the kind of dry goods sold by grocers. Although this combination may seem rather strange, the idea was that someone trained to buy and sell one type of commodity could readily apply that training to the buying and selling of another, so that a mercer could act as a grocer and vice versa.[86]

The trades of the mercer and of the draper were said to be 'as like one another as two eggs', except that the draper dealt mainly with male customers while the mercer 'traficks most with the Ladies, and has a small Dash of their Effeminacy in his Constitution'.[85] The draper dealt in wool and linen cloth whereas the mercer dealt in 'Silks, Velvets, Brocades, and an innumerable Train of expensive Trifles, for the Ornament of the fair Sex: He must be a very polite Man, and skilled in all the Punctilio's of City-good-breeding; he ought, by no Means to be an aukward, clumsy Fellow, such a Creature would turn the Lady's Stomach In a Morning, when they go their Rounds, to tumble Silks they have no mind to buy. He must dress neatly, and affect a Court Air, however far distant he may live from St James's. I know none so fit for that Branch of Business, as that nimble, dancing, talkative Nation the French; Our Mercer must have a great deal of the French man in his Manners, as well as a large Parcel of French Goods in his Shop'.[85] In Margate the distinction between a mercer and a draper was probably less obvious that it was in London.

The token issued by William Savage some time before 1672 showed the Grocers' Arms, so that he was probably a grocer. However, the inventory of a William Savage of Margate, who died in 1662, describes him as a merchant tailor. The inventory lists his shop as having 'Counters and certain shelves' and 'a hatte press'. The stock in the shop was extensive including 'woollen, linen, cloth, silk, buttons, stuffes, serges, Bayes, stockings', worth in total £666 4s 8¾d.[87,88] The inventory of another merchant tailor, John Savage of St John's, who died in 1645, provides more detail of his stock and makes it clear that a merchant tailor of the period could be both a draper and a tailor.[87,88] As well as a large quantity of cloth, John Savage's stock included waistcoats, 'sutes', shirts, short coats, 'gurdles for seamen' and 'gurdles for men and boys', and a variety of hats; his shop contained a 'paire of plaine glasses' and 'counters, shelves and bockes'. It is possible that William Savage the merchant tailor was the son of John Savage the merchant tailor since the Parish Registers describe a William Savage, son of a John Savage, being baptised at St John's in 1629.[10] The deeds for the Tudor House in King Street show that it was once owned by a member of the Savage family, possibly the son of William Savage, and so the shop referred to above could have been located in the house now called the Tudor House.[88]

It has been estimated that in the eighteenth century about half of the shops in a typical provincial town would have sold wearing apparel, not very different from the position today.[89] This was probably also true of Margate, since the majority of the shops for which we have any detailed information were mercers or drapers shops. An advertisement in the *Daily Post*, a London paper, in May 1736 advertised for sale the goods of the recently deceased Mr Laming, a Margate mercer:[90]

For sale by the Candle,
At the Marine Coffee-House in Birchin-Lane [London] . . . by Order of the Executors of Mr Laming, late of Margate, Mercer, decceas'd,
 A large Parcel of Mercery, Drapery and Haberdashery, viz, broad and narrow Stuffs, Calamancoes, Camblets, Inckle, Lustrings, Norwich Crapes, Persians, Poplins, Allopeens, Sarsnets, Bombazeens, narrow Mantuas, broad ditto, 5 8th ditto, rich Silk Shagreens, Sargedesoys, Birds-Eyes, narrow Damask, broad ditto, rich Brocades, broad Ducapes, Half-Ell ditto, water'd Tabbies, unwater'd ditto, black Alamodes, rich black Mantuas, white Sarsnets, black velvets, colour'd ditto, Shaggs, broad Camblets, Hair ditto, Everlastings, colour'd Fustians, printed Cottons, ditto Linnens, dy'd Linnens, Dowlasses, Sheeting Hollands, Cambricks, Muslins, Canvas, Buckrums, a large Parcel of Stays, Boddice, Stomachers, Silk Laceing, Ferrit Laces, Thread ditto, Maidstone Thread, Guilders Thread, whited-brown ditto, Inland ditto, Holland Tapes, Filleting, Gartering, Ribands, Silk Quality, Ferriting, Quality Binding, Silk Handkerchiefs, ditto Sarsner, Manchester Tapes, Boot-Strapings, Sealing Thread, Felliring Thread, Packthread, white Thread Buttons, Metal ditto, Belladine Silk, Mohair and Silk Twist, a Gold chased watch, a Diamond Ring, &c.
 The Goods above mentioned are to be seen in the Grand Sale Warehouse at Leathersellers-Hall in Little St Hellens, within Bishopsgate, from this Morning till the Time of Sale.
 John Bell, Broker.

This advertisement probably refers to William Laming [or Lamming] who died in 1735, and who is described in the parish registers as 'shopkeeper'.[10] He is recorded as supplying goods to the poor of the parish, for example a 'shirt and worsted for Wellens boy' in 1723.[14]

 Another local draper was Michael Traps, more usually spelt Trapps; in 1736 he advertised that he had received a fresh stock of material from London:[91]

Sold by Michal Traps in Margate.
All sorts of printed linens and cottons, strip'd Cottons and Hollands, and all sorts of Cotton and Linnen Checks, and white Linnens and Handkerchiefs, with all sorts of Broad Cloth, Druggets, Kerseys, Plains, Shalloons, Serges &c.
N.B. He has a choice Fresh Stock of the above-mention'd Goods from London.

A few weeks later he advertised that he could now rent out furnishings for funerals, a service previously provided by William Laming:[92]

This is to give notice that Michael Trapps of Margate has furnished himself for serving Funerals the same as Mr William Laming, deceased, of Margate did.
    N.B. He hath the three Velvet Palls and Cloth Palls as did belong unto the said Mr William Laming, &c.

Michael Trapp was later to become a Margate schoolmaster and Parish Clerk, and, in 1747, the master of the Posthouse (Chapter 1).[14]

    Not to be outdone, John Gore let it be known that he was also in the funeral furnishing business:[93]

John Gore of Margate in Thanett, undertakes to furnish Funerals with all sorts of Funeral Furniture at reasonable rates.
    N.B. He has a new Velvet Pall, which he letts at six shillings; likewise a new fine Cloth Pall which he letts at two shillings.

John Gore, like many shop keepers of the time, had many other lines of business, including the sale of patent medicines:[94]

Dr ROBERTS'S Great Tincture.
    Being the most Sovereign and Safe Medicine in the World for those dolorous Pains, the Griping of the Guts, whether the Dry Gripes, or accompanied with a Looseness and Vomiting . . . Also his most Famous Purging Sugar Plumbs.
    To be had of . . . Mr John Gore at Margate.

John Gore was an Overseer of the Poor in 1735, and supplied cloth to the Poor House.[14]
    More informative was an advertisement in 1739 for the stock of Stephen Bennet, a tailor and draper, with a shop 'near the Pier':[95]

To be sold under prime cost, at the shop late of Stephen Bennet, Taylor and Draper, near the Pier at Margate — stock of shop, consisting of broad and narrow cloths, drabs, serges, druggets, kerseys, fearnaughts, cottons, swanskin and bays, flannels, shags, calimancoes, camblets . . . damask table linen, sheeting . . . men and women's hats.

Arthur Rowe identified a number of others in Margate who, based on their supplies to the poor, were likely to have been mercers or drapers, including John Brooman who died some time before 1680, to be succeeded in the trade by his widow, and then by his son, also named John Brooman, and Dudley Diggs, a man of some wealth as he was one of those who lent money for the repair of Margate Pier in 1693.[18,96]

CHAPTER 4

The Poor

Until the middle of the sixteenth century relief of the poor was in the hands of the parish minister. He was expected to 'exhort and stir up the people to be liberal and bountiful' and 'exhort the parishioners to a liberal contribution' for the support of the poor of the parish.[1] Although this might have worked when parishes were small, it failed as the numbers of the poor increased. During the reign of Elizabeth I an increase in the population of England from three to four million combined with a series of poor harvests in the 1590s, led to high food prices and large numbers of homeless and unemployed. The fear that this would lead to a breakdown in law and order led to legislation designed to help the poor. An Act passed in 1572 did away with the reliance on voluntary collections for poor relief and replaced it with a poor rate system based on compulsory assessment and collection.[2,3] A number of ambiguities in the 1572 Act were resolved in later Acts of 1597 and 1601, finally creating the system of poor relief that remained in force for the next two and a half centuries.[4,5]

The intention of these Acts, jointly referred to as the Poor Laws, was to provide support for the 'deserving' or 'impotent' poor, that is, those unable to support themselves, principally the old, the sick, and young children. As described in a guide published for the edification of parish officers 'the statute of *Elizabeth* distinguishes the poor into two classes, the *able-bodied*, or those who are able to work, and the *impotent*; and it directs the manner in which they are to be provided for, namely by setting the former to work, and by furnishing the latter with necessary relief'.[6] The impotent were 'the aged and decrepit, the fatherless and motherless, the lame, the blind, persons labouring under sickness, idiots, lunatics &c'. The Poor Laws recognized the fact that large numbers of men and women were barely able to scrape a living and certainly had no opportunity to save for their old age. Thomas Ruggles, in his *History of the Poor* published in 1797 emphasized the importance of the Poor Laws: 'The occupation of the labourer, as well as the nature of his being, subjects him to acute illness, chronic disorders, and at length to old age, decrepitude and impotence . . . without the aid of his more opulent neighbours, or, what is infinitely to the credit of this nation, without the interference of the godlike laws of his country, this useful class of our countrymen would sink in the arms of famine or despair'.[7,8]

It was up to individual parishes to determine which of its parishioners were deserving of support and to raise the money required to provide this support. The task was delegated to unpaid officers appointed annually by each parish, known as the Overseers of the Poor; each parish was to have between two and four overseers. The overseers were to collect a local tax called the poor rate to be paid by the inhabitants of a parish and by the occupiers of land in the parish.[3,9] The first task of newly appointed overseers was to estimate the poor rate needed to cover the costs for the coming year. They were instructed to obtain 'the balance of money and . . . other parish property and documents from the late overseers' and then to 'minutely examine the state of the parish accounts, ascertain the number of resident paupers in the poor-house, the amount of money paid to out-pensioners, the average disbursements for casualties . . . the arrears of rates due and uncollected, presumed to be good, and generally take an account of the parish fund, so as to enable them to ascertain when and to what amount it will be necessary to levy a rate for the relief of the poor, and for the other purposes to which such rate is applicable'.[6] They would then be in a position to decide on the poor rate for the following year. As described in Chapter 3 the poor rate was levied on property within a parish 'from which a profit is derived', the rate being based on the rental value of the property. The Overseers appear to have had considerable discretion in deciding who would actually pay the poor rate, and anyone deemed too poor to pay the rate was excused.

Those parishioners paying the poor rate would, of course, expect the overseers to keep the rate as low as possible and cynics suggested that many overseers saw their role as being 'to maintain their poor as cheap as possibly they can' and 'to depopulate the parish in order to lessen the poor rate'.[10] Nevertheless, many ratepayers would have been only too aware that they themselves might require relief one day, and this would have ensured a degree of humanity in the system. It is likely though that this humanity would have extended only to the 'deserving' poor and not to the 'undeserving', able-bodied poor, those judged able to work but reluctant to do so. Support for the deserving poor was provided in a number of ways. As explained in *The parochial lawyer, or churchwarden and overseer's guide and assistant*: 'A principal, if not a primary duty of overseers is to find employment for the poor; and this they are bound to do, not only to ease the burthens of the parish, but for the sake of the poor themselves, to whom no greater kindness can be done than by enabling them to earn their own living by labour, instead of suffering them to eat the bread of idleness, by which their habits and morals must soon be corrupted'.[6] This duty was stressed in the guide because 'according to the poor laws, he who is able to labour is to be maintained by labour only, and nothing is to be provided for him but a means of employment.' It was suggested that the able-bodied poor could be set to work by providing them, out of the poor rate, with 'a convenient stock of flax, hemp, wool, thread, iron, or other necessary ware or stuff' with which they could make goods that could then be sold. The money raised in this way would be used to pay the poor for their work and, of course, help to keep down the poor rates. It was suggested that the overseers should persuade local tradesmen to buy the goods produced by the poor, on the grounds that it would be good for the parish.[3] The overseers could also provide employment 'for persons capable of manual labour, but out of employ' by purchasing or hiring land in the parish where they could 'employ and set to work in the cultivation thereof, on account of the parish, any such persons as by law they are directed to set to work, and may pay to such poor persons so employed as shall not be supported by the parish, reasonable wages for their work'.[6] Alternatively, the overseers could rent out parish land 'to any poor and industrious inhabitant of the parish' which they could then cultivate for their own profit. Unfortunately, 'the inconvenience of setting up trades for the employment of paupers under the superintendence of the overseers' was such that the regulations were seldom put into practice and, anyway, were later made redundant by the introduction of workhouses.

The overseers were also charged with providing support for 'the poor by impotency and defect', that is, those unable to work and unable to support themselves, but only in cases where their relatives could not support them: 'the father and grandfather, the mother and grandmother, and the children of every poor, old, blind, lame, and impotent person, and other person not able to work, being of sufficient ability, shall relieve every such poor person according to such rate as a general quarter session shall assess, upon pain of twenty shillings a month, to be levied by distress, &c'.[6] The impotent who needed support from the parish could be placed in the parish workhouse, if there was one, or be supported 'by allowing them small pensions weekly or otherwise, or by occasional relief in money, victuals, or clothes,' payments referred as 'outdoor relief'. Regular support, a pension, was provided only in the most extreme of cases, mostly to aged widows, and was often handed to the recipients once a week in the church porch after the Sunday morning sermon, ensuring that they would be regular attenders at church.[3] The impotent could be supported in their own homes, the parish paying the rent, or the parish could rent or build 'convenient houses of dwelling for the impotent poor, in fit and convenient places' and 'place inmates, or more families than one, in one cottage or house'.[6]

Children who could not be supported by their parents could be apprenticed, or 'bound-out', to work as servants or apprentices to masters or mistresses willing to maintain and train them, the parish paying the apprenticeship fee. Children were usually bound out at between seven and ten years of age, the apprenticeship continuing until the age of 24 for men or until 21 or on marriage for women.[5] Boys could also be sent to sea: 'parish-officers may, with the consent of two justices . . . bind out any boy, of the age of ten years or upwards, who is chargeable to the parish, or whose parents are so chargeable, or who begs, to the sea service, to any master or owner of a ship or vessel, until he is twenty-one years of age. At the time of the binding they shall pay to the master 50s for clothes and bedding, and they shall send the indentures to the port to which the master belongs, and also convey the apprentice thither'.[6]

Overseers were expected to make sure that only the poor belonging to their parish received support from the parish. This led to much wrangling between parishes, one parish arguing that a particular pauper was not theirs, but, in fact, belonged to another parish. The Settlement Act of 1662 tried to clarify the position by defining who was legally entitled to claim to be settled in a parish, that is, who was the legal responsibility of that parish.[11] The provisions of the Act were slightly modified in 1685 and 1692, and, after these amendments, the principal grounds on which settlement could be claimed in a parish were that you had been born to parents who had settlement in the parish, that you rented property in the parish worth more than £10 per year, or that you paid poor rates on property in the parish worth more than £10 per year; married women took the settlement of their husbands.[9,12] The entitlement to settlement for anyone renting property for £10 or more per year would only have been of benefit to the relatively rich since, for example, the average annual rent for a labourer's cottage in the 1700s was about £1 10s.[13] Settlement could also be obtained by serving a full seven-year apprenticeship with a settled resident or by being hired by a settled resident for more than a year and a day, a requirement which, predictably, led to many contracts of just less than a year and a day. Finally, settlement could be claimed by anyone who had lived in a parish for more than 40 days without a complaint having being made against them; a newcomer had to give notice of their arrival in the parish to an overseer and if the overseer thought that the newcomer was likely to become a charge on the poor rate he had 40 days to lodge a complaint with two local Justices of the Peace. These regulations had the unfortunate side effect of reducing mobility and discouraging the unemployed from leaving the parish in which they were born in order to find work elsewhere. The settlement laws continued until 1834 when they were replaced by the provisions of the Poor Law Amendment Act.[14]

The Poor in Margate

The parish of St John's had a few wealthy farmers, merchants, hoymen and maltsters, but the majority of the inhabitants were sailors, fishermen, small farmers and labourers, and their families, and, of course, the destitute. Unhappily, the distinction between the destitute and the labourer was often unclear; many labourers and their families lived at a level barely above subsistence. It has been estimated that at the end of the seventeenth century earnings of about £30 to £40 a year would be required to keep a family, say of a man, his wife, and three children, free from starvation and free from debt.[15] Members of the 'petty bourgeoisie' would typically have incomes of between £50 and £100 a year and a Gentleman would have required a minimum of about £300 to keep up a reasonable style of living.[15] These sums can be compared with the earnings of a typical farm labourer. In 1724 the Quarter Sessions at Maidstone laid down that the rate to be paid for a head ploughman in Kent would be £5 a year, for a ploughman's mate, £3 a year, and for a boy aged between 14 and 18, £2 a year; a farm labourer hired by the day was to receive 14d a day in summer and 10d a day in winter.[16] Labourers in the Isle of Thanet probably received rather more than the average labourer in Kent; John Lewis reported in 1723 that local farmers 'find it very difficult to get servants [farm labourers] . . . so many of them either going to sea or being employed in the hop-gardens; they give very great wages to their servants and day-labourers'.[17] A local guide book of 1763 confirmed that in the Isle of Thanet 'the wages of labourers and servants are very high' and that 'in time of war so many men go into the navy, on the certainty of better pay, or in hopes of prize money, or preferment, that it is no easy matter to procure hands sufficient for carrying on the common business of agriculture, at any price'.[18]

Even with slightly higher than average wages, it is hard to see how a typical labouring man and his family managed to survive. At best they would have had a tasteless, unsatisfying diet, poor housing with no sanitation, little coal for heating in the winter, and hard, back-breaking work with no prospect of putting money aside for their old age. The brutal truth according to Roy Porter was that 'everyone below the income commanded by skilled craftsmen was undernourished'; the experience of many, if not most, people at the time was a life of grinding, hopeless poverty, poverty with no relief and no hope of improvement.[15] The whole family, including children above the age of about seven, would have been expected to work, and the slightest accident or illness affecting any member of the family could result in destitution, turning the family into paupers dependent on charity or the parish for survival. The result was that most inhabitants of Margate would have depended at some time in their lives on the benevolence of others, sometimes their neighbours and sometimes their 'betters'. Indeed, many of those of higher rank saw it as their duty to use some of their wealth to relieve distress among their inferiors. In part, this was a matter of religious belief, of following the teaching of Matthew: 'Lay not up for yourselves treasures upon earth, where moth and rust doth corrupt . . . but lay up for yourself treasures in Heaven.' But giving to the poor also provided a means of controlling their behaviour; channelling support though the church might encourage the poor to attend church, and giving only to the 'sober and upright' might make the poor more abstemious in their ways. It was certainly never the intention of the rich to do away with the poor; both the rich and the poor were thought to have their place in society. William Temple in 1739 thought that 'the only way to make the poor industrious is to lay them under the necessity of labouring all the time they can spare from rest and sleep, in order to procure the common necessities of life'.[19] This was not an uncommon view; in 1771 Arthur Young could write 'Everyone but an idiot knows that the lower class must be kept poor or they will never be industrious'.[20]

The intention of the acts of 1572 and 1597, as we have seen, was to move the responsibility for the poor from the individual to the overseers of the poor who were to raise money by a parish poor rate. Of course, some of the wealthier inhabitants of a parish might still have wanted to perform individual acts of charity and, indeed, a few provided bequests for the poor in their wills. For example, George Collmer, after leaving his land to his wife, left 12s each to 'four seafaring men of St Johns . . . for carrying my body to my grave' and 5s to the poor of St Peter's and 4s to the poor of St John's.[21] Similarly, Roger Laming in his will of 1743 'gave unto the poor of the parish of St John not receiving alms the sum of £10 to be distributed among them'.[22]

Unfortunately, heirs were sometimes less enthusiastic about charitable donations than were the deceased, and the records of the Archdeacon's Visitations to St John's include several such cases.[23] In 1581 a complaint was made about Robert Tittall's widow who refused to sell a house that her husband's will had said should be sold for the poor; making matters worse, the house was being lived in by her son and a woman to whom he was not married:

We find the last will and testament of Robert Tuttall partly suppressed, for that where he gave one tenement or house to be sold to the use of the poor of the parish of St John's and St Peter's, the said tenement is neither sold of his widow, who is yet alive in the parish of St John's.

We find Mother Tuttall do keep the aforesaid house, given to be sold to the use of the poor of the parish, a house of Bawdry; her son and one Agnes Billing, their living together there, and yet not married.

Sometimes annual bequests of money were ignored. In 1581 the Churchwardens complained 'We find the poor of our parish deprived of six shillings given unto them, to be paid yearly out of the land and tenement of John Hartye, by the last will and testament of the said John Hartye, withholden by William Matson, now owner of the said tenement and land.' Similarly, in 1591 'the heirs of John Watson' were reported 'for withholding 6s 8d the year to be paid out of his land to the poor'. Sometimes the problem was a reluctance to hand over a bequest. In 1596 the Churchwardens complained of 'John Baldwin of our parish of St John's, for that the same and report goeth that he keepeth in his hands the sum of £10 given by William Horn, late of the parish of St Peter's in Thanet, unto the reparation of the Church and poor men's box of the said parish, which £10 as the speech is hath been paid into the hands of the said Baldwin who refuses to deliver the same, or to yield any security for the payment thereof. It is seven years ago or thereabout since the said legacies were given, and the Church and the poor have wanted the same, having no benefit thereof as we know'. In 1613 the complaint was about John Thurlo 'for withholding certain legacies or rent from a poor orphan or child dwelling in our parish, named William Adams, for some three or four years past, being 18s 4d yearly, as the same goeth in our parish'. He was called before the Archdeacon's court and confessed 'that there is 12s 6d for three years or thereabout in his hand due to the aforesaid William Adams, but saith that the said Adams is dead and departed this life, and no administration thereof as yet taken that he knoweth, so as he knoweth not to whom to pay the same'. In 1620 Alexander Platt, executor of the last will and testament of John Terry 'late of the parish of St John the Baptist, deceased' was reported to the Archdeacon 'for refusing to pay a legacy of three pounds unto the overseers of the poor of the parish of Westgate, given and bequeathed in the last will and testament of the said deceased, as therein and thereby doth manifestly appear. This Platt dwelleth at Ewell in the parish of Faversham or Goodneston as we are informed'.

Wealthier individuals would sometime leave money to establish charities for the poor. In 1513 Ethelrede Barrowe ordered her executor, William Curlyng, to maintain a yearly 'Give-all while the World endureth', consisting of a gift of 'a quarter of malt and six bushels of wheat and victuals' to the poor people of the parish each year on St James' day; land was bought near Northdown to provide a rental income to fund the gift.[24] John Lewis explained that 'the north chancel of the parish church is dedicated to *St James*; and as it was then usual, in populous towns, to celebrate the anniversaries of their church's dedication with an accustomed fair, so even in the most private parishes were these yearly solemnities observed with feasting, and a great concourse of people'.[25] He went on to explain that 'in this parish there used to be kept, what the inhabitants called a *Fair*, on *St John Baptist's* day, the saint to which the church was dedicated; but I suppose, there being no such fair on *St James's* day, or no provision made for the celebration of it, this devout woman ordered her executor to provide for an annual feast for ever on that day; which is still observed at a place in this parish called *North-downe*, and by the country people called *North-downe Fair;* only instead of a *Give-all* or a common feast for all goers and comers, the corn and meats are ... distributed to poor house-keepers.'

A second charitable gift was that of Thomas Taddy who, in 1566, gave £30 to purchase land at Crow hill, to be rented out and the rent 'yearly for evermore to be distributed, dealt and given unto the most poor and needy of the Parish'. Then in 1594 John Allen, of Drapers, 'gave for ever to be distributed to the poorest people of this parish on *Shrove Tuesday*, 200 of Winchelsea billets, and two bushels of wheat to be baked into bread', a Winchelsea billet being a short, thick piece of firewood, traditionally shipped from the port of Winchelsea. The charity was still in operation in 1837 when 'one gallon of bread' and half a hundredweight of coals were delivered each Shrove Tuesday to 16 poor people.[24] A fourth charitable donation, of unknown date, was made by a Mr Johnson who gave, 'out of his farm at Garlinge', the sum of 6s 8d 'to be paid yearly to the church wardens of the parish, of which 6s to be distributed by them in the time of Lent, to the poorest of the parish, and the 8d to be divided betwixt themselves'. Another small charity was established by Henry Sandford in 1626 who 'gave unto the poor people of this parish every *Sunday* or *Sabbath-day*, throughout the year, six penny-worth of good bread, to be distributed by the discretion of the church wardens and overseers of the poor of the said parish, where most need is'; this charity had ceased to operate some time before 1826.[24]

In 1673 Francis Buller, of Kingston upon Thames, gave to the Parish 'several tenements, and half an acre of land, lying at Church-hill, the rents of which are to be laid out ... in binding poor boys apprentices to some sea-faring employment.' The properties owned by the charity came to include much of Church-square, White's place and Buller's yard, also known by the names of Buller's Court and Parish yard. Buller's yard was used by the parish to house the poor, and is described in more detail below. The largest and best known of the charitable donations to the parish was, however, that of the Quaker Michael Yoakley who, by his will of 1707, established an Almshouse at Drapers, for nine 'poor men or women as are natives or inhabitants of the four parishes of St John, St Peter, Birchington, and Acol', who were to be given 'warm gowns or coats of shepherd's gray for outward garments, and firing, and weekly allowance, at the discretion of the trustees'. Comparing the list of charities given by Lewis in 1736 with that in the report of the Charity Commissioners in 1837 shows that the tradition of establishing charities for the poor ended sometime in the early eighteenth century.[17,24,25]

Despite the importance of these charities, after the Act of 1597 the primary responsibility for maintaining the poor lay with the overseers of the Poor. Four overseers were appointed each year for the parish of St John's.[26-29] Around Easter time each year the parishioners met in vestry to produce a list of those they wished to see appointed as overseers for the following year. This list was submitted to the Mayor and Jurats at Dover, who were the Justices of the Peace for Margate; it was traditional for the Justices of the Peace to appoint those nominated by the vestry.[6] The four new overseers would take up their positions on 25 March or 'within fourteen days after'. The overseers had to be 'substantial householders' resident in the parish. In the period from 1716-1729 the overseers appointed were, on sixteen occasions, farmers, and on three occasions husbandmen (tenant farmers); on five occasions they were mariners and on five occasions they were maltsters (someone making malt to be used in the production of beer); on two occasions they were butchers, and on one occasion each a hoyman, a coal merchant, a cooper, a carpenter and a tailor. Only three men served twice as overseers in this period, Robert Wells and Cornelius Tomlin, both farmers, and Peter Sackett, a maltster.[27,29] The list serves to emphasize the importance of farming, brewing and shipping in the parish before the start of a holiday trade.

Each of the four overseers appointed every year was responsible for one of the four rate collections made in that year, in October, January, May and July. The overseers' accounts started with a reminder of the purpose of the rate, for example:[29]

Assessment made 17 Oct 1716 by the Churchwardens, Overseers of the Poor and other parishioners of the parish towards the relief of the poor and for providing a stock to set them to work and for binding out poor children apprentices and assessing a nine pence on every pound rent and the same sum on every £20 stock or ability within the said parish. To be collected by Robert Wells, Cornelius Tomlin, John Bennett and Richard Laming present overseers of the poor of the said parish.

The reference here to 'rent' refers to the rent obtainable on a property if it were to be rented out. The quarterly rate of nine pence in the pound raised £59 16s 3d in October 1716, £59 12s 3d in January 1717, £59 16s 10½d in May 1717, and £59 1s 3d in July 1717, totalling £238 6s 7½d for a 12 month period.

Inevitably there were sometimes parishioners unable or unwilling to pay. In the sixteenth century such matters were raised with the Archdecon during his visits to inspect the church.[23] In 1574 James Saull, William Reade and Richard Pym were all reported because they 'will not pay to the poor man's box' and even as late as 1598 eight men, William Fleet, Thomas Wood, William Turner, John Watson, Alexander Violett, John Hudson, Arnold Savage, and Ephraim Watson were reported for refusing 'to pay to the poor man's box'. Since the first Poor Law doing away with the reliance on voluntary contributions was introduced in 1574, the references to 'the poor man's box' are rather surprising, this sounding as if the old voluntary system continued. In fact, it is not until 1615 that the first unambiguous reference to a Poor cess (a sess, short for assess, being an obsolete word for a tax) appears in the Visitation reports, in the report of a fine: 'William Saunders, the head tapster at the "King's Arms," for refusing to pay his cess to the poor, being twelve pence.' Unfortunately no records have survived from between 1620, when the records of the Archdeacon's Visitations end, and 1666 when the Accounts of the Overseers begin.

If anyone refused to pay their poor rate, the overseers were expected to obtain a warrant at Dover against the non-payer, allowing them to take away some of their goods and sell them to pay off the debt. Overseers were generally reluctant to take such drastic action against one of their neighbours and debts would build up, to the obvious disadvantage of the other ratepayers. In 1680 the overseers gave 3s 2d to Thomas Markett 'to go to Dover for a warrant of destresse, and for ye warrant' and paid someone 1s 'for writing a letter and a list of those which refused to pay their sesses'.[26] In 1681 the Overseers spent 2s 7d 'at *Goodman Seeleys* when we sent for a Warrant to destrayne' and then paid Thomas Pike 4s 6d 'for a Journey to Dover and 6d for a Warrant'. However, by 1695 the situation had got so bad that the Dover Mayor and Jurats held a special magistrates' session at Margate, with the outcome being recorded in the Overseers' Account Book:[26]

Att a Sessions holden att Margate the 25 June, 1695, before John Hollingbery, Esq, Mayor, and Mr Thomas Scott and Mr Clement Buck, Jurats of the same [of Dover].

  Foreasmuch as Complaint is made to this Court by the Chiefe Parishioners of St Johns That former Overseers of the Poore of the said Parish have been very Negligent in the due execution of their Office in not executing Warrants for takeing Distresses upon Defaulters who Neglect and Refuse to Pay their Several Assessments for the Reliefe of the Poore of the said Parrish. For Preventing of this Mischeiffe for the future It is now Ordered that if any Overseer or Overseers for the Poore of the said Parish shall neglect or to refuse to execute any such warrant or warrants. That the Money due Neglected or Refused to be Collected or Leveyed Shall be Answered and paid by Overseer or Overseers to be Leavied upon his or their Goods in case hee or they shall not Answer or pay the same Money Accordingly.

It is not known whether or not this threat to the overseers had the desired effect. What is known is that the costs of supporting the poor continued to rise throughout the country, despite the best efforts of the nation's overseers, leading to one of the most unpleasant of the Poor Acts, an Act of 1696-7 entitled 'An Act for supplying some Defects in the Laws for the Relief of the Poor of this Kingdome'.[30] The Act ruled that 'persons receiving alms, their wives, children &c' should wear a badge, a large letter P, on the shoulder of their right sleeve, the only exception being for children living at home 'in order to have the care of and attend an impotent and helplesse Parent'. Any poor person not obeying the rule could be committed to gaol and there 'whipt and kept to hard Labour', and any Overseer of the Poor giving relief to a poor person not wearing a badge could be fined 20s, half the money going to the person who reported the offence. It is worth quoting this section of the Act in full:

And to the end that the Money raised onely for the Relief of such as are as well impotent as poor may not be misapplied & consumed by the idle sturdy and disorderly Beggars Be it further enacted by the Authority aforesaid That every such Person as from and after the First Day of September One thousand six hundred ninety seven shall be upon the Collection and receive Relief of any Parish or Place and the Wife and Children of any such Person cohabiting in the same House (such Child onely excepted as shall be by the Churchwardens and Overseers of the Poor permitted to live att home in order to have the care of and attend an impotent and helplesse Parent) shall upon the Shoulder of the right Sleeve of the uppermost Garment of every such Person in an open and visible manner weare such Badge or Mark as is herein after mentioned and expressed that is to say a large Roman P, together with the first Letter of the Name of the Parish or Place whereof such poor Person is an Inhabitant cutt either in red or blew Cloth as by the Churchwardens and Overseers of the Poor it shall be directed and appointed And if any such poor Person shall att any time neglect or refuse to weare such Badge or Mark as aforesaid and in manner as aforesaid itt shall and may be lawfull for any Justice of the Peace of the County City Liberty or Towne Corporate where any such Offence shall be co[m]mitted upon complaint to him for that purpose to be made to punish every such Offender for every such Offence either by ordering of his or her Relief or usuall Allowance on the Collection to be abridged suspended or withdrawne or otherwise by co[m]mitting of any such Offender to the House of Correction there to be whipt and kept to hard Labour for any Number of Days not exceeding One and twenty as to the said Justice in his discretion it shall seem most meet and if any such Churchwarden or Overseer of the Poor from and after the said First Day of September shall relieve any such poor Person not haveing and wearing such Badge or Mark as aforesaid being thereof convicted upon the Oath of One or more credible Witnesse or Witnesses before any Justice of the Peace of the County City Liberty or Towne Corporate where any such Offence shall be co[m]mitted shall forfeit for every such Offence the Su[m]m of Twenty shillings to be levied by Distresse and Sale of the Goods of every such Offender by Warrant under the Hand and Seale of any such Justice one Moiety thereof to be to the use of the Informer and the other to the Poor of the Parish where the Offence shall be co[m]mitted.

The Act was not repealed until 1810.[31] In 1699 the Overseers of the Poor at Margate spent 6s 'for making the Badges for the poor'.[26]

Some idea of how the overseers spent the poor rate can be garnered from the rate books, which survive from 1678.[26-29] One thing that becomes clear is the importance of regular weekly disbursements or pensions, amounting to about half of the total expenditure on the poor. For example, in the first quarter of the financial year starting Easter 1679 the overseers supported 17 people with weekly disbursements of 1s 6d, 2s 6d or 3s a week, costing a total of £21 6s for the quarter.[28] This can be compared to the 'extra disbursements' over the same period, amounting to £17 3s 1d, including payment of 6 people's rent at a total cost of £6 12s, a payment of 1s to Good Knock 'for looking to Widow Ashendon in sickness', and a payment of 7s 6d to Good Raff 'for keeping of Marlow's child'. (Goodwife, usually abbreviated as Goody or Good, was a polite form of address for women, used much as 'Mrs', 'Miss', or 'Ms' are used today; the equivalent for a man was Goodman.) By 1716 the numbers supported by a pension had doubled to 36 in the first quarter of the year, again mostly given to widows, at a cost that had also doubled to £44 18s. These pensions included 1s 6d a week to Widow Tomson who was still receiving a pension in 1718 although by then it had increased to 2s a week, 2s a week to Widow Horton and 2s 6d a week to Elizabeth Roberts; Stephen Pett received a pension of 2s 6d a week. Comparing these names with those in the parish burial registers suggests that Widow Tomson was Ann Tomson who died in June 1718, that Widow Horton was Mary Horton who died in the winter of 1716/17, that Elizabeth Roberts was a 'maiden' who died in 1718, and that Stephen Pett was 'an antient man' who died in the winter of 1717/18. These examples show that pensions were paid mostly to the single elderly at the ends of their life; a pension comparable to the wage of a farm labourer seems not ungenerous although, of course, it should be remembered that a farm labourer's wage was only enough to support a pretty miserable existence. The numbers receiving these pensions were rather small. The 17 pensioners in 1679 represents about 1 per cent of the population of the parish and the 36 pensioners in 1716 represents about 1.5 per cent of the population. This is relatively low on a national scale,[3] suggesting either that the overseers were unusually stingy, which seems unlikely given the level of the individual pensions, or that there was relatively little destitution in the parish.

One of the most important of the overseers' responsibilities was to ensure that the poor had somewhere to live. Sometimes they would pay the rent for a poor parishioner, allowing them to continue to live in their own homes; once the rent was paid even the elderly might be able to support themselves through casual labour.[3] For example, in 1728 the overseers paid £1 10s for Widd Blackbourne's rent and £1 6s for that of Widd Laming, and in 1731 they paid 10s 'towards' the rent of Widd Hatcher. They would also pay for repairs to a house so that the old could continue to live there; in 1679 they paid Robert Pierce 6d 'for thatching Widd Overys house' and in 1683 they paid Stephen Goldfinch, a bricklayer, 2s 'for cleansing of Goodman Knocks Well'.[26] Frequently the overseers would rent rooms for the poor in the houses of other poor people, especially for elderly paupers who could then care for one another; in 1666 Widow Petkin was paid 5s for a year's rent for Richard Harlow, in 1716 Widow Norwood was paid 5s for half a year's rent for Sarah Stevens and Vincent Knot was paid £2 10s for one year's rent for Widow Browne.[26,27] Payments of this kind are, however, relatively rare in the overseers' accounts, and it is likely that many of the parish poor were housed in properties given to the parish as charitable bequests, or in properties rented or built by the overseers. It is clear that the parish had a number of properties of this type, but the overseers' accounts provide frustratingly little detail, and what detail there is is often confusing. In the accounts the properties are referred to as poores-houses, almes-houses, the parish-house, the Pish houses, and Charity-houses, sometimes in the singular but more often in the plural.[26-29] In 1680 the overseers spent 1s on 'the poor's houses' and £3 16s 'for work about the parish house.' In 1681 they spent £7 2s 6d 'for work done to the Charity houses', 1s 10d 'for work done about the Almshouses' and £1 5s 1d 'for work done about the poor's houses'; in 1679 there is reference to the 'Frogg house' and the first reference to the 'Workhouse' occurs in 1727. It is hard to say whether these different names correspond to different buildings or whether some are simply different names for the same building.

We can be fairly certain about one of the houses, the Frog house. Lewis, in his History of the Isle of Thanet published in 1736, listed the parish's charitable benefactions.[25] These include 'two small cottages' belonging to the parish 'at a place called Frog-Hill'. They were built in about 1648 by Christopher Frenchbourn, who 'growing necessitous' sold them in 1662 'to the Church-Wardens &c for the consideration of two shillings a week to be paid to him and his wife, so long as they should live together, and of one shilling a week to the survivor of them'.[25] Frog Cottage is named on Edmunds 1821 map of Margate, at the bottom of Frog Hill, now called Grosvenor Gardens; presumably by 1821 the two original cottages had been combined into one. In 1679 the Overseers paid 6d 'for mending Frog well', and in 1690 John Baker was paid 6d 'for a Bucket for Frogg house'. Frog house had a thatched roof; in 1702 Matthew Constable was paid 4s for thatching the house, in 1706 3s was spent by the Overseers 'for thatching and materials about Frogg house', in 1712 Nicholas Norwood was paid 2s 8d 'for thatching Frogg house' and in 1734 William Castle was paid 15s for 'thatching at Frogg house, and for rods and spindles, and 3 days lowances', the spindles being used to anchor the rods spread across the thatch to hold it down. The Frog house had proper windows; in 1706 John Ovenden was paid 3s 6d 'at Frogg House for Glaseing'.

A second charitable donation that ended up providing housing for the poor was Buller's charity, already described.[17,24] In 1673 Francis Buller gave to the parish 'several tenements, and half an acre of land, lying at Church-hill', the rents from which were to be used 'in binding poor boys apprentices to some sea-faring employment'. The 'several tenements' forming what became known as Buller's square or the Parish Yard were passed to the parish officers of St John's in 1775 who then paid rent to the trustees for the properties, and used them to house paupers. The first specific reference to the Parish yard in the overseers' accounts is in 1735 where there is a record of a payment of £10 'to Mr Robert Brook in full for rent of the houses in the Parish yard, a gift of Mr Buller, which the Parish hires of the Trustees'; Robert Brook was a mariner and trustee of Buller's charity.[26,27] The way in which the Parish Yard houses were run is made clear in the report of a meeting of members of the Margate Philanthropic Institution in 1847 where they discussed the possibility of building alms houses without any endowments, which would allow 'aged and deserving persons a free occupancy'. It was pointed out that with 'the allowance usually given to aged persons by the parish, and the assistance their children or friends might be able to afford them, it was expected they would be able to live, as many persons now do in the parish yard, who enjoy the advantage of having to pay no rent for their room'.[50] The situation was unchanged in 1882: 'the houses . . . in the Parish yard . . . were very nice . . . but were without endowment, and those poor women, although they were very glad to get into those houses, had to depend upon 1s 6d per week allowed them by the parish'.[32]

Figure 9. A west view of the Poor's House at Margate, October 14th, 1781. From John Pridden, *Collection for the History of the Isle of Thanet*.

Joseph Hall's Map of Margate published in 1777 shows a 'Poor house' located to the east of the parish church, on a road corresponding to the road known later as Prospect Place and then Victoria Road (Figure 4).[33] A hand drawn sketch map by John Pridden dating to ca 1781 also shows the 'Poor's house' and its garden on Prospect Place,[34] and Pridden provides a drawing of the Poor's House, showing it to be a fairly large, two storey building (Figure 9). Edmund's Margate map of 1821 again shows the Margate Workhouse on Prospect Place, and William Rowe records that Margate Workhouse was built in 1769,[35] so that John Pridden's 'Poor's house' was, in fact, the Workhouse by another name. Intriguingly, John Harris's map of Thanet published in 1717 shows an unlabelled building to the right of the parish church (Figure 2), a building of sufficient importance in the parish to warrant inclusion on the map. We do not know what this building was, nor its exact location, but one possibility, given its position on Harris's map, is that it was an early Poor's House, either built close to the church, for example on land belonging to Buller's Charity, or on the site where the Workhouse was built in 1769; another possibility is that it is the Parsonage.

The first mention of a poorhouse in Margate is probably that in the accounts of the Pier Wardens which, in 1679, record the receipt of 3s for 'rent of the house and poorhouse'; no similar receipts are recorded in later years.[36] The first surviving volume of accounts for the Overseers of the Poor starts in 1678 and, although there is a reference to 6d being paid 'for mending Frog well' in 1679, the first reference to the 'Poores-houses' does not appear until 1680 when 1s was spent 'at Mr Bushells at sealing the Leases for the Poores-houses' and 17s 2d was paid to 'Mr Denn for writings about the Almshouses'. These large expenditures suggest that something major was being done to house the poor in 1680. In 1681 the Overseers paid Thomas Underdown £6 for the rent of the 'Poores houses', then in 1682, paid £6 'to the Trustees for the Charity houses for rent due at Lady day', and in 1683 paid £6 'to the Feoffees [trustees] one years rent for the Almshouses' followed later in 1683 with £3 to 'Thomas Underdown for half a yeares rent for the Almshouses'; in 1688 the Overseers paid £6 to 'Thomas Underdown, one of the Trustees of the Charity-houses for one years rent due at our Lady day last'.[26] These identical rents suggest that the 'Poores houses', 'Charity houses' and 'Almshouses' were all the same, and were rented out to the Overseers to house the poor by a charity of which Thomas Underdown was one of the trustees. Thomas Underdown was one of an important Margate family, at one time owner of Dane Court.[37] Thomas Underdown himself was a maltster, and, at various times, Churchwarden, Overseer, and Pier Warden;[26,38] the most likely of the local charities to own property like this was Buller's Charity. This would be consistent with an entry in the overseers' accounts for 1737 recording a payment of £6 'to Mr Grainger at taking Edward Whitehead Apprentice to the sea, being the Gift of Mr Bullard [Buller] of the Poor-houses'.[27]

It is less clear whether or not the 'Pish-houses' (Pish being a common abbreviation for Parish) referred to in the overseers' accounts was yet another name for the Poore's House, or was a separate set of buildings. There is no reference to a rent being paid to Thomas Underdown for the Pish-houses, although in 1712 it was recorded that the overseers paid £10 'to the Feoffees rent of the Pish houses'. In 1680 John Turner was paid £3 16s 'for worke and boards about the Pish-house' and in 1682 the overseers paid £4 2s 6d to Dudley Diggs for 'Tyles for the Pish-houses'.

Until about 1727 most references in the overseers' accounts to the Poor's houses are in the plural, but after that date most are in the singular.[27] Assuming that the 'Poores houses', 'Charity houses' and 'Almshouses' do all indeed refer to houses in Buller's yard, it seems that a new, specially built, Poor-house could have been built at about this time. In 1733 the overseers' accounts record a payment of 3s 6d 'to Goodman

Coultroup for work at the Poor-house and Alms-houses' and, also in 1733, a payment of 8s 1d to 'Mr [Joseph] Sandwell per bill for the Poor house and Almshouses', both consistent with the Poor House being an entity separate from the Almshouses. The accounts for 1728 record a payment of £3 'to Mr Petken for half a years rent for the [Poor] house' and in 1731 a further payment of £6 to 'Petken for one years rent of the Poor house'. An Indenture of 1738 between George Upton of Canterbury and William Petken, the Margate brewer, refers to 'all that messuage or tenement with appurtenances, commonly called or known by the name of the poor house' and an Indenture of 1743 between William Petken and Michael Wilkins Conway of Buckingham refers to the messuage 'commonly known by the name of the Poorhouse with the yard, backside garden and appurtenances ... which was lately lent to the Churchwardens and Overseers of the poor ... for the use of the poor ... at yearly rent of £6'.[39,40] It is not known where this Parish House was.

The dread word 'Workhouse' appears in the accounts for the first time in 1727:

> To money spent at Parish meetings and business concerning the Workhouse — 12s
> To money spent at taking an account of the poor's goods — 4s 1d
> To part changing the lease of the Workhouse — 2s 6d

These entries are anything but clear. Knatchbull's Act, *An Act for amending the laws relating to the settlement, imployment, and relief of the poor* had been passed in 1723, with its 'workhouse test' by which a pauper would only be granted poor relief if they were admitted to a workhouse.[41] The act was adopted by many parishes and it has been estimated that by 1732 there were more than 700 workhouses in the country.[12] The aim of the act was to distinguish between the deserving poor, who would be housed in a Poorhouse, and the undeserving poor, that is, those able to work, who would be housed in a Workhouse. Nevertheless, it is doubtful if Margate had a 'proper' Workhouse until a very much later date. In 1777 the Government carried out a survey of the nation's Workhouses and recorded over 1,800, including Workhouses in Birchington and Ramsgate, but the report contains no return for a Workhouse in Margate.[42]

Putting all this information together it seems likely that from 1727 the overseers started to run a new Poorhouse at Margate on more authoritarian lines, but, not wanting to incur the cost of renting any new buildings, made the Poorhouse serve for both the deserving and the undeserving poor. Several items of expenditure listed in the overseers' accounts for 1727 suggest that accommodation for the poor was extended at this time. In 1727 Edward Constant and Gabriel Wilds were paid between them £1 19s 6d 'for a rug and bed' and 'for bed and blanket as per bill', 15s 9d was spent on 'three blankets, rug and coverlid [coverlet] for the poor' and James Stone was paid 4s 6d 'for bed cords'. Also in 1727 Richard Solley, a carpenter, was paid £5 13s 2d 'as per bill' and although no details are given, it is possible that this also corresponded to furniture or work done at the Poorhouse. An entry in the Parish Register for 1728 makes clear the fear engendered by the idea of a workhouse:[43]

On Sunday August 25 1728 hang'd himself John WOOD aged 95, born at Graveney near Faversham out of a dread of his coming to be kept by the parish and put into the workhouse. He had been for some time stark blind, and took the opportunity of his wife being absent at Church, who when she came home found him dead hanging upon his knees

The first master of the Poor house was Robert Peirse who was paid 4s in 1728 as 'his half years salary for the Poor House'.[27] In 1733 John Overy was appointed master at the slightly less miserly salary of £2 a year; during the year John Overy was reimbursed 11s 8d for 'small trifles he disburst' in the poorhouse and for what he had spent 'for necessaries at the Poor house'. The low salary and the fact that he was referred to as 'Goodman Overy' in the overseers' accounts, rather than as 'Mr Overy', suggests that the post of master was not held in high regard. In 1736 Robert Peerse [or Peirse] is back as master of the Poorhouse, possibly with a slightly better salary as the overseers' accounts record: 'To Rob. Peerse for ¼ years salary and other necessaries for the Poor-house - 13s 6d'.

It is after 1727 that relatively large bills for provisions start to appear in the accounts, presumably for the poor at the Poorhouse, starting with a payment of 16s 9d to Henry Petken 'for beer for the poor at the house.' In 1728 John Pummitt, a small farmer, was paid 9s 7d 'for two bushels and a gallon of white peas', William Small was paid £4 11s 9d for 'meal, bread, and flour', William Jarvis, a maltster, was paid £2 12s 6d for '14 bushels of malt for poor house', Matthias Smith, a butcher, was paid £4

6s 5d 'for beef for the poor', and Daniel Pamflett, a hoyman, was paid 18s 9d 'for cheese from London for the poor'. Payment was also made for coal, £4 4s being paid to Peter Wootton, a coal merchant, 'for coals for the poor' with 12s being paid to John Brown, a small farmer at North Foreland, 'for carriage of 8 chaldrons of coals', presumably from the harbour to the Poorhouse; farmers, having horses and carts, were often paid for carting goods around the parish. Also in 1728 the overseers gave 4s 4d 'to the poor people in the house to keep Christmas'. Many more payments for food are included in subsequent years, including payments for pork, beef, mutton, 'neats [cattle] feet and tripes', salt-pork, herrings, salt-fish, peas, French beans, apples, fat, malt, yeast, milk, bread, lots of cheese, and 'wine for the poor in time of sickness'. There are also frequent purchases of 'shop goods', including butter, candles, soap, sugar, raisins, linen, worsted [a variety of woollen yard or thread], linsey [a coarse and stout material of which the warp is linen and the woof woollen], dowlas [a strong and coarse linen cloth], bodices, cotton, thread and tape; in 1731 the overseer's spent 9d on 'cabbage plants for the Poor House' and gave 3d 'to Widd Mainer for herbs to sett at the Poor House Garden'.

In 1731 the overseers started to pay for schooling for children at the Poorhouse, initially for one boy for whom they paid John Prince 3s 11d for schooling over the course of the year and for whom they bought a primer for 1s 3d. The accounts for 1731 also include payments for 'schooling at the Poor House' and for 'schooling for the boy in the Work-house', the use of both 'Poor House' and 'Work-house' again suggesting that these were the same building. In 1732 the overseers gave John Prince 2s, he now being 'in need'; employing him as a school teacher was a way of providing a poor man with necessary financial support. Later in 1732 the overseers paid Widd Norwood 7s 8d for 'Francis Baker's schooling' and Widd Powell 6s 4d 'for schooling for the poor children'. In 1733 a payment of 6s 3d was made 'to Widow Powell and Widow Norwood for schooling for poor children'. The next payment of this type was for 1s 6d paid 'to Wid Sampson for 6 weeks schooling for 3 poor children out of the Poor-house at 3d per week'.

The original Poor Laws emphasised that as well as accommodation, the overseers were expected to provide work for the able-bodied poor by providing them with 'a convenient stock of flax, hemp, wool, thread, iron, or other necessary ware or stuff'.[6] There is little evidence in the overseers' accounts that this idea was pursued at all vigorously in Margate. In 1666 the overseers gave Widow Bell 9d 'to buy yarne for the Girle she keeps' and in 1688 the overseers paid Richard Laming 8s 8d 'for Weaving and for Worke' and 1s 1d 'for making the sacks' and spent 8d for '½lb and 2 oz of Twine to sowe the Sacks'.[26] In 1700 Widow Hall was given 2s for 'spinning one dozen of hemp' and Francis Sanderoff was similarly paid 2s 'for one dozen spinning' but there are very few entries of this type. This reflects the pattern nationally, with unpaid overseers being unwilling to spend the time required to supervise the work of large numbers of poor scattered throughout a parish.[3] Indeed, one of the arguments for the introduction of workhouses was that it would enable the work of the poor to be supervised much more effectively. The overseers' accounts are consistent with the idea that the St John's Poorhouse became more like a Workhouse after about 1727. In 1730 the overseers recorded receiving 7s for '1 dozen of work done at the Poor house', 3s 'for spinning 6 lb of work', and 1s 6d from Thomas Cramp, a shoemaker, 'for work', presumably for shoes made at the Poor house. In 1732 1s was paid to 'the Poor for spinning' and in 1733 2s 8d was paid 'for 1lb of the best wool to spin in the Poor-house' and 10d was paid to 'the poor in the house for encouragement for spinning'. In 1733 the poor in the Poorhouse were given 1s, calculated on the basis of the value of the work they had produced, at a rate of 2d in the shilling, and the overseers invested 6d in the purchase of 'thread, tape and needles' and 1s for ½ a pound of wool for the Poorhouse. The overseers also occasionally gave money to individual men and women to enable them to continue with their trades. In 1679 the overseers paid 1s 'for mending Goodwife Ashendens [spinning] Wheele and for making Richard Knock a Rake'.[26] In 1701 the overseers paid 16s 'for plowing three Acres of ground for Widd Poynter'. In 1730 John Ryes, a poor fisherman, was given 1s to buy a 'whiting line' and 'Goodman Shoemaker's wife' was given 2s 6d in 1738 for a spinning wheel. In 1700 Robert Peirce was given £1 'for or towards byeing him a Boate' and in 1719 James Mount was given 12s 'to mend his boat', although in this case it was noted that the payment was made 'by consent of the parish'.[26,27]

More often the poor were supported through payments for small jobs done about the parish; for men this often took the form of work on the parish houses. For example in 1716 Nicholas Norwood, a thatcher, was paid £1 6s 'for work about the parish houses', although the following year it was necessary for the overseers to give his wife 2s. Women were also employed by the overseers, but largely in caring tasks such as nursing the sick and 'laying out' or washing the dead. In 1666 Widow Bing was paid 1s 6d 'for watching and tending the Wid Witherden', Widow Poole was paid 6s 'for looking to Susan Rendall and her child in her sickness of the Small pox, for one week', and Widow Prickett was paid 1s 'for Entertayning of Susan Rendall and her child in her home for one weeke.' In 1679 Good Knock was paid 1s 'for looking to Widd Ashendon in sickness'. In 1727 the wife of Mathias Mummery, a shoemaker, was paid 3s 6d for 'nursing several people', Widd Everitt was paid 1s for 'washing for sick people', and the wives of Robert Peirse and Richard Blackbourne were paid 1s 4d and 2s 8d respectively for nursing Mrs Hart. Men were paid to help with male paupers; in 1738 Goodman Housden was paid 4s for washing Gabriel Foard, who presumably was lousy at the time. Payments were also made for looking after children. In 1679 Good Raff was paid 7s 6d 'for keeping of Marlow's child' and in 1716 John Salter was paid 12s 6d for keeping 'a parish girl' for one quarter. In 1735 Goodman Kiddal was paid 13s 6d for '11 weeks nursing, at 12d per week, Webbster's bastard child, and other necessaries' and in 1737 John Neal, a weaver, received 12s 'for providing clothing and board for Hedgecock's child'.

Small sums of money could also be earned helping to keep down vermin. In response to a series of bad harvests in the sixteenth century Parliament passed two acts aimed to reduce the numbers of vermin eating seeds and crops, an Act to destroy 'choughs, crows and rooks' passed in 1532 and an Act 'for the preservation of grain' passed in 1566.[44,45] Under these Acts churchwardens had to pay a bounty for vermin killed within the parish, the money coming from the church rate; the vermin covered by the acts included sparrows, rooks, magpies, foxes, weasels, and hedgehogs, hedgehogs at the time being believed to suck milk from the teats of cows at night as they lay in the fields. In 1706 the Churchwardens of St John's paid Thomas Bing 5d for 3½ dozen sparrow's heads, Edward Flagg 1s for three hedgehog heads and Matthew Constable 4d for one hedgehog.[46] Most payments seem to have gone to young boys: in 1705 'Dawson's boy' received 1d for six sparrows heads, 'Edward Bing's boy' received 3d for 1½ dozen of sparrows heads, 'Mr Tomlins boy' received 1s 8d for 5 hedgehogs and 'John Parnell's boy' received 4d for 1 hedgehog. However, some adults also received payments; in 1713 'Mr Cowells

Servant' received 11d 'for 5½ dozen of heads', a 'Mr Grant' received 3d 'for 1½ dozen of heads' and Capt. Omer's shepherd received 4d for a hedgehog and 'Roger Tombe the Shepard' also received 4d for a hedgehog, this probably being Capt. Omer's shepherd again. Payments for heads of rooks, sparrows and hedgehogs continued at least until 1715, in which year £1 9s was paid 'for various sparrow heads and other vermin for whole year'.

Many of the poor, rather than long term help, needed help for just a short period of time, due to illness, lack of work, or some other disaster. Such help was provided either in the form of cash payments or as relief in kind, which could include clothes, shoes, fuel, rent, food or medical care. Examples of cash payments include 'a poor woman in want with two children having lost all they had by fire' who was given 2s in 1679, the 1s given in 1712 'to a poor man that had a great Loss', and the 1s given in 1680 to George Brown 'being a poor man'; the overseers then ensured that George Brown needed no further help from the parish by paying 1s 6d to move him to Canterbury. In 1685 about 60 people received cash relief in the parish, sums varying from 6d to 2s 6d, at a total cost of £14. In 1689 Widow Williams was given 2d 'for a Chamber pott'. In 1716 Widow Jarman received 1s 'in sickness' and Widows Wellen and Grainger each received 2s, also 'in sickness'; Thomas Hewes and Widow Horton received 1s and 2s respectively 'in want' and Widow May received 3s 'in need at several times.' In 1717, Thomas Whithead, a labourer, received 5s 'at five several times in need' and Vincent Watson received 2s 6d 'in his need'. Small one-off payments were also made by the Churchwardens: in 1693, 6d was given 'to a poor man for relief' and, on several occasions, poor men and women received sums of 6d or 1s.[26,46] Money was also given by the churchwardens to men passing through the town, possibly to encourage them not to stay; in 1693 1s was given 'to a poor traveller', 2s was given 'to two soldiers from Deal' and 1s was given 'to a soldier come from Sandwich'.[46] Payments to soldiers and sailors passing though the parish in times of war could be quite large (Chapter 6).

Occasional support was more commonly provided in kind than in cash; payment in kind helped, of course to bolster the local economy, as the overseers bought goods and services from the local shopkeepers and tradesmen. The wide range of goods and services provided suggests that the overseers had a good knowledge of the needs of the poor in the parish. Considerable amounts were spent on replacing and repairing shoes and clothing; large numbers of badly clothed paupers would have been a very public sign of poverty in the parish, suggesting that the parish did not care for its poor.[9] Sometimes individual items of clothing were identified in the accounts and sometimes payments were made to cover quarterly bills submitted by tradesmen. In 1666 Matthew Toarth was paid 2s 6d for three pairs of shoes and 2s 6d 'for one paire [of shoes] for the Girle that Widd Bell keeps, and one paire for the boy that Peter Mosse keeps' and Thomas Emptage was paid 6s 'for shooes for Tho. Tadds Girle, and Jeremy Culmers Girle, and for mending shoes'. Also in 1666 John Laming was paid 8s 'towards cloathes for the boy he keeps', Stephen Cock was paid 2s 'for making a Wastcoate for ye Girle at Adrian Moyses and for Claspes etc.' and 1s 'for making a Wastcoate and pair of breaches for Thomas Tadd'.[26] In 1707 there was a particularly large expenditure on clothes:

> For a Shift and Westcoate for Mary Anderson — 6s 8d
> For a Shift for Mary Phillips — 2s 10d
> For 2 Shirts for George Grant — 6s
> For 2 Shirts for Edw. Norwood — 6s 6d
> For a payer of Briches for old Norwood — 6s 6d
> For a Shift, Apron, Bodys, and other things for Mary Askew — 8s 10d
> For a Gowne and Coate for her, and another shift — 15s 4d
> For a Gowne for Widd Anderson — 11s 6d
> For a shift for Widd Smith — 2s 10d
> For a shift for Widd Russell — 3s
> For a Wastcoate for Widd Horton — 2s 6d
> For a payer of Leatheren Briches for Edw. Peach — 3s 6d
> For a Wastcoate, 2 Handchiefts, tape, a shirt, and a *sock* [a shroud] — 9s 11d
> For 2 Handkerchiffs for Jarmans Girle — 8d
> For a shift for Widd Smith — 2s 10d
> For a Blew Apron for Mary Phillips — 1s 3d
> For a payer of Spactacles and a Case for her — 6d
> For a shroud for Widd Smith — 3s 6d
> For a Rugg for Geo. Grant — 5s 6d
> For a Blew Shirt for old Norwood — 3s 6d

In 1717 Robert Gore was paid for 7s 11d for shoes and Franklin Goldsmith, a tailor and draper, was paid 4s 4d for a 'waistcoat and britches for [the] Wallace boy'. In 1718 Widow Castle was given 1s to allow her to buy 'two capps.' In 1727 three shirts were bought for Thornden's 'young child' for 1s 6d and Richard Dixon's wife was paid 1s 3d for making gowns for Thorden's girls, and two pairs of leather britches were bought 'for poor boys' for 6s. In 1728 John Brooman was paid 12s 8d 'for a gown and a pair of bodies [stays]' and Matthias Mummery was paid 8d for mending a pair of shoes. In 1735 3s was paid 'to the Wid Emtage a shift in need'. In 1735 many of the poor received clothing; Thomas Smith's daughter received a shift costing 1s 6d and two caps costing 1s 1d, John Sanders received a shirt costing 3s 2d, his wife a shift costing 3s, an apron costing 1s 10d, and 5d 'for thread and tape', and his daughter a shift costing 1s 6d, a coat costing 1s 10½d, 'coverings for her stays' costing 1s 5d, and a frock costing 2s 11d, and Franklin Goldsmith was paid 1s 9d for a pair of stays for the daughter of Elizabeth How. In 1728 the overseers spent 6s 6d 'to redeem Widd Reynolds clothes' from a pawnbroker.

The overseers had accounts with a number of the shopkeepers in the town. In 1717 the overseers paid John Brooman, a draper, £3 8s 9d 'as per bill'. Similarly, in 1728, the overseers paid a bill for £1 17s 7d from Solomon Holbourn, a tailor and draper, and also bills for 19s from Thomas Cramp and for 10s 8½d from Robert Gore, both 'for shoes for the poor'. In 1729 William Cobb, a shoemaker, shop keeper, maltster and father of Francis Cobb I, was paid £13 5d 'for shoes for the poor', and Beale, a tailor and draper, was paid 1s 4d 'for gloves and other things'. Again, in 1731 Beale was paid 7d 'for a pair of gloves for Peirce Lawrence'. In 1733 John Commett was paid £3 12s ½d 'as per bill for clothes for the poor'. In 1738 Stephen Bennett, a draper or shopkeeper, was paid £1 7s 6½d for 'shirts and other clothing for the poor'.

There are only a few examples of purchases of food for individual paupers. In 1719 Wid Bubb, probably an inn keeper, was paid 1s 'for victuals and drink for a poor woman' and in 1733 8d was spent to pay for bread 'for Catherine Pattison in her illness'. As we have seen, the overseers started to spend significant sums of money on food for the poor after 1727 when the poorhouse started to operate more like a workhouse. Presumably paupers living in their own homes were expected to pay for their food out of the money given to them by the overseers, if they could not grow it themselves. A number of purchases of coal are also recorded in the accounts. For example, Peter Wootton, a coal merchant was paid £3 13s 6d for coal in 1717 and £2 6s in 1719 for 2 chaldens of coal. In 1718 William Richardson was paid £4 16s 6d for 4 chalder and 5 bushels of coal 'and for carriage to the poor's cellar'. Other payments for coals were made to John Lister, a coal merchant and sexton, to Stephen Baker, a coal merchant and mariner, and to Nicholas Wellen, another coal merchant. It is likely that much of this coal was destined for the cellars of the Poorhouse but some of it could have been given to help the poor living in their own homes. By 1739 the overseers had decided that coal, except in special cases, would only be provided to the poor house:[47]

Whereas there has been for several years last past a large quantity of coals have been delivered by the Officers to the Poor of the parish. It is agreed in this present order of Vestry, there shall be no coals laid in or disposed of, for the use of the Poor, but only, for the Poor house. Except to such people as shall be agreed upon, by an order at Vestry for that purpose.
14 May 1739

The separation of the poor into those receiving regular disbursements and those receiving occasional relief was not immutable; someone starting with occasional relief would often end up relying totally on the parish. An example is provided by the wife of Paul Hart. Paul Hart was an inn keeper and one of Margate's early postmasters but by 1716 the family had fallen on hard times, receiving £3 15s in relief from the parish. By 1726 Paul Hart was dead and 'Widow Hart' was given a payment of 2s and four payments of 1s 6d, being 'in need', but later that year she was paid a pension for 29 weeks of 1s 6d per week. Interestingly, in the overseers' accounts she is sometimes referred to as Mrs Hart, the title 'Mrs' showing that she was of some standing in the parish despite her poverty. In 1727 she received payments of 2s 6d, again being 'in want', followed by periods of 14 weeks and 10 weeks at 1s 6d per week; she was also given 1s 8d for 'a pair of irons', 3s for 'a blanket and rug', and 10s 6d 'at several times in sickness'. Her health had got worse by the end of the year as the wives of Peirse and Richard Blackbourne were paid 1s 4d and 2s 8d respectively for nursing her, after which she was nursed for 15 weeks by 'Blackbourne's girl', who was paid 1s a week for doing so. During this time Widow Hart received a pension of 2s a week for 12 weeks, and 1s 6d a week for the remaining three. She died later in 1727 and the overseers accounts record that 2s 6d was paid for 'burying Widd Hart' with 9s 6d for 'laying her forth, carrying her to church, beer, and other charges'.

The example of Widow Hart shows that the overseers were prepared to pay quite large sums of money to ensure that the poor received a decent burial. Many records in the overseers' accounts show the importance they attached to providing hospitality, particularly beer, after a funeral; this was common in many parishes, the overseers trying to ensure that a pauper funeral did not symbolize 'worthlessness, failure, and anonymity, but the social recognition and personal respectability of the deceased'.[3] In 1716, 2s was paid 'to laying out Widow Foreman when dead', Widow Idley was paid 4d for making her shift, the minister and clerk were paid 2s for her burial, the sexton was paid 2s, and 3s was spent on beer 'at her burying'. Again in 1716, Widow Granger and Widow Hews received 2s for 'laying forth Aythorne's girl' and the minister, clerk and sexton received 3s 6d for burying her, although this time only 1s 6d was spent on beer following the funeral. In 1720 2s 6d was given to Gibbins 'for drink at his fathers' funeral'. Thomas Heros died in 1721 after having received parish relief for a year, and 1s was spent 'to lay Thomas Heros forth when dead', 3s 6d was given to the minister, clerk and sexton 'for his burying' and 2s 6d was spent 'for beer drunk at his burying'. In 1721 there were a series of charges for beer at funerals; 5s 4d for 'eight gallons of strong beer at Fasham's Burying', 4s for 'six gallons strong beer at Widd Blackabee's Funeral' and 4s for 'six gallons strong beer at Widd Castle's funeral'. In 1723 3s was paid 'to the men for laying forth William Goodbourne', 8s was paid for a coffin, 3s 6d for funeral charges and 5s 7d 'for beer at his funeral'. In 1731 Henry Petken, a local brewer and maltster, was paid 14s 8d 'for beer for four funerals' and in 1734 he got 4s 'for 6 gallons of beer for the funeral of Smith daughter'.

In fact, the overseers spent rather a lot on beer. Payments to Widow Dixon, an Inn keeper, often appear in the overseers' records. In 1716 she was paid 5s for beer drunk when the overseers determined the poor rate ['at making my sess']. She was also paid 1s 3d for beer 'at the baptizing of Heros boy' and, sadly, 1s 3d in 1719 'for beer at burial of Heros boy'. In 1717 she was paid 5s 6d 'at making my sess' and 4s 6d at 'choosing officers.' The biggest expenditure though seems to be by the overseers and parish clerk when travelling on parish business, although such payments usually appear as 'charges' or 'expenses'. For example, in 1722 we have 6s 6d 'for charges at Dover about Parish Business' and 1s 'for charges at St Peters'. In the travels of Michael Trapp to Dover and London in 1733 described later, we have 6s 9d spent on 'victuals and drink for 4 of us on a passage to London', and 6s spent on 'expenses for 5 of us'.

One odd feature of funerals at this time was payment for burying in linen. This came about due to an Act of Parliament of 1666, revised in 1678, for 'burying in woollen only'.[48] The aim of the Act was to help the woollen manufacturers of the country and prevent the export of money to buy linen; the Act was not repealed until 1814. A certificate had to be obtained to prove that a body had been buried in a woollen shroud, and, to prevent collusion, the certificate had to be obtained from the vicar of a neighbouring parish; for St John's this was usually the vicar of St Peter's. If a family was determined that their loved one should be buried in linen they would have to pay a fine of £5, but, as long as they reported the fact of a burial in linen to the overseers, £2 10s was returned to them, the remaining £2 10s being distributed to the poor; the result was that burial in linen was a luxury just for the better off.[26] In 1685 4s 6d was paid by the overseers to 'Goodwife Pound and the Widd Ellmor for laying Ann Stokes forth, and for goeing to St Peters to make Oathe that she was buried in Woolen.' Similarly the accounts for 1687 record the death of Katherine Messenger, a Traveller, and that the overseers paid 6s 8d 'for carrying her to her Grave, and for the use of the Pier, and for Drink to one that made Oathe that she was buried in Woolen, and for the Certificate'. In 1686 the overseers record that they had received £2 10s 'of Widd Small for burying her husband in Lynnen' and 'of Widd Wright being buried in Lynnen'. In 1687 they again received sums of £2 10s from 'Widd Price for burying her Husband in Lynnen', from 'Mrs Glover for her Mother being buried in Lynnen', and from 'Tho. Grant for burying his child in Lynnen.' The overseers then record that £7 10s was 'distributed to the poore of the parish'. However in 1688 the overseers record that they 'Received of Tho. Thornden for *burying* his child *in Lynnen* [£2 10s] the which sume was given to him againe, he being a poore man.'

A further tax on burials was introduced in 1695 with the passage of an Act 'for granting his Majesty certain rates and duties upon marriages, births, and buriels and upon bachelors and widowers, for the term of five years, for carrying on the war against France with vigour'.[49] The Act introduced a tax of 4s per burial which, for the poor, had to be paid by the Overseers. In 1696 the Overseers paid 4s as part of the funeral expenses of Widow Pike and in 1698 they record the payment of 14s 'for the Kings Dutyes on Buriall of Peter Marsh, John Fashams wife, Widd Foreman, and birth of Alice Poynters Child'. In 1702 the King's duty had become the Queen's duty, and the Overseers record the payment of 12s for 'the Queens dutyes on the Burialls of Ovenden, Fashen, and Jarvis boy.'

Sometimes the Overseers would sell off the household goods of a parishioner who had died and who they had been supporting. In 1688, the Overseer's accounts record a payment of 4d 'for crying of Edw. Sandwells Goods', in other words, for the Town Crier to announce that Sandwell's goods were for sale; they also spent 1s 6d 'for Bread and Beere at the selling of Edw. Sandwells Goods.' At first sight this might appear to be rather harsh, but the Overseers had spent a significant amount of money at his funeral, in paying off his debts, and in supporting his children:

> Paid Sarah Meakings for a Cask and Beere that Edw. Sandwell had of her — 1s 6d
> Paid John Lister for ½ Chall. Of Coales Edw. Sandwell had of him — 8s
> Paid things at Edw. Sandwells funeral and for Cloath [i.e. for burial suite] — £1 17s
> Paid for Cloath for 2 Shifts for Edw. Sandwell daughter — 4s 3d
> Paid for 12 oz. of Yarne to make Ed. Sandwells Childrens stockings — 2s

In 1702 we have a similar entry, with a payment of 4d 'to Thomas Bishop for Crying the Widd. Baylyes Goods', a widow whose burial was again paid for by the parish.[26]

Medical care for the poor was provided by both professional and amateur healers, the amateurs including bone-setters dealing with broken arms and legs and 'wise women' who cured leg ulcers and fungal infections such as scalled head or favus, a disease of the scalp that used to be common but is now easily treated.[26] In 1680, William Laming's wife was paid 2s 6d 'for the cure of Widdow Roberts Legg', Goody Ford in 1696 was paid 2s 6d 'for cureing Widd Pikes Legg' and in 1697 was again paid 2s 6d 'for cureing Goody Hubbards Arme'; in 1701 and 1702 Goddy Dadds, the wife of Edward Dadds, was paid 1s 6d 'for cureing Jarvis' and £1 'for cureing Punnits head'. In 1702 Thomas Huffam's wife received £1 'for cureing Haselton's Legg' and in 1703 she received 10s 'for cureing Edw. Norwoods fingers'; in 1706 Goody Yeomans received £1 2s 6d 'for cureing Pummett's boys heads'. Widow Avery, apparently an unauthorised practitioner, was given 3s on two occasions in 1718 for 'physick for Rys boy' and in 1722 the parish paid 6d for 'Rys's boy letting blood', hopefully by one of the local doctors.[27] The accounts include very few references to payments for a midwife. In 1706 2s was paid 'to the midwife for the Waygoing woman' and in 1718 Goody Peney was paid 2s 6d 'for delivering or laying of Jane Boys'.[26,27] In 1722 'Mrs Wilds midwife' was also paid 2s 6d; in 1735 she was paid 3s 6d for looking after Ester Mockett, and by 1737, when she was midwife for Pearse Lawrence's wife, her payment had increased to 3s.

The local doctors operating in the parish have been described in Chapter 3. They would submit their bills at regular intervals to the overseers for their work with the poor; in 1717 Nicholas Chewney was paid £4 7s 'as per bill', Edward Jarvis was paid 15s in 1718 'for looking after sick and lame poor people', £2 12s 6d in 1719 'as per bill', and £3 5s 6d in 1724, and George Hammond was paid £3 14s in 1722 'as per bill', and £2 2s in 1724. Thomas Watts appears to have been the first doctor with specific responsibility for the poor; in 1732 he was paid £6 6s 'for medicine for the Poor by Agreement of the Parish'. However, the other doctors also continued to treat the poor; in 1732 Henry Wallis was paid £2 8s 8d 'for physic and looking after the poor', in 1734 Thomas Wheatley was paid £1 3s 11d 'for doctoring and looking after the poor', and in 1736 George Slater was paid £9 4s 10d, also 'for doctoring and looking after the poor'. Simple blood letting cost 6d a time; in 1730 Henry Wallis was paid 6d 'for letting one of the children's blood', which was what had been paid in 1722 for 'Rys's boy letting blood'. The parish even provided spectacles; in 1728 6d was paid for a pair of spectacles for Widd Inward and in 1733 2s 6d was paid to Gabrial Foard 'in need and spactickles [spectacles]'.

With infectious diseases such as small pox special precautions were taken, including cleaning the house where the patient died, putting a lock and staple (for locking with a padlock) on the house door, and being particularly careful during the burial. An example occurred in 1708 when Widow Pegden died; unusually she was both *socked*, 'to sock' being Kentish Dialect meaning to shroud or wrap a corpse in grave clothes, and put in a coffin:[26]

For laying out Widd Pegden — 4s
For *Socking* for her — 3s
For a Coffin for her — 8s
For Grave and all Charges for Minister and Clark — 3s 6d
Paid in her Sickness — 3s 6d
For Carrying her to Church — 3s
Paid cleaning out the house — 1s
For a Lock and Staple — 8d

Complex and costly medical treatments warranted itemised bills in the overseers' account books. In 1725 Edward Jarvis was paid £1 1s 'for setting and curing Bird's arm' and in 1731 Henry Wallis was paid £3 'as per bill for curing Widd Everit's son'. In 1733 George Slater was paid £4 15s for 'curing Margaret Blackbourn's leg' and in 1736 he was paid £5 3s 6d 'for doctoring and looking after Sarah Maynard'. In 1735 Thomas Wheatley was paid 1s 'for doctoring Easter Mockett at the Poor-house' and Walter Plummer was paid £3 10s 6d 'for curing Wid Blackbourn's boy's head and other charges'. One case, that of a young boy, John Barton [Burton], was more complex. In 1728 the overseers spent 4s 6d for a consultation about 'cutting the boy's leg off'. The accounts for 1729 then contain a list of expenses for John Barton:

To a warrant to carry John Barton to Mrs Starks — 7s
To Counsellor Turner for advice on John Barton — 10s 6d
To Mr Turner and my journey to Canterbury at the sessions about John Barton — 11s
To the witnesses journey and expenses — 16s 6d
To Counsellor Turner's pleading fee — 10s 6d

Counsellor Turner was a local lawyer to whom the overseers turned on several occasions for legal advice, but there is no clue as to why this particular case had to go to law. Nevertheless, it was decided to go ahead with the amputation and in 1729 Dr Watts received £5 5s 'for cutting Barton's leg'. The amputation must have been a success since a subsequent entry in the accounts is for 4s 6d 'to a wooden leg for Barton's boy'. Finally, in 1730 the parish agreed to spend £16 to apprentice John Barton to Francis Cobb; it is not known whether or not this Francis Cobb was related to the Cobb family who later became so important in the town.

Some medical cases were thought to be sufficiently serious to warrant treatment in a hospital. In 1732 Widow Grigg was paid 10s 'to get her son in the hospital'. Three payments to hoymen make it clear that patients were being sent for treatment to hospitals in London; in 1734 Henry Petken was paid 4s 6d 'for expenses in getting Smith's daughter into the hospital', in 1735 Stephen Baker was paid £1 6s 'as per bill paid at St Thomas Hospital [London]' and in 1737 John Simmons was paid £1 11s 6d 'as per bill for the use of Robert Bubb and Thomas Dawson at the hospital'. In 1719 James Stone suffered from a stone in the bladder. The minute of a vestry meeting records that a collection had been made in the town 'so that he [James Stone] can be cut for stone'. The meeting decided that if the collection did not reach the required sum, the parish officers could take the balance from the poor's rate. In fact the costs involved were considerable. Stone travelled to and from London in Stephen Pamflett's hoy, for which Pamflett was paid 9s; Pamflett was also given £11 7s 6d 'for the use of James Stone', presumably whilst in London, and a further 4s 6d 'to pay the Apothecary, for the use of James Stone'.

Treatment of the long term mentally ill was particularly harsh. In the period covered by the overseers' accounts there is only one clear case of mental illness — that of John Norwood, a cordwainer or shoemaker. An entry in 1719 records a payment of 1s 4d 'for John Norwood's windows', perhaps mending them or putting bars over them. This was followed in 1720 by payments totalling £1 15s to his wife 'at several times in need'. In 1721 there is a payment of 6d to a barber 'to shave John Norwood,' and in 1722 a payment of 2s to John Norwood himself and a further six payments of 6d a time to Francis Dixon, a barber, 'for John Norwood's shaving'. By 1723 the situation had got worse, both for John Norwood and his wife. In that year his wife was again 'in need' and received 2s 6d, and John Norwood was again shaved by Francis Dixon. However, the accounts now include 5s 'for a new chain for John Norwood', 4s paid to Thomas Sprackling, a carpenter, 'for work about John Norwood's house', and 5s for 'charges for confining John Norwood'. Later in the year 1723 his wife was given a further 7s 6d and a further 1s 3d was spent 'when John Norwood was chained'. In 1724 his wife was given 10s and Francis Dixon was paid 1s 2d 'for shaving John Norwood's head'. The situation had become even more serious by 1725 when 5s 9d was spent for 'four men to help about John Norwood' with 6s being spent 'about

Parish Business, confining John Norwood', with a further 6s 'for straw for John Norwood's house'; he also had his head shaved once again by Francis Dixon for 6d. Later in 1725 it was finally decided that he had to be moved to London, presumably to an asylum. The accounts record a payment of 2s 6d to John Norwood himself and a payment of 9s 6d to get him on board a hoy and 'for several things, as shoes, britches, hat, cap for him' so that he would be properly clothed. There seem to have been two minders looking after him on the journey; Thomas Walton was paid £2 10s 'to carry John Norwood to London' and Mark Browne was paid £1 1s 'for [going] up to London with John Norwood'. Finally Stephen Baker, a mariner, was paid £1 10s 'for charges about John Norwood' and Richard Laming, a hoyman, was paid £6 8s 6d for carrying John Norwood to London, the high charge probably meaning that Norwood and his minders were the only passengers on the hoy. Meanwhile, in Margate, William Cook, a mason, was paid 6s 'for work about John Norwood's house' and Thomas Barber, a carpenter, was paid £5 0s 3d 'for work done at John Norwood's house'. There is no record of what finally happened to him.

The overseers effectively adopted destitute orphan children and supported children whose parents could not themselves afford to support them. This could take the form of weekly payments, referred to as a pension, made to someone in the parish to look after the children, or payments for clothing and shoes. For example, in 1666 Thomas Foster was paid 6s 'for shooes and mending of shooes for severall children that are Pensioners'.[26] The overseers would pay generous premiums so that children could be apprenticed, or 'bound-out', to work as servants or apprentices to masters or mistresses willing to maintain and train them; they would also contribute towards the costs of the children's clothing during their apprenticeship. In 1666 Edward Hurt was paid £2 10s for taking Rendall as an apprentice, and John Freeman was paid £5 for taking Thomas Tadd as an apprentice with a further 10d 'spent at the ensealing of his indenture'; that year the overseers also paid 12s 6d to 'Widd Grant a yeares rent for Rob. Tadd's widow', the death of Robert Tadd presumably driving his wife and son into poverty. In 1721 Daniel Allen was given £3 for taking on a female apprentice, and the parish also paid 10s 'to clothe her more', 4s for making her Indentures and 3s 6d for 'money spent when the Indentures were signed', probably beer to ensure that the event was properly celebrated. In 1719 Nicholas Wellen, a coal merchant, was paid

7s 6d for taking a boy, and 1½d was 'spent at binding the boy'; in 1719 John Kennett, a tailor, was paid 2s 10d 'for a pair of britches for Wellen's boy', in 1721 1s was paid to provide him with a pair of stockings, and in 1723 William Laming was paid 2s 6d 'for a shirt and worsted' for him. In 1728 the overseers paid Mr Wells, a farmer, £5 to take the son of John Thornden, a carter, as an apprentice. John Thornden was ill and in financial difficulty at the time, as in 1728 the overseers gave him 3d for a knife, 6d for a comb, 2s 6d for a hat and 8d for 'a pair of half-legs'; in 1729 the overseers paid 3s 6d 'to bring John Thornden from Brooksend', 3s 6d 'to Widd Sackett for nursing him' and then 6s 'for his funeral charges'. In 1728 the overseers paid Mrs Quince £5 to take Elizabeth Laming as an apprentice; they also paid 8s for a 'hood and petticoat' for her. In 1731 the overseers paid John Kerby, a shoemaker, £1 6s 8d 'for taking W. Pierces girl apprentice', and 3s 6d was spent 'for necessaries for Thomas Huse to sea.' In 1733 the overseers paid £4 5s 'for clothing and putting out Brooks boy to [Francis Dixon] the barber' and 12s to Daniel Butler, an attorney 'for indentures and bond for ditto'.

Of course not all apprenticeships worked out well, and the local papers contained frequent advertisements for the return of run-away apprentices. A typical example appeared in the *Kentish Post* in November 1732 and is particularly interesting in providing details about how a young farm labourer of the time would have been dressed:[50]

Run away from Edward Bings near Margate in the Isle of Thanet, on Sunday the 12th instant, George Simpson, a boy; about 15 years of age, pretty much pitted with the small-pox, and thin brown hair; he had on when he went off, a new light-coloured coat and waistcoat, trimm'd with the same colour, and sheep-skin breeches, with black buttons, and had also with him an old coarse cloth coat, the sleeves turn'd up with blue, and a yellow waistcoat; whoever brings him to the said Edw. Bings, or secures him and sends word so that he may fetch him, shall have satisfaction for the same.

The overseers were less keen to support the children of unmarried mothers, thinking that parents should be made to pay; when they didn't it was necessary to apply to Dover for a warrant to enforce payment. In 1682 the overseers paid 3s 6d 'for fetching the warrants for the bastard children'.[26] In 1739 an entry was made at the front of the overseers' account book:[47]

Whereas complaint has been made to the Justices of the Poor concerning bastard children. And no redress or account has been taken to bring the offenders in that kind to correction. It is mutually agreed by the Church Wardens, Overseers, and the Parishioners whose names are underwritten – being met at a Vestry lawfully called that the Fathers and Mothers of such child or children, who do not provide for them as the law directs in such case and the Justices will not take any account of them as heretofore to bring them to correction or punishment. We do oblige ourselves to look and enquire further into such affairs that the offenders in this kind shall be brought to moderate correction to be whipped or otherwise and to put them to hard labour in order for the maintenance of such Bastard Children. And further it is mutually agreed by us whoes names are underwritten that the charge and expense that shall arise in prosecuting all such offenders above mentioned shall be paid out of the Poor Sess.

The overseers spent much money moving people out of the parish who had no right of settlement and were thought might become a charge on the parish. In 1716 the overseers gave Robert Sackett 2s 9d for 'carrying a woman and three children to Canterbury' and in 1719 John Thornden was paid 3s 'for carrying a poor woman to Sandwich'. In 1720 10s 9d was spent for 'carrying a big bellied woman out of the parish.' In 1728 the overseers gave Widd Jolley £1 'to bear her charges' and gave a hoyman 6s 'for her and her children's passage to London'. In 1730 the overseers paid Daniel Pamflett, a hoyman, 8s 'for the passage of Atkins wife and children to London'. Things could, however, get expensive if the law became involved. In 1723 the overseers spent a total of £1 10s 6d on removing John Hemmings from Margate to Rochester:

> For a warrant and summons to remove John Hemmings — 6s 8d
> To carry John Hemmings to Rochester, expences and journey — 8s
> For a warrant and charges as the Roade, for Hemmings — 6s 8d
> To a journey to Dover for a Warrant for Hemmings — 6s 8d
> To John Hemmings for his charges home — 2s 6d

In another case, in 1731, the overseer's moved Ann Poole out of the parish. They first paid 4s 'for a horse and man to carry Ann Poole to Chislett'. It is unclear why this was done, as the overseers then paid 8s to the Parish Clerk, Michael Trapp, for his 'journey to Ash and Canterbury with Ann Poole' and 2s 'for a warrant and examination', presumably at Canterbury.

The overseers had also to pay 4s 'for horse and man to carry Ann Poole to Ash' and 5s 9d 'for expenses, 2 days, for Ann Poole'. Then in 1732 they paid 10s 6d 'to the Counsel retaining fee', £1 1s 'for myself [Michael Trapp] and both Churchwardens for our journey to Canterbury at the trial of Ann Poole and Isaac Parrau at the Sessions' and £1 11s 6d 'to the Councellers fee for the two causes'. Finally the parish had to pay £1 3s 'to Ash parish by order of court for Ann Poole' and a further 10s 9d for 'our expenses and Court Charges', a total cost for moving Ann Poole from St John's to Ash of £6 0s 6d. And that was not the end of it. In 1738 3s was spent 'on parish business on account of Ann Pool' and 3s 8d on examining Ann Pool at the White Hart in Margate before a Mr Wellard, possibly from Dover, it seeming that Ann Pool was protesting about her transfer to Ash. In 1732 Mary Norwood was also sent to Ash, this time it seeming that the case was settled at Dover. The overseers spent 6s 8d 'for horse-hire and my [Michael Trapp] journey to Dover with Mary Norwood', and they paid 7s 6d to Mr Swinford, a farmer, 'for horse-hire and servant to Dover with her.' A further 2s 6d was spent on unspecified expenses and 7s 'for a warrant and examination to remove her to Ash'. Finally the overseers paid 4s 'for expenses with Mary Norwood', probably incurred at wayside pubs on the route.

An even more extraordinary case dates to 1733 and concerns the transfer of a woman, a traveller or 'stranger', and her child from the Poorhouse to a Poorhouse in London; the cost was £7 13s 10d and occupied Michael Trapp for 9 days:

> To a journey to Canterbury and Councils fee about a stranger and child — 7s 6d
>
> To a journey to Dover, a warrant, examination, and oath — 8s 6d
>
> To money paid for a cart to carry the woman and child to Dover — 15s
>
> To money paid at Dover for a horse and man to go to Sr Bassalls [probably a reference to Sir Basil Dixwell, Governor of Dover Castle] for the mayor and other justices there, 4s, and expenses for 5 of us 6s — 10s
>
> To money paid for ferry for the horse and cart — 2s 4d
>
> To money paid for necessaries the same time — 1s 6d
>
> To money paid for a cart to carry the woman and child aboard of the hoy, and other help — 1s 3d
>
> To money paid for victuals and drink for 4 of us on a passage to London — 6s 9d

To money paid for charges in getting her ashore, with boats and porters — 3s

To money for charges for getting her to Islington, victuals and my [Michael Trapp] expenses with the Officers [of the Poor house there] — 9s 6d

To my charges and expenses the next day to go to Hanvel [possibly Hanwell] with the child — 15s 6d

To my expenses for my self and Feby [Phoebe] and Lodging that night — 5s 6d

To money spent with the Officers of Hanvel — 2s

To money paid for our expenses in getting back to London — 6s 6d

To money paid for lodging, for victuals, for myself and Feby at London — 10s

To money paid for provisions and our passage down [hoy] — 8s

To my expenses to London, 9 days from Home — £1 1s

In 1733 the overseers embarked on a series of forced evictions from the parish. The process started with payment of 5s 2d 'for a warrant from Dover by the News-man', the newsman being one of the men who distributed the local Canterbury paper, the *Kentish Post*, throughout the region. Having obtained their warrant the overseers then paid two men 3s 'for taking charge of Wm. Fisher' and three men 3s 'for taking charge of several men'. It is noticeable that there is no mention of the use of constables on this occasion, and, indeed, the parish records of the period contain no mention of parish constables (Chapter 5).

Having 'taken charge' of the men the real expenses started:

To money paid for a journey to Dover and horse-hire — 6s 8d

To money paid for the Counsellers Fee concerning Elgar — 10s 6d

To money for expenses — 1s

To money paid for examination, warrant and copy for Tho. Smith — 7s

To money paid for removing of Goodman Goatum (Goatham) — 1s

To money paid for examination, warrant, and copy for Hen. Bassett and Jn. Mason, each — 7s

To a warrant to remove Wm. Elgar, Jn. Hubbard, Wm. Pegden, Ed. Coleman each — 4s

To money paid for a Counsel retaining fee and pleading — £2 2s

To money paid for charge at the same time (not allowed) — 1s 6d

To money spent on the Mayor and Jurats of Dover — 1s

To money paid for Wm. Fisher, wife, and children for lodging, drink, and victuals at London — 2s 3d

> To Stephen Baker [hoyman] for their passage to London — 6s
> To Mr. Jewell [Valentine Jewell, White Hart] for 2 horse heirs [hiring of two horses] to Dover — 10s

Also a worry to the overseers were the 'waygoers' or travellers who would, 'if necessitous', be a charge on the parish. Rather than put them in the poorhouse the overseers boarded them out in the parish and then encourage them to move on. Here is an example from 1732:

> To Isaac Reynalls for lodging and nursing a traveller — 4d
> To money paid for charges in removing her — 1s
> To money for wine for the traveller — 1s
> To money for wine for the travelling woman — 1s

Despite the best efforts of the Overseers, the parish rates increased inexorably over this period. Lewis estimated that, based on the Overseers Accounts, the total expenditure on the poor in the years 1663 and 1664 was:[17]

> In the Year 1663 — £84 3s 6d
> In the Year 1664 — £72 16s 8d

By the years 1701 and 1702 the bill had increased dramatically:

> In the Year 1701 — £303 10s 9d
> In the Year 1702 — £279 1s 2d

Lewis attributed this largely to the 'decay of the Fishing here, with the falling off of the foreign trade, and the removal of so many of the substantial Inhabitants on that Account, from this place to London'.[17]

CHAPTER 5

Managing Margate

The Law, the Cinque Ports, and Dover

Local government in England has always been distinctly odd, a hotchpotch of overlapping authorities, developed over long periods of time, interspersed with more or less successful attempts to sort out the mess. Parliament had the ultimate authority but it was a remote institution; local government had more effect on the day to day lives of ordinary people. At the county level administration depended on the Justices of the Peace (the magistrates), men of power and influence responsible both for county justice and county government.[1,2] Although they were amateurs in matters of law, this was counterbalanced by their local knowledge, ensuring that justice was largely a local matter, supporting victims in their wish for compensation.

In Kent there were two separate courts of Quarter Sessions where serious cases were tried by the Justices of the Peace, one for the eastern division of the county, usually held at Canterbury, and one for the western division, usually held at Maidstone. But there were large areas of the county which did not fall within the jurisdictions of either of these two divisions. The most important of these areas, or 'liberties', were the Cinque Ports, of which Margate was a part. The Cinque Ports, from the Norman French for 'five ports,' were first mentioned in a Royal Charter of 1155 and originally consisted of the five ports of Hastings, New Romney, Hythe, Dover and Sandwich; these five ports were known as the Head Ports.[3-5] Rye and Winchelsea joined them as Head Ports in the thirteenth century in what then became 'The Confederation of the Cinque Ports and the Two Ancient Towns of Rye and Winchelsea'. This ramshackle confederation was created to provide ships to defend the Channel in time of war, each port agreeing to supply a specified number of ships and men for the sovereign's service for fifteen days each year. In exchange, the ports were exempted from various taxes and tolls and enjoyed a variety of specific privileges. These were listed in the original charter: 'Exemption from tax and tallage, Right of soc and sac, tol and team, blodwit and fledwit, pillory and tumbril, infrangentheof and outfrangentheof, mundbryce, waives and strays, flotsam and jetsam and ligan.' This might need some interpretation. Exemption from tax and tallage refers to exemption from tax and tolls; right of soc and sac refers to the right of self-government; right of tol and team refers to permission to levy tolls; the right of blodwit and fledwit refers to the right to punish people who had shed blood or had fled from justice; the right of pillory and tumbril refers to the right to punish people for minor offences; the right of infrangentheof and outfrangentheof refers to the power to detain and execute felons; the right of mundbryce refers to the right to punish breaches of the peace; the right of waives and strays refers to the right to take ownership of lost and unclaimed goods after a year; and the right of flotsam and jetsam and ligan refers to the right of ownership of goods thrown overboard or of floating wreckage. The charter gave the Cinque Ports a considerable degree of independence in financial and legal matters.

Over the years many of the original members of the Cinque Ports went into decline. Hastings was almost washed away by the sea in the thirteenth century and was raided and burnt by the French in 1339 and 1377. The town of New Romney was almost destroyed by the Great Storm of 1287 and the River Rother changed course, leaving the town, which had been at the mouth of the river, stranded inland. The declining fortunes of these ports made it difficult for the Cinque Ports to meet their obligation to provide ships for the King, and so between the twelfth and fourteen centuries a number of smaller ports were called upon to help share the burden, in exchange for a share of the privileges. These additional ports became Members (also called Limbs) of their local Head Port; in all likelihood they would have been more than willing to join the confederation, the privileges of membership being as great as they were. The arrangements made with the larger towns were confirmed by Royal Charter; these towns were known as corporate members of their local head port. The corporate members had their own officers and were independent of their head ports except in naval and financial matters. The corporate members of Dover were Folkestone and Faversham. Ports too small and insignificant to become corporate members of the confederation also joined, but in a less formal way and without a Royal Charter, becoming non-corporate members of the head ports, governed by their head port. The non corporate members of Dover were Margate, Goresend, Birchington, Wood or Woodchurch and St Peter's, all in the Isle of Thanet, and Kingsdowne and Ringswold; Ramsgate was a non-corporate member of Sandwich. It is not known exactly when Margate became a non-corporate member of Dover, but it must have been some time before 1229 as an ordinance of that year lists Margate as being a part of the port of Dover.[6,7] As described in the Introduction, the inclusion of Margate as a non-corporate member of the port of Dover led to confusion about the legal position of the rest of the parish of St John's, a problem solved by also making St John's a non-corporate member.[6,8]

Membership of the Confederation of Cinque Ports, even as a non-corporate member, had a number of advantages for a small town like Margate (and the Parish of St John's). It gave Margate a share in the local herring fishery, it meant that it was free from county tolls and taxes, and it enjoyed constitutional and judicial liberties that would normally only have been enjoyed by a wealthy corporation.[4] Not least of the attractions for an area notorious for smuggling was freedom from control by the county magistrates; John Boys of Betshanger, writing in 1794, said that 'the power of the magistrates is rendered of small effect; and many a sturdy rogue escapes the punishment he deserves'.[9] All in all:[4]

whether the Member was a place that had been associated in the service of the Ports from its initiation; whether it had received a charter or was content to let its association rest on the old informal agreements; whether it had voluntarily sought membership as a solution to domestic problems, or had been persuaded by an over-burdened Head Port to accept service for privilege, — the arrangement was one of advantage to both parties, or it could not have been upheld.

Margate was the most important of the non-corporate members of Dover, but the lack of a Royal Charter created problems. In the fourteenth century, wishing to strengthen its position and to clarifying the bargains that it had made with Dover, the 'People of Margate and Barons of the Cinque Ports' petitioned the King and Council asking for a confirmation of Margate's position:[4,10]

The people request that they are able to be discharged of various grievances made to them by the king's ministers according to the purport of an inquisition returned into Chancery, as although they are members of the port of Dover, because Margate is not specified in the charters of the king's progenitors the sheriff of Kent and other ministers disturb them in the enjoyment of the liberties.

The petition was endorsement 'Let the inquisition be viewed before the council', but the outcome is not known. However, in 1424, Margate, the parish of St John's and a group of other parishes in Thanet were recognized in a charter as 'members and advocants of the port of Dover:'[11]

We command you that you allow the men of the Towns of Margate and Gorisende, and the men of the Parishes of SS. John, Peter, Nicholas, and All Saints, of Birchington, Wode in the Isle of Thanet, and the men of Kingsdown, and of the Parish of Ringwold near Dover, which are Limbs and Advocants of the Port of Dover, and the said men avowing themselves to be of the said Liberty, or any one of them, to be quit of this kind of toll, custom, lastage, tallage, passage, kayage, rivage, from pontage, and all wreck, and of every their sale in its sale and re-sale throughout all our land and dominion, with sac and soc, and thol and them, wreck-free, and wit-free, and lestage-free, and lovecop-free, and of shires and hundreds, according to the tenour of the Charters and of the Confirmation aforesaid; and that you do not place, or cause to be placed, them, or any one of them, in any Assizes, Juries, or recognizances held before you for any tenure outside the Liberty, contrary to the tenour of the Charter and the Confirmation aforesaid, nor shall you in any way molest or burden them, or any one of them, contrary to the tenour of the said Charters.

The Cinque Ports fought hard to maintain their rights and privileges, despite the decline in the importance of the ports from their peak in the fifteenth century. A surviving copy of the annual accounts of the Town and Port of Dover for the year 1530 gives a flavour of how Dover spent money keeping the old traditions alive.[12] The total expenditure for that year was £66 14s 2d, including; 16s 1d 'for a supper, wine, ale, and beer at Mr Mayor's election', 10s 'for Mr Mayor's torches at Christmas', 42s 10d for 'expenses at the first general broderyeld', £14 for 'present for the Lord Warden, Sir Edward Guldeford, at the taking of his oath, 20 June', 4s 4d for 'a dinner for Mr old Mayor and Mr new Mayor upon the court day', 30s for 'wine and other pleasures given to the Lord Warden and other noblemen' and 4s 4d 'to the King's minstrels and the Lord Warden's minstrels'. Paying for all this were receipts for the year of £66 8s 3½d, consisting of various fines and taxes on the inhabitants, including 'contributions of our lymmes', one of which was, of course, Margate. Unfortunately Margate was behind with its payments, and the accounts include a debt of 53s 4d, 'the contribution and forfeit of Margate and St John's, in Thanet'. On the other hand, Dover's income did include an item: 'from Valantyne Petytt [Valentine Pettit of Dent-de-Lyon] of Thenett, for striking Thomas Lyncoln, deputy to Mr Dyar, mayor, 40s; of which 21s 8d was remitted by request of divers gentelemen.'

At times things degenerated to the level of farce. In her history of the Cinque Ports, Murray describes a quarrel between the barons of the Cinque Ports and the royal footmen at the coronation of Charles II: 'Dressed in their "large cloaks of garter blue satin with slashed arms of scarlet and red and stockings of dead red", presenting "an appearance perfectly unique", they were involved in an unseemly brawl in which, clinging to their canopy, they were dragged down Westminster Hall by the footmen who were trying to take the canopy from them'.[4] As late as 1682 Dover and the other Cinque Ports were fighting to confirm their independence from the rest of Kent. In that year the Kent Assizes decided to indict some inhabitants of Sandwich, Deal, Dover, and Margate for not attending church. Since the Kent Assizes had no jurisdiction over the Cinque Ports, the Mayor and Jurats of Sandwich wrote to the Speaker of the House of Commons complaining of the action taken by the Kent magistrates, and sent a copy of their letter to the Mayor and Jurats of Dover, asking them to support the complaint:[13]

26 Feb 1682
The Mayor and Jurats of Sandwich to the Mayor and Jurats of Dover. The bearer going to Mr Speaker with a letter for a public contribution for the defence of our townsmen presented at the last county assizes for not coming to church, we knowing that several of your inhabitants are under the same prosecution have ordered him to call on you with this, in which is enclosed a copy of our letter to the Speaker, that, if you think fit, you may likewise recommend it to the Speaker. Enclosed,
The Mayor and Jurats of Sandwich to the Speaker of the Cinque Ports. By an indictment preferred by the Grand Jury of Kent at the last assizes, whereof a copy is enclosed, several of our town and of Deal, one of our members, and of Dover and Margate

are indicted for not coming to church, and proclamation was made that, if they did not surrender at the next assizes, they should stand as convicted Recusants. We, conceiving it the greatest and most dangerous violation ever attempted of our ancient privileges and liberties, which will tend to the utter subversion of our rights and lay us open to the county, think fit that a public defence be made by pleading the Ports' privilege or such other defence as counsel shall advise and desire you to send this letter to all our brethren of the Cinque Ports, praying them to agree that the charge of such defence may be borne by the public as in other cases of less consequence has been formerly requested and submitted to and, as the assizes are to be at Maidstone, 13 March next, we beg you to give such your letters as speedy a dispatch as possible, and that, if our brethren comply with our request, they would in their answers order the delivery of our charter to Mr Pepper or such other as you shall nominate solicitor herein. If counsel shall advise the producing of the same to be necessary, we doubt not of your condescension hereto, for it is but what we have often done for you and other towns, being resolved to live and die constant and bold asserters of the Ports' immunities and franchises.

There was, however, a serious side to all of this. There was, for example, the question of who had the authority to impress sailors into the navy. For the rest of the country the ultimate authority lay with the Lord High Admiral and with a number of Vice-Admirals each responsible for one of the maritime counties. However, in the Cinque Ports the Vice Admiral of Kent had no authority, the authority lying with the Lord Warden of the Cinque Ports. It is unclear whether or not this arrangement was actually to anyone's advantage (Chapter 6). And then there was the question of tax. Margate, as a member of the Port of Dover, was taxed by Dover in a number of ways. In the reign of Richard II, the members paid Dover an annual contribution for the expenses involved in the defence of their franchises, Margate paying 100s and the other Members sums varying from 86s 8d to 26s 8d.[4] Margate also had to contribute ships to the Cinque Ports, although, as described in Chapter 6, this came to be replaced by a contribution in cash to the port of Dover. In the seventeenth century this contribution varied widely from £8 5s in 1621, rising to £54 1s 8d in 1634 and falling to £41 7s 7d by 1640.[14]

In 1692, in the reign of William and Mary, the government introduced a Land Tax to help pay for the war with France, a tax that was not finally abolished until 1963. Each county was told how much tax it had to raise, and, within each county, the tax was imposed on the basis of an assessment made in 1692, based largely on the value of land.[15] The total assessment for Dover and its members was £1923 13s 9d, with Margate's contribution being £502 16s 6d, compared to £349 8s for Birchington and £671 3s for the town of Dover. Over the years, however, Dover gradually increased the assessment of the members, reducing the burden on the town of Dover itself. Not surprisingly 'this gave rise at first to secret murmurings, and finally to open complaints, and they [the members] presented a petition to parliament for redress'.[16] The petition was accepted by Parliament and in the Land Tax bill of 1711 it was enacted that in future 'the parishes of St John, St Peter, and Birchington, in the Isle of Thanet, within the liberty of Dover, shall be deemed and taken to be a distinct division within the said liberty, and in the executing of this Act, shall be charged towards making up the whole sum charged on the town of Dover, and the liberty thereof, according to the proportion which was assessed upon the said parishes by virtue of an Act of Parliament passed in the fourth year of the reign of their late Majesties King William and Queen Mary'.[4,16]

Non-corporate membership of the Cinque Ports gradually came to be seen in Margate as a problem, placing the town in a position subservient to Dover, rather like a colony in the old British Empire. A parliamentary report on municipal corporations in 1835 summarized the position of a non-corporate member rather well:[3]

The Members . . . which have not been incorporated, are under the municipal jurisdiction of their respective Ports: they are within the jurisdiction of the criminal and civil courts, and of the magistrates and coroners of those Ports; they are summoned on the juries, and contribute to the rates, in the nature of county rates, imposed by the justices of those Ports. None of the rights of citizenship, however, can be acquired in the Members, nor have they any share in the election of any of the officers of their respective Ports. Residence within them is not considered as residence within the Port for any corporate purpose.

As a 'limb' of the port and town of Dover, Margate was not answerable to the Justices of the Peace for Kent, meeting at Maidstone and Canterbury, but came under the legal system operating at Dover. Dover, like most of the other corporate towns in Kent, was governed by twelve jurats (aldermen) from whom the Mayor was elected, and thirty six common councillors; the jurats and councillors were chosen from the freemen (all male) of Dover.[3] The Dover jurats acted as Justices of the Peace at what, in the 1800s, had become the Court of General Sessions and Gaol Delivery, a court equivalent to a County Assizes.[17] The lack of surviving records makes the early history of the court unclear, but it is likely that the mayor and jurats of Dover met in this way from before the middle of the sixteenth century, the earlier Hundreds Court gradually evolving into the Court of General Sessions.

This system of law and order, run from Dover, failed Margate in a number of ways. Most importantly, a Jurat of Dover, living in Dover, would not have the local knowledge required to be a good arbiter of events in Margate. There was also the problem that, to report a crime, the victim had to travel the twenty three miles to Dover to present his case to one of the Jurats, usually the Mayor of Dover. If the Mayor decided that the case should go for trial, the accuser, the accused and any witnesses would all have to travel to Dover for the trial and would probably have to stay overnight; if it was decided that the accused needed to be held in detention, it would be in Dover that they would be held. Finally, although the inhabitants of Margate could not be Jurats, as they could never be Freemen of Dover, they were expected to serve on the Grand and Petty Juries, with all the inconveniences and expenses associated with travelling to, and staying in, Dover.

To alleviate some of the problems, the Mayor of Dover appointed an inhabitant of Margate to be his representative in Margate, with the title of Deputy; the Deputy was also High Constable of Margate, with responsibility for overseeing law and order in the town. Until paid police forces were established in England in the second quarter of the nineteenth century there was a collective obligation on all the inhabitants to help maintain law and order in their neighbourhood. For almost 600 years the Statute of Winchester of 1285 laid down what was expected, which was that everyone had a duty to maintain the peace and had the right to arrest an offender.[2,18] The most common crimes were likely to be simple theft or housebreaking, and, if the offender was not caught red-handed, unpaid, part-time constables, often referred to as petty or parish constables, were expected to raise a hue and cry, and, with the help of the inhabitants, to chase the offender through the streets and arrest them. The petty constables were also responsible for presenting offenders at court for trial.

The effectiveness of the system relied on the quality of the petty constables and their willingness, or ability, to perform their duties in an efficient and conscientious manner. These duties were onerous and only someone of 'honesty, knowledge and ability' could be expected to perform the role well.[19] It was accepted that professionals such as clergymen, lawyers, attorneys and physicians could not be expected to fill the office, and so most petty constables were appointed from amongst the tradesmen and craftsmen of a town. The constables had, of course, to earn their livelihoods at the same time as carrying out their constableship duties, and only a man of some economic and social standing would have been able to devote the necessary time to these duties.

How well this system worked in Margate is unclear. The Deputy of Margate was appointed each year by the Mayor of Dover and many of the principal citizens of Margate held the position although later in the eighteenth century the position was taken over by the Cobb family. It is possible that the Margate Deputy, as High Constable, was the only constable in Margate at this time; there is no mention of any parish constables in the parish records. This is certainly suggested by the published report of a case of murder in the parish of St Laurence in 1652.[20] On December 12, 1652 Adam Spracking had 'cut, mangled, and murchered his own wife'. He was apprehended on the night of the murder, 'having his dagger in one hand, and pistol in the other hand' and the next day 'he was carried to Sandwich Jayl'. At his trial in April 1653 he pleaded 'that he was mad when he kill'd his wife, and that he knew not what he did'. At the trial it was described how Humphrey Pudner, the Deputy at Margate, had been called upon to help Edward Taddy at St Laurence to disarm Sprackling, and Pudner described how he had 'to disarm'd Mr Sprackling in an affray, which he made in a Taphouse in St John's Parish':

Edward Taddy deposed, that he being Constable, did assist Humphery Pudner, the Maior of Dovers Deputy, at St Johns parish, and Richard Langley, Deputy to the Maior of Sandwich, at St Laurence Parish, when they three had an Order to disarm Mr Sprackling, and, having taken and secured the Arms in his house, Mr Sprackling assaulted the said Edward Taddy, when he met him some moneths after; and Humphrey Pudner deposed, that he drew upon him also in the street, and, that he being Officer, disarm'd Mr Sprackling in an affray, which he made in a Taphouse in St John's Parish; and William Grant deposed, that in that Parish he drew at him, and had cleav'd his head with his Cutlash, if he had not put by the blow.

Sprackling was found guilty and hanged at Sandwich on April 27 1653.

Until the nineteenth century it was the victim who had to initiate any criminal prosecution: 'not only assaults but virtually all thefts and even some murders were left to the general public. That meant that responsibility for the initial expense and entire conduct of the prosecution was thrown on the victim and his or her family . . . As late as the mid-19th century no public official was responsible for ensuring that even the most serious offences were prosecuted'.[21] A victim would first have to identify the supposed guilty party; this was easy if the suspect was caught red-handed, but, if not, there was no modern police force to provide help. Having identified a suspect, the victim would present his case to the Mayor of Dover, who would decide if there was actually a 'case to answer'. If there was and if the case was sufficiently serious, the Mayor would issue a warrant to his Deputy at Margate for the arrest of the suspect. The suspect would be held in gaol in Dover until the case came for trial. The victim would face the cost of drawing up an indictment and hiring any necessary legal help, and the inconvenience and cost of travelling to Dover with his witnesses for a trial.

At the trial the emphasis was on a personal confrontation between the victim-prosecutor and the defendant. It would have been highly likely that the victim, the suspect and their respective families and friends would have known each other, and their relative social standing was likely to influence the outcome of the trial: 'In making their calculations, judges and jurors were influenced not simply by the abstract character of the various offences . . . Who the prisoner was — his character and reputation — was as crucial a question as what he had done (and even in some cases whether he had done it), and it was centrally the business of the trial to find the answer'.[22] All in all it is not surprising that many victims of crime chose to avoid taking the legal path at all. The *Times* in 1785 suggested that 'nine-tenths of the breaches against the laws escape detection from the trouble and charges consequent on prosecution'.[23]

There were several gaols in Dover where prisoners would be held until their cases come to trial. Until 1722 Dover distinguished between prisoners who were freemen of Dover and those who were not, who they referred to as 'foreigners'; prisoners from Margate, not being freemen, counted as foreigners.[24] The prison for foreigners at Dover was originally at Pennyless Bench, a paved area used by merchants for transacting their business, close to Boldware Gate, also known as Severus Gate, one of the gates in Dover's town wall. The prison for freemen was a tower in the town wall called Standfast, also known as Butchery Gate. In 1722 Standfast became the town jail when the system of having separate prisons for freemen and foreigners died out. Standfast continued in use until 1746 when it was condemned as unfit.

Standfast was not a very secure gaol, as shown by the case of Matthew Pain (or Payne), a Margate man committed to gaol in Dover in 1733, following his confession for robbery:[25]

On Monday night last one John Clun received a sum of money ... and being in company with Matthew Payne of that place [Margate], the latter offered to accompany him home, it being 12 o'clock, which was accepted of; and being got a little out of that Town, they shook hands, and friendly parted, Clun for St Peter's and Payne pretending to return to Margate; but the former had not gone above a mile, when he was knocked down by a person with a club, who robbed him of £6 13s 6d. Clun knowing him, on Tuesday the said Payne was taken up and examined, who at first denied the fact, but at last confessed it, signed his own confession, and was committed to Dover Castle. He was always a loose idle fellow and could never keep any Service.

Then, a month later, the Keeper of Dover gaol, Edward Green, placed an advertisement offering a reward of a guinea for Pain's recapture:[26]

Whereas Matthew Pain, of St John the Baptist in the Isle of Thanet, has broke out of Gaol at Dover, early Yesterday morning, with his irons on, whoever can apprehend him, or give Notice as he may be apprehended and delivered to Edward Green, Keeper of the said Gaol, shall have a Guinea reward. Note, the said Pain is about five feet eight inches high; black hair, full visage, pretty fresh complexion, about 23 years of age, and a stout body'd man.

There is no record of whether or not Matthew Pain was ever recaptured.

Debtors were dealt with differently from other prisoners. Debtors were expected to maintain themselves in prison, buying their own food and drink, clothing and bedding; they were allowed to work in prison, as long as this did not interfere with prison regulations. Although debtors from the town of Dover were generally housed in the town jail, debtors from elsewhere in the Cinque Ports, together with those guilty of offences against the revenue laws, were imprisoned in Dover castle.[16,37] In 1738, Captain Philemon Phillips, Commander of the Customs sloop at Deal, complained to the Customs Commissioners in London that when he applied to Dover for writs for the arrest of some local smugglers he was told that there was no point as there was nowhere to keep prisoners safely in the castle. Robert Wellard, the Register of Dover Castle, reported that 'all the prison rooms in the said Castle do now lay open, there having very lately several of the walls of the said rooms fallen in' and that there was not a single 'close room to put a man in sufficient to detain him for half an hour'.[38] Sometime later Fulbert de Dover's tower in the castle was converted into the prison for Cinque Port debtors and offenders against the Revenue laws.[16]

The complexity and expense of the legal system meant that simple disagreements between the poor would usually be settled in private. Even those with money and more of a social position to maintain would avoid legal action if they could. If a case actually went to court and the accused was found guilty, the judge could order a number of possible punishments. Before 1717 the punishment for all felonies was death except for the felony of petty larceny where the penalty was whipping. For minor misdemeanours the punishment could be a fine, whipping or public exposure in the stocks or pillory; after 1717 possible punishments also included transportation to the American colonies. It was not until the 1820s that many of these punishments were replaced by short periods in gaol, usually with hard labour. Although the court at Dover had jurisdiction over offences up to and including capital felonies, by 1835 'within the liberties of the Cinque Ports . . . capital offences, which are likely to be followed by executions, are generally sent for trial at the assizes of the adjoining county'.[3]

Unfortunately the lack of criminal records for Dover before about 1800 makes it impossible to say much about this period. In 1699 the parish overseers paid 7s 6d 'for a Journey to Dover about the Wench at John Benets, and for a Warrant to distraine' and 6s 3d 'for an Order of Sessions for to Whip the Wenches', the Wenches probably being the local prostitutes.[27] We know that there were stocks at Margate to punish minor offenders. The overseers' accounts for 1706 include payments of 18s 9d 'to Vall. Jewell and Edw. Bing for the new Stocks' and 6s 'to Vincent Barber in part for the new Stocks', the reference to 'new Stocks' implying, of course, that these were replacements for older stocks.[27] In 1712 Thomas Sprackling was paid £1 10s 3d 'for the Stocks', the large sum paid suggesting that these were yet another set of new stocks, and in 1736 Joshua Sandwell, a blacksmith, was paid 6s 6d 'for work done to the Stocks'.[28]

It is likely that Margate had a simple lock-up for prisoners who needed to be held securely before being transported to Dover to await trial; Birchington, for example, had a simple brick structure built in 1787 'at the end of the poor houses to confine ill-behaved riotous persons'.[29] It is not clear when such a lock-up was first built in Margate. John Lewis refers in 1723 to 'two watch-houses, and a watch-bell hung on the cage'.[14] 'Cage' was a term commonly used for 'lock-up' and the overseers' accounts for 1699 show a payment of 2s 6d 'to Andrew Hurst for mending the Cage'.[27] Later, when the Town Hall was built in Market Place, the opportunity was taken to construct under the Town Hall 'a cage to immure offenders against the law, during the pleasure of the magistrate'.[30]

Two types of crime for which Margate had a deserved reputation were smuggling and paultring, the latter being the removal of goods from stranded ships. Smuggling will be discussed separately at the end of this chapter, but as to taking goods from stranded ships, this had a long history at Margate (Chapter 3). In 1723 John Lewis, after praising Margate's sailors for being 'bold in going off to Ships in distress', went on to complain that 'it's a thousand pities that they are so apt to pilfer stranded Ships, and abuse those who have already suffered so much', which 'they themselves call by the proper name of *Paultring*, since nothing sure can be more vile and base, than under pretence of assisting the distressed Masters, and saving theirs and the Merchants' goods, to convert them to their own use by making what they call guile shares'.[14]

Legally, any 'wreck of the sea', 'driven on shore without any living creature upon it' would, in most parts of the country, belong to the King; if any man or beast escaped alive from the ship it was not counted as a wreck and the owner could claim any property saved from the ship within three months, later extended to a year and a day.[4,16] However, things were different in the Cinque Ports; a charter from the reign of Edward I gave the rights to wrecks, including flotsam and jetsam, to the Barons of the Cinque Ports 'to assist them in raising supplies for fitting out their fleet'. The later history of these rights is complex, the rights being taken by the Admiral of the Cinque Ports, an office that eventually became extinct, and then by the Jurats of the port where the wreck had been found, and finally by the Lord Warden of the Cinque Ports. Of course, these rights were of little practical value if a wreck had been stripped before the authorities heard about it, as often seemed to be the case.

What should have happened after a ship was wrecked was an orderly sale of any of the ship's cargo that had been saved, as happened, for example, after the wreck of a ship carrying deals from Norway in 1729:[31]

On Tuesday the 22 inst about ten of the clock in the forenoon will be exposed to Public Sale at the Pier in Margate, a ship's cargo of Deals, in several lots, to the highest bidder.

Note. The said vessel came from Norway, and having struck upon a Sand, was with difficulty brought into Margate Pier on Sunday last, having receiv'd so much Damage that she cannot be repair'd, and could not proceed further on her voyage.

An early example of what actually happened was recorded in 1298:[32]

Commission to Ralph de Sandwyco and Master William de Apperleye, to enquire by jury of Kent touching the complaint by William Martyn, that his ship, laden with armour and other goods, was, on its return to England from Flanders, in jeopardy off the land of Tanet, co. Kent, and that the armour and goods in her, being cast upon the shore, came to the hands of Thomas le Gront . . . and others of that county, to arrest the said armour and goods in whosesoever hands they may be, and restore them to the said William Martyn, or his attorney, on his proving them to be his.

In June 1345 the ship that was wrecked was carrying wine:[33]

To the sheriff of Kent. Order to take diligent information concerning 210 pipes of the King's wines in a ship which was wrecked near the Isle of Thanet, in coming from Gascony to London, the wine being scattered along the coast of that island and elsewhere, found and carried away by the men of those parts, and to cause all that wine which he finds to be taken into the king's hand and kept safely until further order, certifying the king from time to time of his action in the matter.

A few days later the Sheriff of Kent was able to report that 'he had arrested 14 tuns 53 pipes of that wine in divers places' and was keeping it safely until he had received further orders.[33] A pipe (or butt) of wine was 126 gallons, and a tun was equal to two pipes, so that of the original 210 pipes of wine on the ship, the Sheriff had managed to recover 81 pipes, leaving rather a lot unaccounted for.

In July 1579 the Privy Council provided 'A letter of assistance for the recovering of certaine clothes, &c, taken and spoiled out of a certaine hoye in the monethe of November last past by one Walter Dabernall and his complices, about Margate in the Isle of Thennet, divers parcells wherof are said to have come to the handes of divers th'inhubitauntes of the countie of Kent and Dorset about Lullworthe'.[34] Again, in November 1579 the Star Chamber wrote to 'Richard Barey, John Finnox and John Crispe . . . to cause restitucion to [be] made of certen goodes and merchandis spoyled and taken out of three hulkes driven on shore about the Downes by the inhabitantes of the Isle of Tennett and others there aboutes'.[35]

Serious action against paultring was finally taken early in the seventeenth century. In March 1602 Lord Cobham, Lord Warden of the Cinque Ports, appointed George Newman to be Judge of the Admiralty Court of the Cinque Port. Probably as a consequence of this appointment a harder line was taken over the stripping of wrecks. In August of that year an order was made 'in his Lordship's office, to arrest divers poor people prosecuted at the last Admiralty Court for things of small value found by them'.[36] However, the question arose 'whether these persons who dwell far off, by paying the duties due to his Lordship to the droit gatherers [at the various ports], might not be freed of coming hither to the Court on the 17th inst., as their charges in coming would cost them much more than what they have to pay', an arrangement to which the Lord Warden agreed. Also in August 1602 George Newman took depositions from three seamen from Ramsgate and one from Margate concerning a wreck some twenty years earlier off Cliff's End, Ramsgate.[36] The depositions give a better idea of what actually happened following a wreck. The deposition of John Coppyn of Ramsgate was:

Has known the Hope at Cliff's End in Thanet 40 years. A wreck of canvas happened there 30 years since, when the Lord Warden's officers and men took away and enjoyed the goods; 18 or 20 years since, another ship grounded, laden with deals, wax, &c. Deponent and divers others went on board, and the master of the ship desired them to stay, to save the goods from the spoil of the people of the country, which they did until the tide came, when they went on shore until it ebbed; going aboard again at low water, they met one Paramore by the ship's side, with a waggon, and 18 or 20 persons, who got on board before deponent and his company, saying that they would keep possession of the ship and goods, but not claiming any wreck, nor saying for whom they would keep possession. Deponent and his company getting on board, the others went away, the ship perished, and the Lord Warden and his officers had the disposing of the ship and goods. Within his remembrance, they have always had the disposing of wrecks in the Isle of Thanet.

Richard Saunders, also from Ramsgate, made a similar deposition:

Has known the Hope 30 years; 25 years since, a ship laden with cloth, &c. was cast away there, the men drowned, and the goods saved by the inhabitants of Ramsgate were disposed of by the Lord Warden's officers; 20 years since, another ship came aground there, laden with deal boards, wax, and copper, when Thos. Paramore of Minster went aboard with others, in right of Mr Wotton, and when John Coppyn of Ramsgate and others came to go aboard, Paramore willed them to keep off, but when they got on board, Paramore and his company went. All the goods saved and carried to Ramsgate out of that ship were disposed of by my Lord Warden's officers. Never knew any wreck goods saved or found by any inhabitants of Ramsgate, Broadstairs, or elsewhere, but they were disposed of by the Lord Warden's officers.

Finally, the account of John Bussher, of Margate, gave a picture of the competition between the men of Ramsgate and Margate:

20 years since a ship came on ground there [the Hope]; was then dwelling at Minster in Thanet, and Thos. Paramore, then of Minster, and servant to Sir Edw. Wotton, or to Mr. Thos. Wotton, requested him to go on board and seize her to the use of his master, but he refused. On Paramore's return, he said that the men of Ramsgate then aboard had beaten and tumbled him overboard, and had broken three or four of his men's heads, whereupon he wrote for directions to his master, who bade him demand soilage or groundage of the ship, but not any wrecks, as he had no right therewith. Does not know that any has anything to do with the disposition of wrecks but the Lord Warden's officers.

Church and Vestry

A further and vital part of the local government system was the parish. Although originally dealing just with ecclesiastical matters, from the 1530s onwards central government, seeing the parishes as working and available administrative units, started to load them with a wide range of non-religious responsibilities.[39] A statute of 1555 required the parish to maintain the local highways, and required each parish to appoint two surveyors to oversee this work. In 1572 parishes were required to appoint overseers of the poor to implement the new Poor Laws, as described in Chapter 4. Gradually the numbers of these statutory duties increased and, particularly for a town like Margate ruled without representation by Dover, the parish came to be what mattered most to the majority of the population.

The administration of the parish was in the hands of the parish vestry, named after the room in the church, the vestry, used for keeping the church vestments. The members of the vestry were the minister or vicar, any curates who might have been appointed, the churchwardens and various secular officers; they were responsible for the church building, and for setting and collecting a poor rate, for looking after the poor, maintaining law and order, and repairing the roads. The vestrymen would generally hold their meetings in the church vestry and would call meetings of the whole parish in the church, usually attended by all those who paid poor rates. These meetings would discuss all kinds of parish matters, often of a totally secular nature, and when the parish was divided in its views these meetings could become extremely heated and noisy.

The relationship between the minister and the vestry and parishioners was important for the minister as, although the vestry did not appoint him, they controlled the finances of the parish and the minister's income. Until the middle of the sixteenth century the minister's income at Margate was small, just 'a manse, a small glebe, two bushels of wheat, to be paid yearly at Midsummer, and a pension of eight pounds a year, paid out of Salmstone'.[14] In 1553 this was augmented with tithes on that part of the parish that was 'the borough of Margate', this being about a third of the whole parish.[40,41] These tithes were 'tithes of lambs, wool, piglings, geese, flax, wax and honey and other small tithes in the borough of Margate in the said parish'. The income of the minister also included 'all oblations of the four yearly principal days and feasts, and all personal tithes and Easter dues of the parishioners in the same parish'. The glebe land belonging to the vicarage at Margate made up about 15 acres, but about an acre of this land had been lost due to erosion by the sea.[14] Finally, to make a decent living the minster relied on fees for performing services, together with voluntary contributions from the congregation. The fees charged in 1577 were set out in the Parish Register:[14]

Duties belonging to the Vicar of St John's	
For Marriage and Banes	3s 6d
For Burial in a Sheet only	0s 6d
With a coffin	1s 0d
Yf the Corps be brought into the Church	2s 0d
For churching a Woman, but must compound for the Face-Cloth*	1s 0d
And the poorer Sort to pay only	0s 9d
Easter offering per pole	0s 6d

* This refers to the ancient custom of purifying a woman after childbirth, and, if the child died, the face-cloth used to cover the child at its Baptism would be used to wind the child in.

To fulfil their responsibility for looking after the fabric of the church the Churchwardens charged the inhabitants of the parish an annual cess (a tax). The many complaints about non-payment of the cess in the records of the Archdeacon's Visitations to St John's suggest that this was a particularly unpopular charge.[42] In 1592 the Churchwardens reported that Joseph Norwood, Leonard Spracklinge, Samuel Taddie, Henry Platt, and George Fleet were 'behind for a cess made for the Church and refuse to pay'; Joseph Norwood, one of the non-payers, was also a regular non-attender at church, as described later. Francis Parker was another repeat offender; in 1593 the Churchwardens reported that 'Francis Parker refuses to pay a cess made for the reparation of our Church, 6s 8d', in 1598 they reported him for not paying his 14s church cess for that year, in 1600 he was again reported 'for that he will not pay his cess according as he is set, namely at twenty shillings, done by the parish for the Church; and also he is a very negligent subject in coming to Church to Divine Service', and in

1601 he was reported 'for not paying his dues belonging unto the Church, being several times entreated to pay the same.' Alexander Violett, who we will see later caused the Churchwardens many problems, was also reported to the Archdeacon in 1600 'for that he refuseth to pay his cess for the Church, as he is cessed by the parishioners of the parish'. A more surprising name to appear in the records for 1600 was Nicholas Osborne, a former churchwarden. He was reported to the Archdeacon 'for that he will not pay his cess for the reparation of the Church, 8s'. He appeared before the Archdeacon's court in November 1600 when 'he alleged that the parishioners of St John's did owe him . . . £3 or £4 for business done by him about the necessary reparations of the said Church during the time of his churchwardenship, and therefore thinketh he is not bound to pay this present cess referred to'. His argument was supported by Valentine Pettit who declared 'that of his certain knowledge the parishioners of St John's do owe unto Mr Osborne sums of money or some sum of money, amounting to more than the several cesses for which the said Mr Osborne is presented by the churchwardens of the parish; especially they do owe unto Mr Osborne for a suit in law which he disbursed for the said parishioners lately, between them and the inhabitants of the town of Dover.' In 1615, John Johnson, 'a gentleman', was reported 'for not paying his cesses and other duties to the Church, namely, for his cess for the Church, 8s 4d; more for his poor, 7s 6d; more for breaking the ground and the great bell, 10s; more for paving the grave, 6s'. In January 1616 he appeared before the Archdeacon's Court to plead his case: 'he stated: that whereas he is presented for the breaking of the ground and ringing of the great bell for the burial of two of his children, which were lately buried in the Parish Church, the sum of 10s, and for the paving of the graves again 6s. The truth is that he did long since pay and satisfy the said several sums unto Thomas Bussher, late Parish Clerk for the same parish of St John's, who did in his life time collect and gather the same money to the use of the churchwardens'.

The Church played an important part in the life of most inhabitants of the parish. In fact, it would have been very hard to ignore religion at this time, what with the Reformation, the Puritans, and the English Civil War. The Reformation might have started with Henry VIII's attempt to persuade the pope to annul his marriage to Catherine of Aragon but, by the time of his death in 1547, it had turned into a full scale religious revolution. Until the Reformation, English churchgoers 'had been taught to believe that their best hope of salvation lay in leading a good life, and trusting in the range of sacraments and ceremonies supplied by the Catholic Church. Once a year, they confessed their sins to a priest, and were assured of God's forgiveness. Week on week, they attended the mass in their parish church, a service during which Christ became, in the form of bread and wine, as truly present as he had been on the cross of Calvary. They prayed in front of statues of the saints, and petitioned them to assist their plans and heal their ailments. When guilt or piety moved them, they gave alms to the poor, or went on pilgrimage to the great monastic houses, where relics and images of the saints were housed in reverential splendour'.[43]

This traditional form of worship was swept away by Protestant reformers under Henry VIII and his son Edward VI. Popish 'flummery and superstition' and the belief that salvation could be found in 'good works' was to be replaced by the belief that salvation could only be achieved by placing one's faith in the once-for-all sacrifice of Jesus Christ. In this the Bible was all important, and, in English translation, its words were to be preached in Church and read by ordinary people at home. In 1538 churchwardens were ordered to buy a Bible for their churches, and to extinguish the candles and lamps that used to burn before the images of saints and extinguish all the other lights used for religious purposes, except for those on the altar and before the Easter sepulchre. As described by John Lewis:[14]

In the Times of Popery, besides the High-Alter, as it was called, at the East end of the middle Chancel, there were Altars in this Church [St John's], dedicated to St George, St John and St Anne, and very probably, others for other particular saints. On, or over them, in Niches, stood the Images of the several Saints, before which were burnt Wax Lights, to whose Maintenance People used to contribute when alive, and leave Legacies when they died

The removal of these lights represented a very visible sign of the changes taking place. Charles Cotton lists a number of testators who had left money in their wills to maintain the lights in St John's:[44]

William Rooke, in 1448, left inter alia one peck of barley to the light of St George within this Church. Thomas Draper, also in 1448, left one peck of corn to the light of Corpus Christi. In 1414 John Sandere left 5s to the high altar, together with the other altars in the same Church; also 20d to the light in the presence of the image of the crucifix; also to John, the Vicar there, twelve pence; also to the light in the presence of the image of St John, 8d; also to the image of St Anne one quarter of barley in the hands of William Culmerhouse, for the making and sustaining of the light in the presence of the said image.

These lights or tapers were made in two houses called wax-houses, which used to stand on the south side of the churchyard, but burnt down in 1641.[44]

In 1547 it was ordered that all shrines and pictures of saints should be destroyed and many religious houses were closed. In 1548 four of the major ceremonies of the religious year were banned and any remaining religious images were ordered to be removed from parish churches. The effects on religious life over this short period were profound; most of the seasonal rituals of the English Church had been done away with, along with the ornaments that were such a part of them. From 1549 services were held in English, based on a new liturgy set out in the Book of Common Prayer.

The Protestant Reformation came to a sudden end in July 1553 with the death of Edward VI and the accession of the Catholic queen, Mary I. Edwardian statutes concerning alters and lights were repealed, and ceremonies and processions were reintroduced. However, in November 1558 Mary I died and her Protestant sister Elizabeth I came to the throne. In April 1559 Parliament passed a statute requiring the use of a new Protestant liturgy, based on that of 1552. An Act of Parliament in 1563, the Supremacy of the Crown Act, required schoolmasters and others to acknowledge on oath the royal supremacy, and the first canons of the new Church of England issued in 1571 laid down that 'it shall not be lawful for any to teach the Latin tongue or to instruct children, neither openly in the schools neither privately in any man's house, but whom the bishop of that diocese hath allowed and to whom he hath given licence to teach under the seal of his office.[45]

Radical Protestants, unhappy with the settlement of 1559 and its many compromises, believed that every remnant of 'popery' should be swept out of the Church of England. They were called Puritans by their enemies, a mocking reference to what was seen as their obsessive concern with purity of life and doctrine, but called themselves the 'godly'. Their vision was of a society in which everyone led a strictly ordered life, according to the mandates of the bible; behind their preaching and campaigning lay a deep concern with the final destiny of the individual soul. They obsessively scrutinized their own behaviour for signs that they were members of the 'elect' and would be saved, and were equally willing to condemn others for conspicuous failings such as drunkenness and fornication which would inevitably lead to damnation.

Until the 1630s most Puritans were content to press for reform within the Church of England but then more radical groups started to splinter off from the mother church. The English Baptist movement started in exile in Amsterdam in 1611 and then established itself in London, preaching the belief that only adults should be baptised. In 1633, a group believing in Calvinistic predestination broke away to form the Particular Baptist Church, those remaining with the original body becoming known as the General Baptists; many General Baptist churches later became Unitarian. To their opponents, both Particular and General Baptists were known as Anabaptists, a term that was also used loosely for many other Protestant Dissenters.

A further convulsion in English religious life followed the English Civil War of 1642-6 and the brief second Civil War of 1648 which led to the execution of Charles I in January 1649. The period of republican government that followed is referred to as the Interregnum or Commonwealth; in 1653 Parliament was dissolved by the army and Oliver Cromwell became Lord Protector, to be succeeded upon his death by his son Richard. The Interregnum lasted until the Restoration of Charles II in 1660. Over the period 1661-1665, following the Restoration, four acts were passed that effectively re-established the supremacy of the Anglican Church and put an end to a period of toleration for dissenting religions. The Acts became known as the Clarendon Code, after Edward Hyde, 1st Earl of Clarendon, who was Charles II's Lord Chancellor. The Acts reintroduced a system of licensing by Bishops to ensure that schoolmasters subscribed to the Thirty-nine Articles of the established church, and forbade conventicles [meetings for unauthorized worship] of more than 5 people who were not members of the same household. The second of the acts, the Act of Uniformity, made use of the Book of Common Prayer compulsory in all religious services and over two thousand clergymen who refused to comply with the act were expelled from the Church of England.

Those who refused to accept the Clarendon Code were referred to as Nonconformists or Dissenters and included Baptists, Presbyterians (who rejected government by bishops) and Quakers (members of the religious Society of Friends established by George Fox). For short periods in 1669 and 1672 Nonconformist meetings were allowed, as 'licensed conventicles' and, in 1689, after the Glorious Revolution in which the Roman Catholic James II was replaced by the Protestant William of Orange and his wife Mary, Nonconformists were allowed to license their meeting houses for public worship. A letter of 1675 from John Glover to Sir John Williamson, head of the government's intelligence network, reported on an attempt to build a conventicle house in Margate:[46]

February 12 1675: John Glover to Williamson.
The fanatic party are building a conventicle house here where we never had any before, and I know not why they go about it now unless it be in spite of the proclamation against them. They make great haste to get it up, and I tell them it may be it will be pulled down as fast ere long.

The records of the Archdeacon's Visitations to St John's reflect the upheavals of the time.[42] These records start in 1560, two years after the death of the Catholic Mary I and the succession of the Protestant Elizabeth I, and show that at the time the church building was in a poor state of repair. The vicar was Thomas Hewett who had been appointed in 1546, and so survived the changes from Catholic to Protestant, back to Catholic, and then finally back to Protestant again.[47] This might make him sound rather lacking in principle, but public opinion was generally against violent change, and clergy who avoided controversy and went on quietly attending their flock were left in peace. Thomas Hewett did not die until 1563, but at the end of his life he seems no longer to have been active in the parish as an entry in the records of the Archdeacon's Visitation in 1560 reads 'they have no vicar'.[42,47] In 1561 it was reported to the Archdeacon that 'their vicarage house is in ruin and that our chancel is unripped [that is, without tiles or slates]. That the nether part of the body of the Church is unrepaired. They have neither Vicar, nor hospitality kept.' In 1562 the report was that 'the vicarage is in decay for that the fruits [income] are not able to keep the same in repair. They lack the Homilies for the gang [i.e. Rogation] days, and the little book of prayers set forth by the authority of the Archbishop of Canterbury.' The Homilies refers to the *Book of Homilies*, a collection of sermons explaining the reformed doctrines of the church in greater depth than in the 39 Articles, and designed for vicars who lacked the experience and education needed to write their own sermons.

In 1565 'the churchyard is not sufficiently repaired. The vicarage is in ruin and decay. The place where the altar stood is not yet paved' and in 1569 'we lack a Bible in the largest Volume, and the Paraphrase of Erasmus which was stolen out of the Church a year ago'; the Paraphrase of Erasmus refers to Erasmus's *Paraphrase of the New Testament*. Despite these obvious signs of poverty there was at least a vicar in the parish, William Lesley [or Lester], who was reported to be 'hospitable according to his power', but he was not a graduate and was 'no preacher or licensed to preach'.[42]

In 1578 the Churchwardens reported 'that they lack the first part of the Homilies, the Paraphrase, [and] a cover of silver for their Communion Cup'. In 1581 the state of the building was still a problem: 'the nether part of our Church is not paved nor sufficiently repaired, and that they used to lay there lime, tiles, sand, and other rubbish, which serveth to their use of repairing the Church, and that they set there the parish ordnance [weapons], very unseemly for that place'. In 1585 'they lack a convenient book of Common Prayer, also a convenient and comely surplice. The pulpit is not comely and decently placed. There is no cloth for the pulpit, nor cloth of linen for the Communion Table', and again in 1586 'the pulpit is not decent', and in 1592 'we lack a cloth for the Communion Table; also the first part of the Book of Homilies'. Now, however, the Archdeacon finally came up with a solution: 'the churchwardens were ordered to provide a cloth for the Communion Table, a silk cloth for the pulpit, and the Book of Homilies'.

In 1591 the problem was with the vicar, Robert Jenkinson:

1. We present our Minister for being absent from service four Sabbaths together, from the 10th of October to the 1st of November. And at other times since Midsummer, two Sabbath Days.
2. Our Minister, for keeping the Register Book so that we know not whether the christenings and burials be entered into the book, yea or no.

3. Our Minister, for that his houses are not so largely maintained as heretofore they have been, and between the hall house and the barn there is a house burnt down and not set up again. Also the dove-house is let fall down, that belongeth to the Vicarage.

Despite these complaints, the parish continued largely untroubled by religious controversy. Only one parishioner, Richard Sharpe, was examined at an Archdeacon's Court for Puritan views, and that was in 1599; the grounds for his summons were detailed as follows:[42]

1. He hath of late published and affirmed that the Book of Common Prayer is heresy.
2. That the Litany in the Book of Common Prayer is a charm.
3. That no ministers are to be allowed in the Church but preaching ministers.
4. That the Sacraments are no Sacraments, being administered without a sermon.
5. That Common Prayer is not needful in Churches, because it may be read at home.
6. That where in the Litany we pray for travellers by sea and land, and for women labouring with child, that we do but pray for 'theeves and hawes'.
7. That Holy Days are not to be kept, because they be ordained by men, not God.

His defence to the charges was as follows:

To the first he denieth that he uttered the same; also the second.
To the third he confesseth that he hath said that he knew not whether unpreaching ministers were ministers or not.
To the fourth, he confesseth that he said he thought that the Sacrament was not Sacrament without a sermon.
To the fifth, he confesseth that he said that Common Prayer was not sufficient, because they received nothing thereby, and they could utter it at home.
To the sixth, he confesseth that he said he disliked the prayer, for then we prayed for the Spaniards and other enemies of the truth of God.
The seventh he denied the same. He owned and alleged that he hath not, nor doth obstinately affirm as before he hath confessed, but only uttered his opinion what it was; wherein so far forth as he hath erred, he is sorry and willing to be informed and reformed.

The Judge must have been impressed by Sharpe's contrite manner as he simply ordered that Sharpe 'go to Mr Simons, Vicar of St Nicholas in Thanet, or to Mr Jenkinson, Vicar of St John's, and confer with them or either of them, touching these matters for his instruction'.

Not surprisingly, disagreements would sometimes arise in these very difficult times between the ministers of neighbouring parishes. One such occurred in 1620, between the vicar of St Peter's the Apostle and William Stone, described as 'Minister and Lecturer at St John the Baptist':[42]

A presentment made by the Vicar of [the] parish of St Peter's the Apostle in Thanet, of the delinquents whose names and qualities hereunto are certified: —
1. Forasmuch as Thomas Elwood, a parishioner of this my parish, coming unto myself upon the 4th day of October last past, between the hours of eight and nine of the clock in the morning, about the baptizing of a son of his own, born unto him on Friday before in the evening, and then at the time of his coming to me pretended to be weak, having answer from me that I was even then ready to do my ministry, and replying that he had not as then his witnesses ready, but that he had to fetch them from Sandwich, which is a town five miles from us, did not only defer the baptism of his child until the next day, on the which I told him I had to be from home, but also without my leave and against my will procured Mr William Stone, Minister and Lecturer at St John the Baptist in the same Isle of Thanet, to baptise the same. I do by these presents present both him the same Thomas Elwood, the father of the child, and him the same William Stone, the Minister of the Baptism, unto your Court as delinquents against the wholesome and laudable constitutions of our Venerable Church, and humbly desire of the same your Reverend Court their correction.
2. Again, forasmuch as on the Sunday following, which was the 8th day of October, at what time the child baptized was brought into the Church according to another constitution of the same our Venerable Church, there to have the baptism thereof to be published unto the congregation, and with all to be further proceeded with all, according to our Venerable Church Order and Rites as by the last rubric in private baptism is appointed, the forenamed William Stone standing there at the font, as both the Minister of the former act and as one of the godfathers, did at what time I offered to minister unto the child the ceremonies receptant thereof into pastoral charge, together with the consignation, make strong and peremptory opposition, whose example was followed both by the forenamed Thomas Elwood, the father of the child, and also by Henry Joanes of the parish of St John the Baptist, who stood at my font as the other

godfather, and also by John Howman's wife of the parish of St Lawrence in Thanet, the midwife and holder of the child, who refused to deliver me the child or suffer me to minister unto it in her arms. I do by these presents present unto your Reverend Court all these same four forementioned persons, to wit, William Stone, Thomas Elwood, Henry Joanes, and good wife Howman, as open either contemners of our Church Order, or at the least disturbers of the Minister in his Ministry. By me, Leonard Rowntree, Vicar.

In 1620 the vicar of St John's was Humphry Wheatly, and the fact that William Stone was described as a Lecturer suggests that Wheatly was not a preaching Minister.[14] There is no record of the outcome of the complaint.

Wheatley died in 1631 to be replaced by Peter Criche [or Oriche or Creech] who drowned with his parish clerk on a voyage to London in a hoy.[14] Peter Chriche was replaced by John Banks who resigned the position in 1647 having been offered the 'rich rectory' of Ivy Church, in Romney Marsh.[14] One of Banks's innovations was, in 1641, to take an inventory of the contents of the church:[47]

A note of such goods and imployements as are belonging to the pishe church of St-John's ye Baptist, in the Isle of Thanett.
Comprising two silver cups, with one silver cover, used at the time of administering the Holy Communion.
Item — three pewter flaggones used at the like occasion, and were given by Mr Valentine Pettit, deceased.
Item — a deske; three books, one of Jewell's workes, the other two of the Acts and Monuments of the Church [Foxe's].
Item — a Bible, two bookes of Comon Prayer, a booke of Cannons, a booke of Homileyes, and other smalle bookes of paper appointed to bee read for several purposes.
Item — a Communion table, and a carpett thereunto belounging.
Item — two old tables, and one cushion.
Item — a newe pulpitt cloath and cushion, both of greane cloath.
Item — one old pulpitt cloath and cushion, both of silke.
Item — a surplus and a hoade.
Item — two chestes one with three lockes, and the other with one locke.
Item — one old trunke, and one pewter bason.
Item — foure laddera, a spade, a shovel, a spud, a ladle, and mattock.
Item — ten setting formes, one planke forme to worke on, and sixe old bell-wheels not serviceable.
Item — in the vestry, three tressells, a shoote for leade, and parte of a fourme for the sheets to runne; certaine old leade, and foure small piggs of leade.

Item — a saint's bell, a beer to carry the dead corps on, and xviii of bell metle.
Item — five peeces of new timber cont. by estimacton, two tun lyeing in Edward Mussared's place.
Item — one spill pin, one drift pin, an iron chisell, and some olde iron.
Item — a table cloath of linnen, and a napkin for the Communion table.
Item — in the steple, certaine posts of timber and planke to trusse the bells, three long peeces of timber, and two winch rowles.
Item — a new stoole to sett the coffins on in sermon time.

An inventory was taken each year up to 1653 and remained substantially the same. The mention of 'ten settinge formes' is interesting, and could refer to benches or simple pews for the parishioners. Thomas Staveley, in his *History of Churches in England* published in 1773, describes the early history of the pew:[48]

Now the churches were always furnished with some necessary seats for ease and convenience; yet those of that sort which we now have were set up but at, or since the Reformation, for many ceremonies, and processions, and other services, could not be performed, if seats had been posited as now they are. And for regulating the ancient seats, such as they were, I find this constitution in a synod held at Exeter by Peter Wivil, Bishop of that diocese, in the fifteenth year of King Edward III. 'Whereas we are given to understand, that the Parishioners do often quarrel about the seats, to the great scandal of the church, and disturbance of Divine Service, frequently two or more challenging the same seat; we do ordain that from henceforth none shall claim any property in any seat in the church except noblemen and patrons: And if any come into the church to say their prayers, let them do it in what place they please.' From this constitution, and for other reasons, I apprehend, that before Henry VIII his time, that is, before the Reformation was begun, there were not any pews or seats to be seen in our churches, except some that were appropriated to persons of quality and distinction: and some are apt to think, that those which our ancestors then had were moveable, and the property of the incumbent; if so, consequently at his disposal. For before the Reformation, it was the use for the people to thrust up together near the priest, without respect to the condition and qualities of persons: and some would place themselves near to some altar, pillar, or tomb, with the convenience of a matt, cushion, or some small stool or form, to rest upon. But when the service of the mass (performed generally at the high altar, the priest turning his back to the people) was laid aside, and Divine Service ordered to be read in a desk, then both that and the pulpit were placed for the most convenience of the people's hearing; and the whole church furnished with seats for that purpose; the ordering of the same being in the power of the ordinary [the minister], who placed the people and their families therein in decent manner, according to their respective ranks and qualities, as we see them continued to this day; and thereupon in time, some seats become appropriated to some certain capital messuages [houses] within the parish.

Certainly there was some form of seating in St John's church by 1615 as in that year, during the Archdeacon's visitation, the Churchwardens reported 'the wife of Robert Young and the wife of John Cosbye, for not taking their places that were appointed to them' and then 'on the 5th of May, Young appeared in Court and confessed: that she is now contended to take the place in the Church of St John in Thanet that is appointed unto her by the Commissioners'.[42] In fact, Mrs Young was still dissatisfied, and was called once again to appear at the Archdeacon's court on October 23 to announce again to the court that 'she is contented to sit in the seat appointed unto her by virtue of a commission taken out of this Court, and she do sit in the said seat appointed unto her'.[42] In another case, in 1626, two boys, Thomas Creed and Christopher Russell, had been fighting in church; Thomas Creed was questioned by the Churchwardens and his defence was that he had hit Russell with his elbow 'unawares' after Russell had pulled him 'out of his seat wherein he did peaceably sit to hear Divine Service'.

An entry in the parish registers reports that in 1714 a private gallery had been erected in the church, generating a long running argument about ownership of a pew in the gallery, which was only settled after a legal opinion had been obtained:[49]

In the year 1714 Mr Edward Bing & several other persons at that time Parishioners of St Johns Thanet, by the consent of the then Minister, Churchwardens & Inhabitants, erected a Gallery in the middle Chancel at the East end of the Parish Church there at their private expence, each of the Subscribers taking a separate Pew for the use of himself & his Family. Several of these Pews have been transferred at different times from one to another as Personal Property.

Mr Edward Bing died many years since possessed of his Pew in this Gallery leaving an only son Edward Bing his Executor & Residuary Legatee.

Mr Edward Bing the son enjoyed this Pew without interruption for his life. He died in or about the year 1774 leaving a Will, by which . . . [after] certain specific Legacies therein contained not comprehending this Pew, He gave all the residue of his personal estate to his Wife Ann Bing for her life & after her decease to his nephew Benjamin Solly his Executors & administrators.

In or about the month of May 1765 Edward Bing junior a Son of the last Mr Bing intermarried with Alice Cowell the Niece of Mrs Bing his Mother. He died in or about the year 1770 in the life time of his Father the last Mr Bing leaving the said Alice his Widow him surviving. She hath since intermarried with Mr Robert Eason & is now living.

Upon & for some time previous to the present Mrs Eason's marriage with the late Mr Edward Bing junior she was permitted, owing as it is presumed to the family connection by Mr Bing her Father in Law during his life & after his decease, by Mrs Bing his Widow & residuary Legatee for life during her life to have a Seat in the Pew above mentioned. This Seat having been enjoyed by Mrs Eason upwards of twenty years under such permission, Mrs Eason now claims a right hereto, which Mr Solly the substituted residuary Legatee of the last Mr Bing [denies].

The before mentioned Gallery is erected over a Chancel being private property & all the Galleries in the Church have been considered private property & locked up for security from being interrupted, & by long custom have been transferred from one to another & Pews in the Gallery have been customarily let & hired for different lengths of . . . [time?] as parties have agreed upon, Mr Solly having sold his part of [another] Gallery in the Church & taken possession of the above mentioned Pew.

Your Opinion is therefore requested Whether the Sole Property of this Pew is not vested in Mr Solly & whether he cannot maintain the same against Mr [sic] Eason's claim of a right to a seat therein. Upon the state of this Case I cannot see how Mrs Eason can maintain a claim of Right to a seat in this Pew, the Presumption is very strong indeed, to me it appears more than presumption, I think it to be very plain from the case stated, that her original & [continued] use of the Seat was from Family courtesy only, such courtesy as no Family that was not divided, could deny & such as one shou'd think wou'd never induce any one to set up a claim under. I think the property of the Pew, such as it is, is in Mr Solly . . . that he can maintain it against Mrs Eason.

E. Benson, Cant [Canterbury] 2 July 1785.

In 1643 the English Parliament decreed that a covenant should be taken by every Englishman over the age of eighteen, agreeing that the church would be reformed 'according to the word of God and the example of the best reformed churches'. In 1643 John Banks, then the minister at St John's, summoned the parishioners to the church where they swore 'to the solemn league and covenant', and the churchwarden's accounts include a charge of 3s 'for writing the covenant and parchment'.[47] Puritan families in many parts of the country at this time rejected traditional Christian names associated with Catholic saints for their children, and instead used names from the Old Testament or newly minted names descriptive of Christian values, such as 'Lovewell', 'Do Well' and 'Temperance'. This fashion did not catch on at St John's, the only new names appearing in the register being only mildly odd, such as 'Godlie', 'Mercy', 'Godgift' and 'Freegift'.[47] It seems the parish was continuing its tradition of religious moderation.

In 1653 Parliament ordered that the parish registers were to be taken out of the hands of ministers and given to a registrar, chosen by the parish and sworn in by a justice of the peace. Although no record of the administration of this oath is included in the registers for St John's, there is a record of the event in the neighbouring parish of St Peter's, and presumably the oath taken at St John's would have been very similar:[47]

The oath of John Baker for marriages, births, and burials, in the parish of St Peter the Appostle in the Isle of Thanet, administered before me, Thomas White, of the towne and port of Dovor, Jurat and Justice of the Peace there, and in the limbes and precincts thereof, this 1st day of June, 1654.

'You shall sweare that you shall duely and truly during the tyme you shull coutinew register Register all marriages, and birthes of children, and burialls of all sorts of people within the said parish of St Peter the Appostle in the said isle, and the names of everie of them, and the dates of the moneth and yeare of publicacion of marriages, births, and burialls, and ye parents, guardians and overseer's names, whereof you shall have notice according to the Act of Parliament in that behalfe made. So helpe you God.'

THO. WHITE

Many ministers protested when the registers were taken out of their hands. The following note occurs in the St John's register after a baptism on December 11, 1653:[47]

Henceforward untill [blank] you must look to have this register somewhat confused, for it was kept in confused times, and when the government was broken and imprisoned, when Hypocrisy reigned and proclaimed herself by the name of Religion, and this poore nation lay under an arbitrary government, our lives, libertyes, and estates for divers year last past being subject to be taken away by a vote of a piece of an House of Commons without any legall tryall or judgment by peers, according to the law untill ye Lord Generall of ye army took on him ye government and then we began to have some rules to live by.

The first registrar chosen at Margate was Edward Culmer, a member of a family renowned for its puritanical fervour; it was one of the Culmers who destroyed the stained glass windows of Canterbury Cathedral. It seems probable, from the way that he signed his name, that he could not write, but he did not hold the office for long, as he died in 1656. After his last signature in the register someone has written 'Exit Culmer'.[47] Culmer was replaced by the parish clerk, Francis Cory, who was able to write, and who held the post until 1693 when he died.

During the Interregnum marriages were generally, although not always, performed by magistrates rather than by a minister in a church. For example, on December 26, 1653, 'Edward Paine and Elizabeth Nash were married by Justice [he is sometimes called Major] Foach at his house at Monkton', and 'Richard Younng, Bach. and Ann Egender, Virgin ... were married by Justice Foach the 9th day of October, 1656'; marriage bans were sometimes published in the parish church and sometimes 'in Sandwich markett'.[47] It is not clear why Major Foach, a Justice of the Peace at Monkton, was marrying couples from Margate, as this would seem to represent an extension of the jurisdiction of the Kent magistrates into the Cinque Ports. Major Foach is probably the troop leader addressed in a letter from the Council of State in 1651 asking him to keep the peace in Kent:[50]

August 27, 1651. Council of State to Major Foach. We ordered you to march up to London, with your troop for strengthening the guards of the Parliament and city, since which, upon information received, we think you should remain in the quarters in which you were before our last order to you, in [Kent], and have a special care to prevent any trouble or insurrection in those parts by enemies to the peace, by hindering their meetings, and passing up and down the country, and stopping all persons who are suspicious, and cannot give a good account of their occasions. Be very careful in this business, there being more than ordinary cause.

John Banks was followed as minister in 1647 by John Laury [or Lawrey]; John Lawry died in 1655 and John Lewis reports that for the following few years there was no permanent minister at Margate.[14] It seems that the Churchwardens worked hard to find a suitable successor to John Lawry as their accounts include several charges for journeys to consult the former vicar, John Banks, who had moved to Ivy Church.[47] In 1657

Edward Riggs moved to the parish from Deal and, John Lewis reports, 'for [his] encouragement a collection was made that same year for building the chalk-wall round the Vicarage Green' and the Churchwardens accounts for 1658 contain the entry 'Paid to Francis Parker for two posts to make the Gate on Mr Riggs his Wall'.[14] Edward Riggs remained vicar until at least December 1659 when he married a couple in the church, but it is not known what happened to him after that; it is possible that he had to resign his position at the Restoration.[47] His successor, appointed in 1660, was Thomas Stephens [or Stevens], previously vicar of St Peter's. This was a strange appointment; Lewis records that he was removed from St Peter's 'for Incontinency', meaning that he had led a licentious life, and Lewis adds, he had 'some way or other rendered himself very obnoxious and unacceptable to the People of both Parishes [St Peter's and St John's]; but he did not continue here long.' In fact, he was buried at St John's on January 2 1662. 1662 was a momentous year for the Church of England as the passing of the Act of Uniformity that year, requiring the clergy to take an oath to follow the rites, ceremonies, and doctrines prescribed in the Book of Common Prayer, led to the expulsion of over 2000 clergymen from the Church. Four ministers were 'ejected' in this way in the Isle of Thanet, from St Peter's, St Lawrence, Monkton, and St Nicholas, but not from St John's.[51] It is not clear quite what implications can be drawn from this fact as John Lewis claimed that no minister was ejected from St John's simply because 'there was no settled minister' there at the time to be ejected.[51] However, a contemporary diarist recorded on July 27, 1662 that 'Mr [Stephen] Street, at St John's in this island, was silenced and put by preaching by Capt. Rook, by special order from the king himself, because the book that was set out concerning the execution of Col. Oakey and two others was seen at his house'.[51] The Colonel John Oakey referred to here was a religious radical, actively involved in the trial and execution of Charles I, who fled abroad but was arrested and executed in 1662. Possibly Stephen Street was a curate or assistant to the vicar at St John's; his daughter said 'that he only preached in this island [the Isle of Thanet] for some time occasionally'.[51]

What is clear is that Thomas Stephens was replaced by John Overing, previously curate at Minster. Overing had made himself very popular at Minster and the Churchwardens at St John's had requested that Overing move there after the departure of Edward Riggs, but had been unsuccessful in their request. After the death of Thomas Stephens they again applied to the Archbishop of Canterbury asking that Overing be appointed, and this time they were successful.[14,47] Unfortunately, they soon came to regret their decision, and in 1665 they made a number of serious complaints against Overing. One complaint was that he had been absent from the parish for a long period of time. This was a serious issue. If a minister was away from his parish he was expected to pay for a curate to carry out his duties during his absence; the 'cure [or care] of souls' by instruction, sermons and administration of the sacraments was seen as the prime responsibility of a parish priest. Failing in these duties could lead to sequestration [removal] of the assets of the parish such as tithes and glebe lands, which would be held by the Churchwardens until a new priest was appointed.[52] Unfortunately for Overing he had also fallen out with his Churchwardens, and the Archbishop took the decision that the assets of the parish should be sequestered. In July 1665 Overing applied to the Archdeacon's Court at Canterbury to have the sequestration lifted:[42]

On the 11th day of July 1665 Mr John Overing, cleric, Vicar of St John the Baptist, appeared in Court, and said: That he was absent from his Vicarage for about the space of three or four months at several times, but did in such his absence take care with the churchwardens for the supply and serving of the Cure, and see it was accordingly done, as he believeth, he promising the said churchwardens to allow according to the proportion of the living, and the said churchwardens and parishioners did seem to be therewith satisfied and contented.

And as to the obliterating of some letters in the Church, he said that whereas John Crampe, one of the churchwardens of St John's, had his name written or painted upon the wall of the said Church, by the name of John Crump, but he understanding his name to be John Crampe (he being commonly called by that name) did with his staff endeavour to make an "a" of the "u", which was all he did.

And as to his calling the sequestration a bug-bear, he said and confessed: That upon the churchwardens and some others of the parishioners telling him that by virtue of that sequestration he had lost his living, and had nothing to do there, he told them that as to that the sequestration was but a bug-bear, but he did not speak in any such contemptuous manner as is specified.

And as to the two days presented, namely, the 5 April and the 29 May last past, he saith that he wrote to the churchwardens to provide for the supplying of those days of the said Church, and he did know nothing to the contrary but that the Cure was served accordingly. Wherefore he humbly prayeth that the said sequestration may be decreed to be released, promising that he will constantly reside upon his said living and duly discharge the Cure thereof in all respects as by the Canons is required. Then the judge admonished him that he do reside upon his vicarage of St John's and duly discharge the Cure according to the Canons.

It is not clear what then happened to John Overing. The *Calendar of State Papers* for 1664-5 include a letter written to Joseph Williamson:[53]

5th February 1665. John Wakefield, Queen's College, Oxford, to Joseph Williamson. The Vicarage of St John, Isle of Thanet, worth £100 a year, is void by the removal of Mr Overing to Old Fish Street, London; it is in the gift of the Archbishop of Canterbury. Begs assistance to obtain it, if he thinks it worth the having.

In fact, John Overing never moved to a parish in the Diocese of London and certainly John Wakefield did not become Vicar of Margate; the next vicar of Margate was Nicholas Chewney, who was appointed in 1665 and died in 1685.[14,42,54] Chewney was followed by Gilbert Innys [Innes] who resigned in 1692 to go to Maidstone. John Lewis reports that the parish was so poor at this time that to encourage Innys to take the post 'the Principal Inhabitants of this Parish, obliged themselves to pay him yearly an Augmentation of £40'.[14] Innys was followed by George Stevens [Stephens] who left in 1697 to take up the post of vicar of Shrivingham, and, as reported resignedly by John Lewis, 'ever since . . . this poor Vicarage has been under sequestration, and served by . . . curates', John Johnson (1697-1703), John Warren (1703-1705) and John Lewis himself (1705-1747).[14,54] Lewis was certainly right that the position of vicar at St John's was a poor one. There were some tithes in the parish that went to the vicar, and some Glebe land, originally of about 15 acres, although about half an acre of Glebe land at a place called Sea-Deales and half an acre at Rockinstairs had been washed away by the sea. In 1709 the value of the living was estimated to be just £49 2s 6d a year.[14] However, this was not Lewis's only source of income, as, from 1708, he was also vicar of Minster in Thanet, worth £250 a year and held positions at Eastbridge and Saltwood, worth £30 and £80 a year, respectively.[55] Why St John's was in sequestration from 1697 is not known; after Lewis's death in 1747 the parish again obtained a vicar, so that the sequestration had presumably been lifted by then. John Lewis is, of course, best known to us as the author of his invaluable history of the Isle of Thanet, published in a first edition in 1723 and in a second edition in 1736.[14,40]

Surviving parish documents, apart from the registers of births, marriages and burials, are concerned mainly with the management of the poor (Chapter 4). However, entries in the volumes of the Visitations of the Archdeacon of Canterbury give us a picture of what petty crime and misbehaviour were like in Margate in the sixteenth and early seventeenth centuries.[42,56] During a visitation any 'improprieties', any matters of public scandal in the parish, would be reported by the churchwardens to the Archdeacon. The Archdeacon would then issue orders for any changes he thought necessary in the parish, together with a list of any individual penances he had imposed. Such penances were usually a simple 'Declaration Penance,' a confession to be read publicly in the church, reciting the offence and expressing penitence, although the penance could be performed in private if the churchwardens thought the offender was of generally good character or of good social standing. Those accused of more serious offences were summoned to appear before the Archdeacon's court in Canterbury.

Complaints made to the Archdeacon often concerned purely church matters such as regularly missing Sunday services. For this a parishioner would first be fined but, if they refused to pay the fine, they would be reported to the Archdeacon. In 1597 the churchwardens complained of Joseph Norwood, Nicholas Seare, and Robert Kirkby 'for that we demanded twelve pence apiece of them for their absence from Church, and they refuse to pay it.' Joseph Norwood was reported again in 1614 'for not coming to our Parish Church this twelvemonth to hear Divine Service'. Norwood was summoned to the Archdeacon's court later that year where Stephen Strong, a notary public, appearing on his behalf, said of Norwood 'that for three quarters of that year . . . he was so continually grieved with sickness and disease in his body, that he could not go unto his Parish Church, and for the rest of the time there were four other just and lawful causes that hindered him'. Norwood was fortunate to have a legal representative to speak for him; he could afford it as he was a member of one of the principal families of Margate.

Parishioners working on a Sunday were a common cause for complaint. Thomas Deale was reported in 1581 'for being absent from Common Prayer on the Sabbath Day, and for grinding with his windmill', Richard Knowler was reported in 1593 for using his beer-cart on the Sabbath Day, and in 1611 Robert Spracklinge was reported for 'reap[ing] the wheat of Thomas Spracklinge on the Sabbath day'. Drinking and playing sports instead of attending church was also frowned on. In 1600 'Alexander Borage, William Parker, Ralph Tebb, with the rest of their associates' were reported 'for playing at Bowles in time of Divine Service, forenoon and afternoon.' In 1605 William Huffe and John Taylor were found drinking in the house of Robert Harbie, a victualler, instead of attending church. In 1615 John Cosbie, another victualler was reported 'for entertaining of divers persons at sundry times, playing and drinking in time of Divine Service upon the Sabbath Days.' Cosbie's defence was that 'upon one Sunday in harvest time last past the churchwardens of the parish of St John's, coming into his house in the time of Divine Service in the afternoon, found two persons in his house going to play at tables, but what their names were he knoweth not, for that they were strangers, poor harvesters'; 'tables' was a popular game similar to backgammon, played on a flat board.[57] In 1610 Roger Coleman and his wife were reported 'for keeping victualing in the time of Divine Service on Trinity Sunday 1610, and since upon another Sunday, at which times they kept ill rule by selling drink and entertaining divers disordered persons in their house in Service time.' Roger Coleman was also reported 'for being a man given to excessive drinking and drunkenness,' and his wife for being 'a very malicious and contentious person among her neighbours, railing on them and troubling them.' Railing and scolding were seen as largely female vices likely to result in discord in the community. In 1561 Ann, the wife of Henry Paine, and Elizabeth Druett were reported as common scolds, and Ann was ordered to 'behave in future.' In 1598 Margaret Cates, the wife of Charles Cates, had also been reported 'for a railer and scolder, coming into the Church and misusing the schoolmaster in evil words, and throwing a stone at him in the Church, among the children.'

The churchwardens complained several times about fighting in and around the church. In 1578 they reported that 'Austen Carpenter did fight with one Gilbert Wimark in the churchyard, and there drew bludd.' In 1612 John Savage was reported for striking Paynton's servant in Church: he claimed that 'he and Paynton's servant being in the Church together, did then wrestle and strive together in jest, and some blows passed between them, but all was in merriment without any malice or anger between them.' In 1617 the minister accused Winter Churchman, a weaver, of 'striking of Leonard Browne, Parish Clerk, in the churchyard of St John's aforesaid, who would not desist from beating him till I myself came and pulled him from the said Leonard, lying under him.' Another case, already described, involved two boys, Thomas Creed and Christopher Russell, who 'did in the Church, in the time of Divine Service, strike each other with their hands or arms.' Creed was called to appear at the Archdeacon's Court, and claimed in his defence 'that he did unawares hit the said Russell with his elbow on the face, and thereby caused his nose to bleed' when Russell pulled him out of his seat.

Particular complaint was made of the general behaviour of John Covell, or Cavell. He was reported by the minister in 1613 'for that by the space of two years or at least twelve months last past or thereabouts, [he] hath been and is a great ale-house haunter and given to drunkenness, or at the least to excessive drinking, and for that in the said time he hath been and is at the said ale-house such a common gamester, and an enticer of others to excessive drinking, unthriftness, and drinking. Also that within the time aforesaid he hath attempted the chastity or offered very incontinent behaviour and gesture, with or unto divers women, hereafter if need require to be named. Also for that within the time aforesaid he hath been and is vehemently suspected to live incontinently with divers women, hereafter, as occasion shall need, to be named. Also for scoffing at and abusing me the said Vicar in divers ale-houses in the time aforesaid, by virifull speeches uttered before people, and by scurrilous and base gestures to the great contempt and depraving of my person and calling.'

The churchwardens also had problems with Alexander Violett. In 1588 he was first reported for being often absent from church on a Sunday; his excuse, when he appeared in Court was 'that he came not to the Church in that time for that he was bitten with a dog, and by manner thereof was not able to go to the Church'. Ten years later he was again reported for not attending church and for refusing to pay for 'four or five Sundays' absence, being demanded of him.' His excuse this time 'was for that he was not well, but grieved with a pain in his head and teeth so as he feared to come abroad, and also saith that many have died lately in the parish of St John's, as it is suspected of the plawge [plague], which also somewhat moved him to absence from Church'. He was reported yet again in 1603 for not coming to the Church for a whole year, for not receiving Communion for the last three years and for 'living most suspiciously in his house,' 'living suspiciously' being a phrase used to describe any behaviour of which the churchwardens disapproved, but particularly referring to sexual misconduct.[58] Benet Wayte, Alexander Violett's female servant, was also reported 'for not using to come to the Church, and for not receiving the Communion, living also suspiciously in the said house.' More seriously, Alexander Violett had been reported in 1597 for consulting with a 'witch or sorcerer'; his explanation was 'that he had a child was sick, and there came one Chambers, a woman that told him his child had the "yelow jandis," and gave his child medicine for it.' Paul Rigden was also accused of consulting with Chambers: Rigden confessed to the Court 'that his wife was sick and there was one mother Chambers that had done some good unto divers others that were sick; he sent for her, but not as a sorcerer or witch as alleged.' In fact witches were not particularly common in Margate. Alice Busshe of St Lawrence, but previously of St John's, had been convicted of being a witch in 1561 and was ordered to perform a penance at Christ Church, Canterbury and in the Market Place in Canterbury; she failed to appear on two occasions and was excommunicated.[56] In 1582 Goodwife Swane was reported 'for that she is vehemently suspected to be a witch, and she herself hath reported that she can make a drink, which she saith if she give it to any young man that she liketh well of, he shall be in love with her. And that she hath threatened one of her neighbours and upon words fell out with her, and told her that she would make her repent her falling out with her. And it is come to pass this same woman her neighbour hath never been well since.'

The Churchwardens were also responsible for ensuring that local schoolteachers and surgeons were properly licensed, and as described in Chapter 3, had occasion to report both unlicensed schoolteachers and, more worryingly, unlicensed surgeons such as Francis Carpenter, 'who being a smith by trade, doth practise surgery without license'. The impression given from reading these cases is of churchwardens trying to maintain good order in the community, particularly among the poor; the poor, of course, probably saw this as their 'betters' trying to interfere in their private lives. The number of cases of sexual wrongdoing, excessive drinking, and 'scolding' were rather small, only one or two cases being reported by the churchwardens at each visitation, but then Margate at the time was also very small.

Smuggling and the Customs at Margate

The nearest Margate got to organized crime was smuggling; Margate was well known as a smuggling town. In *Letters of Momus from Margate* published in 1777 Margate was described as being 'almost central to a great number of little villages ... which were originally the habitations of farmers and their dependants, but are now the receptacles of contraband goods. Indeed the whole Isle of Thanet exhibits only a general jumble of lawless confusion; everything is conducted by trick, and law and gospel are dispensed by smuggling'.[59,60] A writer to the *Morning Herald* in 1784 described Margate as a 'dirty, imposing, smuggling village'.[61] The Kent coast was, of course, ideally suited for smuggling, being close to both the continent and to London. Large scale smuggling started in England when the government tried to protect the manufacturers of woollen cloth by imposing a tax on the export of wool and yarn.[62] Smuggling then changed in the eighteenth century to the illegal import of a variety of goods, including jewellery, lace, silks, and, most importantly, tea, wines, spirits, tobacco and snuff, after the government started to impose duties on these goods to fund a long succession of wars. The peak of the smuggling trade was reached in the years 1700 to 1840; it was estimated that in 1773 15,000 men were engaged in smuggling in Kent alone, with an average of 1,500 gallons of Geneva (gin), 450 gallons of brandy and 4½ tons of tea being smuggled through Kent and Sussex per *day*, by 1783.[63]

The government took a number of steps to combat the smugglers and protect its revenues. A national customs system was created in 1275. The coastline of England was divided up into administrative regions, referred to as *ports*. Each port consisted of a *head port* and, usually, one or more *member ports*, together with a number of smaller landing places, called *creeks*.[64] Custom officials were based at the head port and at any member ports, but not at the creeks. Initially there were 13 head ports but, during the reign of Elizabeth I, this was increased to 21. One of the head ports was Sandwich, included in which were the member ports of Rochester,

Customs Officers

Coast-waiter: the officer who supervised the unloading of goods from ships from a British port.

Collector: the Customs official responsible for collecting customs duties in a port.

Comptroller: an alternative name for the Controller.

Controller: an official whose role was to check on the Customer.

Customer: originally the principal Customs official in charge of a port, and originally responsible for collecting customs duties in the port, a task later passed to the Collector. The post eventually became largely redundant, the most important official in practice being the Collector.

Land-surveyor: the officer in charge of the coast-waiters and land-waiters.

Land-waiter: the officer who supervised the unloading of goods from ships from foreign ports.

Riding officers: officers patrolling the coast line on horseback.

Searcher: an 'indoor' official who did not actually search ships or passengers, but supervised the import, export, and coastal business of the port.

Tide-surveyor: the officer in charge of the tide-waiters.

Tide-waiter: the officer who met ships arriving on high tide and ensured that all cargo was discharged into the custody of the land-waiter.

❋ ❋ ❋

Milton, Faversham and Dover, together with creeks at Queenborough, Whitstable, Margate, Ramsgate and Deal.[62] From time to time the membership changed, with Deal and Dover becoming head ports in the eighteenth century and Ramsgate and Folkestone achieving head port status in the nineteenth century.[62] It was not until 1732 that Margate became a member port rather than just a creek.

A confusingly large set of officers were responsible for running the customs establishments at these ports. There were originally three principal officers appointed by the Crown at each head port, the *customer*, the *controller* and the *searcher*.[65] The most important of these was the *customer*, who was responsible for the collection of customs duties in the port. With time the job of actually collecting the duties was passed to another official, the *collector*, and the job of the customer became that of returning the accounts each year to the Exchequer in London, and of monitoring the coastal trade of the port to prevent goods from being smuggled abroad. Later, the roles of customer and collector merged into one post that was sometimes called customer and sometimes collector. The second Crown appointment was the *controller*, who was appointed to act as a check on the customer. The controller was expected to keep an independent account of the port's overseas trade, sitting next to the customer in the customs house and making his own record of all overseas shipments and the duties paid on them. Each year the accounts of the controller were also sent to the Exchequer so that they could be checked against those of the customer. Although this might seem wasteful duplication, it was designed to minimize fraud.

The third of the Crown appointments at a headport was the *searcher*. His role was to supervise the import and export and coastal business of the port. Despite his name the searcher did not actually search either ships or passengers. Rather, he had two basic duties. The first was to confirm that the goods on a ship matched what was declared at the customs house which he did by overseeing the loading and unloading of cargoes. The second involved boarding outbound ships to inspect their cargoes and check that these matched the certificate of customs paid, known as a *cocket* or *coquet*, a word derived from the Latin phrase *quo quietus est*, meaning 'by which it is cleared'. The searcher was always the most likely of the customs officers to be corrupt because he could defraud the customs without any of his fellow officers knowing about it. The job of the searcher, like that of the customer, gradually changed with time and other, more junior, officials were appointed to carry out many of tasks he used to perform, particularly the *tide waiters*, the *land waiters*, and the *coast waiters*. *Tide waiters* met ships arriving on the high tide and made sure they tied up at the appropriate place on the quay; the tide waiters were overseen by a *tide surveyor*. A number of boatmen were employed to get the tide waiters on and off ships when they were anchored off shore. Once a vessel had tied up at the right place the unloading of goods would be supervised by a *land waiter*, if the ship was from foreign parts, or a *coast waiter*, if the ship was from a British port; the land and coast waiters were supervised by a *land surveyor*. Finally, *riding officers* patrolled the coast line on horseback for up to about 10 miles inland, to combat smuggling. Riding officers were often shared between head ports.

The Customs officials had to administer a complex set of laws, with an associated complex set of paperwork. The *coquet* was a small parchment receipt for the payment of export duties; goods carried along the coast required a coquet from the port of origin. Goods that had been brought in from abroad and on which duty had already been paid were allowed to go from port to part without the payment of any further duties, under a document called a *transire*. Documentation of this type was not, however, required for items of low value, judged not worth importing illegally; such goods, including timber, iron, hemp, rope and other 'heavy' goods, were referred to as '*gruff*' goods, in contrast to '*fine*' goods such as cloth, wine, jewellery and so on. Gruff goods were allowed to move from port to port without documentation, under '*let pass*' or 'sufferance'.

Despite the long history of the Customs service, it was not until 1671 that a permanent Board of Customs was established in London. The Board, as well as collecting customs revenue for the Treasury, was responsible for preventing and detecting smuggling, for which purpose they operated a fleet of boats patrolling the coast, referred to as the *water guard*.[63] The water guard and the smugglers were in constant competition over who had the fastest boats.[65] Initially the water guard only had modest smacks and sloops, but cutters and cruisers were then added, together with six-oared boats, although, unfortunately the smugglers response was simply to use light, open craft that could hide in the shallows where the large customs boats could not go. In 1698 a new branch of the Customs was formed to help in the fight against smuggling, known as the *Land*

Guard, consisting of 'surveyors and riding officers' who patrolled the coast on horseback, searching for contraband that had eluded the Revenue cutters; the service continued until 1865. Each officer of the Land Guard would normally patrol alone but could, in principal, call on help from the Army who, in the absence of a civilian police force, played an important role as guarantors of civil order.[66] In practice, although small local units of dragoons (regular mounted soldiers) might be called on for help, many dragoon officers resented taking orders from a revenue man and so provided little help.[63]

Customs officials, as part of their jobs, were expected to guard the coast and prevent the entry of people thought for one reason or another to be 'undesirable'; they were also expected to search people entering the country for letters that might help enemies of the Crown. Margate's proximity to the continent meant that it was often a source of worry to those in power. In 1326 a commission was issued to William de Grey and John de Shelvyng 'to guard all places along the coast of the Thames between Recolvre, Gruyston and Whitstapel and search in all places where ships put in, both those entering the realm and those leaving the realm, and to arrest all who are carrying letters prejudicial to the crown, and send such letters with all speed to the king: as he is informed that many persons, to evade the scrutiny of the persons appointed in the several ports for the capture of such letters, are frequently landed there in ships and boats'.[67] At the same time an equivalent commission was issued to Ralph de Sancto Laurencio and Thomas Pusserum for 'the coast of the isle of Thanet and the ports of the towns of Margate and Stanregg'.[67]

In 1345 the Abbot of St Augustine's, who owned much land in Thanet, kept a 'keeper' at Margate to control arrivals and departures from the town:[68]

Oct 13 1345. To the abbot of St Augustine's, Canterbury. Order to cause the port of Margate and all other maritime places in his lordship in those parts to be safely guarded, and to cause all those bringing letters from parts beyond or taking them thither, except letters of the king or from those of his alliance to him, to be arrested with their goods, without delay, and to keep them safely until further order, sending such letters to the king and council, so that after they have been examined the king may cause what seems good to the council to be done, certifying the king in chancery of the names of those arrested and their goods, although the king by divers writs ordered the mayors and bailiffs of ports on the sea coast of co. Kent to arrest such persons in the said form, yet certain persons bringing bulls [Papal edicts] and other things prejudicial to the king and the community of the realm have newly come to the port of Margate, through the default of the abbot and his keeper in that port.

In 1354 a proclamation was issued stating that no one could cross to the continent from Margate because of the lack of control there:[69]

To Bartholomew de Burgherssh, constable of Dover castle and warden of the Cinque Ports, or to him who supplies his place. Order to cause proclamation to be made that no one shall cross from England at the place of Mergate, or at other privy places on the sea coast in Kent, other than in one of the said ports where the king has ordained a scrutiny to be made so that none of those crossing may carry things prejudicial to him, and that no one coming to the realm from parts beyond shall land elsewhere, and to arrest any crossing or landing without the said ports after the proclamation, unless they are driven by a storm, with the goods found with them, and keep them and the goods until further order, as the king is informed that numbers of men cross to parts beyond the sea at Margate and other privy places in the said county, and land there with letters prejudicial to the king and his people.

In 1358 the prohibition was renewed, making it clear that no one should cross to the continent from Margate, but only from Dover:[70]

To Roger de Mortuo Mari, earl of March, constable of Dover castle and warden of the Cinque Ports, or to him who supplies his place in the port of Dover. Order not to permit any one to cross from any port or place in the liberty of the Cinque Ports, even if they have the king's licence to cross from any port, or from the port of Dover without special licence, to cause proclamation to be made that no one shall enter a ship or boat to cross or shall presume to cross at Sandwich, Mergate or elsewhere than Dover, upon pain of forfeiture, and if he finds any crossing after the proclamation contrary to the form of this order, to arrest them with their horses, harness and goods and keep them safely until further order, certifying the king in chancery from time to time of the persons and things and the value of the things so arrested.

A copy of the order was sent 'to the bailiffs of Mergate', bailiffs probably being an alternative name for the Pier Wardens.

The Cinque Ports treated their independence very seriously and all communications between the Crown and the ports were expected to be directed to the Lord Warden of the Cinque Ports. The Lord Warden of the Cinque Ports, who also held the post of Constable of Dover Castle, would then pass instructions on to the Deputy Constable, formerly known as the Lieutenant of Dover Castle. In February 1606 Henry Howard, first Earl of Northampton and Lord Warden of the Cinque Ports, wrote to Sir Thomas Fane, Lieutenant of Dover Castle, passing on a message he had received from the King, asking for a short, red-haired man to be arrested if he arrived in one of the ports:[71]

The Lord Warden to Sir Thomas Fane.
The matters I wrote to you about I am to recommend from the King's own mouth to myself. "I must require you with all speede possible to awake the Portes and charge them to putt on all their eyes of caution and curiouse observation whether any man do lande in port or creeke that is of little personage, a sharpishe nose, a shrimpishe face, a beard light auborne or somwhat more enclyninge to a reddishe yellowe, that he may be either stayed, till I have word or sent up, with sure garde of two or three, with so great care in the keepinge him from accesse or specche of any man till he be brought to me as I may answer both for myself and for the diligence and discretion of those that are putt in the leike trust in my absence to have an eye to these occurrences under me. It is likely that he will not tell his name, but he is northerly, which circumstance in his tongue may geve you some light also wherby to gesse at the right man, yf it be so happy that he fall into their handes, that knowe the right waye howe to handle him."

It is not recorded whether or not the man was spotted.

In May 1606 when the Lord Warden again wrote to the Lieutenant of Dover Castle, the problem was Irish beggars arriving unchecked at Margate:[72]

The Earl of Northampton to Sir Thomas Fane
I hear that the commissioners for passage at Dover and Margate have been of late very remiss in suffering great numbers of Irish beggars to be brought over and landed here, contrary to the express directions from my Lords of the Council. I pray you let them understand from me that if it be true, as it is reported, they shall not only run into danger themselves by their negligence, but cause an imputation and blame upon me.

In 1635, the Lord Warden, now Theophilus Howard, 2nd Earl of Suffolk, wrote to Henry Crispe, Comptroller of the Customs at Dover,[73] complaining that proper procedures for recording those arriving at the Cinque Ports, including Margate, had not been put in place:[74]

The Earl of Suffolk to Henry Crispe.
Whereas uppon notyce given by me to his Majestie and the Bord of the landinge of great numbers of strangers in the Portes within my government whoe in respect of troubles abord desyre to retyre into this kingdome for theire better safetie, his Majestie commiserating theire estate with the advise of the Bord was then pleased to admitt them passage and did in May last order and command me to give directions to keepe a particular booke or register of the names, surnames, qualities and professions of all such strangers as then were arived or from thence forward should arrive at any of the said Portes with an intent to reside in this realme, and that they should from tyme to tyme send up a true copye or transcript thereof. And that I should direct and charge the Maiors and others whome it should concerne not to permit the said strangers so landinge to dwell and reside in any of the said Portes [but] to repaire to any of the said inland townes and more remote from the seas. According to the purport of which order I did address my letters to the Porte townes in generall to put the same order in execution, and som of them did only make return unto me of the persons that landed, but have not caused them to departe the Porte townes; neither have they since theire last certificates in Michlemas terme last past made known unto me of the great numbers of people since arrived, wherein they deserve much blame no more to regard his Majesty's command in that behalfe, it beinge so dangerous to this kingdome that if any enimy should arise, the numbers of strangers might neere equalize if not exceede the strength of those townes, and secondly the tyme of yeare cominge on it is dangerous for infection of the plague and other infectious deseases, and thirdlie verie incommodious for theire owne inhabitantes in raysing the prizes of victualls; but not the least of all to myselfe in my accompte to his Majesty when I shall be called thereto, touchinge the performance of this service by them hitherto neglected. And therefore these are to praye and require you to send copies of this my letter unto all the Maiors of the townes within my government to require them that they spedilie put the said oider in presente execution in all particulars. And that they shall also spedille give an accompt thereof, especially from the townes of Dover, Sandwich, Margate, and Rye. . . .

And of all this I require as speedy an accompt as may be, because I knowe not how sone I shall be thereto called myselfe.

There were still problems with controlling entry at Margate in 1695:[75]

Sir William Trumbull to the Commissioners of the Customs. I am informed that a vessel, coming, as was pretended, from Ostend, landed lately at Margate about twenty persons, supposed to be foreigners and some of them officers, and it being a thing which may have very ill consequences if men coming from beyond seas are permitted to land without passes without any notice taken of it, I desire you will give orders to your officers at Margate and on that coast to look more diligently about them, and not suffer passengers to be put on shore without examining them, and taking a strict account of them; and if they are foreigners or his Majesty's subjects (unless officers in his Majesty's army), and have not passes, they are to detain them and give immediately an account thereof to me, together with their names and what they can discover of them, lest dangerous and disaffected persons to his Majesty's government be invited thither, when they find there is so easy an entrance into the kingdom and that they may pass unobserved.

In 1696 Sir William Trumball wrote to the 'Principal Officer of Customs at Margate' about three foreigners of 'evil design' expected to land at Margate:[76]

I send you herewith the descriptions of three foreigners, who are expected shortly to land at Margate or thereabouts, with some evil design. I therefore desire you to be very watchful over persons coming to your port from abroad. If you find any who come near these descriptions, you are to secure them and give immediate notice to me thereof; also if any such persons have already gone, I desire you to give me notice of them, and where they may probably be found.

Appended is a description of three suspected persons: —

The first is a large, tall, well-shaped man, with broad shoulders and handsome legs, pretty full eyes and very black, his eyebrows thick and rough; he has great hands, and black hair upon his fingers. He now wears a periwig, but intends to leave it off, his hair being jet black and frizzed. He is about 48 years old, and has a tanned complexion.

The second is a man of wit, and bold. He is large, rather high-shouldered, and hangs his head down a little. He has a light brown complexion, small eyes, a great nose, hanging cheeks, a long chin, a large mouth, and his teeth are white as ivory. His left arm is somewhat shorter than his right, which happened by a wound he received. His legs are ill-shaped, he is much wrinkled between his eyebrows, has a very fierce look and a sort of bullying air. He wears a very light periwig, but designs to leave it off. He is 55 years old.

The third is related to ------. He is little, broad-shouldered and long-waisted for his height. He has a large head and forehead, black eyes, and his eyebrows hang a little over his eyes, a great round nose, and cheeks like a trumpeter, a handsome chin and red lips, pretty white teeth, a hand like a ploughman, and well-shaped legs. He is considered a very good soldier, and is drawn in upon hopes of preferment.

The following year Sir William Trumball wrote to the Commissioners of Customs about several Irish men expected to arrive in Margate:[77]

I have received advice from Holland that several Irishmen, belonging to a marine regiment in the service of the French King, design to come over to England from Holland or Flanders, intending to make an attempt upon the King's person. You are to give directions immediately to your officers at the several ports, especially at Margate, whither the Flemish convoys usually come, to be very careful what passengers they permit to land, and to apprehend all persons, with their papers, who come without passes or whom they may have reason to suspect, sending notice thereof to me. I have as yet no other description of the persons, than that the sergeants wear blue coats with yellow trimming, and the private soldiers red coats with yellow trimming, if they have not changed their habit; but, even if they have, they may be distinguished by their speech, and discovered to be Irishmen.

Although the early history of the customs at Margate is obscure, we do know that in 1485 Thomas Creys, 'one of the yeomen of the King's chamber', was appointed to 'the office of searcher within the ports of Margate and Feversham, Kent, with wages &c out of the customs and subsidies of the said ports'.[78] In 1660 a letter from the Council of State to the Commissioners of Customs warned them that John Glover 'customer and searcher at Margate, and late postmaster there, is very intimate and holds correspondence with disaffected persons', for which reason he had been dismissed as postmaster; the Council suggested that the Commissioners of Customs 'remove Glover from being customer and searcher of that port [Margate], and to put Hooke into the employment, if you hold him qualified'.[79] It is not clear whether or not Glover was actually dismissed as customer and searcher but in 1672 we find him employed as commander of a Customs smack at Margate, with 'one mate, 6 men and a boy'.[80] Glover lived in some style in Margate in the town's largest house, the

Mansion House, but it seems that he over-reached himself financially and he died in debt in 1685 (Chapter 1).

Locating a customs smack at Margate was clearly not a success as in 1675 the smack was removed to Queenborough, and Glover was dismissed 'as an unnecessary officer'.[81] However, moving the smack to Queenborough was also not a success, and in 1676 it was decided to get rid of it and to use the money saved to increase the salary of the waiter and searcher at Margate from £20 a year to £40, so that he could keep a horse to be used 'for taking care of the Isle of Thanet'.[82] At the same time John Smith, the existing waiter and searcher at Margate, was sacked.[82]

At small ports like Margate it was common for one person to fill several posts, and the searcher at Margate was also the tide and land waiter. In 1682 John Hunt was referred to as 'surveyor, waiter and searcher' at Margate; in 1684 he was dismissed and replaced by Christopher Merett, previously waiter and searcher at Sandwich, even though it was suggested that Merett 'was too aged and infirm for that employment'.[83,84] In 1685 it was decided to remove the element of the waiter and searcher's salary that paid for him to keep a horse, and to use the money instead to maintain a boat and two men at Margate to protect the coast.[85] The hope was that a 'fit' boatman would be able to 'do the duty of waiters and searchers at land and be frequently in motion in their boats at sea occasionally as shipping shall approach their coasts'.[85] In August 1687 Thomas Ryder was appointed 'to be waiter and searcher and have the command of the boat and boatmen [at Margate] at £40 *per an.* salary'.[86] However, Thomas Ryder was dismissed in October 1687, to be replaced by Thomas Child.[87] In 1690 Thomas Child was dismissed to be replaced by Abraham Hough, although Hough was appointed just as waiter and searcher, suggesting that the idea that a boatman could do it all had not worked out.[88] For many years Abraham Hough was paid an extra £10 per year for 'keeping the wool register in the Isle of Thanet, being 10 miles from Sandwich, the principal port, and having often occasion to visit the wool growers there and to inspect the disposition of their wool'.[89] Abraham Hough was married to Hannah, one of the daughters of John Glover, the former waiter and searcher and postmaster at Margate.[90] Unfortunately no reasons are given in the Treasury Entry Books for why any particular customs officer was dismissed, but the frequency of dismissals at Margate suggests that the Board of Customs was unhappy with the way that the customs establishment was operating there.

In 1718 it was decided to base a tide surveyor and a boat and a boatman at Margate to board ships at anchor in Margate Road, because ships not being monitored by a tide surveyor had 'great opportunities ... for running their goods on shore' and 'several ships came into Margate from Holland and other parts without being inspected by any officer'.[91] However, by 1729 the Customs Commissioners had concluded that putting tidesmen and mariners on board ships at Deal and Margate had been 'of little service' and, instead, decided to establish 'four additional sloops at certain stations in the ports of Deal, Sandwich, Rochester, and London, to accompany ships up the river till they come under the care of the tide surveyors at Gravesend'.[92]

Successful smugglers, by the very nature of things, leave few written records to tell of their exploits, but we do at least know a little about their less successful colleagues. Some light is thrown on the kind of low-level smuggling that was probably common at Margate by two linked cases from the 1690s, involving a customs official, John Watkins, a one-time customs official Thomas Child, the local postmaster, Paul Hart, a local mariner and would-be spy, John Lethered, and Richard Laming, a wealthy Margate hoy-owner. The tale of John Lethered (or Lithered or Letherhead), part mariner and part spy, has been told by Rachel Weil in her book, *A plague of informers*.[93] In the early 1690s the Earl of Nottingham, the Secretary of State, arranged for spies to be sent to France to provide information about Jacobite plots against the Government and about the effects of the English blockade of Dunkirk. One of those recruited by his agent William Carter was John Lethered, a mariner who lived at Margate, owned his own boat, and made frequent trips between Margate and Dunkirk where he would usually stay about two weeks, arranging deals with the local merchants.[94,95] To enable him to report on the state of the French defences, Lethered was given a Royal Pass allowing him to travel freely to the coast of France. Lethered was expected to provide his first report to William Carter early in May 1691 but was delayed for a few days by a lack of wind.[95] When Carter visited Lethered's wife in Margate on May 27 Lethered had still not returned from France:[95]

William Carter to Nottingham, May 27 1691

Having been at Margett in the Isle of Thanet in expectation to have met with Jo. Letherhead back from Dunkirk, etc., but his wife hearing nothing from him since he went away puts her upon doubts of [his] being lost, for that he usually made two or three voyages in the time; but I suppose while any part of their Majesties' fleete lyes on the French coasts no English vessel, tho' never so constant a trader, will be suffered to come out of their ports.

Carter added in his letter that Lethered's wife 'intends this day to go to Canterbury amongst their merchants to see if any letters are come from Dunkirk. I could not get any of their names from her'. Her reluctance to give up any of the names suggests that some of Lethered's business might not have been totally legal.

It turned out that Lethered had experienced a number of problems while he was in Dunkirk, explaining his delayed return to Margate. He was later to attribute these problems to the actions of one the customs officers working at Margate, Abraham Hough. Little is known about Hough except that in November 1685 he had applied for a post in the Customs, 'he having been bred a merchant', and that he had been appointed waiter and searcher at Margate in April 1690, as a replacement for Thomas Child who was 'lately dismissed'.[96,97] Lethered claimed that Hough would not at first allow him to go to sea, 'which obliged him to show the said Huff [Hough] his pass', which sounds as if Hough was simply doing his job.[94] However, Lethered went on to claim that, having seen his pass, Hough told others about it and, feeling that his mission was now widely known about, he decided he should provide cover for his spying mission to Dunkirk by acting like a smuggler, buying goods in Dunkirk to smuggle back to Margate. Lethered arranged that an officer in Margate would seize these 'smuggled' goods, but then, in private, would 'quit the seizure', returning the goods to him, allowing him to sell them and regain his money. This plan failed, again because of Huff. According to Lethered, on his arrival back at Margate 'the said Huff with one John Anderson, pretending to have share in the seizure, the said Huff requiring some of the said goods to make cherry brandy, and being refused it, he made the designs of the deponents voyage ... public', putting at jeopardy any future spying trip to France. When Lethered finally met Edward Russell, Lord of the Admiralty, on June 2 1691, to report on what he had discovered in Dunkirk, the meeting did not go well. Russell reported to

Nottingham that 'I do not find his report very probable', but added that 'the custom house officers have been a little hard with him, which may frighten others from going on the like service'.[98]

Despite these setbacks, William Carter wrote to Nottingham in July saying that he had persuaded Letherhead to undertake a second journey, although he had to provide him with money as 'he was straitened for money (and the more for that his last return is still under seizure) but I have borrowed some for to set him out and promised to remit more to his wife in his absence... I shall be as frugal as the thing will bear in my own expense'.[99] Nottingham replied to Carter a few days later:[100]

I have received your letter, and have had an account that the man you employ has in a public house talked very openly of his designs, by which it may seem that he does not intend to act honestly, and therefore is in no fear of being discovered, or else by his own indiscretion he will bring his life in danger, so that if you are satisfied he will be true to his trust, you may do well to advise him to be more cautious in his behaviour and discourse.

Meanwhile it had become common knowledge, both at Margate and at Dunkirk, that Lethered was a spy and 'his merchant' at Dunkirk advised him not to go, but Carter devised a way 'to obviate that difficulty [by] not going into Dunkirk with his vessel, and yet to effect his design another way', which seems to have been by sailing to Calais.[99] At Margate though, Hough and Francis Diggs, the Deputy at Margate had, according to Lethered 'used all means to prevent his going the second time which so discouraged the seamen that when ready to sail they deserted this deponent [Lethered] being informed they would all be hanged'.[94] Lethered was only able to sail after John Watkins, described as 'an Officer to their Majesties Voluntary', as 'Messenger extraordinary for preventing the exportation of wool', and as a 'King's Officer', had agreed to sail with him, which encouraged the others.[94,101] Despite their cunning plan, Lithered was arrested as soon as he arrived in Calais, 'his design being made known at Dunkirk, by means of an information sent [there] from an officer in the Isle of Thanet'; John Watkins claimed that the information had come from Abraham Hough, or, at least, 'by his means.' Meanwhile feelings were running high in Margate: 'it was commonly reported that [Lethered] was gone to France almost as soon as he got out of sight, and his wife was abused by the mob, who rent her clothes from her and her flesh in several parts, telling her her husband was a rogue and gone to France to sell us'.[102]

Luckily for Lethered the Calais merchants spoke up for him and his crew, and they were all released. However, John Watkins explained that 'the said Lithered was forced (to prevent suspicion) to bring from there, some other prohibited goods' and, 'to keep his designs private' Watkins, together with Thomas Child, seized the goods when the boat arrived in Margate. The intention was then for the boat to continue on to London, 'but the vessel proving leaky, was forced to land the goods at Romansgate [Ramsgate].' The goods, nine parcels of thread, silk, and lace, were then carried from Ramsgate to Margate where John Watkins arranged for them to be left with Paul Hart the Postmaster at Margate until he could come to take them away. However, sometime later 'the said goods were forcibly seized, and taken out of the possession and custody of the said Paul Hart by Mr Wallford, Collector of Sandwich, Mr Fisher another officer of Sandwich, Mr Hough Surveyor of their Majesty's Customs at Margate, and Mr Francis Diggs, Deputy at Margate who assisted them'.

All this had cost Lethered dear. He presented a bill of his costs to the Commissioners of Customs asking them to pay 'what your Lordships shall think fit:[94]

The particulars of the Goods I was obliged to bring from [France] to colour my design and to save all our lives the Second Voyage (being discovered, viz)

53	pcs Black Lace	£158 9s
30	pcs White Lace	£167 19s
1	p coll of Lining	£13
220	Gallons of Brandy	£60 15s
5	Gallons of Wine	
4	p colls of Thread	£45
1	p coll of Silk cqt 4 remnants	

The value of my goods lost to me by Huff's [Hough's] interruption £445 3s
The Charges of my first voyage

	At Dunkirk for my vessel	£3 16s 6d
	For victualing	£5
	For a new cable and anchor	£5
	Mens wages	£12

The Charges of my second voyage

At Calais for my vessel	£4
For victualing	£3
Mens wages – The enterprise being dangerous by the discovery, and opposition was made by Abraham Huff and Frances Diggs who slighted their Majesty's pass and your Lordships authority	£24
Extraordinary charge I have been put to in fees and attendance and soliciting for my goods to save their majesty's charge	£12 4s 9d
Sum	£67 11s 3d
Total	£512 14s 3d
Received –	£22
	£490 14s 3d

At the end of July Lethered wrote to Nottingham asking that John Watkins 'who freely ventured his life along with me to encourage my seamen to go with me, may be employed to bring the said goods to London, he being the first that did seize them for their Majesties' use'. He also complained that 'my goods having by stress of weather received wet, will be much damnified should they lay long, being I have not the liberty to open them'.[101]

In July Lethered also launched a lengthy complaint against Hough with the Treasury, claiming that Hough 'having obtained a sight of [his] pass from his Majesty he forthwith published the same and the service that the said Lethered was engaged in, whereby their Majesty's service was greatly obstructed and the said Lethered put in danger of his life'.[94] This complaint was treated seriously by the Treasury in London who wrote to the Collector and Comptroller at Sandwich directing him 'forthwith to send the said Hough hither to answer the said charge'. The Collector was instructed to look into the complaint and 'inform yourselves by the best means you can of all the circumstances of the said publication ... and what public notice was taken thereof ... and what happened thereupon at Margate', all this 'without acquainting the said Hough' with what you are doing. At the end of September the Collector at Sandwich sent his conclusions to the Treasury:[94]

In obedience to your honours of the 26 instant touching the complaint against Hough the officer at Margate, upon all the inquiry that can be made there, Hough had a view of Lethered's pass, by reason the embargo was not then out and as he was officer upon the place we judge it was his duty so to do for had he not produced his pass to him he was obliged to have given bond before he departed the port, but how and by whom the pass came to be divulged is not known nor any person in Margate will charge him with it, neither will any person in Margate say but that he is well affected to the present government and we believe him to be such, in the whole we are able to inform your Honourables and that Hough will attend the Board speedily to make his defense.

The case was referred to the Commissioners of Customs for a hearing but, unfortunately, Hough was taken ill and could not meet them until early October. John Lethered suggested, unkindly, that Hough was indeed indisposed, 'but rather in mind than body' and that this had been brought on by the pressure of getting people in Margate to sign multiple affidavits and petitions in his favour, or, as Lethered put it, the true reason for Hough being unwell was 'that he has been all this time tampering with several persons to set their names to what he was pleased to form and draw in manor of certificates, which I suppose will be sent to your Lordships'.[102] Lethered said that he would be able to demonstrate 'by affidavits from most of the substantial and well-affected persons in and about Margate, that the majority of those who signed his [Hough's] certificates are criminals in this affair, as well as himself, especially Francis Diggs, John Baker, Valentine Jewell, Edward Bilting and several others, who are as true French [ie Jacobites] and self-interested persons as Mr Wells, the officer at Sandwich was. . . or as Mr Hough himself, when an officer in Sussex, or Sir Nicholas Butler when a Commissioner of the Customs, and I wished we had no great reason to suspect that there were some "of the same kidney" at that Honourable Board at this time.'

The Commissioners of Customs concluded that Lethered had no fresh evidence supporting his claim against Hough, which was based largely on unsubstantiated hearsay. Hough, on the other hand, had laid before them 'several certificates under the hands of most of the chief inhabitants at Margate testifying his good affection to the present Government', several of whom also affirmed that 'the first notice they had of the said Lethereds being in France was from one Egerton who went with him to Dunkirk [on] the former voyage and had publicly declared the same'; they concluded that they could find no support for the charges against Hough. They also concluded that John Watkins had no authority to seize Lethered's goods, a seizure which had, of course, been meant to be a sham, and that Hough was the only one legally entitled to the right of seizure. The Commissioners were, however, clearly worried that if Lethered was seen to have lost a lot of money on the two trips, this would discourage others from undertaking similar spying missions for the Government. The Commissioners therefore suggested to the Treasury that 'one half part of his [Hough's] moiety of the value of the [seized] goods may be disposed of between the said Watkins and Lethered. And as a further reward and encouragement to them for their diligence in the public service, that your Lordships will be pleased to become a means that they may be recompensed with their Majesty's moiety of the said goods after condemnation thereof'.

The final decision reached by the Treasury was even more favourable to Lethered:[103]

Lords of the Treasury to the Customs Commissioner to deliver to John Lethered that part of the goods seized by Abraham Hough, surveyor of Margate, to enable him [Lethered] to make up his account in order to his receiving satisfaction for the loss he has sustained; provided same be not of the growth and manufacture of France and that you have nothing to object hereto.

Thomas Child and John Lethered re-appear in the second case, a local smuggling case of 1693 involving Roger Laming, a rich local hoyman. Laming had been found guilty and fined at the Court of Exchequer in London for carrying to London six hundred pounds weight of French Silks and two hundred and fifty pounds weight of French Lace, prohibited goods at the time.[104,105] Penalties imposed by the Court of Exchequer could be severe, including seizure of the smuggled goods, forfeiture of the boat which carried the goods, fines amounting to several times the value of the smuggled goods, and imprisonment of those engaged in the smuggling.[65] Laming claimed that the fines imposed on him 'would prove the utter ruin of him and his family'. His defense was that the goods were put on his hoy by Thomas Child when only his servant John Edgington was on the boat, and, he said, that as a hoyman he 'comes to London virtually every fortnight and never opens parcels or trusses that are put on his hoy nor enquires what is put on board the same.'

In 1698 Laming addressed a petition to the King asking for the judgement against him to be reconsidered:

Petition of Roger Laming, of Margate in the island of Thanet, hoyman; setting forth that he has for many years been a hoyman and common carrier to and from Margate and London. In Oct., 1693, one Thomas Child, then an officer of the Customs at Margate, put on board the petitioner's hoy some goods for London, which were seized at London by Peregrine Bertie, Esq., an officer of the Customs, as prohibited goods: and the petitioner is informed that the goods, proving to be French silks and French lace, were afterwards condemned in the Court of Exchequer. And, although the goods were seized and condemned, yet in Trinity Term, 1696, an information of Devenerunt [a type of writ] was exhibited in the Court of Exchequer against the petitioner, in the name of Sir Thomas Trevor, for their value; and on the 1st inst. a verdict was given against him for £760 damages. The petitioner was not present when the goods were put on board, but they were taken on board by his servant, John Edgington. The petitioner never knew what was in the packets, as appears by affidavits annexed, nor was he to have a farthing more for carrying them than is given for other goods. The petitioner has a wife and many children. The servant had no reason to suspect the goods being put on board by an officer of the Customs. He prays that the Attorney General be directed to cause satisfaction to be entered upon the judgment.

Although Roger Laming described Thomas Child as 'then an officer of the Customs at Margate', this is probably not correct, as Thomas Child had been dismissed as waiter and searcher at Margate in 1690.[106] Nevertheless, Thomas Child might have still held an official position at Margate in 1693 as it is known that in 1696 he was 'deputy to the Sergeant of the Admiralty' at Margate; the Sergeant to the Admiralty was the principal droit gatherer appointed by the Lord Warden of the Cinque Ports with responsibility for enforcing orders of the Admiralty Court.[4,107]

The King referred Laming's petition to the Treasury for their decision and in July the Commissioners of Customs heard the case.[105] The principal prosecution witness was a Mr Saunders, described as 'a Common Importer and Conductor of prohibited goods.' Saunders laid before the court 'a book fairly kept containing the accompt of this transaction between him and his employers and partners, and the money by him expended in the carrying on their practices. Amongst which were diverse sums charged to be paid to the Letter **L** for the conveying of several parcels of prohibited goods, which sums are much above the common rates for carriage in the ordinary course of trade. And the said Saunders viva vow in the presence of the Petitioner, explained his accompt; that under the character **L** in that part of the said accompt was means the Petitioner Laming, and that the said severall sums were actually paid to him, for carrying goods from Margate to London.' Roger Laming, however, claimed, that he had never received any money from Saunders 'other than the sum of two shillings for the passage of him the said John Saunders in his [Laming's] hoy from Margate to London.' Supporting Roger Laming's claim was John Leathered who said that he was the mysterious '**L**' in Saunder's book; Lethered said that he had been acquainted with Saunders for about fourteen years 'and that during that time he hath received of the said Joseph Saunders several sums of money for bringing goods from France to England which he believeth are the sums entered in the said Joseph Saunder's book under the letter '**L**' and saith that at any time since his acquaintance with the said Joseph Saunders he never delivered any French or other prohibited goods whatsoever to Roger Laming ... or to any of his servants or agents either by the order of the said Joseph Sanders or for his use or by the order of any other person whatsoever.' Unfortunately for Laming, Lethered's evidence was not believed by the Commissioners as a note on the back of a report of the proceedings reads 'Read 16 Aug 98 – The petition is rejected'.

This was not the last we hear of Lethered. In 1697 he had been caught by Joseph Beverton, one of the riding officers of the customs at Canterbury, for 'going to France in the time of the late war'.[108] He was taken to Canterbury gaol and there 'he confessed his employers, to wit, Joseph Saunders, --- Eveden, and many others'. On the basis of his evidence Saunders was charged with the import of £760's worth of French silks. Earlier in 1697 it was reported that a vessel called the *Mary and Jane*, of

23 tons, of which Joseph Saunders had been 'late master' was 'seized in the port of Margate, and condemned in the High Court of Admiralty for coming out of France'.[109] In 1697 Paul Hart had been dismissed as Margate postmaster for 'assisting in the running a parcel of lace', presumably some further business with Lethered and Saunders.[110]

Saunders was to reappear in the House of Commons in 1698 at a discussion of 'Foreign Lustrings, and Clandestine Trade', lustrings being a type of glossy silk fabric.[111] There he reported that on the 11th of November 1692 'he sent a boat from Margate to Calais, John Lethered went master about eight voyages between that time and May 1694, and brought from 12 to 20 packets each return; only once he brought but seven; and generally 9 or 10 pieces in a packet'; he also reported that 'Mr Letherhed, master of the vessel Mr Saunders sent to Calais, had, at three times, five packets of silks from Gilbert at Calais', and that 'in 1694 he received from Arthur Goodwin, of Wivenhoe, in Essex, by the hands of Thomas Child, 4 packets of silks'. He went on to explain that 'he commonly sent his vessels over in ballast, but once sent over 10 bags of wool' and that 'he was paid 5s per pound weight freight for silks, and 6s per pound weight for lace'. There seems little doubt that Lethered had tried to use spying and his Government pass as a cover for his own smuggling.

In the eighteenth century the Customs officers based at Margate were responsible both for finding smuggled goods on the ships passing to and from London through the Margate roads, and for capturing smuggled goods landed locally. Although smuggling of wool was concentrated around Romney Marsh, the main area of wool production, woollen goods were sometimes captured by the Customs station at Margate.[62] In 1724 it was reported that 'some days since Mr Purnell, Surveyor of his Majesty's Customs at Margate, seiz'd thirteen casks of fine worsted yarn, on board of a ship bound for France, clear'd out of the Custom-House at London, as flour, which proves a very considerable seizure'.[112] It was not unknown for smugglers to try to recapture goods such as these, seized by the customs. In 1688, 'John Underdowne, gent., Customs officer at Margate, Kent' had seized a load of wool which he then stored in the barn of Thomas Fleet, at St Stephen, Kent, but which was then rescued by the smugglers:[113]

Treasury warrant, to Serjeant Ryley to arrest Thomas Price of Sterry [Sturry] and — Iverson of Canterbury and Thomas Fleet of St Stephen, Kent; the said Price and Iverson having with 50 persons unknown on the 5th Mar. inst. repaired to the barn of the said Fleet with clubs and staves and forcibly rescued and carried away towards the sea side 14 horse load of combed wool which had been seized that day by Jno. Underdowne, gent., Customs officer at Margate, Kent, the said officer and his assistant being beaten, bruised and wounded in the said rescue.

Despite the undoubted profits that could be made from smuggling wool, spirits and tobacco were more to the smuggler's taste. In 1686 the Customs Commissioners decided 'to sell a parcel of 109 cwts of tobacco stalks seized at Margate and to pay £10 to the seizer for his encouragement'.[114] The Commissioners, thinking that the tobacco stalks were only worth 'an inconsiderable value, viz., only £15 0s 6d' had at first decided to destroy them. However, they were informed that following the imposition of a new tax on tobacco, 'great quantities of tobacco stalks were imported into England from Holland and that by a new invention of rolling and pressing, it supplies the [place and] use of tobacco to the great prejudice of the revenue' and that the stalks were in fact worth the best part of £200; the Commissioners changed their minds, hence the sale.

In 1723 'Mr Purnall, a Custom-House Officer at Margate, having Intelligence of three open boats coming from France with brandy, went off in quest of them; but their friends on shore making a signal to them, they made off to sea; however Mr Parnall came up with one of the boats, and made a seizure of about 42 half anchors of brandy [a half anchor or half anker was a small barrel containing about 4 gallons]'.[115] In October 1726 30 small casks of French brandy were advertised for sale to the highest bidder in the Margate Customs House and a further 190 gallons of French brandy were advertised for sale 'in several Lotts' during August 1729 at 'the King's Warehouse in Margate'.[116,117] In 1753 it was reported that 'yesterday came up three smuggling boats, supposed to be laden with brandy and other accustom'd goods. Two of the Tidesmen belonging to this place went out in the evening, and seized ten half anchors of brandy, as they were running them ashore; but the smugglers got off with the rest of their cargoes'.[118]

Although the Customs Service had a waiter and searcher stationed at Margate to supervise the loading and unloading of goods, there was no quay for the transaction of foreign trade and it was the Collector at Sandwich who had responsibility for the customs at Margate.[119] By the 1720s the customs duties collected at Margate amounted to close to £2000 a year and, to save unnecessary trips to Sandwich, 'from time out of mind' the Collector at Sandwich had allowed the duties on foreign goods landed at Margate under the supervision of the landwaiter to be settled at Margate rather than at Sandwich.[120] However, this dispensation came to worry the Customs Commissioners in London and in 1728 they ordered an inquiry 'into the conduct of the collector of Sandwich in granting sufferances for landing wines and other fineable goods at Margate'.[120] The inquiry uncovered a range of abuses at Margate. One concerned wine from Spain and Portugal landed at Margate; it was found that 'the gauges of the casks appeared to be at least five or six gallons less than the lowest gauge of the like casks from the same places [imported] into the port of London, whereby the Crown lost in about nine years the Duties of above twenty five tons of wine'. There were similar problems with 'Linnen, fruit &c' landed at Margate, 'it not appearing they had been measured or weighed'. The Commissioners therefore 'gave strict directions to the Collector and Comptroller [at Sandwich] to observe the law and not to permit wine or any other foreign goods except timber, deal boards, hemp and other gruff goods to be landed at any other place than the lawfull keys' as 'should such indulgence be granted to the people at Margate the like will be expected by the traders of all other creeks and places where there are no lawfull keys which has often been desired and always refused and would subject the Revenue to great abuses and losses.'

The inquiry also found abuses in the coastal trade. Masters of coasting vessels loading just small quantities of foreign goods on which the custom duties were less than 20s, were allowed to take out a 'let pass' or 'transier' rather than having to take out a 'cocquet' and provide a bond. This system was abused in a number of ways, with the 'connivance or negligence' of customs officers. One abuse was for a ships' master to arrange for foreign goods of low value to be inserted in his let pass or transier but not to actually load these goods; the ship would then travel to a foreign port or meet another ship at sea and load up with goods of high value. An alternative was to obtain a let pass or transire for 'damaged or decayed' goods of low value that were actually on the ship, and then, having left the port, to 'fling the goods overboard' and then 'take in other goods of a better quality to the great precudice of the Revenues.' This type of fraud was sufficiently common for the Commissioners to give directions in 1728 'not only to Sandwich but to the Officers of all the other ports to oblige all Masters of coasting vessels loading any foreign goods to be carried from one port to another the dutys whereof mounted to twenty shillings and upwards to take out a cocquet and give bond according to Law'.

These new tougher regulations meant a lot of extra work for the mariners at Margate and so in 1731 the 'freeholders, traders, fishermen and other inhabitants' of Margate petitioned the Treasury 'that for their ease and the encouragement of the fishery and foreign trade a proper officer may be established at Margate to receive the Customs, to land all foreign goods, and to give the necessary dispatches to the hoys, &c'.[121] The petition explained how under the new system 'they have been obliged after payment of the duties on the arrival of a ship with wines in Margate Road to take the wines out and carry them to Sandwich in open boats, there to land them and in open boats to bring them round the Northforeland which is fifteen miles by sea back to Margate, by which the wines run a much greater hazard of leakage and perishing in quality than in the voyage home; besides the danger of losing the goods and the customs; and in a war with France small privateers often lurk under the Highlands that a foreign trade would be impracticable'. They also explained that the inhabitants of the Isle of Thanet 'in a great measure subsist by the fishery particularly that of herrings' and that 'by a late Order they cannot ship their herrings for foreign parts but in the presence of an officer from Sandwich which is eight mile and the delay of such officer's coming is frequently the loss of a Market'. There was also a problem with corn shipments: 'that the Growth of the island being chiefly corn and the inhabitants having no market but London keep hoys to carry the same weekly to Bear-Key the masters of which hoys are obliged to send to Sandwich for sufferances to load and for transires to clear to their great delay and expence'. The final problem was with importing coal: 'the said Island having little or no wood [they] are obliged to fetch coals from Newcastle, and the pier not being capable of receiving ships of great burthen they are frequently in danger of being lost for want of a proper Officer to receive the customs or to permit the Masters to lighten their ships'.

The Commissioners of Customs produced their response to the petition in January 1732.[120] Having rehearsed all the abuses at Margate, their report concluded: 'It will not be safe to comply with the petition without appointing a new set of lawful officers, with a custom house and lawful quay, distinct from Sandwich. This would be a great expense'. Fortunately the petitioners' rebuttal of the report persuaded the Commissioners to change their minds:[122]

Mr Francis Wyatt and Mr Robert Brooke attended the Commissioners with a Memorial by way of reply to the said report and the Commissioners on considering the said Memorial did agree in order to ease the traders of Margate as far as was consistent with their duty and in their power to direct the Customer and Comptroller to appoint Deputys at Margate to grant dispatches for all goods brought or carried coastways and corn and fish exported and to receive the dutys on coals and to discharge gruff goods on a special sufferance from the Officers at Sandwich as has been done in some other places . . . And the Customer and Comptroller of Sandwich having very lately appointed Deputys at Margate, orders will be sent down next week to the officers at Sandwich to admit them to their duty.

In August 1733 it was reported that a deputy-controller and deputy searcher had indeed been appointed at Margate, which was now a port rather than a mere creek: 'Treasury Warrant – Henry Petkin [Petken], Deputy Controller at Margate at £40 and ---- deputy searcher there at £35 for the accommodation of the traders of the Isle of Thanet and the town of Margate, now made a port'.[123] Henry Petken's career as a local brewer and maltster has been described in Chapter 1.

Lewis's 1736 map of Margate shows the Customs establishment at Margate, consisting of the King's watch house and the King's warehouse at the entrance to the Pier (Figure 3); the King's warehouse was a building provided by the Crown where the Customs officers could lodge goods securely, and where confiscated goods could be auctioned off.[40,124] It was usual for the Customs to rent suitable premises for their use.[65] At Margate premises were rented from the Pier wardens; the pier accounts for 1733-34 include a payment of £8 from the Collector at Sandwich for a year's rent and those for 1744-45 show that this rent was for 'the storehouse and Watch house'.[125]

By Christmas 1743 the Customs establishment at Margate had gown to one supervisor, one tide surveyor, one waiter and searcher, and seven boatmen, together with four riding officers who had to cover Margate, Ramsgate and Kingsgate.[126] The Margate men had an average age of almost 42, as follows:

	Age
Thomas Ketcherell, Supervisor	32
Gervas Cowper, Tide Surveyor	34
7 Boatmen	
Thomas Moulden	53
Henry Bassett	52
Bradwell Brothers	44
Edward Marshall	51
John Dibock	34
Thomas Malpas	36
John Friend	32
William Hewett, Waiter and Searcher	49

Despite their age, it was reported that 'the officers above mentioned are in good health and are able to do their duty'. At Christmas 1749 the size of the establishment was the same, as were the personel, except that John Friend had left and been replaced by Charles Crickett.[127] Noticeable are the large number of boatmen, manning the boats now patrolling the coast. In 1743 the Tide Surveyor at Margate, Gervas Cowper, wrote to the Customs House in London requesting a new vessel as 'the six oared Boat there is quite worn out and not fit for the Service'.[128] In 1749 he reported 'that the old boarding boat is so bad that she is not fit to go to sea in, and that to repair her would cost more than she is worth' and he requested permission to order a new boat, costing 'twenty four pounds sixteen shillings and a penny'.[129]

While the water guard protected the coast from the sea, riding officers protected it from the land. A riding officer had been appointed as early as 1697 to patrol the Thanet coast:[130]

Copy of a letter from the Commissioners of Customs to the collector of Dover. They agreed to present Jeoffrey Haford to be established by the Lords of the Treasury, as a riding surveyor, for the guard of the Isle of Thanet and the adjacent coast; and that he should reside at Margrett [Margate]

By 1735 Riding Officers were no longer based at Margate but two were stationed at Birchington to cover the coast from Reculvers to Margate, together with one each at Ramsgate and Broadstairs to cover jointly the coast from Sandwich to Margate.[131] John Collier, the Surveyor General of Riding Officers in Kent, judged that the two Riding Officers stationed at Birchington in 1735, Gervas Cowper and Thomas Thunder 'are both brisk young men & very capable of performing their duty but on inspecting their Journals & enquiring of their Supervisor have reason to believe they have of late been remiss in observing their Instructions as to patrolling their district but on admonishing them have promised to be very careful and diligent'.[131] Collier was able to report in 1736 that having 'admonished' Cowper and Thunder, they 'are more diligent in discharge of their Duty' but he now had a problem with Edward Elsted, the Riding Officer stationed at Broadstairs: 'Elsted was a little lame on my survey and I observed but little duty done by his Journal & on enquiry of his brother Officers, for which I reprimanded him & he promises a future diligent behaviour & I directed his Supervisor to have a particular eye over him.' In 1740 Elsted was more active having, with Edward Bunting the Riding Officer at Ramsgate, seized 'forty gallons and a half of foreign brandy.' Unfortunately though, in 1740 Collier again found fault with Cowper and Thunder, as, although they had 'very good horses and arms', he found 'but little done by them having since my last survey made but one Seizure of 17 gallons of Rum which belonged to William Born and John Darker of Margate; on examining these Officers and their Journals they gave an account of several persons in the Island they suspected to carry on the Smuggling Trade but did not find they had proof against any of them. I charged them with being Indolent in the Execution of their Duty and that on my report Your Honours would be displeased with them and think them very remiss and that if they did not more exert themselves they must expect to be dismissed and more vigilant persons employed. And they promised to be very careful and diligent'. Cowper and Thunder had a better year in 1741: 'These Officers since my last Survey have made ten Seizures consisting of a horse, a boat, 49 Gallons of rum, 4 Gallons of brandy, 80 pounds weight of tea, 28 pounds weight of coffee, 80 pounds of tobacco, 68 yards of handkerchiefs and a parcell of all spice & beads. These Officers prosecuted before the Justices of the peace of the County, Benjamun Damaster, Roger Fagge, and Peter Dunskin, three persons in whose custody part of the above Goods were found but the Justices would give no penalty against them'. Gervas Cooper was promoted to the position of Tide Surveyor at Margate in 1743, in place of John Barber, 'the late Tide Surveyor'.

John Collier also reported on the customs establishment at Margate, where, from 1734 to 1742, the Tide Surveyor was John Barber, who, Collier noted, was also responsible for keeping the Wool Register.[131] In 1734 Collier reported that 'I found at [Margate] and at Ramsgate and Broadstairs considerable quantities of Wine and Brandy which was taken up floating at sea and is secured in warehouses in a safe manner'. In 1735 John Barber reported that one more boatman was required at Margate, as he only had six boatmen and six men were required to take the Margate boat out to sea; an extra man would allow one man 'to be on shore and on the Pier when he [John Barber] is out with his boat' and 'it would be of very good service and more than compensate the charge thereof'.[131] In 1736 Collier reported that the extra boatman had been appointed at Margate; the new boatman 'one John Debock . . . is a stout active man & the Tyde surveyor thinks him to be of great service to the Revenue in preventing the clandestine landing of goods'. In 1740 Collier 'mustered the seven Marriners belonging to the Boat and found them well in health and of ability to do service' and added that William Hewett, the Waiter and Searcher at Margate was 'a diligent and good Officer'. He reported that they 'appeared to be wanting a Jack Flag for their Boat and a new Ensign to hoist on the Flag Staff on shore as a Signal to Captain Long or other Sloops and vessels in the service of the Revenue'.

In 1744 Gervas Cowper, now the Surveyor at Margate, wrote to London reporting that 'a shed is . . . necessary to shelter their Great Boat particularly during the summer season' and 'that there is a shed already built at the expense of Capt. Long, late Commander of the Princess Caroline Sloop, and in which he used to keep the Great Boat, which has been valued by indifferent persons who think the same to be reasonably worth thirty shillings and that to erect a new one would cost a great deal more'; he asked that he be given an 'allowance for the said shed as it stands, seeing himself obliged to have one if that is taken away by Capt. Long'.[132] It seems that Gervas Cowper was allowed his shed since in 1745 London enquired about the price of the shed 'for the service of the Surveyors boat' and were assured that 'it is a very good shelter and is worth thirty shillings'.[133]

There are surprisingly few reports of the capture of smugglers in the Isle of Thanet and widespread collusion was suspected between the smugglers and the Custom officers.[134] A letter sent by Gervas Cowper in 1743 provides another possible explanation — the large numbers of men in the smuggling gangs and their willingness to use violence. Cowper explained that on one occasion 'he and his men were out along the coast and at night five of them met with a Gang of Smugglers, arm'd about 24 in number who beat the said officers very much, particularly Henry Bassett, whose head is in such a miserable condition that the surveyor thought proper to put him under the care of a surgeon which we humbly hope your Hons. will approve of'.[135] The Surveyor reported that smugglers 'travel in such Gangs and so well-armed that it is impossible for the officers to cope with them, there being seldom or never less than 30 in a gang who bid defiance to all the officers when they meet them'.[135]

The customs officers at Margate were themselves armed. In 1745 Gervas Cowper was asked 'to explain the necessity of firearms for his people, and when they were last provided'.[136] The arms available were, in fact, not always sufficient. In 1747 Gervas Cowper wrote to London about a seizure of tea asking for 'an allowance to be made to . . . several people of Margate and Birchington . . . without whose assistance with firearms the seizure could not have been made' as the officers at Margate only had four pistols and two blunderbusses between them.[137] It was agreed that the 23 inhabitants involved in the seizure should receive rewards totalling £70, individual rewards varying between £4 4s and £1.[138]

CHAPTER 6

Riots and War

Riots

In June 1381 the Peasants' Revolt, the major uprising of the Middle Ages, broke out, mainly in southern and eastern England, the wealthiest parts of the country, and despite its name, involved towns as well as countryside.[1,2] The background to the riots was a simmering discontent with the local gentry and the Church and the ways in which they tried to control the lives of the poor, some of whom were unfree serfs forced to work on their lord's lands for a period of time each year. What finally sparked off the riot was, however, the imposition of a poll tax on both rich and poor. Under the leadership of Wat Tyler the Kentish rebels marched on London to be joined by rebels from Surrey and Sussex. There, with the support of the London mob, they unleashed an orgy of destruction, freeing prisoners, lynching lawyers, and burning buildings; the chancellor and treasurer of England were seized and summarily beheaded. King Richard II, then only 14 years old, conceded the rioter's demands and granted a free pardon to all, although Wat Tyler was killed in a scuffle with the Lord Mayor of London. The rebellion lasted only a few days before the authorities regained control and executed the leaders of the revolt.

In Kent the rebellion started in early June. Sir Simon de Burley, a courtier close to Richard II, had imprisoned a Kentish man, Robert Belling, in Rochester Castle, claiming that he was a serf escaped from one of his estates. After a meeting at Dartford, a large crowd travelled to Maidstone, where they stormed the gaol, reaching Rochester on 6 June, breaking into the Castle and releasing Belling. Although many of the rebels then dispersed, some, under the leadership of Wat Tyler, advanced to Canterbury, entering the city without resistance on 10 June. There they attacked properties in the city, murdered the Archbishop, Simon Sudbury, and others they considered to be their enemies, and released prisoners from the city gaol. The next morning Wat Tyler with several thousand rebels left Canterbury and proceeded to London. Inspired by the arrival of Wat Tyler and the rebels in Canterbury, the Thanet revolt broke out at St Lawrence (Ramsgate) on 13 June and at St John's on 24 June, that at St John's being led by a local curate, William ate Stone the younger.[3] At St Lawrence six men, including 'John Tayllor, Sacristan of the Church of St John in Thanet, and John Bocher, Clerk of the said church of Thanet', made a proclamation that the house of William Medmenham in Manston should be attacked; Medmenham was Steward of several Manors and keeper of their Court Rolls, as well as Receiver of the King's Taxes for the County of Kent. The intention was not only to burn his rolls and books but to pull down his house and, if they could find him, to 'kill him, and cut off his head from his body'. A crowd about 200 strong attacked his house. They 'feloniously broke open the gates, doors, chambers, and chests of the said William and carried away his goods and chattels to the value of twenty marks' and burnt his 'books and muniments' but, fortunately for him, did not find Medmenham himself. The proclamation made at St John's on 24 June was milder, 'that no tenant should do service or custom to the lordships in Thanet, as they have aforetime done'. On 8 July Medmenham's house in Canterbury was also looted and John Boucher [Bocher], the clerk at St John's, led a raid on the Canterbury house of John Wynnepeny 'and feloniously compelled him to pay a ransom of thirty-two shillings'.[3]

The enquiry into these events was heard by two jurors of the Hundred of Ringslow, William Daundelion (Dent-de-lion) and Thomas Edrich and three constables, Stephen Colluere (Collier), Gervase Saghiere (Sayer) and Simon Fygge, and are recorded in 'Presentationes de Malefactoribus quie surrexerunt contra Sominum Regem, 4 et 5 Ric. II'.[3] Two presentments relate to the rebels at St John's:

I. Presentments of malefactors who have risen against our Lord the King (4. and 5. Ric. II.)
Be it remembered, — that, on St John the Baptists Day, in the fourth (fifth) year of the reign of King Richard the Second after the conquest (June 24th, 1381), at St John's (Margate) in Thanet [Tanet], William Tolone, John Jory, Stephen Samuel, William atte Stone the younger, and John Michelat, raised a cry, that no tenant should do service or custom to the lordships in Thanet, as they have aforetime done, under pain of forfeiture of their goods and the cutting off of

their heads. And also, that they should not suffer any distress to be taken, under the above-said penalty.

And also, the aforesaid men raised another cry, on the day of the Feast of Corpus Christi, in the above-said year (June 13, 1381), at St Laurence in Thanet, that every liege man of our Lord the King ought to go to the house of William Medmenham, and demolish his house and level it with the ground, and fling out the books and rolls found there, and to burn them with fire, and if the said William could be found, that they should kill him, and cut off his head from his body, under like penalty; and they ordered a taxation to be paid for maintaining the said proceedings against the lordships throughout the whole Isle of Thanet, except the tenants of the Priory of Canterbury and the franchise of Canterbury.

By virtue of which cry, the Jurors of the hundred of Ryngslo say, that these same entered the house of the said William, and burnt the aforesaid rolls and books, and did no other harm to the said William.

And further they say, that they raised the cry that no tenant should do service or custom, as is above said, and that they made the taxation.

II. RYNGSLO to wit

The Jurors to inquire concerning the malefactors who rose against our Lord the King and his people, from the Feast of Trinity, in the fourth year of the reign of King Richard the Second, continuing at intervals, from the day and year aforesaid until the morrow of Corpus Christi next ensuing (from June 9 to 14, 1381), say, upon their oath, that William the Capellan, officiating in the Church of St John in the Isle of Thanet, and Stephen Samuel, on Thursday in the Feast of Corpus Christi in the aforesaid year (13 June, 1381), rose and proclaimed, against the peace of our Lord the King, that all and singular ought to unite, and go to the house of William Medmenham, under the penalty of death and the forfeiture of their goods and chattels, and to pull down the house of the said William Medmenham. Whereupon, the aforesaid William and Stephen entered the house of the aforesaid William Medmenham, on the day and year aforesaid, together with others who were driven by them to this, and burned the books and muniments of the foresaid William Medmenham at Manston, in the foresaid Island, to the damage of the said William of twenty shillings. The rest well.

Custodes of the said Hundred,
William Daundilioun, Thomas Eldrych.
Names of the Constables,
Stephen Coluere, Gervis Saghiere, Simon Fygge.

There is no evidence to suggest that any Thanet men were involved in the riots in London, and none are recorded amongst those hung, although six men from Canterbury were.[4]

A second revolt occurred in Kent in 1450, led by Jack Cade. This revolt was centred on Ashford and at least eleven Thanet men were involved.[4] Their grievances included local concerns such as the perceived corruption of the Dover courts and corruption surrounding the election of knights of the shire, and more general concerns such as anger over the debts ran up to pay for years of warfare against the French. Cade marched on London but, when the rebels started to loot the city, the citizens turned on them and forced them out. Cade fled but was fatally wounded in a skirmish with Alexander Iden, a future High Sheriff of Kent. There is no evidence to suggest that the inhabitants of the Cinque Ports took any concerted part in this rising.[5] A further riot occurred in 1495 following the introduction of a new statute to replace the national wage rates for labourers established in 1446.[6] Disturbances occurred in Wingham, to the east of Canterbury, and in the parish of St Nicholas at Wade, in the Isle of Thanet. Nine men were indicted for the disturbances, but it was suggested that at least 160 men were actually involved in the Isle of Thanet.

Wars

Margate's position on the coast gave it a strategic importance. Margate Roads, a deep-water anchorage just north of Margate, protected on the seaward side by the Margate Sands, was used by the Royal Navy as a fleet anchorage and to guard the mouth of the Thames. On the cliffs to the east of the harbour at Margate was a small fort built to protect both the harbour and ships going round the North Foreland into the Downs. In the twelfth century the need to protect the English Channel led to the formation of the Confederation of the Cinque Ports, a confederation consisting of the five ports of Hastings, New Romney, Hythe, Dover and Sandwich (Chapter 5). We know that Margate had become a non-corporate member of the Cinque Ports by 1229 as an 'ordinance touching the service of shipping' issued by King Henry III in 1229 listing 'the Ports of the King of England having liberties which other ports have not' included 'Dover, to which pertaineth Folkstone, Feversham, and Margate, not of soil but of cattle'; unfortunately the meaning of the phrase 'not of soil but of cattle' has been lost.[7,8] The original charters specified that Dover, with the help of its corporate and non-corporate members, was to provide for the King 'twenty-one ships, and in every ship twenty-one men with one boy, which is called a gromet', the word 'gromet' coming from the Dutch word *Grom*, meaning a stripling. These ships were to be provided each year 'for fifteen days at their own cost' the fifteen days to be counted 'from the day on which they shall hoist up the sails of the ships to sail to the parts to which they ought to go'.

The agreement to provide just twenty one men and a boy for each ship might have been sufficient when the ships were just 30 to 60 tons, but by the fifteenth century most naval ships were of 100 tons, needing crews of at least 65 men.[5] These large fighting vessels were either specially built royal ships or large impressed merchant ships from ports on the East and West coasts; the ships provided by the Cinque Ports, mostly fishing vessels, were by then used mainly for relatively menial transport purposes. As emphasised by Murray:[5]

During the thirteenth century the reputation of the [Cinque] Ports' fleet was established, but as pirates rather than a national force: their importance was temporary, arising out of a condition of civil war and the fact that their profession as fishermen involved the possession of seaworthy vessels available in an emergency when other sources failed. The terms of their service were unsuited to the big naval expeditions which became more common in the fourteenth century. They were only bound to serve for fifteen days at their own costs, and this time was often spent in reaching the meeting-place before the campaign began ... In expeditions of this kind the Cinque Ports played no special part; they were not exempt from general service with the impressed ships of other ports, and their boats formed only a fraction of the total fleet.

As the Cinque Ports lost naval power and, with it, effective control of the Channel, they also lost political influence; when a royal navy came to be built its headquarters were at Southampton, and not in the Cinque Ports.[5] This loss of importance is clear in the small numbers of ships provided by the Cinque Ports for the continental campaigns of the fourteenth century. The Cinque Ports provided just 36 ships crewed by 1,084 mariners in 1325 to transport the forces of Edward II to Gascony, and in 1326 their contribution was just 35 ships, 26% of the total, manned by 1,262 mariners, 46% of the total, none of the ships apparently coming from Dover.[9] Indeed, this earned the constable of Dover castle a rebuke from Edward II: 'Although the king ordered the mayors and bailiffs of the towns of Hethe, Dover, and Faversham, which are within the liberty of the Cinque Ports, to cause all owners of ships of those towns and the members thereof of the burthen of 50 tuns and upwards to come to Portesmuth with their ships on Sunday after the Decollation of St John the Baptist last, to set out in his service for the defence of the realm against the attacks of the French . . . the said mayors and bailiffs have not hitherto caused certain of the ships to come to the said place'.[10] As a sign of his displeasure:[10]

> the king has now ordained that twelve ships of Kent and the city of London, each provided with 40 armed men and victuals and other necessaries, of the ships that have not come to Portsmouth, shall remain on the sea coast near Forland in the Isle of Thanet for the repulse of the French and other enemies, if they endeavour to enter the realm there, at the cost of the men of the towns to which the ships belong who shall have no ships there, and have no part in the ships, and are not now in the king's service aforesaid, whilst other ships that have come to that place by virtue of the orders aforesaid and that have set out in the fleet . . . shall remain in that service; of which twelve ships the king wills that two shall be of the town of Hethe, two of the town of Dover, and the fifth of the town of Faversham; the king therefore orders the constable to cause the said five ships to be chosen out of the best ships of those towns that have not set out in the king's service as is aforesaid, and to cause each of them to be provided with 40 armed men and victuals and other necessaries at the expense of the aforesaid men, and to cause the necessary charges for the mariners and armed men to be levied, and to cause the ships to come to the coast aforesaid, so that they be there on Sunday the feast of St Matthew next at the latest.

The Cinque Ports also contributed little to the great naval engagements of the Hundred Years war lasting from 1337 to 1453. For example, at the siege of Calais in 1347 only about a quarter of the Southern Fleet came from the Cinque Ports, Margate providing 15 ships and 160 mariners and Dover 16 ships and 336 mariners; the relative numbers of mariners per ship emphasises how small the Margate ships were, even compared to those of Dover.[5,11] The cost of the war with France was immense, and large numbers of merchant vessels were impressed for these expeditions, some 735 for the siege of Calais in 1347. Merchants whose ships had been impressed would, of course, try to get them back as quickly as possible. In 1343 Edward III ordered the arrest of a large number of ships that 'went with the King to Britanny' but 'departed from the port of Brest, where the King landed, contrary to his prohibition'.[12] Of these ships two were from Margate, *la Godbiete* and *la Luk*, Simon Lioun and Salomon Lithere, masters.

In 1544 Dr Richard Layton, Dean of York and Henry VIII's agent in Flanders, was requested by the privy Council to 'prest 200 hoys' to provide transport for the war with France over Boulogne; it was reported that he had managed to press '10 for Margate'. These hoys were from 110 tons down to 35 tons and were each large enough to carry between 30 and 35 horses.[13,14] When a survey of the ships at Margate was taken in 1584 as part of the preparation for the abortive expedition sent to Flanders, only one of the 12 was listed as suitable for carrying ordnance, and that was a barke of 70 tons.[15] Eventually Margate ceased to provide any of the 21 ships that Dover had to contribute to the Navy, making instead a cash contribution to Dover every year.[16] However, in 1628 Margate did provide one hoy to the fleet used in the relief of la Rochelle:[17]

Whereas there are imprested for his Majesties service twenty Hoyes and Catches, being to attende the Fleete which is to be employed for the reliefe of Rochell, although six of that number, viz. the *Mary* of Margat, the *John*, the *Marygold*, the *Samuell*, and the *Michell* of Sandwich and the *Edward* of Feversham, belonging to places within the jurisdicion of the Cinque Ports; yet in regarde of the present and necessarie use of them, there being no other meanes to have a sufficient number of such vessels: It is hereby ordered that they shalbe employed in his Majesties service, for which they are imprested notwithstanding anie priviledge or direction to the contrarie: Whereof the principal Officers of the Navy are hereby required to take notice, and to see the same performed accordingly.

The Home Guard

The strategic importance of the Isle of Thanet meant that it needed to be properly protected at times of war, but until late in the seventeenth century England had no standing army. In the same way that the inhabitants of a town were expected to enforce law and order themselves, as there was no police force until the nineteenth century, so every able-bodied Englishman was required by law to be prepared to fight in defence of the realm.

In April 1338, at the start of the hundred years war, Edward III ordered that all archers in Kent should be sent with the King's forces to France, except for those living close to the coast, who were to stay where they were: 'Order not to lead any archers away from the maritime parts of that county, to wit, within 12 leagues of the sea, but to permit them to stay there to repel attacks'.[18] An order of May 1338 made it explicit that this order applied to the Isle of Thanet:[19]

To the electors and arrayers of archers for the king's service in co. Kent. Order to supersede the leading of archers out of the isle of Thanet, but to permit them to remain there for the defence of the island, while danger is imminent or until further orders; the king also orders them to elect as many archers as they elected in the island, elsewhere in the county and to lead them to the town of Great Yarmouth, to be there on Wednesday in Whitsun week next at latest, as the men of the island have besought the king to order such archers to stay there and to provide for the assistance of other men for the defence of the island, as aliens in galleys and ships of war are ready to invade the island, thinking to do injury there more quickly than elsewhere.

Also in May 1338 Edward III made it clear that he wished the large local landowners, 'the abbots of St Augustine's, Canterbury, and Faversham, and the priors of Christ Church, Canterbury, Dover, and Rochester' together with 'priors, earls, barons and others in Kent and Sussex having land near the sea coast, to cause their servants and others of their retinue to be arrayed at arms, and to be led to their manors near the sea and to stay there for the defence of the realm' because 'certain aliens of France, Normandy and elsewhere have assembled a great fleet of galleys and ships of war to attack the realm'.[19] It was recognized that concentrating so many men close to the coast might result in a shortage of food and so it was also ordered that the forces going to France should not take 'any victuals except wine within 12 leagues of the sea in co. Kent, while there is danger of foreign attack there, and while the lieges are staying there for the defence of those parts'.[18]

The threat to the coast was real; in March 1338 a large French force took Portsmouth and, having plundered the town, set it alight, and in October the French, supported by their Scottish allies and by Genoese mercenaries, landed at Southampton and sacked that town as well. In 1339 the French forces sailed up the coast as far as the Isle of Thanet, and

Hastings, Thanet, Folkestone, Dover and Rye were attacked and partly burnt; it was reported that the French 'were prevented from doing much mischief, except to the poor'.[11] An order was given in 1339 that some of the men of Sarre should remain on the Isle of Thanet for its defence:[20]

To William de Clynton, earl of Huntingdon, constable of Dover castle and warden of the Cinque Ports and of the maritime land in co. Kent. The mayor and community of Sandwich have shown the king that although they have ordained ships of that town to set out to sea with the fleet towards the west, for the defence of the realm, and certain men of Sarre in the isle of Thanet, a member of the port of Sandwich, are ordained to set out in those ships, yet the men assert that they are staying in the island for its defence by order of the keepers of the island, and are forbidden by them to leave the island, and it is more expedient for them to remain in the island for its defence than to set out in the said ships, and they excuse themselves to the mayor and community who have besought the king to cause those men to set out; the king orders the warden that if the town is a member of the port of Sandwich, then to cause certain of those men to set out in the fleet, as he sees fit, and certain to remain in the island.

In July 1345 'measures were taken for the protection of the Isle of Thanet, in consequence of the French, whom the King styled his "enemies and rebels," having collected numerous ships, galleys, barges, and flutes, for the purpose of landing on the English coast, to commit all kinds of injuries'.[11] In 1378, although a truce had been negotiated with the French, 'lest the French should again invade England, on 16 March a general array of soldiers was made in the Isle of Thanet to prevent the enemy from landing there'.[11] In 1385 the English army invaded Scotland but was driven off by the joint forces of Scotland and France, a situation made worse by the threat of an attack on England's southern coast by the French fleet. The need to defend the Kent coast was urgent, and was to be paid for by a tax of 1d on every basket of fish landed at the ports:[21]

January 18 1385, Westminster
Appointment of Simon de Burley, constable of Dover castle and warden of the Cinque Ports, John de Cohham of Kent, John Devereux and Edward Dalyngrugg, upon information that the French with a large army intend to land within the liberty of the Cinque Ports to destroy them, to levy from the seller a penny upon every basket of fish coming to Rye, Wynchelse, Hastynges, Promhell, Lyde, Pevenyse, Romene, Hethe, Folkstone, Dele, Walmere,

Recolvere, Wytstaple, Sesaltre, Mergate in the isle of Tenet, Redlyngweld, Bourn, Codyng, Bolewarehethe, Iham, Odymere and Plvdenne, and to expend all sums arising therefrom upon the defence of those ports and the country adjacent, and to take masons, carpenters and labourers for the fortifying of Rye, with power to arrest and imprison the disobedient until further order.

For whatever reason the level of the tax seems to have been changed, before implementation, to '3d on every noble's worth of fish landed' (a noble was a gold coin worth 6s 8d, or a third of a pound sterling).[21]

Also in January 1385 it was ordered that all the able-bodied men in Kent were to proceed to the coast 'and other places where danger threatens', and that the beacon warning system should be overhauled:[22]

Commission, in view of imminent invasion by the French, to Simon de Burle, constable of Dover castle, John de Cobeham, John Devereux, Arnald Savage, Thomas Brokhull, Roger Wygemore, Thomas Sbardelowe, John eta Frenyngham, James de Pekham, Richard de Berham and the sheriff of Kent, to array all men-at-arms, armed men and archers who live in that county, and arm all able-bodied men, both those who have the wherewithal to arm themselves and those who have not, each according to his estate, and to assess, apportion and distrain all who in lands and goods are capable but by feebleness of body incapable of labour, to find armour in proportion to their lands and goods, and to contribute to the expenses of those who will thus labour in defence of the realm, those staying at their houses for the purpose of defending them are not to take wages nor expenses therefor. These men-at-arms they are to keep arrayed and to lead to the sea coast and other places where danger threatens, and if any resist they are to arrest and imprison them until further order. Moreover the signs called 'Bekyns' are to be placed in the accustomed spots to warn the people of the coming of the enemy.

By April 1385 the threat of invasion was thought to be so serious that all the inhabitants of the area were ordered to go with their families to Dover castle, Rye or Sandwich for protection:[23]

Appointment until All Saints, of Simon de Burle, constable of Dover castle and warden of the Cinque Ports, upon information that the king's enemies of France, Spain, Flanders, and Brittany are leagued together to destroy the people and fortalices on the English coast by an invasion within a brief time, to cause proclamation to be made in Sandwich, Dover and Rye, and all places where he shall deem it expedient within the islands of Thanet and Oxeye and six miles round Dover castle and the said towns of Rye and Sandwich, that all the inhabitants within those islands and six miles round, with their families and goods, withdraw before 3 May under pain of imprisonment to the said castle and towns for safety, ecclesiastics only excepted.

Presumably the order must have been withdrawn a few weeks later when the expected invasion failed to occur. Anyhow, the order was re-imposed on April 31 (*sic*) 1386, withdrawn on May 14 and then again re-imposed on June 18, when the inhabitants were ordered to take their victuals with them.[24,25] The policy was clearly to stop people from fleeing inland and to concentrate manpower at the major ports where they could mount an effective defence. Nevertheless, in February 1392 it was reported that people were leaving the Isle of Thanet because its defences against enemy landings were in ruins:[26]

Commission of oyer and terminer to Arnald Savage, William Rikill, William Makenade, Nicholas atte Crouche, Stephen Bettenham, William Elys, William Berton and William Titecombe, on information that inhabitants of the isle of Thanet having lands and houses therein are continually leaving it, and that the turreted walls both upon and below the cliff of the island, as well as certain dykes formerly constructed there for defence against hostile attacks, are weak and in ruins, while divers persons who are bound to repair the causeways of the ferry on either side of the water of Serre and to find and maintain boats and other vessels for the passage and carriage of men and animals have long neglected to do so. They are to examine the condition of the island in all these respects and enquire who are bound to find boats and vessels, repair the causeways and walls and cleanse the dykes, and compel them thereto and to stay in the island or find others in their place for its defence.

In March 1410 a renewal of hostilities seemed so likely that a commission of array was issued to the abbot of St Augustine's and other senior county figures for the defence of the Isle of Thanet, a commission of array being a commission issued to the local gentry to muster the able bodied men of an area for its defence:[27]

Commission of array to the abbot of St Augustine's Canterbury, Arnold Savage, Richard Cliderowe, Robert Clifford, William Notebem, John Whithede, John Dreylonde, Thomas Marehaunt, John Scheldwych, and the sheriff of Kent within the Isle of Thanet for defence against the king's enemies.

In 1451 another muster 'of all men at arms, hoblers and archers' was taken in the Isle of Thanet and at the same time the beacons were put in order:[28]

Commission to George, abbot of the monastery of St Augustine by Canterbury, William Manston, Roger Manston, John Septvans and Thomas Saintnycholas, appointing them to array and try all men at arms, hobelers and archers within the isle of Thanet and to lead them to the sea coast and other places in the Island to resist the king's enemies, and to take the muster of the same from time to time, and to set up 'bekyns' in the usual places and cause wards and watches to be kept, arresting and imprisoning such as refuse to keep the same, until they find security for their obedience.

Simply mustering large numbers of the local men would not be sufficient to ensure the safety of the country if those men were untrained in the use of weapons. On 1 June 1363, Edward III wrote to his sheriffs and commanded:[29]

[a] proclamation to be made that every able bodied man on feast days [including Sundays] when he has leisure shall in his sports use bows and arrows, pellets or bolts, and shall learn and practise the art of shooting, forbidding all and singular on pain of imprisonment to attend or meddle with hurling of stones, loggats, or quoits, handball, football, club ball, cambuc, cock fighting or other vain games of no value; as the people of the realm, noble and simple, used heretofore to practise the said art in their sports, whence by God's help came forth honour to the kingdom and advantage to the king in his actions of war, and now the said art is almost wholly disused, and the people indulge in the games aforesaid and other dishonest and unthrifty games, whereby the realm is like to be kept without archers.

The proclamation was followed by a series of similar laws over the next two centuries including statutes from Edward IV, Henry VII, and Henry VIII who, in 1512, clarified that the requirement to practise applied to all men 'not lame, decrepute or maymed' under 60 years of age.[30]

The risk of invasion by the powers of Catholic Europe increased after Henry VIII's break with Rome, and to guard against such an invasion Henry VIII, in 1538, implemented a programme of military and naval preparations along the southern and eastern coasts from Kent to Cornwall. The French ambassador Marillac reported in 1539 that 'In Canterbury, and the other towns upon the road [to Dover], I found every

English subject in arms who was capable of serving. Boys of seventeen or eighteen have been called out, without exception of place or person . . . Artillery and ammunition pass out incessantly from the Tower [of London], and are dispatched to all points on the coast where a landing is likely to be attempted'.[31]

In February 1545 Stephen Vaughan, an English merchant and royal agent, reported to Henry VIII that he had heard a rumour of a planned French invasion of England, to start at Margate:[32,33]

'A French broker,' he [Stephen Vaughan] said, 'hath secretly called upon me. He asked me if there was not in England an island called Sheppy, and a place by it called Margate, and by those two a haven. I said there was. 'Then,' said he, 'you may perceive I have heard of these places, though I have never been there myself. To the effect of my discovery,' said he, 'you shall understand that the French King hath sent unto this town of Antwerp a gentleman of Lorrayne named Joseph Chevalier. The same hath sent out of this town, two days past, a Frenchman, being a bourgeois of Antwerp, named John Boden, together with another man that nameth himself to be born in Geneva, but indeed he is a Frenchman. These two,' he said, 'were sent from hence in a hoy by sea, and had delivered unto them eleven packs of canvass to be by them uttered and sold in London, and the money coming thereof to maintain their charges there. The said Joseph Chevalier, besides these two, hath sent another broker named John Young, also of this town; he speaketh singularly well the English tongue. These three shall meet together in London, and shall lodge in a Fleming's house dwelling by the Thames, named Waters. The first two shall have charge to view and consider the said Isle of Sheppy, Margate, and the grounds between them and London; what landing there may be for the French King's army, what soils to place an army strongly in. For,' said he, 'the French King hath bruited that he will send forth this summer three armies, one to land in England, the second in Scotland, and the third he mindeth to send to Boulogne, and Guisnes, and Calais. But his purpose is to send no army to Scotland, for he hath appointed with the Scots that while his armies shall be arrived, the one at Margate and the other at Boulogne, they shall set upon the north parts of England, with all the power they can make. The French King proposeth with his army that he appointeth to land in the Isle of Sheppy and at Margate, to send great store of victuals, which shall be laden in boats of Normandy with flat bottoms, which, together with the galleys, shall then set men on land. This army shall go so strong that it shall be able to give battle, and is minded, if the same may be able, to go through to London, where,' said he, 'a little without the same is a hill from which London lyeth all open, and with their ordnance laid from thence they shall beat the town.'

In May 1545 Henry VIII received a report on the defence of the sea coasts of England.[34] The report identified a possible landing place for French forces at Margate, 'between rock and rock, a great quarter of a mile fair landing', and said that 'Mr Auchar and the gentlemen of Tenet undertake, with certain artillery and 300 men in garrison, the defence of the Isle'. It was suggested that 'for the present defence of the said isle to grant the inhabitants 6 or 8 pieces of good ordnance with men practised to handle it, and to command the inhabitants to make a trench in the corner next Canterbury adjoining the Marsh, where they may sustain attacks from the enemy until aid come. The King to appoint three or four gentlemen at any fire given within the isle with three or four hundred men for their succours'.

In 1557, two new Acts were passed, 'An Act for the having of horse, armour and weapon' and 'An Act for the taking of musters', jointly referred to as the Arms Acts.[35,36] The first of these Acts divided the population into ten bands depending on their wealth, and defined what was expected from each of them. At the top of the scale, anyone with an income of £1000 a year or more was expected to provide six horses for men-at-arms carrying the shorter lances used in battle (demi-lance), ten geldings equipped with armour and weapons (light-horse), 40 corslets (suits of armour), 40 almain rivets (studded jackets), 40 pikes, 30 longbows each with a sheaf of arrows (24), 30 skulls or steep caps, 20 bill or halberd, 20 hackbuts (simple firearms), and 20 morions or sallets (helmets). At the bottom of the scale were gentleman, knights and esquires, and substantial yeoman farmers with an annual income between £5 and £10 a year; they were required to supply one coat of plate, one bill or halberd, one bow with arrows, and a steel cap. The second of the Acts concerned the gathering of the military forces, a *muster*, for training and inspection. The Act was designed to prevent some of the corrupt practises that had developed over past years. As described in the Act 'a great number hath absented them from the said Musters, which ought to have come to the same, as also for that many of the most able and likely men for that service have been through friendship or rewards, released, forborn and discharged of the said service'. In future, anyone missing a muster without good reason would be imprisoned for ten days and anyone in charge of a muster accepting a bribe would be fined 'ten times so much as he shall so receive'. A further development came in 1573 when it was ordered that 'a convenient and sufficient number of the most able' men at the muster would be selected to be 'tried, armed and weaponed, and so conveniently taught and trained' to form an elite band, referred to as the *trained band*.[37] The militia as a whole would be mustered just once a year, or less, but the trained band would meet more often, sometimes as frequently as once a week, for training in the use of their weapons. The records of the militia at Canterbury include a payment of 6s 8d 'paid to the trayned shott when they went to Margate', possibly to help with the training there.[38] In 1679 the records of the Overseers of the Poor for the parish of St John's included an item: 'Paid for clearing Matt. Mummereyes musquett 2s', which does rather sound like something from an episode of *Dad's Army*.[39] The muster system was to remain, more of less unchanged, until 1757 when 'An Act for the better ordering of the Militia Forces in the several counties of that part of Great Britain called England' was passed, leading to the awarding of 'Commissions to a proper number of Colonels, Lieutenant Colonels, majors and other Officers . . . to train and discipline the Persons so to be armed and arrayed'.[40]

The musters were held over two days and became something of a social occasion. They were usually the responsibility of the Lord Lieutenant of the county but for the Cinque Ports the responsible official was the Lord Warden of the Cinque Ports, who appointed a muster-master to oversee the process. In 1677 Edward Randolph, the muster-master for the Cinque Ports, complained 'that he has several years' salary due to him', totalling £79 5s 10d, calculated 'according to the rate agreed on in 1617 and paid until 1665'.[41]

Margate, St Peter's and Birchington together formed two companies of militia, a 'select company' and a 'general, not selected company' which were inspected at an annual muster by the Deputy Constable of Dover Castle, acting on behalf of the Lord Warden.[16,42] Lewis commented on the considerable cost of these musters, giving as an example the costs involved in 1615 when Thomas May was the Deputy at Margate:[16]

To the messenger who brought the Warrant to warne the Musters — 1s
More, moneys layed out when Sir Robert Brett took Muster at Mergate the 12 and 13 daies of October for his diet and his followers — £3 18s
More, to Mr Warde — 10s
More, to Mr Packenhum — 10s 8d
More, to --- Dibbe — 5s

More, to the Trumpeter — 5s
To the two Dromers — 5s
    To Sir Roberte's servants
First, to his Chamberlen and Purse bearer — 6s 8d
More, to the serving men — 2s 6d
More, to the Coachman, footman, and horse keepers — 4s 6d
More, to Mr Rawworth, the Clarke of the Musters — 3s 4d
More, to Mr Packenhum's and Mr Ward's men — 2s
More, to the Muster Master — 9s 2d
More, to Mr Raworth for writing and ingrosing of our Muster Role — 6s
To the Ferryman for passing Sir Robert and his company over the haven at Sandwich — 8s 7d

The muster role for the select and general companies of the Isle of Thanet in 1599 shows 364 men in all, of whom about half came from St John's:[43]

Role	St John's	Birchington	St Peter's
Officers	4	1	4
Calivers	36	14	30
Musket	39	18	27
Armed men	13	6	10
Pike men	38	15	19
Bills and halberds	16	11	37
Pioneers	9	4	7
Wagoner	2	0	1
Drummer	0	0	2
Clerk	1	0	0
Total	158	69	137

About half the men carried hand weapons such as pikes and halberds (including those listed simply as 'armed men') and half carried fire arms such as calivers and muskets; the lower orders made up the 'pioneers', equipped with picks and shovels. The three wagoners were responsible for transport and the two drummers were there to ensure that the soldiers kept pace when marching. Calivers and muskets were precursors to the rifle. The caliver had a barrel between 39 and 44 inches in length, giving the weapon an overall length of about 55 inches; it weighed between 10 and 12 pounds. The musket was much larger and heavier than the caliver, with a barrel between 45 and 55 inches long, and a weight of about 20 pounds; its weight was such that it had to be supported by a forked rest during aiming. The pikemen, who were expected to be 'the strongest men and best persons' had to fight at close quarters and so had body protection in the form of a corslet, a metal shell around the body, with pouldrons, vambraces and tassets which were metal plates to protect the shoulders, arms and thighs, and gauntlets. To protect their heads the pikemen wore a steel cap or morion well stuffed for comfort, tied with a scarf under the chin. The halberd was a shorter weapon, some 7 to 8 feet long, with a metal point like the pike for thrusting, a heavy blade for cutting and a hook for dragging horsemen from their saddles.[31,44,45] The general company of 1599 was about half the size of the select company, with 76 coming from St John's.[46]

The muster role for 1572 for St John's, St Peter's and Birchington combined shows 170 men in the select band and 204 in the general band, giving 374 in total, a total figure very similar to that for 1599. The Muster Role for 1619 shows that the Select Company then contained 147 men, including 3 officers and 2 sergeants, and the General Company contained 172 men including 3 officers and 2 sergeants.[42,47] In the Select Company 60 were Corsletts, pike men named after their corslets or body armour, and 80 were Musquets, with a clerk and a drummer and two waggons looked after by two wagoners. In the General Company 30 were Corsletts, 76 were Musketts, and 60 were 'Dry Pykes' who, it seems, were pike men who wore no armour; there was also one drummer.[48] The officers of the Select Company were listed as 'Paul Cleybrooke, captaine, esquire, Manasses Norwood, Lietenant, gen., and William Cleybrooke, ensigne, gen.' and those of the General Company were listed as 'Valentine Pettit, gent., captayne, William Parker, Liuetenauntt, and Thomas Busher, Ensigne.' Paule Cleybrooke was from Fordwich, Manasses Norwood from Dane Court (Chapter 1), William Cleybrooke from Nash Court, Valentine Pettit from Dent de Lyon, and William Parker from Minster, illustrating once again the importance of the large farming families in the Isle of Thanet. Gradually the organization of the trained band became more professional and in 1684 commissions were given to 'Lieut. Andrew O'Neale to be lieutenant and to Ensign Stephen Greedhurst to be ensign of a company of trained band soldiers of St John's in the Isle of Thanet ... in the second regiment of the Cinque Ports'.[49]

Musters were generally held on some convenient open ground, usually somewhere in the countryside.[31] Arthur Rowe made the suggestion that the muster in Margate might, however, have been held in the spot close to the harbour and Fort known as Cold Harbour. This idea was based on the belief that Cold Harbour was a name used throughout the south of England for the mustering place of the trained bands.[39] There is, however, little or no evidence for this, and the name Cold Harbour is usually thought to derive either from the name for a refuge for the destitute or from the name given to a station on the line of a Roman road. It seems more likely that the Cold Harbour at Margate got its name simply from being a cold and windy spot close to the harbour and, anyhow, it would be too small an area for holding a muster.

Perhaps because of its membership of the Cinque Ports, the Royal Navy never maintained much of a presence at Margate, although a brass plate in St John's church records the death in Margate in 1615 of Roger Morris, one of the principal Masters of Attendance of His Majesty's Navy Royal.[85] The Principal Master of Attendance was a rather ill-defined post, but a holder of the post was essentially a local representative of the navy, generally responsible for the naval side of a royal dockyard. What he was doing in Margate is not known; he might have simply retired there or he might have been posted to Margate to look after the interests of the navy. Nevertheless, an extract from a manuscript, *The life of Mr Phinear Pette, one of the Master shiprights to King James the first*, shows just how useful he could be to any senior navy officers who happened to be in the area:[86]

1612: The 15th [April], London, we came to an anchor in Margate road; the next day the Lord Admiral went ashore at Margate, and lay there three daysh, at Mr Roger Morris's, one of the four masters of his majesty's navy, and then returned aboard. The 21st, the lady Elizabeth, his grace the Palsgrave, and all their train, came to Margate, and were embarked in barges and the ships boats, and were received on-board the admiral, and lay there all night. The 22d the wind getting Easterly, and likely to be foul weather, her highness and the Palsgrave, and most part of her train, were carried ashore to Margate. The 25th they were all brought on-board again.

Press Gangs

The charters establishing the Cinque Ports required them to provide both ships and sailors in time of war, but only for fifteen days a year; although the burden of manning the ships fell largely on coastal communities, the burden was manageable. However, by the eighteenth century naval ships were very much larger, with much larger crews, scattered all over the world for long periods of time. Manning the navy had by then became a problem and relied increasingly on the use of press-gangs.[50] The term 'pressing' for the procedure is something of a misnomer, as in fact the men were 'impressed' or 'imprested', the word *imprest* meaning to pay someone in advance to guarantee their service; in the army this took the form of paying a man 'the King's shilling' so that it could be claimed that they had volunteered to join.

Navy press gangs were meant to operate within clearly defined limits, although as press officers were paid an allowance for each man they recruited these limits must often have been broken.[51] The intention was to recruit seamen with few family. At sea, pressing was not permitted from outward-bound vessels, and so press gangs would board homeward-bound ships to find their 'volunteers' although even then they had to leave enough men on board to enable the ship to reach its destination safely. On shore the press gangs were meant to recruit just able bodied mariners, between the ages of eighteen and sixty and would concentrate on places with large numbers of seamen, such as Wapping and Rotherhithe along the Thames.

Who actually had the authority to impress men within the Cinque Ports became something of a contentious issues in the sixteenth century. The head of the navy in England was the Admiral of England, later to be known as the Lord High Admiral, an office created around 1400. In the sixteenth century the post of Vice-Admiral was also created, with one Vice-Admiral being responsible for each of the maritime counties. The first Vice-Admiral of Kent was Sir John Tregonwell, appointed in 1525.[52] The responsibilities of the Vice-Admirals included impressing men for naval service but, based on long custom, it was accepted that 'the Lord Warden is Admirall within the Ports', so that within the Cinque Ports it was the Lord Warden of the Cinque Ports rather than the Vice-Admiral of Kent who was responsible for pressing men.[5] Although the offices of

Vice-Admiral of Kent and Lord Warden of the Cinque Ports were separate offices, they were occasionally held by the same man, as, for example, by William Brooke, tenth Baron Cobham, who was appointed Lord Warden of the Cinque Ports in 1558 and Vice-Admiral of Kent in 1559.

There are a number of records from the 1560s of payments to press officers for impressing men from Margate and other places in Kent.[53] In August 1562 Butolph Moungey was paid £16 13s for 222 mariners 'by him prested from Folkestone, Hythe, Margate, Lydd, Rye, Winchelsea, Hastings, Newhaven, Brighton, Kingston, Heene, Worthing, Lancing, Old Shoreham, New Shoreham, and in divers places thereabouts in Kent and Sussex' and for conducting them to Gillingham, 'at 18d every man'. On July 6 1563 Lancelot Tristram was paid 'for the conduct of Jeffrey Fraxson, Robert Sutton, John Dowes, Henry Cowper, Thomas Beate, Richard Pissinge and 10 other mariners by him prested from Dover, Kingsdown, Sandwich and thereabouts in Kent to serve in Her Grace's ships at Chatham, distant 36 miles, at 18d every man — 24s; [and] for the conduct of Thomas Parker, John Bayllie, Thomas Houghe, Christopher Parkins, Thomas Homan, William Tompson, George Browne and 25 other mariners by him prested from Deal, St Lawrence in Thanet, St Peters, St John's [Margate] and thereabouts in Kent to Chatham, distant 24 miles, at 12d every man — 32s'. On July 10 he was also paid £9 8s 6d 'for the conduct of John Hatley, William Goodson, John Castell, Thomas Atkynson, Robert Clarke, Thomas Tuckar, Henry Readman and 102 other mariners by him prested from Dover, Folkestone, Hythe, Lydd, Rye and thereabouts to Chatham, distant 36 miles, at 8d every man — £8 3s 6d; and more to him for the conduct of Robert Harrys, Henry Martyn, James Bennet, Richard Hemmynge and 21 other mariners by him prested from St Peter's, St John's and divers other places in Thanet in Kent to serve in Her Grace's ships at Chatham aforesaid appointed to the sea, distant 24 miles, at 12d every man — 25s'. On the same day he was paid his expenses 'for the charges of him and his horse, travelling about the presting of 134 mariners out of sundry places in Kent and Sussex to serve in divers Her Grace's ships appointed to the seas, by the space of 8 days, at 3s 4d *per diem* — 36s 8d; more for so much by him paid to John Hewson of Dover for his charges and horse-hire riding into Thanet for the like presting of mariners for the said service — 11s 4d; more by him paid for a letter of attendance had from Dover castle — 2s 6d; more paid to William Browne for his charges riding from Dover alongst the coast to Rye with precepts — 4s 6d; and more to him for the hire of post horses from Dover to London, and also for other charges incident to the premises — 10s. *Summa* — £2 15s'. Tristram's charges for attending at Dover castle and for taking precepts [a warrant] to Rye suggest that his pressing in the Cinque Ports was done with the agreement of the Lord Warden.

In January 1602 Cobham, as Lord Warden of the Cinque Ports, was ordered to impress a hundred sailors from the Cinque Ports to keep the fleets manned and help patrol the Irish coasts after the defeat of the Spanish and Irish at Kinsale:[54]

> Her Highness pleasure and commandment is that your Lordship cause a general muster to be taken of all the mariners and seafaring men fit for service within the Portes of your Lordshipps lieutenancie and wardenrye from the age of sixteen to three score years owt of which ther shalbe choice made of one hundred of the most able and sufficient.

Cobham, however, decided that only about half of the men should come from the Cinque Ports with the other half coming from the rest of Kent, as 'I find the Portes have ben extraordinarily chardged of service for the shippes upon every small occasion'.[54] In fact, 57 men were mustered from the Cinque Ports, of whom 6 were from the parish of St John's, 4 from Ramsgate, 4 from Broadstairs and 7 from Dover. The arrangement for the impressment was somewhat different from that for soldiers, the sailors being given twelve pence for impress money with a half-penny per mile from their home port to Chatham; they were charged 'uppon payne of death to present themselves before the officers of the navye by the laste daie of the present January to be disposed into soch shippes as shalbe meete'. The order sent to Cobham included a reminder that many of the drafted men would present themselves 'unarmed and naked without anie convenyent clothes'. As this was both a danger to themselves and a cause of infection he was to ensure that those that could 'sholde furnish themselves' and those without means should be fitted out 'by their parents, masters or friends with swords and daggers and all necessarie apparell'.[54]

The convention that the Lord High Admiral had no authority to impress in the Cinque Ports continued into the seventeenth century. When George Villiers, 1st Duke of Buckingham and Lord High Admiral from 1619, wished to impress 'three score seamen in the Cinque Ports, to man the Victory and Dreadnought' in 1621 he had to write to Lord Zouch, the Lord Warden, asking him to issue the appropriate order.[55] Again in 1623 when the Privy Council and the Commissioners of the Navy wished to issue instructions concerning the impressing of sailors in the Cinque Ports, the instructions had to be addressed to Lord Zouch.[56,57] The instructions sent by the Privy Council concerned seamen who ran away:

The punishments will henceforward be heavy against all seamen who run away from their ships, enter foreign service, or endeavour to avoid the prest, particularly as regards the fleet now preparing for Spain; 150 mariners are required from the Cinque Ports; all such as endeavour to escape are to be apprehended, and all abuses of presters, in impressing unfitting persons, or discharging for favour or money those who are fitting, are to be punished. Whitehall, March 9.

The instructions from the Commissioners of the Navy concerned the choice of men to be impressed: 'To be observed in the presting of mariners. All seamen are to be summoned to appear, according to lists previously sent in, and efficient men to be chosen with discretion, so as to injure trade as little as possible.'

The Duke of Buckingham, as Lord High Admiral, disliked having no authority to impress in the Cinque Ports, as he explained in 1626: 'The king's service is much hindered; for the most usual and ordinary rendezvous of the king's ships being at the Downs, and that being within the jurisdiction of the lord warden; the lord admiral or captains of the king's ships have no power or warrant to press men from the shore, if the king's ships be in distress'.[58] Buckingham's solution to the problem was, in 1624, to purchase the Lord Wardenship of the Cinque Ports from Lord Zouch who was then an old man and no longer wished to hold the position.[59] This, for a while, put an end to the clash of interests between the Lord Warden and the Lord Admiral and united the entire naval administration of the country in one man, him.[59] The arrangement was, however, short lived and ended with Buckingham's assassination in 1628; the two offices were only once again to be held by the same man, and that was between 1702 and 1708, by Prince George of Denmark.

The year before his assassination Buckingham had led an expedition to fight against the French at La Rochelle, in support of the Huguenots. As part of his campaign Buckingham had ordered a 'general muster throughout England of all mariners [and] mid-seamen' to be held in June 1626.[60] Papers in the archives of the Cinque Port of Rye show that this was linked to a 'strict stay of all ships and vessels going forth' from any of the Cinque Ports.[61] In practise this proved impossible to enforce, much to the annoyance of Buckingham, who addressed a stiff letter to the Mayor and Jurats:[61]

Whereas I am credibly informed that notwithstanding the strict order and commaund given for a generall restraint of all shipps, barques, and vessels, there doe dayly passe out of your porte or the members thereof aswell sloopes as barkes and other vessels to the infringement of the King's expresse comaunds and prejudice of his Majesty's service. Wherefore these are to will and require you not only to inquyre and certifye me what barques or vessels (since the said restraint) have passed out of your porte, and by whose directions, licence, helpe, and meanes, and whether they have gonne, but to take a more strict and vigilant course, that noe shippe, barque, sloope, or other vessell whatsoever of what quallity or condition soever, whether belonging to his Majesty's subjects or straingers doe by any meanes passe or goe forth of your said porte, roade, or harbor untill further order from me or the Lieutenant of Dovor Castle.

The restrictions on ship movements also applied to Margate and led, in June 1627, to a petition from the inhabitants of Margate asking Buckingham for an exemption: 'Petition of Inhabitants of Margate, member of the port of Dover, to Buckingham. Pray for removal of the restraint from their trade with small hoys and vessels laden with corn to London'.[62] It is not known whether or not Margate got its wish but in 1628 permission was given for hoys from a number of ports, including Margate, to ship corn abroad, as long as it was to 'his Majestie's friendes':[63]

An order granted to the inhabitants of Feversham, Milton, Rochester, Whytstable and Marget to transport corne into forreigne partes in good amitie with his Majestie by virtue of the generall order of the 27th of February 1627, they first putting in bonde to carry the same to none but to his Majestie's friendes.

During the reign of Charles II the Admiralty began to impress sailors in the Cinque Ports without bothering to first get permission from the Lord Warden. In 1668 a petition was addressed to James, Duke of York from the Cinque Ports claiming that 'their liberties since "the late distraccions" have been much impeached and infringed so that many have left the Ports, and the towns are decayed and they therefore place before him their grievances'.[64] The petition listed seven specific grievances of which the third read: 'The officers of the Admiralty Court often impress seamen without the knowledge of the chief officer of the town and instead of making arrests themselves send warrants to the mayor, bailiffs and jurats with their common officer making them thereby but servants liable to contempt'. By the eighteenth century any rights of the Cinque Ports over the impress of sailors arising from 'ancient customs and privileges' were largely ignored.[65] An incident in 1702 led to a petition from Deal to Prince George of Denmark, who was both Lord High Admiral of England and Lord Warden of the Cinque Ports at the time:

The Humble Petition of the Mayor, Jurats and Commonalty of the free town and Borough of Deal, a member of the Cinque Ports, Sheweth — That great privileges and immunities have been anciently granted to the Cinque Ports for their signal service at sea, which have been confirmed by Magna Charta and preserved to them hitherto.

In grateful acknowledgment whereof they have constantly supplied the kings and queens of this realm with great numbers of able and efficient seamen to serve in the wars at sea. That, by the customs and privileges of the Cinque Ports, all seamen thereunto belonging are to be impressed and raised only by the officers of the Lord Warden within the said ports, or the Mayor and Magistrates of each town thereof, and in this manner great numbers of seamen, whenever it has been required, have been provided by the said ports. That your Petitioners have on all occasions distinguished themselves by their readiness and zeal for Her Majesty's Service. As an instance thereof, have encouraged and compelled about four hundred seamen to go on board Her Majesty's ships of war, by the Magistrates of this little town of Deal, who are now actually in the public service, and this hath been the custom of furnishing the Royal Navy from the Cinque Ports, and not otherwise. The impressing of seamen by persons unauthorised by the Lord Warden is not only in opposition to the liberties and privileges of the Cinque Ports, but is frequently attended by disturbances, riots, tumults, and sometimes bloodshed: and it happened so in the town of Deal on the fourth instant, when some strangers, led on by the Marquis of Carmarthen to impress seamen, laid hold of one, Phillips, and thereupon drew their swords and grievously wounded several townsmen, in particular, one of the Magistrates who came to suppress the riot and prevent murder, and also one, Simmons, who came to the assistance of the said Justice, receiving no less than five several wounds; and soon after, the said Marquis of Carmarthen, without any provocation whatever, seriously assaulted the Magistrate by striking him in the face, in the execution of his office, which had well nigh produced considerable disturbance. The energy and zeal of the Magistrates succeeded at last in preserving the peace, so that, in return for the assault, the marquis nor his party received any injury; but the marquis and his followers persisted in this irregular and unreasonable way of impressment, and, therefore to prevent further mischief the Mayor was compelled to raise a strong watch to keep the peace to the great charge of your Petitioners. That unless seamen in Deal are impressed in conformity to the ancient customs and privileges of the Cinque Ports and by the officers only appointed by the Lord Warden, or by the Justices of the town of Deal (who best know who are fit to serve), it will be difficult to maintain order and preserve the peace within the said town of Deal for the time to come — for your Petitioners have been in danger of their lives continually. Wherefore your Petitioners humbly pray your Highness will be pleased to redress the affronts done to the Magistrates and inhabitants in endeavouring to preserve Her Majesty's peace, and graciously to consider of this matter and to give suitable directions thereon as your Royal Highness shall think fit, whereby your Petitioners may enjoy their ancient privileges and lie safe in their lives and estates, and not exposed to the affronts and insults of strange Impress Masters not residing within the said port of Deal.

And your Petitioners will ever pray.

Witness our Seal of Corporation, the eleventh September, 1702.

The response to the petition was an order by the Queen in Council, dated, 27th September, 1702:[65]

Upon reading this day the memorial forwarded to His Royal Highness from the Mayor, Jurats, and Common Council of the Borough of Deal, complaining of divers irregularities committed on the inhabitants of Deal in impressing of seamen for the Royal Navy, contrary to the rights and privileges of the Cinque Ports, by the Marquis of Carmarthen, — it is this day ordered by Her Majesty in Council, that a copy of the said memorial be transmitted to the marquis who has appointed the second Council day in November for hearing the complaint aforesaid, of which all parties concerned are to take notice to govern themselves accordingly.

That seems to be where the matter was left. As the author of a later history of the town of Deal complained: 'this was a somewhat equivocal manner of appeasing the indignation of the Deal folk at the decided violation of their liberties. But later on in the century the rights of self-selection for service were entirely disregarded, and Deal became one of the most frequent haunts of the press-gang'.[66]

Dover's response to a similar incident was more robust. In 1743 when the lieutenant of the *Devonshire* impressed six men in Dover 'many people of Dover, in company with the Mayor thereof, assembled themselves together and would not permit the lieutenant to bring them away'.[50] This angered the Admiralty Commissioners who ordered a Captain Dent of the *Shrewsbury* to send a press-gang ashore at Dover and press the first six able-bodied seamen they saw, as long as they were bachelors and not householders.[50] In this way it was finally made clear that the Cinque Ports had lost any immunity they might once have had against the press-gangs, and it is known that a press-gang was active in Margate in 1803.[67,68]

Wars with Spain

Margate was threatened on several occasions during the wars with Spain in the sixteenth and seventeenth centuries, particularly during the Spanish Armada scare that started in 1587.[69] The Spanish plan was for a two-pronged attack by the Duke of Medina Sidonia, the Commander of the Armada fleet, with some 16,000 Spanish infantry, and the Prince of Parma with some 30,000 men who were to cross the Channel from the Netherlands. The plan was described in detail in a letter from the King of Spain to the Prince of Parma.[70] The first step was for the Duke of Medina Sidonia to 'sail up the channel and anchor off Margate point' and then land his troops to establish a beach head at Margate. The instructions given to the Prince of Parma were: 'when you see the passage assured by the arrival of the fleet at Margate, or at the mouth of the Thames' you are to 'immediately cross with the whole army in the boats which you will have ready'. The plan was for the two men to 'cooperate, the one on land and the other afloat, and with the help of God [you] will carry the main business through successfully'. The King emphasised the importance of taking Margate: 'the fact of his [the Duke of Medina Sidonia] having taken possession of that port [Margate] will cut the communication of the enemy, and prevent them from concentrating their forces to some extent.'

In 1587 all the maritime counties were told to ensure that their forces were ready to repel any invasion by the Spanish.[71] Six thousand men were assembled in a camp at Sandwich, with a camp at Northbourne to watch the coast between Deal and Ramsgate.[72,73] The Isle of Thanet was recognized as one of five 'dangerous places' in Kent 'fittest to be putt in defence to hinder th'enemye'.[71] Edward Wotton was put in charge of the troops in Thanet with Captains Crispe and Partridge in charge of two companies of 250 and 200 trained men, respectively, and Captains Charles Hales and John Finch in charge of two companies of 120 and 150 untrained men, amounting to 720 men in all.[71] Martial activity slackened off in the spring of 1587 when it became clear that the dispatch of the Armada had been delayed, but then built up again in the autumn with the expectation of an attack the following spring. An order had been given to keep all ships in harbour but at the end of August 1587 this order was relaxed for fishing boats: 'Lord Cobham to geve order for the releasing of shippes and barkes belonging to fishermen which were taken at the last Generall Restraint of all shippes, &c, at Sandwich, Dover and Hith, &c'.[74] It seems that some 'gentlemen' had taken the opportunity of this lull to leave the island, but they were now ordered back: '[Lord Cobham] to give commaundment to such gentlemen as did withdraw themselves from the Isle of Thennet, where they inhabited before, to returne againe to their houses in the said Isle for the better strength of the same'.[74]

On June 18 1588 the Privy Council wrote to Lord Cobham 'being advertised that the kinge of Spaine's navie is alreadie abroade on the Seas and gone to the coast of Biscaye'[71] On June 27 Sir John Norrys was sent to inspect the defences on the Isle of Thanet and the Isle of Sheppy, another possible landing place for the Spanish:[75]

A letter to the Deputy Lieutenantes of Kent; her Majestie having receaved speciall advertizment that the Duke of Parma had intent and purpose to attempt the landinge of his forces about the Isle of Tennet or Sheppy, and so to take those Isles to serve for further invacion, because her Highnes did consider the neernes of that coast to the Dukes forces, and the weaknes that the same was in as yet for to make defence, her Majestic sent Sir John Norrys, knight, to take the viewe of those Isles and the coast neere adjoyninge, and other places there of danger, that he might consider what should be meet to be donn for the resystaunce and repulse of the ennemy yf he should goe about to invade those partes and to lande his forces there; therefore they were required that they would accompany the said Sir John Norrys in this service with soche of the Justices of the Peace as inhabyted those partes, and meet with him at soche places as he should appoint, that they might take the viewe of those places together and enforme him what had allready ben donn by them, or in performance of those orders their Lordships sent them in that hehalfe, and to see soche thinges performed and executed as he should thincke meet to be donn for the better strength[en]inge of those Isles and other places subject to the landinge of forraine forces.

In the event the Armada was, of course, defeated by the English fleet led by the Lord High Admiral, Lord Howard of Effingham, with Sir Francis Drake as second in command. The battered Armada fled, with Howard and Drake in pursuit, as far north as the Firth of Forth. The English fleet returned to anchor in Margate Roads but there a violent sickness broke out in the fleet, probably related to typhus or gaol fever. Howard did what he could for his sick mariners and on August 9 1588 wrote to Sir Francis Walsingham that 'Col. Morgan is at Margate with 800 soldiers: victuals must be provided for them'.[76] The following day, in a letter to William Cecil, Lord Burghley, Elizabeth I's premier councillor, he explained that he could not find adequate accommodation for the mariners in Margate and so was obliged to lodge them in barns and outhouses:[77]

August 10 1588 — Howard to Burghley.
My good Lord: — Sickness and mortality begins wonderfully to grow amongst us; and it is a most pitiful sight to see, here at Margate, how the men, having no place to receive them into here, die in the streets. I am driven myself, of force, to come a-land, to see them bestowed in some lodging; and the best I can get is barns and such outhouses; and the relief is small that I can provide for them here. It would grieve any man's heart to see them that have served so valiantly to die so miserably.

He adds in his letter that 'the Elizabeth Jonas had lost half her crew' and that 'of all the men brought out by Sir Ric. Townsend he has but one left alive.' He goes on to propose 'that £1,000 worth of new clothing should be sent to the fleet, as the men were in great want'.[78] On August 22 he wrote:[79]

The infection in the fleet is so great that many of the ships have hardly men enough to weigh their anchors. Lord Tho. Howard, Lord Sheffield, and other ships at Margate are so weakly manned that they could not come round to Dover. Recommends that the fleet should be separated into two divisions, the one to remain in the Downs and the other at Margate so as to let the men go ashore. The men are discontented that they have not received their full pay.

Defence of the southern coast remained a worry for many years. In 1596 Elizabeth I sent a letter to Lord Cobham, Lord Warden of the Cinque Ports, asking for a careful check on the state of preparedness of the coast for any attack:[80]

The Queen to Lord Cobham. Although we have long had proof of your faithful service, as Lieutenant of Kent, and Warden of the Cinque Ports, by your continual directions to your deputy lieutenants, and your lieutenant of Dover Castle, for mustering, furnishing, and training horse and foot thought convenient to be put in order for service of the country, yet upon considering the present state of affairs, and for the strengthening the maritime counties, you are immediately to repair along the sea coast, view all the forts, castles, and port towns, and see that they are properly furnished with officers, soldiers, ordnance, and ammunition. We have given warrant to the officers of ordnance to supply the defects in the latter . . . You are also to view the state of the port towns, havens, creeks, and passages; to consider as to their strength, and what number of able people they have to serve for their defence, and to cause them to be armed and furnished, at the common charge of the inhabitants; if in a conference with the officers of the towns, you shall find any opportunity to make them stronger against all attempts, either by building sconces, intrenching, or by reparations of the walls or otherwise, you are to procure the inhabitants to yield some contribution towards the charges. Also there should be a number of men, under able conductors, always in readiness to repair to the towns, forts, and castles, for their defence, upon warning by beacons or otherwise.

The previous day Lord Cobham had received a letter from the Privy Council concerning the Isle of Thanet, 'for the surveye whereof your Lordship is to take order that it may be knowen what defence the inhabitantes are hable to make, and what the whole state of the said Isle is in respect either of offence to be receaved or resistance to be made, and that the inhabitantes may be mooved to be at some charge for the strengthning of themselves with making some sconces or entrenchinges or such like meanes'.[81]

In January 1599 England had armies deployed in both the Low Countries and Ireland as part of the Nine Years War of 1594-1603 between England and a force of Gaelic Irish chieftains supported by Spain. On

January 10, 800 soldiers were to be shipped from Margate, most probably to the Low Countries, but, unfortunately, the expected transport failed to arrive from London:[82]

A letter to the Maiour and officers of the port of Margett. Whereas the number of 800 soldiers leavied in the counties of Kent and Sussex have bin appoynted to be in readines for their emkarquing at the port of Margett by the 10 day of this instant, who as we understand came thither at the tyme appointed and have attended for shippinge which should have comme thither from London before this tyme, as it was purposed, to take in the saide souldiers at that port and therefore it was supposed it should be needeles to take order for the lodginge and victualinge of them for the tyme there. Now for as much as the stay of the shippinge at London beyonde the tyme prescribed is the cause of the attendaunce of the souldiers at that port of Margett, we doe pray and require you in the meane while till the shippinge shall come downe thither to take order for the lodginge and victualinge of the saide number of souldiers at reasonable rates in the towne of Margett or neere thereaboutes, so as it exceede not the rate of eight pence the day for a man, the chardges whereof we will cause to be repaide and satisfied uppon your certificate to be sent up unto us.

Also in 1599 a letter from the Privy Council to Lord Cobham reported that the King of Spain was expected to attack London and that to do so he would 'attempt to land his forces either in the Downes or at Margett.' Cobham was to 'consider where and how some provision may be made, by casting up trenches or any other way [of] impeachment, at their [the Spanish] likest landing places, either in the Downs or at Margett, which may serve also for defence of those forces which shall be used against them'.[83] In 1628, at the start of the reign of Charles I, when a treaty was signed between France and Spain for the invasion of England, moves were again made to protect the Isle of Thanet by moving troops into the Island. About 35 soldiers were billeted in Margate from January 1628 for between 4 and 7 weeks.[84] Fifteen of the soldiers were billeted in three 'victualing houses', those of Simon Evans, John Pritchard and Ralph Tebbs. The other twenty soldiers were billeted in the private houses of the more important of the local inhabitants.

The Fort

A little above this Town of *Mergate*, to the *Northward* on the Cliff is a small piece of ground called the *Fort*, which has been a long time put to that Use, and was formerly maintained by the Deputies here, at the charge of the Parish. A large and deep ditch is on the land Side of it next the Town, which used to be scoured and kept clean of Weeds and rubbish. At the entrance into it, towards the East was a strong gate which was kept lock'd, to preserve the Ordnance, Arms, and Ammunition here. [16]

The Fort was paid for out of an assess (tax) allowed each year to the Margate Deputy 'to bear the charges he was at, in the execution of his office'; the costs of the annual muster were also paid for out of this assess.[16] Lewis reported that the assess was discontinued in about 1703, which, said Lewis, 'is like to prove of no service to the place, tho' they who see not afar off, are well pleased with its being drop'd as saving them a little present money'.

The Fort seems to have been built sometime in the reign of Queen Elizabeth. In 1569 the Spanish Ambassador, Guerau de Spes, reported to the King of Spain that the English 'are making plans to fortify Margate', so that any existing fortifications at Margate were likely to have been fairly primitive.[87] In a second report, in 1570, he described how Charles Howard had arrived in Margate to take charge of a squadron of ships that, as a mark of friendship, was to accompany a fleet of Spanish ships during its passage through the English Channel, carrying Ann of Austria to Spain for her marriage to the Philip, King of Spain. He reported that Charles Howard 'has his look-out on the hill close to Margate, and when our Queen's fleet is sighted they will go out to salute and receive her'.[88] The 'hill' is presumably the hill overlooking the harbour on which the Fort was to be built, and the reference to just a hill again suggests the absence of any extensive fortifications at the time. In 1588 the Venetian Ambassador in France wrote in a report to the Doge in Venice that 'there is a scheme for fortifying all the coast on both sides of Margate, which is the place where a landing might most easily be effected, and where it was discovered that the Spaniards actually intended to land. This can be done at very small cost, and in a very short time'.[89]

The first defences to be constructed at Margate would have consisted of little more than simple earthworks on which to mount guns. In March 1558 steps had been taken to provide Margate with some ordinance:[90]

A lettre to Sir Richard Sowthewell, Master of thordinance, to geve order that for the better defence of thisle of Thannett in Kent there may be sent furthewith unto Sir Henry Crispe, knight, thies parcelles of ordynance and munycion following; viz.. thre pieces of ordinance called sacres of yron, three fawcons either of yron or bras, foure demibarrelles of powlder, and for every piece xx[ti] [twenty] shott; indenting nevertheless, with the saide Sir Henry for the redelyvery of the same pieces hereafter to the Quenenes *(sic)* Majesties use.

Sacres (or sakers) and fawcons were field guns designed to be moved from place to place, sacres using five pound balls and fawcons two pound balls.[91] It is likely that the six guns were mounted on small platforms on the hill overlooking the harbour. A comment contained in a petition dating from September 1625 suggests that earthworks had been constructed on the hill at about this time.[92] The petition, from the inhabitants of the parishes of St John's and St Peter's and addressed to George Villiers, 1st Duke of Buckingham and the King's chief minister, asked 'that the sconce of fortification erected there in the time of Queen Elizabeth, but then much ruinated, may be repaired'. A sconce was a small protective fortification, such as an earthwork often placed on a mound as a defensive work for artillery, and was much used from the late Middle Ages until the 19th century.

In October 1625 the Privy Council wrote to the Earl of Montgomery, Lord Lieutenant for Kent, agreeing to improvements in the defences of the Cinque Port in general, and of Margate in particular:[93]

Wee have taken into our consideration the letters of the 9th and the 19th of September written from your deputy lieutenantes unto your Lordshipp and communicated unto us, wherein wee find just cause to commend the care and industry which they have used to view and take order for the sea-coast within the precinct of your Lieutenancye; and first wee have thought fitt to advertize your Lordshipp that wee have sent the said letters to our very good Lord, the Duke of Buckingham, inclosed in others of our owne, to praie and require him to take order for those matters mencioned in the said letters which concerne the Cinque Porta, and ... [with regard to] the redoubt at Margate raised in the Lord Cobham's time, if the deputy lieutenauntes shall send unto us any man whome they shall make choyce for the repayring of it, order shall be given for the setting of the worke in hand ... [and] wee doe likewise well approve and commend the vise of your Lordshipp's deputy lieutennauntes for a new troope of horse to bee raised in the island of Thannett which wee praie and require your Lordshipp to see put in execution according to what number you thinke fitt and the countrey maie well beare.

In 1627 the Privy Council wrote to the Earl of Totnes, the Master of the Ordinance, asking for the five guns then at Margate to be properly mounted:[94,95]

Whereas wee have beene made acquainted by our very good Lord, the Lord Admirall, that Margett and the partes there aboutes are often infested by the ennemie who dailly chaseth in shipps thether, that it were of no small consequence for the securitie of those partes to cause such peeces of ordinance as are alreadie at Margett to be theire mounted together with a proporcion of powder, shott and other necessaries to be sent thether on that behalf, wee, uppon consideracion had thereof, have thought good hereby to pray and require your Lordshipp to cause the said five peeces of ordinance to be there accordingly mounted and withall to cause a fitt proporcion of all necessarie provisions for the mounting and furnishing of the same to be forthwith sent thether.

In November 1627 a letter from the Privy Council to the Earl of Montgomery ordered him to ensure that the inhabitants of Thanet should 'assist and reinforce the garde and watch' in the area:[96]

Whereas it greatly importeth his Majesty's service in these tymes of danger, that all possible care and meanes be used for the well garding of the Cinque Portes and of every part and member thereof; wee have therefore thought fitt hereby to pray and require your lordship to give presente and effectuall direccion and order, that the inhabitants of the Isle of Thanet, who lye without the jurisdiction of the sayde Cinque Portes, shall neverthelesse assist and renforce the garde and watch which is held in those parts that are next adjoyning unto them in such a proporcion of number as shalbe competent and fit for that service.

Lewis reported that the Fort was extended in 1624, paid for out of the Deputy's assess already described:[16]

Out of the same rate or assess were built AD 1624 two watch-houses, and a watch-bell hung on the cage; windows made to the court of the guard here, and another watch-house built in the Fort, which was fortified with a large dike and gates, the expence of which was paid out of this Assess. By the same means were provided two brass Guns for the Fort, and Carriages for them, Muskets and Drums for the Watch, Powder, Musket-bullets, Match, Rests, Bandeleers, Pitch, and a barrel for it to set upon the beacon. Out of the same Assess were the charges defrayed of filling up the sea gates made in the Cliff, to prevent rogues coming up into the Country that way from the sea to steal and plunder, especially in time of war.

It is poissible that Lewis's date of 1624 is slightly out, and that the improvements to the Fort actually occurred over the period 1625-1627, as outlined above.

Although the Fort was equipped with 'five pieces of Ordnance' it was still very small, as made clear by Sir John Manwood in a letter of 1639:[97]

Sept. 26 1639. Deal, Sir John Manwood to Sec. Windebank
Last night a Holland man-of-war took out of the road at Margate two English ships that were freighted with Spaniards. There is a poor fort there and more poorly furnished, which shot the ship through fore and aft twice, howsoever they carried them away.

In 1672 John Evelyn described the Fort as 'a small fort of little concernment'.[98] In 1689, at the start of the Nine Years War (1689-1697) between France and a European-wide Grand Alliance led by William III, the government agreed to pay for a Gunner to take charge of the guns and ammunition at the Fort.[99] The position was filled by local men, first by William Cock followed, after Cock's death, by Roger Omer. The gunner was also responsible for searching for illegal immigrants in the town: 'March 24 1690: Warrant to William Cock [The name scratched out and that of John Gibbons put in its place], then gunner of the platform at Margate, to search for persons, clandestinely coming from France and going thither, in Margate Roads or places adjacent'.[100]

In June 1693 the inhabitants of Margate petitioned parliament asking that the £20 paid each year for the gunner should be given to them as an allowance to help maintain the Pier, saying that they would supply their own gunner.[101] It seems likely that this request was turned down, but anyhow the Government ceased to pay for a Gunner at Margate sometime after the end of the Nine Years War in 1697. Nevertheless, following the declaration of another war with France in 1702, part of the War of the

Spanish Succession, the Deputy and inhabitants of Margate rather illogically applied to the Queen for a reinstatement of the position of Gunner:[99]

To the Queen's most excellent Majesty in Council.
From Deputy and Inhabitants at Margate.

That Margate is a port situate between the Buoy of the Nore and the Downes, exposed to the French more than any other and is a place of trade having a peere for Shipping and coasting vessels. That in the Reign of King Charles and King James the second, and the late King William a platform or Fort on a place called the Fort green at Margate of 12 Guns was the only defence of the Town and peere and coasting vessels. And there was always one principal Gunner constituted, that commanded the Fort, and with the Deputy of Margate for the time being, had the keeping of the Stores and Ammunition, and was accountable for the same to the board of Ordnance, for which such Gunner was allowed out of the Office of Ordnance by bill and debenture £20. And that one William Cock in his lifetime, and after him Roger Omer, were constituted such Gunner and received such salary till the late peace when King William retrenched the same. That during this War, there is an absolute necessity for this Fort to be maintained, but the Guns and Carriages being out of order, and there being no powder or shott the peere and the Town are in great Danger to be plundered, and their vessels to be burnt or took in the Harbour, and hundreds of Shipps and Coasters like to be taken by privateers, for want of the Signals and Fireings from this little Fort as by the annexed certificates appears. That the Earl of Romney constituted the said Roger Omer to be Gunner in 1693 as by a copy of his warrant appears.

Your Petitioners therefore humbly crave leave to lay this matter before your Majesty in Council and pray the said Fort at Margate may be again supported, and that a Gunner may again be constituted by the Major General of the Ordnance and his salary paid as it was before and that the Guns, Carriages, ammunition and stores may be supplied in such manner as your Majesty in your great wisdom shall think fit.

The petition was sent to the Principal Officers of the Ordnance for consideration and their reply was guardedly supportive:[99]

We humbly return that during the late War the said Place was furnished by this Office with Gun Carriages and Ammunition and a Gunner appointed to take care thereof from 1 January 1689 at the pay of £20 per Annum, viz. first William Cock and at his decease, Roger Omer and the Deputy of the Place for the time being, which upon the peace was reduced as an unnecessary charge then but the

Platform or Fort was maintained by themselves. We have no objection but the charge it brings upon the Office for which no provision is made by Parliament, nor to the Establishing a Gunner there during the present War, but that it will be the only place in England, that is not a Garrison that will have a Gunner maintained at your Majesty's Charge, all which is most humbly submitted to your Majesty by

Office of Ordnance 3 November 1702

A newspaper report of March 1704 showed just how deficient the defences were at Margate:[102]

On the 9th Instant, in the Morning, a Hoy of the Queens Stores, was taken out of Margate Road, by a French Boat, about 8 or 9 Hands, and 6 Oars; and so well Guarded are our Coasts, that it's a Wonder they do not come and Plunder all our Houses; some Honest People would have gone off and recovered her, but the Custom Officers would neither give them Commission, nor furnish them with Ammunition; nor indeed was there enough on Broad-Stairs before which Village she lay some Hours, to Discharge one Gun.

Fine Work, indeed! All our Coast, and within the Mouth of the River too, not able to Rescue a Hoy of the Queens Provisions, from a Six Oar Boat, and not one great Gun!

However, Lewis's description of the Fort in 1723 makes it clear that by then the Government had reinstated the position of Gunner at Margate, at least when the country was at war:[16]

In War time this Place is still made Use of; a Gunner is appointed by the Government with a Salary of £20 *per Ann.* and a Flag staff erected to hoist a Flag upon occasion. There are likewise sent hither from the Tower 10 or 12 Pieces of Ordnance, Carriages, &c. with Ammunition for them. This Provision is not only a Safeguard to the Town, but a great means of preserving Merchants Ships, going round the North Foreland into the Downes, from the enemies privateers, which often lurk there-about to snap up ships sailing that way, which cannot see them behind the land. But as these lurking thieves lie open to the Places on the other side of the Foreland, particularly *Broadstairs*, an account of them is sent to the Gunner of this Fort or Platform, who gives notice to the ships, sailing that way, of their danger, by hoisting a flag and firing a Gun.

Pirates and Privateers: ours and theirs

Piracy was common in the Channel, with English, French, Spanish and Dutch ships all seeking prizes: 'low-level piracy was an ever present activity within the Channel, where, with a good lookout and a favourable wind, a pirate could sail after breakfast, seize a passing ship and return in time for supper'.[91] Indeed, Murray in her history of the Cinque Ports emphasised the importance of piracy to the very existence of the Cinque Ports:[5]

It was indeed the fact that the Cinque Ports were the worst pirates of the time that gave them their great importance. Their fierceness and lack of scruple increased their efficiency as guardians of the Channel and their value to the king, and it also gave them a reputation abroad. This was of great significance, since at that time the pirates from either side of the Channel were recognised as mercenaries whose services were for hire, and whose only demand was for opportunities for plunder. This placed an effective weapon for blackmail in the hands of the Portsmen, the threat of desertion to the enemy was known to be one which it was only too easy to carry out. The Ports had realised the strength of their position by the beginning of the [thirteenth] century, and their customary response to a proposal to punish them was that they would 'forthwith forsake their wives and children and all that they had, and go to make their profit on the sea, wheresoever they thought they would be able to acquire it'.

The extent of piracy during the fifteenth century led many merchant communities such as that at Bristol to arm and equip ships at their own expense to protect their trade.[103] These privately owned ships, referred to as privateers, were licensed by the crown and had the authority to attack foreign vessels deemed to be pirates.[104] Privateers were also referred to as picaroons or pickeroons, from the Spanish word for a pirate, picarón; the lightly-armed vessels used by the Dutch for privateering were often referred to as Dutch capers. Privateering provided a way to mobilize armed ships and sailors at no cost to the government, and with no commitment of naval officers; the cost of a privateer was borne by investors who would profit from any prize money earned from captured cargo and vessels. Privateers were particularly useful at disrupting the trade of a foreign power and were an important component of naval warfare between the sixteenth and nineteenth centuries. Although we associate privateering with major figures such as Sir Francis Drake and Sir Walter Raleigh, most privateering was actually undertaken by owners of small vessels, just offshore, usually taking 'modest prizes (wine, salt fish, etc. rarely worth more than £200), selling the plunder cheap in minor seaports or plunder marts'.[105] Both privateers and pirates would raid and plunder ships, the distinction between the two being that only the privateers had government permission for what they did. Foreign privateers were active in the channel at times of war with the French and Dutch and their presence would have disrupted trade in and out of the harbour at Margate.

Possibly the earliest recorded cases of piracy off Margate occurred in 1315. One case concerned a ship carrying wool from London to Antwerp.[106,107] Several London wool merchants had hired a ship called *la Petite Boyard* from John le Priair in London to carry a cargo of 120 sarplars of wool to Antwerp (a sarpler was a bale of wool weighing 728 pounds, about 330 kilograms), worth £1,200. The ship sailed down the Thames without mishap, but off Margate it ran into a pirate fleet led by the Admiral of Calais with 22 armed ships. In fear for their lives the crew grounded the ship off Margate on the ebb tide, probably on the Nayland Rock to the west of Margate. The ship was then attacked by the pirates; some of the crew were wounded and some slain, but others managed to escape into Margate, taking with them the sail and the rudder of the ship, hoping in this way to immobilize it. However, 'the admiral with his company approached that town and caused the sail and rudder to be carried back to the ship and afterwards carried off the ship, detaining her and the goods'.[108]

This happened in late summer 1315 and in November Edward II wrote to the Louis, King of France and Navarre, requesting that 'restitution and satisfaction' be made to the London merchants. A year later nothing had been done despite the fact that Edward II had frequently 'by his letters requested Sir William de Castellion, the constable of France, to cause restitution to be made to the merchants and mariners of the goods, or satisfaction and competent amends for the losses they had incurred.' After nearly three years of fruitless requests Edward II, in June 1318, ordered the Sheriffs of London 'to arrest goods of the men and merchants of the king of France within the city [of London] to the value of £600, and to cause them to be kept safely until the said merchants have been satisfied for that sum or until otherwise ordered', and Edward II 'also ordered the sheriff of Southampton to arrest goods in like manner to the value of £400, the bailiffs of Great Yarmouth to arrest goods to the value of £200, and the bailiffs of Ipswich to arrest goods to the value of £133 6s 8d'.[109] As a result 'certain goods of the merchants of the city of Amiens were arrested; and the king of France a short time since signified to the king that the citizens and merchants of Amiens, whose goods were so arrested in this realm, had come to him and prayed him for a remedy, and it was contained in the king of France's letters that due restitution had not been made to the king of England's merchants owing to negligence of the officials and ministers of the king of France'. Philip, then King of France and Navarre, requested Edward II 'to desist from such counter seizures and to restore the goods of the merchants of Amiens thus arrested, and promised to cause such satisfaction to be made to the said merchants of this realm before All Saints next as should content the king of England'. Edward II accepted this promise and in August 1318 he ordered the execution of his order to be delayed until All Saints next 'and to release any goods that they may have arrested in execution of the above order, as the king of France will do justice to the aforesaid merchants concerning this robbery before the aforesaid feast, as he has promised to do by his letters patent to the king remaining in chancery'. Unfortunately Philip did not keep his word and in January 1319 Edward II issued another order to the Sheriffs of London 'to arrest goods of the men and merchants of the king of France to the value of £402 1s 10d, the residue of the sum of £600' with similar orders to the Sheriff of Norfolk and Suffolk 'to arrest goods to the value of £333 6s 8d' and for the Bailiffs of Southampton 'to arrest goods to the value of £400'. The officials were ordered 'to certify the king of their proceedings in this matter, keeping safely the goods arrested by virtue of this order until further orders'. The execution of this order was delayed 'at the frequent requests of the king of France' but, with no settlement achieved, it was again put into effect in August 1320 with the only change being that, instead of involving the Sheriff of Norfolk and Suffolk, the 'bishop of Winchester's bailiffs of St Giles's Fair, Winchester, [were] to arrest goods to the value of £333 6s'. Presumably this brought the matter to a close, nearly five years after the first complaint had been sent to the French king.

The second case of piracy in later summer 1315 also concerned an attack by pirates from Calais on a ship grounded on the ebb tide off

Margate.[110] Again Edward II wrote to Louis, then the King of France to complain:

To L[ouis], king of France and Navarre ... letters concerning an attack by malefactors of Calais, who lately attacked by their barges and boats a ship of John Brand, citizen and merchant of London, laden at London by him and Henry de Boure, Nicholas Fissh and Siward de Bokham, merchants of the Almain Hanse [an organization of traders in Germany], dwelling in this realm and enjoying the privileges of the king's merchants, with 34 sacks of wool to take to Andwerp, the said malefactors having captured the ship whilst she lay upon land near Mergate, in the isle of Thanet, owing to the ebb of the sea, when they took her and her crew and cargo to Calais.

The outcome of the complaint is not recorded.

Later the problem became one of pirates from Flanders, a country with which England had a complex relationship.[111,112] Treaty relationships between England and France required England to act against Flanders when, in 1315, renewed war broke out between France and Flanders. On 1 September 1315 Edward II duly declared that all Flemings must leave England and that English merchants were forbidden to provide arms or food to the Flemish. Unfortunately, this coincided with a period of famine in Flanders, and the Count of Flanders had to resort to piracy to provide food for his country. However, the formal ban on the presence of Flemings in England was removed at the end of 1316 when Louis of France informed Edward II that he had made peace with Flanders but the resumption of diplomatic relations between England and Flanders did not end the fighting at sea and, in particular, hostilities continued between the Flemish sailors and those of the Cinque Ports.

In March 1317 pirates from Flanders attacked and seized the ship *la Swalowe* off Margate and, following an investigation by the Sheriff of Kent, Edward II wrote to the Count of Flanders asking for 'restitution or satisfaction':[113-115]

To R[oyal] count of Flanders. Because it was lately found by an inquisition taken by the sheriff of Kent that certain malefactors of the count's power took by armed force a ship of Robert Youn, Alan atte Warfe, and Thomas Tuk, citizens and merchants of London, called *'La Swalewe'* of London, laden with wines, linen cloths, canvas, and other goods of Robert, Alan, Thomas, and of Henry le

Palmer, whilst anchored at Mergate within the king's power, and slew the master and mariners of the same, and took away with them the ship and her tackle, price 200 marks sterling, together with the goods and merchandize found in her, to wit 25 tuns and 7 pipes of wine, price £171 sterling, canvas, linen cloth, and other goods to the value of £24 sterling, silver cups, beds, robes, armour and other small necessaries, price £30 sterling, and £60 sterling in money by tale, and carried the same to La Swyne within the count's dominion, detaining the same from the said merchants to their damage of £100 in addition to the above sums, the king frequently requested the count to cause restitution or satisfaction to be made to the said merchants; and the count at length replied that he was in ignorance in this matter, as he was not informed concerning the above deed nor of those who committed it, adding that he would punish them if found within his power; as it is now testified before the king that Lambesin White, William Hoscard, William Denel, Christian Wolpyn, John Spaynard, William Reinald, Quintin Hereman, Quintin Broun, Hanekyn Colure, Richard Rawel, John Malefit, Quintin le Penson, John le Moselere, John Lemesone, and Peter Seeman committed the said trespass and robbery, and that they took with them to Flanders a boy found in the said ship, having slain the mariners and all others found in her, which boy stayed in Flanders for nearly a year with some of the trespassers aforesaid and with John le Gos, then the count's bailiff of Leschufe, and that the wines found in the ship were delivered by the said malefactors to John Tripet of Male for the count's use, which John appropriated to himself a dog found in the ship together with the charter of the freight of the ship, and that the aforesaid Quintin Lempescue (*sic*) sold the said ship to John Lompesone, his brother, who repaired it otherwise than it was before in order that it should not be recognised; wherefore the king signifies the premises to the count in evidence of the affair, and requests him to cause restitution or satisfaction to be made to the said merchants of their ship and goods and their damages without further delay, according to the contents of the count's aforesaid letter, so that it may not behove the king to provide them with another remedy. He is desired to write back an account of his proceedings by the bearer.

A year later the Count had done nothing and Edward II ordered 'the sheriffs [of London] to arrest goods of the count's men and merchants to the value of £118 6s 8d in part payment of £418 6s 8d, the value of the ship, wine, money, and other goods, and of £100 for the estimated damages, and to detain the same until the merchants have been satisfied for the first-named sum or until further orders, certifying the king of their proceedings in this matter. The king has ordered the sheriff of Kent to arrest goods in like manner to the value of £100; the sheriff of Suffolk to arrest goods to the value of £100; the sheriff of Southampton to arrest goods to the value of £100; and the bailiffs of Great Yarmouth to arrest goods to the value of £100'.

A letter written towards the end of 1317 records another occasion on which a ship, the *le Bon An*, carrying wine from Bordeaux to London was attacked by pirates from Flanders who 'lying in wait upon the sea took the ship laden with the said wines by violence at Merkat [Margate] near the Isle of Thanet whilst on her voyage to London, and carried her and the wines away with them to Flanders'.[116] Again, in 1319 a ship, *la Arounde*, carrying wine from Leyburn [Libourne] in Gascony to London was attacked by 'certain malefactors of Flanders and elsewhere, [who] lying in wait for the said ship, attacked her on the coast near the land between Mergate and Recolvre, co. Kent, where she was anchored, and, having slain the mariners thereof, carried off with them to Le Swyn the ship and wines'.[117,118] This time Edward II ordered 'the sheriff [of Lincoln] to arrest goods of the men and merchants of the power of the count of Flanders to the value of £306, in part satisfaction for the wines and goods aforesaid, and to keep them safely until further orders, certifying the king of the goods arrested by virtue of this order. The king has ordered the sheriff of York to arrest goods in like manner to the value of the remaining £300.'

Edward II was apparently unaware of the ongoing feud between the sailors of the Cinque Ports and those of Flanders and, on hearing of it in September 1317, sent an apology to the count of Flanders:[119]

> The king, whilst staying in the northern parts of his realm, heard with regret that dissensions have arisen between the barons and men of the Cinque Ports and the count's men, and he has sent W. [Walter Reynolds] archbishop of Canterbury and John [John Hotham], bishop of Ely, his treasurer [Lord High Treasurer], to the barons and men of the Cinque Ports to prohibit their grieving or damaging the count's subjects under pain of forfeiture; wherefore he requests the count to issue a similar prohibition to his subjects; and he further requests him to send certain of his subjects to this realm with full power to treat concerning the damage suffered by both sides and to reform lasting peace, as the king proposes shortly to appoint certain of his subjects to enquire concerning the aforesaid damages, and to do full and speedy justice to the sufferers.

Fresh diplomatic overtures were made between England and Flanders following the death of Robert III, Count of Flanders, and a truce was agreed: on 5 April 1323 the Lord Warden of the Cinque Ports was ordered to proclaim the truce throughout the Cinque Ports.[112]

Trouble with Flanders flared up again in the sixteenth century. In 1537 Henry VIII appointed Sir John Dudley to patrol the Channel with four ships to prevent the seizure of English ships.[91] A particular nuisance was a Flemish ship, the 'Admiral of Sluys' or 'Admyrall of Slews'.[120] It was reported that '"This Admyrall of Slews" took from the crayer of John Masters of Sandwich two barrels of white herring and 17 barrels of beer. He and Capt. Meker landed at Margate, broke up the house of Thos. Hewse, took out two Frenchmen and carried them to Flanders.'

A hundred years later there was still trouble. In August 1649 'fishermen of Ramsgate, Broadstairs, and Margate' petitioned the Admiralty Committee 'for a convoy this season of herring fishing; and desiring that a guard may be provided for them'.[121] Two days later the Council of State instructed Capt. James Henley, of the Minion, that because of the 'considerable losses being sustained by well-affected people of Sandwich, Margate, &c. by reason of pilfering sea rovers from Ostend, Dunkirk, &c. that lie between Lee Road, the Gore, and the North Foreland' he should, 'laying aside all other commands whatsoever, . . . carefully ply between Lee Road, the Gore, and North Foreland, and the mouth of the river, sometimes looking into Margate Road, and use your best diligence to destroy those sea rovers.[122]

In November 1649 the Navy Commissioners hired James Coppin and his ketch 'to be employed as a man-of-war between Dover, Sandwich, Margate, and Tilbury Hope, for the guard of that part of the river from pirates, and convoying of vessels trading to London'.[123] James Coppin was a Margate man who married Mary Smith at St John's in April 1642 and had five children, all baptised at St John's.[124] On November 9 1649 a warrant was issued 'to contract with Jas. Coppin, for his ketch to be employed as a man-of-war in the winter guard' and 'to supply the Sea Flower, Jas. Coppin's ketch, with six sacker cuts, tackle, muskets, pistols, pikes, shot, powder, &c'.[125] In the middle of November James Coppin was sent his instructions:[126]

Many vessels have been surprised by sea rovers and pickeroons, lurking under the headlands on the Kentish shore, in the mouth of the Thames. You are therefore to repair with your vessel to the mouth of the Thames, and ply to and from Dover, Sandwich, Margate, and Tilbury Hope, which places have been much prejudiced of late by pirates and sea rovers; also to give convoy to such vessels and small craft as shall be laden with grain, &c., between Dover, Margate, Sandwich, and London. If you meet with any man-of-war of the enemy, you are to force him to your obedience, or otherwise to fight with him; in case he will not yield, you are to kill the men, and in case of extremity, fire or sink the vessel.

Later in November, 'Capt. Coppin of the Sea Flower' was ordered 'to sail to Dunkirk, and endeavour to bring back the vessels taken out of Lee Road, taking the advice of Geo. Blake therein' and, in December a warrant was issued, 'to supply Capt. Coppin, of the Seaflower ketch, with arms and ammunition'.[125] In 1650 Capt. James Coppin was chosen to be the captain commanding one of 'the Parliament Ships appointed for the next summer's service', the 'Margaret ketch', with 40 men.[127] In 1651 he was appointed captain of a frigate, the Hart, with 60 men and 14 guns, part of the Winter Guard protecting the Northern Coast and convoys between Newcastle and the Downes.[128] In May 1652 he received a warrant ordering the Heart [Hart] 'to convoy the Godspeed, and five other ships, of Hull, and the Employment, and three others of Lynn, to their ports'.[129] Sometime between May and October 1652 he died on the Hart frigate, in a battle with the Dutch; a warrant was issued on October 20 1652 by the Council of State for Payments of Money by Collectors for Prize Goods 'to Marie, widow of Capt. James Coppin, of the Hart frigate, for her loss by his death £40 a piece for herself and four children'.[129]

Pirates did not come only from the other side of the Channel; the Cinque Ports had their own. Piracy by ships of the Cinque Ports reached a peak in the first half of the fourteenth century and then declined following the appointment of an Admiral of the Cinque Ports, an appointment designed to impose some discipline on the ports.[5] The writ describing the appointment of the Earl of Arundel to the position in 1345 explained that 'no one can chastise them or rule them [the sailors] unless he be a great man'; the role of the Admiral was to be 'governor of the mariners . . . to rule them and uphold them in all their laws and customs'.[5] A letter from

Edward II to the Lord Warden of the Cinque Ports in 1323 had reported an attack on two galleys loaded with 'divers cloths, silver, copper, tin and other merchandise, to the value of £610' belonging to a merchant 'lately trading in Flanders', that took place when one galley was off Calais and the other off Sandwich: 'divers persons from those ports and the county of Kent and elsewhere in the king's dominions with divers ships attacked them piratically, seized the galleys and took them to the Isle of Thanet, co. Kent, and carried away part of the goods, and then took the galleys with the residue of the goods to Sandwich, within the liberty of the Cinque Ports, and there divided the residue of the goods amongst themselves, and having robbed the masters and mariners of their goods and clothing permitted them so to depart'.[130]

A case, more of theft than of piracy, that took place in Margate harbour was reported in a letter of February 1340:[132]

To the bailiffs of Margate. The king has received the plaint of Arnald Kayard of Ardenburgh in Flanders containing that certain men of Mergate entered a ship of his anchored there, by night, and took herrings, white bread, salt, onions, garlic and other goods found therein to the value of £45, and unjustly detain them from Arnald, whereupon he has besought the king to provide a remedy; the king, considering the services of the men of Flanders to him, and therefore wishing to deal graciously with them, orders the bailiffs to take an inquisition on the matter, upon sight of these presents and to cause the ship and the herrings etc. to be restored to Arnald or his attorney without any diminution, and the price thereof if they do not exist, compelling the malefactors to do this by distraints, and the taking of their goods and persons, so that the plaint may not be repeated to the king, knowing that if they are remiss in the execution of this order the king will cause the price of the ship and goods to be levied of their goods and chattels and of those of the other men of Mergate, and delivered to Arnald or his attorney. The king also orders them to punish the malefactors so that their punishment may serve as an example to others.

Another case described in a letter of July 1404 specifically mentions a sailor, John Rose, from Margate:[131]

Commission to Robert Markeley, Serjeant at arms, to appraise a ship called *la Jambard* with its gear and certain goods and merchandise now under arrest and to deliver the same to James Naunnesson of Harlam in Holand in part satisfaction of the value of goods and merchandise captured from him, and to arrest

Walter Berneville of Wykham, Michael Berneville of Wykham, Stephen Yonge of Wykham, Thomas Hastyng of Sarre, Robert Twytham of Haddesham, Walter Deryng of Fordewich, William Hunte of la Batell, John Mawer of Brolan, David Walssheman, 'taillour,' John Elys of Sandewich, John Gosnale of Sandewich, William Kendale of Sandewich, John Royston of Sandewich, John Preston of Sandewich, John Rose of Mergate and Richard Cornewaille of the county of Essex and imprison them until they fully satisfy the said James. Lately, on information that they and others being at sea in the said ship captured the said James, who for no small time before had been victualler to the realm, on his return from the city of London to his own parts and despoiled him of divers goods and merchandise of his to the value of £100 6s 8d in a ship of his called *la Godmerade*, the king by the advice of the council by divers writs ordered the constable of Dover Castle and warden of the Cinque Ports and the sheriff of Kent to arrest the said ship called *Jambard* and the said Walter and others and all the goods and merchandise captured and to put the ship, goods and merchandise in safe custody and cause the said evildoers to come before the king and council; and the ship with its gear and divers of the goods and merchandise at Sandewich and Fordewich and elsewhere within the said county were seized and are still detained, and the said Walter Berneville and Michael being arrested and brought before the king and council departed from thence without licence.

A letter sent in 1551 to Charles I, Holy Roman Emperor and first King of Spain, complained of the support given at Margate to a Scottish pirate who was attacking Spanish ships:[133]

January 21 1551, Vienna, Jehan Scheyfve to the Emperor.

Sire: In accordance with the Queen's commands expressed in her last letters of December 19th, which I received on the 28th of that month, I presented myself before the Council and made declaration to them of the peace concluded between your Majesty and Scotland, together with the inclusion in it of the King of England and his dominions . . . I also told them I had heard that a certain Scots pirate was being welcomed and supported at Margate, the inhabitants of which place openly purchased from him goods seized from your Majesty's subjects, and that most of the crew of the pirate ship were English; wherefore I demanded the punishment of these pirates, purchasers and abettors, according to their offences. The Admiral stated that the said pirate had been arrested, and should be punished. I praised this good deed, and added that, a few days before, the same pirate had taken three vessels from Flushing, which ought promptly to be restored. He replied that he knew nothing about such prizes, and supposed they had already been sold to the French.

In a subsequent letter to the Queen Dowager of Spain the complaint was about French men of war using Margate to attack Spanish ships:[133]

January 14 1552, Vienna, Jehan Scheyfve to the Queen Dowager.
At the ... meeting I reminded them of my former complaints that three or four French men-of-war put in to Margate now and then, to lay in wait for and pillage the Emperor's subjects' vessels entering or leaving the Thames. Now they had gone ashore and seized some boats belonging to the Emperor's subjects; and the Frenchmen were supported and caressed by the inhabitants of the place, for they had sold their booty taken from the said subjects to some of the King's officers and other Englishmen. Moreover, one of the King's pinnaces was now at sea, and usually stood off Margate, boarding every vessel belonging to the said subjects that went by, and holding them up until the Frenchmen could make ready to attack. ... They replied that this complaint surprised them greatly, for the French ambassador said that his Majesty's ships were daily plundering the French in English waters, and even in English ports. Nonetheless, they had had the bailiff of Margate arrested for having bought some of the Emperor's subjects' property. As for the pinnace, they were not aware that there was one at sea, or near Margate; but they would obtain information and take such steps as should seem necessary.

Three references to this arrest of the 'bailiff' of Margate appear in the Acts of the Privy Council, the bailiff probably being another name for a Pier Warden.[134] The first, on December 1551 records a letter to the Keeper of the Kings Bench Prison in London for the arrest of the bailiff of Margate: 'A lettre to the Keper of the Kinges Benche to receyve the *body* of the Baylyf of Margat, and se hym kept so as none speake with hym but by ordre from the Lordes.' The second, on February 1 1552, names the bailiff as Alexander Norwood and gives the condition of his bail: 'Alexaundre Norwood, Baylif of Margat, bounde in recognisaunce of two hundreth poundes. The condition to be forth cumming at all tymes when he shalbe uppon reasonable warning called for to aunswer unto suche complaintes as ar by certaine merchauntes layed to his charge; and thereuppon the sayd Norwood was discharged of his enprisonement'. The third, on February 11 1552, orders the bailiff of Margate to release the ship and goods taken by the French: 'To the Baylif of Margat to delyver to David Garraud certayne goodes taken by the Frenchemen remaining in his custody'. That presumably was the end of the matter.

In 1565, Margaret, Duchess of Parma wrote to Elizabeth I protesting about English pirates waiting around the mouth of the Thames to attack Flemish and French ships, putting at risk attempts to restore normal commercial relationships between England and the Netherlands.[135] The Privy Council duly wrote to the responsible officials in all the maritime counties complaining:

dyvers evill disposid persons, as it apperythe, forgettinge the feare of Almightye God and the duetye of good subjectes, have of late in sundry vessells and shippes frequentyd the seas upon the coast of this our realme, robbinge and spoylinge honest quyett merchauntes and others, both of our owne subjectes and of other princes being presentlye in legue and good amytye with us, which cometh chiefly to passe by reason the said pyrattes, whereof parte are knowen also to be of other nacions, are at the handes of a number of disordered persons, dwellinge within or nere the havens, crekes and landinge places of this our realme, secretly refresshed with victualles, furnyshed with munytion and other necessaries, and sundrye other wayes by byeng of the stollen wares ayded and relyved, to the manifest contempt of us and our lawes and the grete sclaunder of this our realme.[136]

A letter was also sent specifically to Lord Cobham because it was suspected that men from the Cinque Ports were involved in these attacks:[136]

A letter to the Lord Cobham signyfieng unto him that the Queen's Majestic is daylye importunately complained unto by the French and Spanyshe Embassadours resident here of spoiles commytted by Englishe pirattes upon the King's, their masters', subjectes upon the Narrow Seas, and be, as is vehemently to be suspectid, harborid, victuallid and maineteynyd by some dwelling in the V Portes, whereunto his Lordship is required in her Majesties name to have espetiall regard, and yf any of the said pyrattes shall happen to come into any porte or creke of his rule, to gyve order that he may be stayed and committed to safe warde, and to use the like with all their aydours, and to cawse all such goodes as have ben brought in by them to be stayed and commytted to safe custodye, after perfect inventorye taken first thereof, and to advertise hither what he shall have donne herein.

One of those caught up in the action against the English pirates and privateers was William Herle, an Elizabethan 'intelligencer,' or spy, and agent of the Secretary of State Sir William Cecil, Lord Burghley. In

1565 Herle was accused of associating with a privateer operating under a Swedish letter of marque and suspected of seizing goods from a neutral merchant vessel from Antwerp while it was off the North Foreland. The case against Herle was made in a disposition by Luke Sprackling, a searcher at Margate, and was investigate by the High Court of Admiralty; Luke Sprackling was a son of Nicholas Sprackling, one of the Sprackling family of St Lawrence, Ramsgate.[135] Luke Sprackling had been trying to find Herle for some time as Herle owed him £4 17s; the previous August Herle had lodged at Sprackling's house for thirteen days, borrowing about three pounds from him, and running up a bill for his food.[137] On July 4 1565 two sailors told Sprackling that Herle was on board the privateer *Tiger* laying off the North Foreland. Sprackling boarded the *Tiger* to try to recover his debt from Herle, but Herle was not there. While on board the captain, Charles Morehouse, provided Sprackling with 'gentell entertaynment' and also 'sent to the sayd searchers wife a smale rowlet of iij [three] gallons of wine called Taynt, a holand chese and two barrels of powdred cods, and offered to sell xx [twenty] barrels of fishe more at xiij^s iij^d [13s 3d] the barrel which he refused'.[137] Although Sprackling did not buy the goods offered him by Morehouse, presumably plundered, he did accept the gifts for his wife; Morehouse was already known to Sprackling because he had lodged in Sprackling's house the previous year when Herle had also been there. The *Tiger* remained off the North Foreland until 10 July and Morehouse asked Sprackling to sell him provisions of beef, biscuits, and beer for the ship, but Sprackling refused after he had heard rumours in Margate that Morehouse was involved in piracy. Morehouse claimed to Strackling that as the *Tiger* had a license from King Erik of Sweden 'to apprehend and take all suche shipps and goods as did appertaine to any of his enemies' he was doing nothing illegal.

Mary Best, another inhabitant of Margate, claimed in her deposition to the High Court of Admiralty that Herle and four others had lodged at her house for one night, which she thought unusual as Herle 'was accustomably used to lodge at the sayd searchers [Sprackling's] howse'.[180] Also strange was the 'great bage' filled with 'divers peeces of goold' carried by one of Herle's companions, possibly spoils from pirating. In his defense Herle claimed that he was only on board the *Tiger* because its owner, William Wilson, owed him money and intended to repay him in plunder acquired under his Swedish letter of marque, although, he added, he had left the ship before any acts of piracy had actually taken place. Later, Herle was to send a detailed diary of his movements to Lord Burghley, designed to prove that he had not been involved in piracy.[138] In the diary Herle described his stay in Margate as follows: 'I lay & supped the sayd tewsday [3 July] at night in Margate with a vyttayler there, & by occupatyon a shewmaker, nether desgysed as som pretend nor yet unknowen in that towne, departing erlye the next morning on foote to Sandwiche', a rather different account from that provided by Sprackling.

The final decision reached by the Admiralty Court is not known, but there is nothing to suggest that the case against Herle actually went to trial, perhaps not surprising given the difficulty in proving that Herle was actually on board the Tiger when the alleged act of piracy took place.[135] It seems likely that the Privy Council decided to make an example of Herle by taking him to the High Court of Admiralty because of the complaint from Margaret of Parma about piracy. Whatever the actual outcome of the case, it does point to a rather cosy, if not corrupt, relationship between the customs officials at Margate and the pirates and privateers operating off the town's coast.

Problems with pirates continued. In 1570 Elizabeth I complained to Lord Cobham of ships captured by pirates being brought into English ports and 'caused a Proclamacion to be published within all the shires of this her realme lying upon the sea costes, whereby a former Proclamation is revived forbidding the bringing in or uttering within any of her havens, crekes or portes of any shippes, wares or goodes taken by any rovers or others upon the seas'.[139] In particular, she complained that 'Englishe and Frenchemen toguithers, have taken a hulk coming out of Portingall, with ij [2] other Flemishe shippes, and the same brought to Mergat.'

As well as the close relationships with foreign pirates revealed by these letters, Margate had problems with its own pirates. In 1578 the Privy Council wrote to Lord Cobham:[140]

that wheras their Lordships are gi[ven] to understande that one Nicolas Petite hathe of late committed sundrie spoiles upon divers hulkes and other shippes hanting the river of Thames, who (as their Lordships are informed) is presentlie at Margate where he inhabitethe; his Lordship is therefore required fourthewith uppon the receipt hereof to give order for his apprehension, and being apprehended to se him safelie delivered unto this berer, who hathe charge from their Lordships to see him safelie delivered at London.

In September 1579 the Privy Council wrote again 'in answer of a letter sent from him [Lord Cobham], that ... touching such pirates as were staied at Margate, he should geve order that they should be proceaded with according to lawe and such Commission as hathe ben heretofore addressed unto him in that behalf'.[141] Also in 1579 the Privy Council provided a 'letter of assistance' for recovering material taken from a hoy off Margate: 'A letter of assistance for the recoveringe of certaine clothes, &c., taken and spoiled out of a certaine hoye in the monethe of November last past by one Walter Dabernall and his complices, about Margate in the Isle of Thennet, divers parcells wherof are said to have come to the handes of divers th'inhabitauntes of the countie of Kent and Dorset about Lullworthe'.[142]

The Anglo-Dutch wars and more wars with France

The real importance of Margate and its Fort became apparent during the second (1665-1667) and third (1672-1674) Anglo-Dutch Wars, wars essentially over control of trade routes.[143] A number of major and minor naval battles in the first Anglo-Dutch war (1652-1654) exhausted both the English and Dutch forces and led to a peace treaty that, unfortunately, failed to resolve the commercial rivalry between the two nations. The second war was provoked by the English who believed that a combination of English naval force and privateering would cripple the Dutch and lead to a favourable peace. In fact, the Dutch raid on the Medway in June 1667 by a flotilla of ships led by Admiral de Ruyter is considered one of the most humiliating defeats in English military history, and the war ended with a Dutch victory. The third Anglo-Dutch war started when Charles II came to the assistance of Louis XIV in the Franco-Dutch War; a series of victories by de Ruyter against the Anglo-French fleet forced Charles II to make peace.

Margate's role in the first Anglo-Dutch war was just to provide a church tower from which to observe the movements of the Dutch fleet in the Channel. In November 1652 General Blake wrote to the Council of State that 'since evening intelligence is brought me that from off the steeple of Margate there was observed above 400 sail'.[144] The town was, however, more involved in the second and third wars, and much information about this period of Margate's history is provided by the letters sent from

Margate to Sir Joseph Williamson, Under Secretary to the Secretary of State and head of the government's network of informants. In November 1666, one of these correspondents, John Smith, informed Williamson that although '70 sail of Ostenders have passed by' Margate, 'no Dutch capers have been near lately'.[145] Again, in May 1667 he reported that 'the coast is clear of pickeroons, and the mackerel men fish quietly, with the Blackamoor pink [a small, square-rigged ship with a narrow stern] as convoy'.[146] Privateers were more active during the third Anglo-Dutch war; in July 1672 Richard Watts wrote from Deal to Williamson about a Dutch fleet of capers that took four Margate vessels 'so that several vessels that yesterday and to-night resolved to go to Newcastle, have laid up in the several piers of Thanet and Sandwich' threatening the supply of coal (Chapter 2).

The main threat to Margate came, however, from the Dutch navy. On 16 October 1665 Samuel Pepys wrote in his diary: 'The newes for certain that the Dutch are come with their fleete before Margett, and some men were endeavouring to come on shore when the post come away, perhaps to steal some sheep'.[148] A letter of 15 October 1665 to Henry Muddiman gave more detail: 'In Margate roads are 80 Dutch men-of-war; they have shot 100 pieces of ordnance at the town, breaking chimneys, and maiming most of the vessels in the harbour, and they have landed 40 men'.[149] In July 1666 John Smith reported that 'the Dutch fleet is in view, hovering between Margate and Orford-Ness; they have not yet joined the French fleet; the ships seen near Dungeness might be merchant vessels bound southward; good guard is kept, and Sir Rich. Sandys has brought his foot and horse company into the island'.[150] The same day Richard Watts and Captain S. Titus sent similar reports from Walmer and Deal:[150]

July 1 1666, Walmer. Ri. Watts to [Williamson].
The Dutch fleet is said to be 90 or 100 sail; four are cruising at South Sands, on the back of the Goodwin. The Pearl is gone up to London, with two Swedish frigates laden with masts, which they say will serve the best ship in England. The plague breaks out in fresh houses in Deal. A regiment of foot is gone to the Isle of Thanet.

July 1 1666, Deal Castle, Capt. S. Titus to Lord Arlington.
Was obliged to go through the companies of his regiment to put them in order. On Friday, the Dutch fleet of 90 sail appeared before the North Foreland.

On Saturday, it was thought they meant to do mischief at Margate, but they put off to sea, and nothing has been heard of them since. In the Isle of Thanet are 300 men of his regiment, two of the county companies, and two small troops of horse under Sir Rich. Sandys and Lieut. Col. Rooke. Dares not quarter any companies in Deal, it is so dismally affected. Will draw men from Sandwich if needful, but hopes not to be besieged longer than men can conveniently fast.

On July 10 1666 John Smith reported that 'there has been a general muster of horse and foot, Lord Middleton, the general, being present' and John Lindsey from Walmer reported that 'two Dutch men-of-war came into Margate bay, but did no harm'.[151] On July 27 Smith reported that 'guns have been heard, and they are believed to have been engaged two days' and that 'a smack is being manned with soldiers to take a French sloop hovering on the North Foreland'.[152] On August 31 Colonel Thomas Culpepper at Canterbury reported that he was going to the Isle of Thanet 'to inquire of the enemy's fleet' which he found 'at anchor off the North Foreland' and reported that he had ordered 'two companies to guard the coast'.[153] In August further steps were taken to protect the Isle of Thanet: on August 29 a warrant was sent from Whitehall to the Commissioners of Ordnance 'to deliver 12 pieces of ordnance, well mounted and fitted, to Col. Silius Titus, governor of Deal Castle, for defence of the Isle of Thanet' and on the same day a message was sent from the King to the Lord Lieutenant of Kent that 'Capt. John Boyse's company of militia, being chiefly from the Isle of Thanet, is to associate with Colonel Titus' regiment in defence of that coast, being nearer to it than to that to which it properly belongs, that there may be good and sufficient guard for the coast, and to obey Colonel Titus as their superior officer'.[154] On April 8 1667 Smith reported that Margate 'is in a good posture of defence, with two or three companies of the Scotch regiment there. Col. Titus has ordered a meeting of the trained bands to-morrow; they are to have their ammunition with them, and their arms well fixed'.[155] On May 17 he reported that there was 'a rumour of a great fleet of Dutch and French ships coming, and the wind is fair for them' so that 'the coast is put in a posture of defence, and the trained bands mustered'.[156] However on May 21 he reported that he had heard 'of no Dutch nor French men-of-war on the coast' and that 'the fishermen have not been molested' but still 'the trained bands of the Isle of Thanet have been mustered'.[157] At the end of May 'the trained bands have mustered again' as although 'no French nor Dutch men-of-war are seen off the coast . . . the wind blows fair to bring them in'.[158]

On June 25 Smith reported that 'near the road are six Holland men-of-war, one a vice-admiral, and a galliot hoy. Others show themselves near the shore, and go away again'.[159] On July 5 it was reported from Dover that 'a squadron of the Dutch fleet, appearing off the North Foreland, causes all to be in arms, lest they should have some design on the Island [of Thanet], Sandwich, or some place near'.[160] A similar report came from Colonel Titus in Deal: 'At 8 am part of the Dutch fleet was discovered, standing in the North Foreland; 14 ships beside galliots, &c.; the flags of one vice-admiral and two rear-admirals were discerned; expected they would have visited the Downs, as they had wind and tide, but they anchored before the Foreland. Either Margate or Deal are ready for them, if they come not too many'.[160] The second Anglo-Dutch war ended with a peace treaty signed on 21 and 31 July 1667; peace was proclaimed at Margate 'with the ringing of bells and firing of guns'.[161] Smith reported in September that merchant vessels started to sail again from Margate: 'The vessels there are fitting to go for coals, and three are bound to Rotterdam'.[162]

Margate was particularly vulnerable during the third Anglo-Dutch war from 1672-1674. John Glover, who had taken over from Smith as Williamson's main informer from Margate, reported on May 11 1672: 'About sunrise this morning the whole Dutch fleet came in upon the Foreland, and lay off and on Margate, there most of the forenoon with their sails haled up. They were so near in that we could see their hulks very plain, but now they are beating off to sea again'.[163] His report of May 13, however, makes it clear that the Dutch fleet remained off the Forelands:[164]

[I] am very glad that Capt. Coleman and the rest are stopped at the Middle Ground, for about seven last night it suddenly cleared, after a thick fog all day, and then we saw the whole Dutch fleet off the Foreland, standing to sea under all sail, so that we thought they had seen our fleet, but it was not so, for about ten this morning we saw about 40 of them as far from the Foreland as we could discern their sails, and about six this evening six sail of them stood in close to the beach near the Goodwin, and all lay by there till it was near dark, and then stood off to sea again. I presume they came in to see what was in the Downs.

The following day he reported on a shortage of gunpowder and shot for the fort: 'Colonel Roocke, being all last week at Dover with the horse, is come here this morning and desires me to remind you that about ten days ago he gave you an account of our dangerous condition here for want of powder and shot for 14 good guns we have here, and he and all the country desire you to stand our friend, that we may have powder and shot sent us with all speed'.[165] On May 16 the guns on the Fort fired two shots at a Dutch ship: 'About 3 this afternoon came in upon the Foreland four of the Dutch fleet, and two tenders, that went out of harbour this high-water, and my boat being in the Road, they came up towards the town, and the tenders ran into the pier again, and our smack stood away before them. When they were almost as high as the town they tacked, and stood down again, and the headmost, being near the town, fired one shot ashore in the rocks, and we from the fort sent him two for it, and so our fight was ended, and they are standing off to sea again'.[166]

On June 10 there was a false alarm that caused much panic in the town:[167]

Our last night's alarm was occasioned by two small tenders in the fleet that came down to this road, and being drinking together and parting about one this morning, took leave of each other by firing several guns. This gave such an alarm to both town and country that the women were running away with their children, which would have been a fair riddance, and some of the men were almost at their wits' end, and would not believe but that the Dutch fleet were come into the roads to land, for one told me a shot went through one house. I called my boat ashore by a fire on the hill, who told us the reason of the guns, but could not satisfy the people till daylight, when we saw three ships standing off and on the North Foreland, which they would have to be the Dutch scouts that were in the road and fired last night. I manned a boat and rowed off, and found them to be the Falcon and the Warwick with another flyboat bound for the Downs. This gave them satisfaction, but I fear did not stop the alarm, which was got to Canterbury by nine next morning, and by this time may be got to Whitehall.

The third Anglo-Dutch war ended with a peace treaty signed in February 1674. Even though these wars resulted in little if any physical damage to the town, trade by sea must have been affected adversely. The large numbers of sick and wounded men landed from the ships at Margate must also have created problems for the town. John Smith reported during the second Anglo-Dutch war that 'many sick and wounded men were set ashore at Margate, and no provision made for their reception'.[168] The situation was particularly serious after the third Anglo-Dutch war. John Knight was the Chirurgeon General of the Forces and was responsible for appointing regimental surgeons, for finding provision for the army medical stores, and for arranging for the reception and dispersal of the casualties of war.[169] In March 1672 he reported to Williamson complaining that Smith was so incompetent that he had to stay in Margate until he had put the sick and wounded 'in so good a condition that scarce his [Smith's] ignorance can injure them'.[170] Knight estimated the number of wounded at Margate to be about 100, in agreement with Smith's estimate that the number of wounded put ashore at Margate was about 70, coming from the St Michael, the Resolution, and the Gloucester.[170,171]

The problem facing Knight was that fighting was so fierce, the numbers of wounded so high, and the weather so bad, that the wounded could not be kept for long on board ship. The result was that the wounded had to be brought ashore at the nearest sheltered anchorage rather than be taken to places where accommodation was available.[169] The burden created by billeting the sick on the inhabitants of towns such as Margate was made worse by the great difficulty the inhabitants had in recovering the money owed to them. John Evelyn reported in September 1672 that he needed to be sent money to pay for the care of the sick and wounded men that had been landed at Gravesend: 'I am at present £3,000 indebted to miserably poor people, and have near 3,000 sick creatures dispersed amongst them'.[172] Evelyn went on to report:

there are no fewer than eight . . . places, namely, Dover, Deal, Margate, Faversham, Milton, Sittingbourne, Chatham, and even as far as Deptford, on my hands, where I have multitudes of sick men, that daily increase, and of which divers have malignant and putrified fevers, complicated with the scorbut [scurvey], all which I beseech your Lordship and the Board to consider seriously, and not to take alarm at the noises of such accidents as may happen, upon sudden inundations of sick people, when they are set on shore in numbers, and in places where it is impossible to keep good order

The same problem with sick and wounded landed at Margate arose after later naval battles, as recorded in the parish burial records. The following is the list of those landed after the Battle of Beachy Head in July 1690, a battle against the French which was won by the French:[173]

Currier – August 2 – Buried Thomas Currier brought a Shoare sick out of their Maties Ship Defiance

Stevens – August 2 – Buried Nathaniel Stevens brought a Shoare sick out of their Maties Ship Defiance

Gyles – August 11 buried James Gyles which was brought a Shaore sick from their Maties Ship the Defiance

Jarrett – Then also buried William Jarrett which was brought sick out of their Maties Ship the Cambridge

Saterwhite – October 24 Buried John Saterwhite servant to John Brook of London which was brought ashore sick out of their Maties Ship called the Happy Returne

2 Soldiers – November 3^d Buried two Soldiers that were brought ashore sick out of their Maties Ships and died heere

4 Soldiers – November 4th Buried four Soldiers that were brought ashore sick out of their Maties Ships and dyed heere

7 Soldiers – November 5th Buried seven Soldiers that were brought ashore sick out of their Maties Ships and dyed heere

3 Soldiers – November 6th Buried three Soldiers that were brought ashoare sick out of their Maties Ships and dyed heere

2 Soldiers – November 7th Buried two Soldiers that were brought ashoare sick out of their Maties Ships and dyed heere

1 Soldier – November 8th Buried one Soldier that was brought ashoare sick out of their Maties Ship and dyed heere

1 Soldier – November 9th Buried a Soldier that was brought ashoare sick out of their Maties Ship and dyed here.

4 Soldiers – November 10th Buried fower Soldiers that were brought ashoare sick out of their Maties Shipps and dyed here

5 Soldiers – November 11th Buried five Soldiers that were brought ashoare sick out of their Maties Ships and dyed here

1 Soldier – November 14th Buried a Soldier brought a Shoare sick and died here

5 Soldiers – November 16 Buried five Soldiers ought ashoare sick out of their Maties Shipiand dyed here

2 Soldiers – November 18th Buried Two Soldiers brought ashoare sick out of their Maties Ships and died here.

1 Soldier – November 20th buried a Soldier brought sick a Shoare and died here

2 Soldiers – November 22th Buried Two Soldiers who were brought ashoare sick out of their Maties Ships Sick and dyed

1 Soldier – November 24th Buried a Soldier brought a Shoare sick and dyed

2 Soldiers – November 25 Buried two Soldiers brought ashoare sick out of their Maties Ships and died here

A Drummer – November 27 Buried Thomas son of William Roberts of Leonard Shoarditch neere London which said Thomas was Drummer to the Company whereof --- is Commander and was brought a Shoar sick and dyed here
1 Soldier – November 29 Buried a Soldier brought ashoare sick and died here
1 *Soldier* – December the first Buried a Soldier brought ashoare sick and died here

What to do with the large numbers of wounded seamen became a major problem for the government. Those meant to be looking after the interests of the seamen were the Commissioners for Sick and Wounded Seamen, but they could do little until the Treasury provided the necessary money. The Treasury papers contain many warnings from the Commissioners, of which the following from 1693 is typical:[174]

June 28 1693. Representation of the Commissioners for sick and wounded seamen, &c to the Lords of the Treasury, stating that the want of money to pay the quarters for the sick and wounded and the dearness of provisions had destroyed the poor people's credit, and they were then unanimously resolved not to trust any longer, so that the wounded seamen set on shore for the future "would be exposed to perish without, or to be starved within doors"; praying for a speedy and proportionable supply.

Later that year the worry was that 'at the return of the fleet great numbers of sick seamen would be put on shore at Dover, Deal, Chatham, and Rochester' and that although the Commissioners had promised payment to those providing accommodation for the seamen, referred to as the 'Quarterers', they had been unable to honour that promise.[175] The result was that 'the quarterers had refused to receive the sick men, then lately sent from their Majesties' ships, into their houses; alleging that they and their families are like to starve, and they had better let the sick men die without, than hunger them within'.[175]

The Receiver for the Sick and Wounded Seamen did not pay 'the old debt for the sick and wounded seamen at Deptford, Gravesend, Rochester, Deal, Dover, Sandwich, Margate, and Ramsgate' incurred in 1695 and 1696 until October 1700.[176] The accounts for Margate show that both seamen and prisoners were accommodated in the town, with payments made both for accommodation and for 'cures' for the sick:[176]

Abstract of Payment: At Margate

Mich quarter 1695	For quarters	£14 5s
	For cures	£4 6s 8d
Xmas quarter 1695	For quarters	£11 7s
	For cures	£1 6s 8d
Lady Day quarter 1696	For quarters	£27 3s
	For cures for seamen	£8
	For quarters	£1 2s
	For cures for prisoners	£1
Midsummer quarter 1696	For quarters for seamen	£23 19s
	For cures for seamen	£6 13s 4d
	For quarters for prisoners	£2 8s

The problem on the Isle of Thanet was largely confined to Margate; the accounts include just a single payment at Ramsgate, of £1 11s for quarters for the Michaelmas quarter 1695.[176]

The defeat of the English by the French at the Battle of Beachy Head in 1690 had been a shock, as was a subsequent attack on part of the English fleet by the French. It was clear that regaining control of the Channel would involve strengthening the English fleet and increasing the number of harbours along the South Coast suitable for naval use. It was decided in 1698 to undertake a survey of the south west part of the coast, from Dover to Lands end and, in 1699, Lord Cobham, Lord Warden of the Cinque Ports, received an order to send Sir Thomas Wilford to report on the fortifications at Margate, but the outcome of that survey is not known.[177,178]

Finally, a last example of the effect of war on Margate. The end of England's involvement in the War of the Spanish Succession led to large numbers of poor and sick seamen and soldiers passing through Margate in 1712 on their return from the continent. Many received support from the Churchwardens and overseers, as recorded in the overseers' accounts, even though they were not parishioners:[39,179]

To three poor Seamen. Came with the Deputy — 1s 6d
To six poor Souldiers put on Shore here from Ostend — 1s 6d
To two poor Seamen late taken by the French — 8d
To a poor Seaman broth (brought) to me by the Deputy — 1s 6d
To eight poor Seamen came from Flanders — 2s
To a young man Sick putt on Shore here out of a smak — 1s

To a poor woman and child whose husband was prest (press-gang) — 1s
To two poor Sick Souldiers come from Flanders — 1s
To poor Souldiers when the Duke of Marlbrough come over — 9s 9d
To three poor Dutch Seamen — 1s
To ten poor Souldiers putt on shore from Oastend — 2s 6d
To a Soulders wife when brought to bed — 2s
To the soulders wife more and carriage of her away — 8s
To five Souldiers and three Seamen — 2s
To two Souldiers and a woman — 1s 4d
To a French prisoner — 2d
To six lame Souldiers — 2s 6d
To a Souldiers wife — 2d
To ten Souldiers — 1s 8d

The Future

The story presented here ends in 1736, with Margate's days of glory still to come. As little more than a large village, albeit one with a harbour, it had rather little on which to survive. True, there seems to have been no actual starvation in the town, the rich arable land of the Isle of Thanet and the fishing seeing to that, but there were no great families and few landed gentry either in Margate or in the parish of St John's. There was little in the way of industry, except for those associated with farming and with the sea. There were few shops and no market, although the easy contact with London and the continent by sea meant a ready supply of goods, some smuggled and cheap. Many labourers worked both on farms and at sea; William Camden referred to them as *'amphibii*, as both land-creatures and sea-creatures', being 'fisher-men and plough men, as well husband-men as mariners'.[1] Some of the young would have travelled to London to serve an apprenticeship or to enter domestic service; in the seventeenth century over 300,000 people, about one in every sixteen of the total population of England, lived in London, and London had an insatiable demand for fresh young workers.[2] Other young men would, at time of war, have joined the navy 'on the certainty of better pay, or in hopes of prize money, or preferment'.[3] The result was that in the Isle of Thanet 'the wages of labourers and servants are very high' and farmers found it difficult to hire workers 'at any price'.[3]

John Lewis, in his history of the Isle of Thanet published in 1723, reported that times were hard in Margate at the start of the eighteenth century.[4] He presents a picture of a town suffering from a decline in all its major sources of employment. Fishing in the sea off Margate was in decline because of reduced fish stocks in the local waters, and it had become more difficult to find herring in the English Channel and the southern part of the North Sea. The decline in the herring fishery had, in turn, caused the fishermen of Margate to sell off their large boats, keeping just boats so small that, according to Lewis, they no longer dared 'to venture out of the Peer in a fresh gale of Wind'.[4] Perhaps Lewis somewhat exaggerated the decline in fishing as other observers said, in 1721, that Margate was 'chiefly inhabited by Mariners and Fishermen' and, in 1754, that Margate was 'a fishing town'.[5,6] However, there had certainly been a loss of maritime trade, partly attributable to the poor state of the storm-damaged pier and partly due to a move to newer merchant vessels, too large to lay up in the harbour at Margate. But not all was gloom; the corn trade remained buoyant, shipping locally corn grown corn to London, and there was a valuable trade in barley, shipped to London for the brewing trade.[4,7] Lewis reported that it was by the corn trade that 'the Pier and Harbour are chiefly maintained'.[4]

Linked to the fishing industry was the local trade in curing herrings, a trade which employed many of the poor in Margate and which continued even when the herrings were no longer caught by local fishermen.[4] The herrings were cured in buildings called herring-hangs, where the herrings were hung on wooden rods to dry, in purpose-built drying-houses designed to keep the herring out of the sun and so prevent the fat from becoming rancid. In Kent the drying process was generally performed over a low fire, giving the herrings a smokey flavour. The smell of the herrings combined with that of the smoke issuing from the herring houses must have been quite a feature of the town. Even at the end of the nineteenth century there were about two dozen herring houses remaining in Margate, although many of these were small, private herring houses, not involved in trade.[8] Adding to the smells of the town were the smells coming from the many malt houses, although the number of these had declined by the 1720s from a peak of about forty.[4] The decline in malting was attributed by Lewis to a decline in the popularity of the locally brewed ale, Northdown ale, in favour of North County beers.

The loss of jobs in the town led inevitably to an increase in the numbers relying on the parish for survival. The amount spent by the Overseers' of the poor increased from about £84 a year in 1663 to £279 a year in 1702, although some of this increase can be attributed to a significant increase in population over the period.[4] Some of the poor were housed in a 'Poor house' which, even if it was not strictly a 'Workhouse', still shared some of its more unpleasant characteristics. Nevertheless many of the poor were supported in their own homes by parish pensions, and the overall impression given by the Overseer's accounts is of a generally humane approach to the poor.

All in all, Margate was in a rather sad state at the start of the Georgian era, in 1714. The whole parish of St John's contained only about 600 families, corresponding to a population of roughly 2,400.[4] The built-up area of the town was very small, being limited largely to the areas around the harbour, around the church, and along the line of the old creek, later to become King street; the road between the church and the harbour area, later to become the High street, was 'but a long dirty lane, consisting chiefly of malt-houses, herring-hangs, and the poor cottages of fishermen'.[9] The town lacked most of the facilities expected of a town, having no market, few places of entertainment, and no independent local government, the town being governed by Dover. There was little in the way of law and order and smuggling was rife. It did though have a working pier and harbour, despite disagreements in the town about how they should be paid for, and the town had survived several threated invasions, suffering no more than very occasional hits by cannon balls. The lack of development within the town was eventually to prove an advantage, ensuring that plenty of land would be available on which to build a new town, designed for the new holiday trade.

The Georgian period saw a growth in the number of 'middling' people – masters, craftsmen, shopkeepers, legal men and clerks, people with significant disposable incomes. One way of spending this income was by visiting a spa town, where it would be possible to meet friends, arrange marriages for any unmarried children, possibly mix with one's betters, and, finally, to improve one's health by drinking spa water or bathing in hot or cold water baths. The boom in consumer spending in the Georgian era, linked to improvements in communications, led to the establishment of a number of new spa towns to supplement the older spa towns such as Bath and Tunbridge Wells. One of these new spa towns was Scarborough, established in the 1720's to serve the northern gentry. The mineral springs that were the raison d'être of the spa were down on the beach and it must have occurred to many that 'sea water is in fact a mineral water to all intents and purposes'.[10] Indeed, Dr Robert Wittie, the author of *Scarborough Spa*, had suggested bathing in the sea as a remedy for gout as early as 1667, and Floyer's *An Enquiry into the Right Use and Abuses of the Hot, Cold and Temperate Bath in England*, published in 1697, did much to advertise the efficacy of cold bathing. Celia Fiennes, who visited Scarborough in 1697, described what she saw: 'On this Sand by the Seashore is ye Spaw [Spa] well wch people frequent, and all the diversion is ye walking on the sand twice a day at ye Ebb of the tide and till its high tide and then they drink [the water]'.[11] Gradually, walking on the sands, boating, and swimming in the sea came to rival the drinking of spa water; a famous engraving of Scarborough in 1736 by John Setterington shows people bathing in the sea and using bathing machines, the first record of such machines. At about this same time a regular bathing season had started at the little fishing village of Brighthelmstone, as Brighton was first called. The Rev. William Clarke wrote from Brighton in 1736: 'We are now sunning ourselves on the beach at Brighthelmstone . . . Such a tract of sea; such regions of corn . . . My morning business is bathing in the sea, and then buying fish; the evening is riding out for air, viewing the remains of old Saxon camps and counting the ships in the roads and the boats that are trawling'.[12]

It was about this same time that a few intrepid bathers first explored the possibilities of Margate as a seaside resort. Margate was, of course, conveniently close to London with good access by sea and by road, the London to Dover road, running through Canterbury, being one of the most important roads in Britain. And, once having reached Margate, a visitor found 'a smooth pleasant shore' and a bay of 'fine clean sand, perfectly free from rocks, stones, sea-weed, and all manner of soil and sullage', with 'so gentle and regular a descent' that it was possible to 'go into the water in the open ocean with security and ease'.[13] But despite all its natural advantages, Margate lacked most of the man-made amenities expected by a visitor of the time, such as assembly rooms, libraries, theatres, and accommodation suitable for the fastidious visitor. What it did have, however, was the space where these amenities could be built. Harris's map of the Isle of Thanet in 1717 (Figure 2) and Hall's map of 1777 (Figure 4) show just how close the open fields came to the centre of the town. The map of 1717 shows buildings around the bay and along the road that was to become the High Street leading to the church. In 1777, although buildings are now shown along the future King Street, the land between the High Street and King Street and that between King Street and the cliffs is still undeveloped, and there are no buildings to the west of the High street, before the small settlement at Westbrook. It was on all this undeveloped land that the new Margate was to be built; Cecil Square, Hawley Square, and Union Crescent between High Street and King Street, and Fort Crescent, East Crescent Place, and West Crescent Place along the cliffs beyond the Fort. Developments to the west, the future Marine Terrace, came later, after suitable flood-defences had been built along the coast line. The potential for development, and the potential for making money, attracted 'numbers of adventurers in building' to the town, and a new future for Margate opened up, as one of London's principal playgrounds.[14]

Notes

Introduction

1 Lucy Toulmin (Ed.), *The Itinerary of John Leland in or about the Years 1535-1543*, Vol IV, 1964.
2 E. S. de Beer (Ed.), *The Diary of John Evelyn*, Vol III, Oxford, 1955.
3 *Seventh report of the Royal Commission on Historical Manuscripts*, p 204a, 1879.
4 Daniel Defoe, *Curious and diverting journies through the whole island of Great Britain*, 1734.
5 John Lewis, *The history and antiquities ecclesiastical and civil, of the Isle of Tenet, in Kent*, 1st ed., London, 1723.
6 Edward Hasted, *History and Topographical Survey of the County of Kent*, Vol 10, 1800.
7 http://en.wikipedia.org/wiki/Adam_Willaerts.
8 Arthur Rowe, *The origin and decadence of the creek and the brooks at Margate*, Margate Public Library, manuscript Y06005.
9 Mick Twyman and Alf Beeching, *The old Tudor house at Margate*, Margate Historical Society, 2006.
10 George Saville Carey, *The Balnea: or, an impartial description of all the popular watering places in England*, London, 1799.
11 *A new description of Kent divided into fyve lathes ther of and subdivided into baylywiekes and hundredes, with the parishe churches conteyned within every of the same hundreds, By the travayle of Phil. Symonson, of Rochester gent*, Engraven by Charles Whitwell.
12 Arthur Rowe, *The streets of Margate in 1800*, Vol 2, Margate Public Library, manuscript Y060.182.
13 Kent Archives, R/U774/T443, Title deeds of land near the Dane.
14 Arthur Rowe, *Notes on the History of Margate*, Margate Public Library, manuscript.
15 Canterbury Cathedral Archives U3/140/5/1, U3/140/11/2, Parish of St Johns, Overseer's Rates.
16 John Lyon, *The history of the town and port of Dover*, Dover, 1813.
17 Samuel Jeake, *Charters of the Cinque Ports, Two Ancient Towns and their Members*, London, 1728.

18 John Harris, *The History of Kent*, London, 1719.
19 Felix Hull (Ed.), *A calendar of the White and Black books of the Cinque Ports, 1432-1955*, Her Majesty's Stationary Office, 1966.
20 *Calendar of State Papers, Letters and Papers, Foreign and Domestic, Henry VIII*, Vol 4, Part III, 1529-30.
21 *Archaelogical notes on Thanet*, Archaeologia Cantiana, 12, 329-419, 1878.
22 Carolyn C. Fenwick, *The Poll taxes of 1377, 1379 and 1381*, Part 3, Cambridge University press, 2005.
23 Margaret Bolton, *The Isle of Thanet*, Lulu.com, 2006.
24 J. M. Gibson, *The 1566 survey of the Kent coast*, Archaeologia Cantiana, 112, 341-353, 1994.
25 Arthur Hussey, *Visitations of the Archdeacon of Canterbury: St John's in Thanet (Margate)*, Archaeologia Cantiana, 26, 17-50, 1904.
26 R. K. I. Quested, *The Isle of Thanet Farming Community*, 2nd ed., 2001.
27 W. Benham, *A study of an old parish register*, Macmillan's magazine, 43, 190-200, Nov 1880-April 1881.
28 W. E. Tate, *The Parish Chest*, Cambridge University Press, 3rd ed., 1969.
29 *Gentleman's Magazine*, p 447, October 1781.
30 Jacqueline Bower, *Kent Towns, 1540-1640*, in *Early Modern Kent: 1540-1640*, Michael Zell (Ed.), Boydell Press, 2000.
31 Mary Dobson, *Population 1640-1831*, in *The Economy of Kent, 1640-1914*, Alan Armstrong (Ed.), Boydell Press, 1995
32 Alan Armstrong (Ed.), *The Economy of Kent, 1640-1914*, Appendix IIIA, Boydell Press, 1995.
33 *Newcastle Courant*, November 17 1739.
34 *Kentish Post*, June 26 1736.

Chapter 1. The Town

1 John Lewis, *The History and antiquities ecclesiastical and civil, of the Isle of Tenet, in Kent*, 1st ed., London, 1723.
2 John Lewis, *The History and antiquities as well ecclesiastical as civil, of the Isle of Tenet, in Kent*, 2nd ed., London, 1736.
3 John H, Andrews, *The Thanet Seaports, 1650-1760*, in *Essays in Kentish History*, Margaret Roake and John Whyman (Eds.), 1973.
4 Mick Twyman and Alf Beeching, *Piering into the past – storms and some thoughts on the Turner Centre*, Bygone Margate, Vol 9, No. 2, pp 16-24.
5 Charles Cotton, *The Church of St John the Baptist, Margate*, Archaeologica cantiana, 25, 64-74, 1902.

6 *A description of England and Wales containing a particular account of each county*, Newbery and Carnan, London, 1769.
7 Arthur Hussey, *Visitations of the Archdeacon of Canterbury: St John's in Thanet (Margate)*, Archaeologia Cantiana, 26, 17-50, 1904.
8 *Daily Journal*, May 20 1723.
9 D. R. J. Perkins, *Jutish glass production in Kent*, Archaeologia Cantiana, 120, 297-310, 2000.
10 George Saville Carey, *The Balnea: or, an impartial description of all the popular watering places in England*, London, 1799.
11 *Calendar of State Papers, Domestic, William and Mary*, July 4 1691.
12 *Public Advertiser*, September 1 1766.
13 *A description of the Isle of Thanet*, 1765.
14 Z. Cozens, *A Tour through the Isle of Thanet*, J. Nichols, London, 1793.
15 Peter J. Hills, *Dane Court, St Peter's in Thanet*, 1972.
16 *Acts of the Privy Council of England*, Vol 3 1550-1552, 21 February 1551.
17 John Cheesman Norwood, *A Kentish Descent*, The Gentleman's Magazine, 288, 320-339, 1900.
18 Arthur English, *A Dictionary of words and phrases used in ancient and modern law*, Vol 2, Washington, 1898.
19 Arthur Rowe, Margate Public Library, manuscripts, Deeds of 47 and 49 High Street.
20 *A new description of Kent divided into fyve lathes ther of and subdivided into baylywiekes and hundredes, with the parishe churches conteyned within every of the same hundreds, By the travayle of Phil. Symonson, of Rochester gent*, Engraven by Charles Whitwell.
21 Jenny West, *The Windmills of Kent*, Charles Skilton, London, 1973.
22 *London Evening Post*, November 2 1732.
23 Irene Josephine Churchill (Ed.), *East Kent Records*, Kent Archaeological Society, Vol 7, pps 47, 48,1922.
24 Arthur Rowe, *The streets of Margate in 1800*, Vols 1 and 2, Margate Public Library, manuscript Y060.182.
25 Arthur Rowe, Margate Public Library, manuscript, Deeds 125 High Street, Y060.188B.
26 *Kentish Post*, February 3 1733.
27 Peter Brimblecombe, *The Big Smoke: A history of air pollution in London*, Methuen & Co., London, 1987.
28 Arthur Rowe, Margate Public Library, manuscripts, Deeds relating to property on north side of Mill Lane, Y060.182.
29 Kent Archives, R/U1063/T39B, Deeds of Dean Chapel and windmill.
30 Arthur Rowe, *Notes on the History of Margate*, Margate Public Library, manuscript.

31 *Canterbury Journal*, September 1 1772.
32 *Public Advertiser*, September 1 1766.
33 Kent Archives, U1453/T2B, Cobbs Brewery Yard Deeds.
34 Edward White, *List of Deputies and Pier Wardens*, Margate Public Library, manuscripts.
35 Arthur Rowe, *Accounts of the Poor House 1666 to 1716*, Margate Public Library, manuscript, Y060.755.
36 Kent Archives, R/U20/T4, Deeds of Jumble house Church Hill.
37 *Isle of Thanet Directory and Guide*, Hutchings and Crowsley, 1883-4.
38 Kent Archives, R/U774/T457B, Deeds at Church Hill.
39 Arthur Rowe, *Accounts of the Poor House 1716 to 1733*, Margate Public Library, manuscript, Y060.755.
40 Kent Archives, R/U774/T457A, Dixon High Street deeds.
41 Arthur Rowe, Margate Public Library, manuscripts, Deeds Covells Row, Y060.188.
42 Arthur Rowe, Margate Public Library, manuscripts, Deeds 122 High Street, Y060.188.
43 Arthur Rowe, Margate Public Library, manuscripts, Deeds 106A and 106B High Street, Prince of Wales' yard, Y060.188.
44 Arthur Rowe, Margate Public Library, manuscripts, Deeds of 98, 100, 102 High Street, Y060.188.
45 Kent Archives, U1453/T6, Deeds of the Fountain.
46 Kent Archives, U1453/T8, Foley House Deeds.
47 Arthur Rowe, Margate Public Library, manuscripts, Abstract of deeds for Pump Lane, Y060.188.
48 Kent Archives, U1453/T2C, Cobb Brewery Yard Deeds; translation from http://theme.wordpress.com/credits/thingsturnup.wordpress.com/.
49 Kent Archives, U1453/T2B, Cobb Brewery Yard Deeds.
50 Kent Archives, U1453/T2F, Deeds, Garden and offices at back of Dwelling House.
51 Kent Archives, R/U45/No 62, Margate Pier Accounts 1678 to 1724.
52 *Morning Post*, August 28 1805.
53 *Kentish Gazette*, October 5 1810.
54 Kent Archives, R/U1063/E1, Charles James Fox's Land, malthouse and land near the Fort Green, map surveyor I. Hodskinson, 1774.
55 Mick Twyman and Alf Beeching, *The Old Tudor House at Margate*, Margate Historical Society, 2006.
56 Kent Archives, U1453/T2D, Brewery Road deeds.
57 Kent Archives, R/U774/T443, Deeds for Lucas Dane.
58 Alan Everitt, *The marketing of agricultural produce*, in *The agrarian history of England and Wales*, Joan Thirsk (Ed.), Cambridge University Press, Vol 4, 1967.

59 Kent Archives, R/U774/T525, Deeds for Lombard Street.
60 Kent Archives, R/U696/T4, Deeds for Queens Arms.
61 Kent Archives, R/U696/O5, Waterhouse Solicitors Collection, Margate Pier, letters 1755-1779.
62 Arthur Rowe, Margate Public Library, manuscripts, Deeds Broad Street, Y060.182.
63 Kent Archives, R/U58/T1, Deeds of Puddle Dock.
64 Kent Archives, R/U696/T1a, Deeds Old Kings Arms.
65 Nigel Barker, Allan Brodie, Nick Dermott, Lucy Jessop and Gary Winter, *Margate's Seaside Heritage*, English Heritage, 2007.
66 Arthur Rowe, Margate Public Library, manuscripts, Deeds Lombard Street, Y060.188.
67 Kent Archives, R/U20/T19, Deeds of Lombard Street.
68 National Archives, PROB 11 382.186, will of John Glover.
69 National Archives, Court of Chancery C 11/2754/19 and C 11/9/29, Spooner v Glover.
70 C. I. Elton, *The tenures of Kent*, John Parker, London, 1867.
71 Anna Glover, *Glover memorials and genealogies - An account of John Glover of Dorchester*, Boston, 1867.
72 E. S. de Beer (Ed.), *The Diary of John Evelyn*, Vol III, Oxford, 1955.
73 *Calendar of State Papers, Domestic, Charles II, 1677-1678*. Vol 19, Mar 1677-Feb 1678, November 27 1677.
74 *Applebee's Original Weekly Journal*, November 12 1720.
75 *London Gazette*, May 25 1717.
76 National Archives, PROB 11/788, will of Stephen Baker 1 Oct 1739.
77 National Archives, PROB 11/914, will of Elizabeth Baker May 19 1764.
78 *Gazetteer and New Daily Advertiser*, February 28 1766.
79 *Kentish Gazette*, August 3 1768.
80 *Parker's General Advertiser and Morning Intelligencer*, July 3 1782.
81 Malcolm Morley, *Margate and its Theatres*, Museum Press, London, 1966.
82 *The Times*, July 6 1791.
83 *Kentish Chronicle*, June 24 1791.
84 *Kentish Gazette*, July 19 1796.
85 William Cortez Abbott, *The writings and speeches of Oliver Cromwell*. Vol 4, The Protectorate, 1655-1658.
86 *Calendar of State Papers, Domestic, Interregnum*, Vol 11, June 1657-April 1658, April 22 1658.
87 *Calendar of State Papers, Domestic, Interregnum*, Vol 13, July 1659-May 1660, January 28 1660.
88 *Calendar of Treasury Books*, Vol 3, 1669-1672, Entry Book January 9 1672.
89 *Calendar of Treasury Books*, Vol 4, 1672-1675, Entry Book January 13 1675.

90 *Calendar of Treasury Books*, Vol 5, 1676-1679, Entry Book June 15 1676.
91 Susan E. Whyman, *Postal censorship in England 1635-1844*, a paper delivered at the Censorship Conference at the Centre for the Study of the Book, Princeton University, 2003, web.princeton.edu/sites.
92 Peter Fraser, *The intelligence of the secretaries of state and their monopoly of licensed news 1660-1688*, Cambridge University Press, 1956.
93 *Calendar of State Papers, Domestic, Charles II, 1671-1672*, Vol 12, May 10, 11 1672.
94 *Calendar of State Papers, Domestic, Charles II, 1672-1673*, Vol 14, November 12 1672.
95 *Calendar of State Papers, Domestic, Charles II, Addenda 1660-1685*, Vol 28, undated 1675.
96 *Calendar of State Papers, Domestic, Charles II, 1673-1675*, Vol 16, February 12 1675.
97 Ralph F. Chambers, *The Strict Baptist Chapels of England*. Vol III, The Chapels of Kent.
98 Joseph Ivimey, *History of the English Baptists*, Vol 4, 1830.
99 Taylor, John, *The honorable, and memorable foundations, erections, raisings, and ruines, of divers cities, townes, castles, and other pieces of antiquitie, within ten shires and counties of this kingdome*, Printed for Henry Gosson, London 1636.
100 National Archives, WO/30/48, *Abstract of a particular account of all the inns, alehouses (etc.) in England with their Stable Room and Bedding in the year 1686*.
101 National Archives, WO/30/49, *Inns and alehouses, 1756*.
102 *Kentish Post*, June 26 1736.
103 *Kentish Post*, June 20 1753.
104 *Kentish Post*, December 3 1729.
105 Brian Austen, *English provincial posts*, Phillimore, 1978.
106 *A new journey to France with an exact description of the sea-coast from London to Calais*, J. Baker, London, 1715.
107 Mr Oldmixon, *The History of England during the reigns of King William and Queen Mary, Queen Anne, King George I*, London, 1735.
108 *Calendar of Treasury Books 1660-1667*, Vol 11, January 30 1697.
109 *London Evening Post*, July 7 1737.
110 *Kentish Post*, February 14 1747.
111 *General Advertiser*, May 26, 1747.
112 *Kentish Post*, December 19 1747.
113 *Kentish Post*, April 19 1760.
114 *Kentish Post*, May 28 1760.
115 *Kentish Post*, July 29 1761.

116 *Kentish Post*, December 26 1747.
117 *Kentish Post*, April 28 1750.
118 *Kentish Post*, March 7 1759.
119 *Kentish Gazette*, January 2 1770.
120 *Kentish Gazette*, April 23 1774.
121 *Kentish Post*, May 28 1760.
122 *Kentish Gazette*, July 16 1768.
123 *Kentish Gazette*, May 3 1769.
124 *Kentish Gazette*, March 10 1770.
125 *Kentish Gazette*, April 25 1786.
126 *Kentish Gazette*, February 10 1789.
127 Kent Archives, R/U20/T5, Deeds of the Ship.
128 Kent Archives R/U20/T12, Deeds of the Ship.
129 Kent Archives R/U774/T581, various deeds.
130 *General Evening Post*, April 11 1761.
131 *Weekly Journal or British Gazetteer*, September 12 1724.
132 *Kentish Post*, March 20 1765.
133 *Kentish Post*, April 30 1729.
134 *Kentish Post*, July 11 1733.
135 *Kentish Gazette*, September 18 1795.
136 Joseph Strutt, *The sports and pastimes of the people of England*, Methuen and Co., London, 1801.
137 *Kentish Post*, June 10 1730.
138 *Kentish Post*, June 27 1730.
139 *Kentish Post*, September 6 1732.
140 Ogilby, *Britannia, or an illustration of the Kingdom of England*, London, 1675.
141 Theo Barker, *Road, rail and cross-channel ferry*, in *The Economy of Kent 1640-1914*, Alan Armstrong (Ed.), Boydell Press, 1995.
142 2 and 3 Philip and Mary, c8, 1555
143 Elizabeth Melling, *Kentish Sources. I. Some roads and bridges*, Kent County Council, Maidstone, 1959.
144 Terence Lawson and David Killingray (Eds.), *An historical atlas of Kent*, Phillimore, 2004.
145 B. H. Hiscock, *The road between Dartford and Strood*, Archaeologica Cantiana, 83, 229-247, 1968.
146 Joan Parkes, *Travel in England in the seventeenth century*, Clarendon Press, Oxford, 1925.
147 M. Exwood and H.L. Lehmann (Eds.), *The Journal of William Schellinks' Travels in England, 1661-1663*, London, Royal Historical Society, 1993.
148 Thomas De Laune, *The present state of London*, 1681.
149 *City Mercury*, July 4 1692.

150 *Kentish Post*, March 19 1729.
151 *Kentish Post*, March 24, 1736.
152 *London Gazette*, September 18 1701.
153 J. A. Chartres, *Road carrying in England in the seventeenth century: myth and reality*, Economic History Review, 30, 73-94, 1977.
154 Paul Hentzner, translated by Horace, late Earl of Oxford, *Travels in England during the reign of Queen Elizabeth*, 1797.
155 Samuel Sorbiere, *A voyage to England*, J. Woodward, London, 1709.
156 William Brenchley-Rye, *Visits to Rochester and Chatham made by royal, noble and distinguished personages*, Archaeologica Cantiana, 6, 43-82, 1866.
157 M. Grosley, translated by Thomas Nugent, *A tour to London or new observations on England*, Vol 1, London, 1772.
158 1 Henry VII, 22 Aug 1485 - 21 Aug 1486.
159 Frederick Clifford, *A History of Private Bill Legislation*, Vol 2, Routledge, 1887.
160 *Kentish Post*, May 7 1729.
161 Arthur Rowe, *The origin and decadence of the creek and the brooks at Margate*, Margate Public Library, manuscript Y06005.
162 *A Description of the Isle of Thanet and particularly of the Town of Margate*, Printed for J. Newbery and W. Bristow, London, 1763.
163 Robert Edward Hunter, *A Short description of the Isle of Thanet*, London, 1796.
164 *Kentish Post*, December 27 1735.
165 Cranfield, G. A., *The development of the provincial newspaper, 1700-1760*, Clarendon Press, 1962.
166 National Archives, Court of Chancery, C11/2736/35 Beale vs Jarvis and C11/518/2 Beale vs Turner.
167 *Original Weekly Journal*, November 22, 1718.
168 *Weekly Journal or Saturday's Post*, October 29 1720.
169 *Kentish Post*, December 3 1729.
170 John Whyman, *The significance of the hoy to Margate's early growth as a seaside resort*, Archealogica Cantiana, 111, 17-41, 1993.
171 John Taylor, *The carriers cosmographie*, Printed by A[nne] G[riffin], London, 1637.
172 *A brief director for all those that would send their letters to any parts of England, Scotland or Ireland*, 1710.
173 *Grub Street Journal*, April 15 1731.

Chapter 2. The Pier and the Harbour

1 *Patents rolls of the reign of Henry III, 1216-1225,* 1225.
2 *Calendar of the Patent rolls, Edward III, 1330-1334,* December 29 1331.
3 *Calendar of the Patent rolls, Edward III, 1367-1370,* June 11 1369.
4 *Calendar of State Papers, Edward III, 1374-1377,* March 11 1377.
5 *Calendar of the Patent rolls, Richard II, 1377-1381,* February 6 1380.
6 Lucy Toulmin (Ed.), *The Itinerary of John Leland in or about the Years 1535-1543,* Vol IV, 1964.
7 John Lewis, *The History and antiquities ecclesiastical and civil, of the Isle of Tenet, in Kent,* 1st ed., London, 1723.
8 *Calendar of State Papers, Domestic, James I,* Vol 3, 1619-1623, August 1 1621; National Archives SP 14/122 f. 167.
9 J. H. Andrews, *The Thanet Seaports 1650-1750,* in *Essays in Kentish History,* Margaret Roake and John Whyman (Eds.), Frank Cass, London, 1973.
10 *Calendar of State Papers, Domestic, James I,* Vol 3, 1619-1623, September 12 1621.
11 *Calendar of State Papers, Domestic, James I,* Vol 3, 1619-1623, April 2 1622.
12 *Calendar of State Papers, Domestic, James I,* Vol 3, 1619-1623, January 14, 1623.
13 John Lewis, *The History and antiquities as well ecclesiastical as civil, of the Isle of Tenet, in Kent,* 2nd ed., London, 1736.
14 John Smith, *Two petitions. TO THE Honourable House of COMMONS, Now assembled in Parliament: The humble Remonstrance of John Smith, in behalf of the Inhabitants of MARGATE.* London, 1646; *To the right honourable the Lords and Commons now assembled in Parliament the humble petition of John Smith of Sandwich Draper, in behalfe of himself and the inhabitants of Margate.* London, 1647.
15 C. H. Firth and R. S. Rait (Eds.), *Acts and ordinances of the Interregnum, 1642-1660,* 1911.
16 British Library, Harleian manuscript, 7598.
17 *House of Lords Journal,* Vol 9, March 26 1647.
18 *Sixth report of the Royal Commission on Historical Manuscripts,* Part 1, Calendar of the House of Lords Manuscripts, p 166, March 26 1647.
19 *House of Lords Journal,* Vol 10, February 24 1648.
20 *House of Commons Journal,* Vol 5, March 1 1648.
21 *Calendar of State Papers, Interregnum,* Vol 1, 1649-1650, June 28 1649.
22 *Calendar of State Papers, Interregnum,* Vol 1, 1649-1650, July 23 1649.
23 *Calendar of State Papers, Interregnum,* Vol 1, 1649-1650, July 26 1649; National Archives SP 25/123 f. 44.

24 *Calendar of State Papers, Interregnum*, Vol 1, 1649-1650, November 22, 1649; National Archives SP 25/123 f. 76.

25 *Calendar of State Papers, Interregnum*, Vol 1, 1649-1650, November 28, 1649; National Archives SP 25/123 f. 80.

26 *Calendar of State Papers, Interregnum*, Vol 2, 1650, May 23 1650; National Archives SP 25/64 f. 381.

27 *Calendar of State Papers, Domestic, Charles II, 1667-8,* January 5 1668; National Archives SP 29/232 f. 44.

28 *Calendar of State Papers, Domestic, Charles II, 1667-8*, September 28 1671.

29 Kent Archives, R/U45 Item No 62, *Pier Accounts 1678 to 1724.*

30 *Calendar of State Papers, Domestic, James II*, Vol 3, June 1687- February 1689, January 8 1688.

31 *Calendar of State Papers, Domestic, William and Mary*, July 4 1691; National Archives SP 44/235 f.151.

32 Kent Archives, R/U686/01, *Waterhouse Solicitors Collection.*

33 *Calendar of State Papers, Domestic, William and Mary*, June 23 1693; National Archives SP 44/236 f.333.

34 National Archives, PC 1/1/153 and PC 1/1/221, *Fort petition and reply*, August 5 1702 and November 3 1702.

35 Kent Archives, U1453/Z50/1, *Orders, decrees, and rates, time out of mind used by the Inhabitants of Margate and St John's MARGATE and St JOHN's ... for and towards the perpetual maintenance and preservation of the Pier and Harbour of Margate,* 1693-4.

36 *Calendar of State Papers, Domestic, William and Mary*, May 12 1696; *Calendar of Treasury Papers*, Vol 37, 1696, May 12 1696; National Archives T1/37/64.

37 Kent Archives, R/U696/O3, Bond of Indemnity, Waterhouse Solicitors Collection.

38 Kent Archives, R/U696/04, Case and legal opinions, Waterhouse Solicitors collection.

39 Edward White, *List of Deputies and Pier Wardens*, Margate Public Library manuscript.

40 Daniel Defoe, *The Storm, or A collection of the most remarkable casualties and disasters*, 2nd ed., 1704.

41 Daniel Defoe, *An historical narrative of the great and tremendous storm which happened on Nov. 26th, 1703*, London, 1769.

42 *An Act for the Repair of Dover Harbour*, 11 Will. III, c5, 1698.

43 *An Act for enlarging the term of years granted by an Act passed in the session of Parliament, held in the eleventh and twelfth years of King William the Third, for the repair of Dover Harbour*, 2 and 3 Ann, c7, 1703.

44 *House of Commons Journal*, Vol 18, February 28 1717.

45 *An act for enlarging the term of years granted by the acts of the eleventh and twelfth years of King William the Third, and second and third years of Queen Anne, for the repair of the Dover harbour*, 4 Geo. I c3, 1717.
46 *House of Commons Journal*, Vol 20, December 1 1724.
47 *House of Commons Journal*, Vol 20, December 14 1724.
48 *Parliamentary Papers, Sixth Parliament of Great Britain, 2nd session*, January 9 1725 – April 24 1725.
49 *An Act to enable the Pier-wardens of the Town of Margate, in the County of Kent, more effectually to recover the ancient and customary Droits, for the Support and Maintenance of the said Pier*, 1725.
50 *Daily Post*, January 4 1737.
51 *A description of England and Wales*, London, 1769.
52 Dennis Baker, *Agricultural process, production and marketing, with special reference to the hop industry: north-east Kent, 1680-1760*, Garland Publishing, 1985.
53 William Sutherland, *Britain's Glory or ship-building unvail'd*, London, 1717.
54 John Whyman, *The significance of the hoy to Margate's early growth as a seaside resort*, Archealogica Cantiana, 111, 17-41, 1993.
55 T. S. Willan, *English Coasting Trade 1600-1750*, Manchester, 1938.
56 *Sir William Monson's Naval Tracts*, p 281, 1703.
57 *Calendar of State papers, Letters and papers, foreign and domestic, Henry VIII, 1544*, Vol 19, Part I, May 10 1544.
58 J. M. Gibson, *The 1566 survey of the Kent Coast*, Archealogica Cantiana, 112, 341-353, 1994.
59 *Calendar of State papers, Domestic, James I*, Vol 3, 1619-1623; National Archives SP 14/140 f. 116.
60 R. K. I. Quested, *The Isle of Thanet Farming Community*, 2nd ed, 2001.
61 J. Harris, *The History of Kent*, p 314, 1719.
62 *Calendar of Close Rolls, Richard II*, Vol 4, 1389-1392, October 24 1391.
63 *Calendar of the Patent Rolls, Henry VI*, Vol 5, 1446-1452, May 15 1449.
64 *Calendar of State Papers, Foreign, Elizabeth*, Vol 3, 1581-1582, February 19 1581.
65 William Cunningham, *The growth of English industry and commerce*, Vol 1, Cambridge University Press, 1968.
66 *Acts of the Privy Council of England*, Vol 12 1580-1581, February 26 1581.
67 *Calendar of State Papers, Foreign, Elizabeth*, January – June 1583 and Addenda, February 17 1582.
68 *Calendar of State Papers, Foreign, Elizabeth*, Vol 21, Part 1, 1586-1588, March 21/31 1588.
69 Mavis E. Mate, *Trade and economic developments 1450-1550: the experience of Kent, Surrey, and Sussex*, Boydell Press, 2006.

70 *Calendar of State Papers Relating To English Affairs in the Archives of Venice*, Vol 6, 1555-1558, October 1 1555.

71 T.S. Willan, *Some aspects of English trade with the Levant in the sixteenth century*, The English Historical Review, 70, 399-410, 1955.

72 Fernand Braudel, *The Mediterranean and the Mediterranean world in the age of Phillip II*, Vol 1, University of California Press, 1995.

73 *Acts of the Privy Council of England*, Vol 14, 1586-1587, March 20 1587.

74 *Acts of the Privy Council of England*, Vol 44, 1628-1629, July 10 1628.

75 John Taylor, *The carriers cosmographie*, Printed by A[nne] G[riffin], London, 1637.

76 *A brief director for all those that would send their letters to any parts of England, Scotland or Ireland*, 1710.

77 *Grub Street Journal*, April 15 1731.

78 Kent Archives, R/U45 Item No 14, *Pier Accounts 1732 to 1749*.

79 J. Whyman, *Aspects of holidaymaking and resort development within the Isle of Thanet, with particular reference to Margate, circa 1736 to circa 1840*, Arno Press, New York, 1981.

80 William Camden, *Britain, or, a Chorographicall Description of the most flourishing Kingdomes, England, Scotland, and Ireland Brittania*, 1st ed., translated by Philemon Holland, London, 1610.

81 *London Gazette*, September 13 1737.

82 *London Gazette*, October 1 1737.

83 *Calendar of State Papers, Domestic, Charles II*, Vol 13, 1672, July 24 1672.

84 *Calendar of Treasury Books*, Vol 31, 1717, January 3 1717.

85 Samuel Baldwin, *A survey of the British Customs*, London 1770.

86 *Journal of the House of Lords*, Vol 21, 1718-21, 6 Geo 1 c. 14.

87 House of Lords Record Office, Main Papers, 1720/578.

88 *Journal of the House of Lords*, Vol 21, 1718-21.

89 Mr Senex, *A new general atlas containing a geographical and historical account of all the empires, kingdoms, and other dominions of the world*, 1721.

90 James Joel Cartwright (Ed.), *The travels through England of Dr Richard Pococke*, Cambden Society, Vol 2, p 86, 1889.

91 William Crowne, *A true relation of all the remarkable places and passages observed in the travels of the right honourable Thomas Lord Hovvard, Earle of Arundell and Surrey, Primer Earle, and Earle Marshall of England, ambassadour extraordinary to his sacred Majesty Ferdinando the second, emperour of Germanie, anno Domini 1636*, London, 1637.

92 *Seventh report of the Royal Commission on Historical Manuscripts*, p 204a, 1879.

93 *Calendar of State Papers, Domestic, William and Mary*, October 20 1691.

94 *Post Man and the Historical Account*, April 20 1697.

95 J. P. Barrett, *A History of the Ville of Birchington*, Margate, 2nd ed.

96 E. S. de Beer (Ed.), *The Diary of John Evelyn*, Vol V, p 273, Oxford University Press, 1955.
97 *The London Gazette*, 18 July 1698.
98 *The London Gazette*, 1 June 1699.
99 *The Calendar of State Papers, Domestic, William III*, January 1699-March 1700, p. 217, 1937.
100 *Cobbetts Parliamentary History of England*, Vol 5, p 1323, 1701.
101 *The life of William III late King of England and Prince of Orange*, London, 1703.
102 *Calendar of Treasury Papers*, Vol 2, 1697-1702; National Archives T76/58.
103 *Calendar of State Papers, Domestic, William and Mary*, Vol 11, 1700-1702, November 4 1701.
104 http://catchlove-research.org/page33.html.
105 *The case of Thomas Blunt, John Searing, Charles Sewell, Thomas Holland, Thomas Storey, Cornelius Rose, and the rest of the eight hundred licensed Hackney Coachmen*, London, 1716.
106 *Original Weekly Journal*, November 22 1718.
107 *London Daily Post and General Advertiser*, December 4 1736.
108 *The Annals of Europe for the year 1740*, George Hawkins, London, 1742.
109 *Universal Spectator and Weekly Journal*, September 13, 1729.
110 *Daily Post*, September 15 1729.
111 *Daily Post*, September 16 1729.
112 Edward White, *List of Deputies and Pier Wardens*, Margate Library manuscript.
113 *Daily Post*, September 13 1729.
114 *British Journal or The Censor*, October 4 1729.
115 *Universal Spectator and Weekly Journal*, September 13 1729.
116 *London Magazine*, p 394, September 1745.
117 *Notes and Queries*, 6th series, Vol 3, p 227, March 19 1881.
118 National Archives, Court of Chancery C 11/2754/19 and C 11/9/29, Spooner v Glover.
119 *Supplement*, May 4 1709.

Chapter 3. The People of Margate

1 William Harrison, *The description of England*, George Edelen (Ed.), Cornell University Press, 1968.
2 R. K. I. Quested, *The Isle of Thanet Farming Community*, 2nd ed., 2001.
3 J. Harris, *A history of Kent*, 1719.
4 John Lewis, *The History and antiquities ecclesiastical and civil, of the Isle of Tenet, in Kent*, 1st ed., London, 1723.

5 Charles Cotton, *The Church of St John the Baptist, Margate*, Archaeologica cantiana, 25, 64-74, 1902.
6 W. Benham, *A study of an old parish register*, Macmillan's magazine, 43, 190-200, Nov 1880-April 1881.
7 *London Daily Post and General Advertiser*, September 17 1743.
8 *London Daily Post and General Advertiser*, September 30 1743.
9 Kent Archives, R/U696/T5, Deeds of Pier Green.
10 St John the Baptist, Margate, Parish Registers, Kent Family History Society, CD27.
11 http://www-personal.umich.edu/~bobwolfe/gen/person/p20344.htm.
12 National Archives, Will of Roger Laming, Gentleman of Saint John Isle of Thanet, Kent, October 6 1743, PROB 11/729.
13 Kent Archives, R/U20/T5, Deeds of the Ship.
14 Arthur Rowe, *Accounts of the Poor House 1716 to 1733*, Margate Public Library, manuscript, Y060.755.
15 National Archives, C 11/2754/19 and C 11/9/29, Courts of Chancery Glover case, 1716.
16 *Kentish Post*, December 3 1729.
17 Stephen Pritchard, *The history of Deal and its neighbourhood*, Deal, 1864.
18 Arthur Rowe, *Accounts of the Poor House 1666 to 1716*, Margate Public Library, manuscript, Y060.755.
19 Edward White, *List of Deputies and Pier Wardens*, Margate Public Library manuscripts.
20 Canterbury Cathedral Archives, PRC/17/101/420, will of Richard Sackett.
21 Kent Archives, R/U45 Item No 14, *Pier Accounts 1732 to 1749*.
22 William Camden, *Britain, or, a Chorographicall Description of the most flourishing Kingdomes, England, Scotland, and Ireland Brittania*, 1st ed., translated by Philemon Holland, London, 1610.
23 *Calendar of the Patent Rolls, Henry VI*, Vol 4, 1441-1446, April 15 1442.
24 Irene Josephine Churchill (Ed.), *East Kent Records*, Kent Archaeological Society, Vol 7, pps 47, 48, 1922.
25 Dennis Baker, *Agricultural process, production and marketing, with special reference to the hop industry: north-east Kent, 1680-1760*, Garland Publishing, 1985.
26 J. Whyman, *Aspects of holidaymaking and resort development within the Isle of Thanet, with particular reference to Margate, circa 1736 to circa 1840*, Arno Press, New York, 1981.
27 E. S. de Beer (Ed.), *The Diary of John Evelyn*, Vol III, Oxford, 1955.
28 Edward White, *Miscellaneous extracts relating to the Isle of Thanet*, Margate Public Library, manuscript.

29 Alan Everitt, *The marketing of agricultural produce*, in Joan Thirsk (Ed.), *The Agrarian History of England and Wales*, Cambridge University Press, Vol 4, 1967.
30 Daniel Defoe, *The complete English tradesman. In familiar letters: Directing him in the several parts and progressions of trade*, 2nd ed., London,1732.
31 John Taylor, *The honorable, and memorable foundations, erections, raisings, and ruines, of divers cities, townes, castles, and other pieces of antiquitie, within ten shires and counties of this kingdome namely, Kent, Sussex, Hampshire, Surrey, Barkshire, Essex, Middlesex, Hartfordshire, Buckinghamshire, and Oxfordshire: with the description of many famous accidents that have happened, in divers places in the said counties. Also, a relation of the wine tavernes either by their signes, or names of the persons that allow, or keepe them, in, and throughout the said severall shires*, Printed for Henry Gosson, London, 1636.
32 Robert Herrick, *A Hymne to the Lares*, 1646.
33 *Calendar of State Papers, Domestic, Charles II*, Vol 6, 1666-1667, December 3 1666.
34 *Calendar of State Papers, Domestic, Charles II*, Vol 8, 1667-1668, March 12 1668.
35 Samuel Pepys, *Diary*, London, 1949; www.pepysdiary.com.
36 Henry Teonge, *The Diary of Henry Teonge, Chaplain on Board H.M.'s Ships Assistance, Bristol, and Royal Oak, 1675-1679*, p 238, Charles Knight, London, 1825.
37 Canterbury Cathedral Archives, PRC/17/77/49b, will of John Prince.
38 *Encyclopaedia Britannica*, 1st ed., 1773.
39 *Kentish Post*, March 1 1755.
40 *Public Advertiser*, September 1 1766.
41 *Kentish Post*, July 19 1755.
42 Z. Cozens, *A Tour through the Isle of Thanet*, J. Nichols, London, 1793.
43 John Lewis, *The History and antiquities as well ecclesiastical as civil, of the Isle of Tenet, in Kent*, 2nd ed., London, 1736.
44 Arthur Rowe, *Notes on the History of Margate*, Margate Public Library, manuscript.
45 Edward Hasted, *History and Topographical Survey of the County of Kent*, Vol 10, 1800.
46 *Calendar of State Papers, Domestic, James I*, Vol 2, 1611-1618, June 1616.
47 *Calendar of State Papers, Domestic, James I*, Vol 2, 1611-1618, April 13 1617; National Archives SP 14/91 f.47
48 *Daily Journal*, May 20 1723.
49 D. R. J. Perkins, *Jutish glass production in Kent*, Archaeologica Cantiana, 120, 297-310, 2000.
50 Kent Archives, U1453/T1, Deeds King Street.

51 *The Margate Guide*, 1770.
52 Samantha Williams Shaw, *Poverty, gender and life-cycle under the English poor law, 1760-1834*, London, 2013.
53 Canterbury Cathedral Archives, U3/140/11/2, Parish of St John's Overseers Rates, 1716-1726.
54 Samantha Williams, *Poverty, gender and life-cycle under the English poor law 1760-1834*, Boydell Press, Woodbridge, 2011.
55 *A general valuation of the lands and tenements in the parish of St John, the Baptist, 1801*, Margate, 1802, Margate Public Library Local Collection.
56 Edward Graham, *The Harrow life of Henry Montagu Butler*, Longmans, Green, 1920.
57 *Notes and Queries*, 69, p 311, 1905.
58 *Kentish Post*, November 23 1726.
59 Ian Mortimer, *A directory of medical personnel qualified and practicing in the Diocese of Canterbury, circa 1560-1730*, Kent Archaeological Society, www.kentarchaelogical.ac./authors/021.pdf.
60 R.S. Roberts, *The personnel and practice of medicine in Tudor and Stuart England: Part 1: the provinces*, Medical History 6, 363-382, 1962.
61 Ian Mortimer, *A directory of medical personnel qualified and practising in the diocese of Canterbury, c. 1560-1730*, Archaeologia Cantiana, 126, 135-169, 2006.
62 Ian Mortimer, *Diocesan licensing and medical practitioners in South-West England, 1660-1780*, Medical History, 48, 49-68, 2004.
63 Arthur Hussey, *Visitations of the Archdeacon of Canterbury: St John's in Thanet (Margate)*, Archaeologia Cantiana, 26, 17-50, 1904.
64 Ian Mortimer, *The Triumph of the Doctors*, Transactions of the Royal Historical Society, 6th series, 15, 97-116, 2005.
65 Peter Fraser, *The intelligence of the Secretaries of State and their monopoly of licensed news 1660-1688*, Cambridge University Press, 1956.
66 John Churchill, (Ed.), *A collection of Voyages and Travels*, Vol 6, London, 1745.
67 *Calendar of State Papers, Domestic, Charles II*, Vol 6, August 1666 – March 1667, October 1666.
68 *Calendar of State Papers, Domestic, Charles II*, Vol 6, August 1666 – March 1667, December 13 1666.
69 *Calendar of State Papers, Domestic, Charles II*, Vol 7, April – October 1667, May 17 1667.
70 *Calendar of State Papers, Domestic, Charles II*, Vol 7, April – October 1667, July 19 1667.
71 *Calendar of State Papers, Domestic, Charles II*, Vol 8, November 1667 – September 1668, December 28 1667.
72 *Calendar of State Papers, Domestic, Charles II*, Vol 9, October 1668 – December 1669, November 11 1668.

73 *Calendar of State Papers, Domestic, Charles II*, Vol 12, December 1671 – May 1672, March 18 1672.
74 *Calendar of State Papers, Domestic, Charles II*, Vol 12, December 1671 – May 1672, March 20 1672.
75 *Kentish Post*, August 23, 1732.
76 National Archives Court of Chancery, C11/2736/35 Beale vs Jarvis and C11/518/2 Beale vs Turner.
77 *Kentish Post*, April 3 1731.
78 John Lawson, *Mediaeval Education and the Reformation*, Routledge 2007.
79 www.dbtheclergydatabase.org.uk.
80 *Calendar of State Papers, Domestic, Charles II*, Vol 8, November 1667 – September 1668, May 13 1672.
81 John Lyon, *Short description of the Isle of Thanet, and particularly of the town of Margate*, 1763.
82 William Boyne, *Trade tokens issued in the seventeenth century*, London, 1889.
83 Arthur Rowe, *The streets of Margate in 1800*, Vols 1 and 2, Margate Public Library, manuscript Y060.182.
84 www.margatelocalhistory.co.uk; Rule by the Margate Local Board of Health: 2 Margate in the Middle of the Nineteenth Century.
85 R. Campbell, *The London Tradesman: Being a Compendious View of All the Trades*, London, 1747.
86 William Bohun, *Privilegia Londini: Or, The Rights, Liberties, Privileges, Laws, and Customs of the City of London*, London, 1723.
87 Canterbury Cathedral Archives, PRC/3/36a/186 and PRC/17/71/354b.
88 Mick Twyman and Alf Beeching, *The Old Tudor House at Margate*, Margate Historical Society, 2006.
89 Hoh-cheung Mui and Lorna H. Mui, *Shops and shopkeeping in eighteenth century England*, Routledge, London, 1989.
90 *Daily Post*, May 4 1736.
91 *Kentish Post*, March 3 1736.
92 *Kentish Post*, March 17 1736.
93 *Kentish Post*, April 14 1736.
94 *Fog's Weekly Journal*, September 11 1731.
95 *Kentish Post*, May 9 1739.
96 Kent Archives, R/U45/No 62, *Margate Pier Accounts 1678 to 1724*.

Chapter 4. The Poor

1 W. E. Tate, *The Parish Chest*, Cambridge University Press, 3rd ed., 1969.
2 *An act for the punishment of vagabonds, and for the relief of the poor and impotent*, 14 Elizabeth I, c5, 1572.

3 Steve Hindle, *On the Parish*, Oxford University Press, 2004.
4 *An act for the relief of the poor*, 39 Eliz I, c3, 1597.
5 *An act for the relief of the poor*, 43 Eliz I, c2, 1601.
6 James Shaw, *The Parochial Lawyer or churchwarden and overseer's guide and assistant*, 2nd ed., Sherwood, Gilbert and Piper, London, 1829.
7 Thomas Ruggles, *The History of the Poor: Their rights, duties and the laws respecting them: In a series of letters*, London, W. Richardson, 1797.
8 Susannah R. Ottaway, *The Decline of Life: Old age in eighteenth-century England*, Cambridge University Press, 2007.
9 Steven King, *Poverty and welfare in England 1700-1850*, Manchester University Press 2000.
10 R. Burn, *The History of the Poor Laws*, London, 1764.
11 *An act for the better relief of the poor of this kingdom*, 14 Cha II, c12, 1662.
12 Paul Slack, *The English poor laws, 1531-1782*, Cambridge University Press, 1995.
13 Gregory Clark, *Farm wages and living standards in the industrial revolution*, Economic History Review, 54, 477-505, 2001.
14 *An act for the amendment and better administration of the laws relating to the poor in England and Wales*, 4 and 5 Will IV, c76, 1834.
15 Roy Porter, *English Society in the 18th century*, Penguin Books, 1991.
16 R. K. I. Quested, *The Isle of Thanet Farming Community*, 2nd ed., 2001.
17 John Lewis, *The history and antiquities ecclesiastical and civil, of the Isle of Tenet, in Kent*, 1st ed., London, 1723.
18 *A Description of the Isle of Thanet and particularly of the Town of Margate*, Printed for J. Newbery and W. Bristow, London, 1763.
19 William Temple, *Vindication of Commerce*, 1739.
20 Arthur Young, *The Farmer's Tour Through the East of England*, 1771.
21 Canterbury Cathedral Archives, PRC17/63/299, will of George Collmer.
22 National Archives, PROB 11/729, will of Roger Laming, 6 October 1743.
23 Arthur Hussey, *Visitations of the Archdeacon of Canterbury: St John's in Thanet (Margate)*, Archaeologia Cantiana, 26, 17-50, 1904.
24 Parliamentary papers, *Commission of Inquiry into Charities in England and Wales: Thirtieth Report*, 1837.
25 John Lewis, *The History and antiquities as well ecclesiastical as civil, of the Isle of Tenet, in Kent*, 2nd ed., London, 1736.
26 Arthur Rowe, *Accounts of the Poor House 1666 to 1716*, Margate Public Library, manuscript, Y060.755.
27 Arthur Rowe, *Accounts of the Poor House 1716 to 1738*, Margate Public Library, manuscript, Y060.755
28 Canterbury Cathedral Archives, U3/140/11/1, *St John's Parish Churchwardens accounts 1678-1716*.

29 Canterbury Cathedral Archives, U3/140/11/2, *St John's Parish Churchwardens accounts 1716-1726*.
30 *An Act for supplying some Defects in the Laws for the Relief of the Poor of this Kingdome*, 8 and 9 William III, c30, 1696-7.
31 *An act to amend so much of the 8 & 9 William III as requires poor persons receiving alms, to wear badges*, 50 Geo III, c52, 1810
32 *Thanet Guardian*, January 28 1882.
33 J. Hall, *A Map of the Isle of Thanet*, Margate, 1st ed., 1777.
34 John Pridden, *Collection for the History of the Isle of Thanet*, Kent Archives, EK/U203/1.
35 Arthur Rowe, *Notes on William Rowe's Church Book*, Margate Public Library, manuscript.
36 Kent Archives, R/U45 Item No 62, *Pier Accounts 1678 to 1724*.
37 Dane Court, *St Peter's in Thanet*, Peter J. Hills, 1972
38 Edward White, *List of Deputies and Pier Wardens*, Margate Public Library, manuscripts.
39 Kent Archives, U1453/T2C, Cobb Brewery Yard Deeds.
40 Kent Archives, U1453/T2B, Cobb Brewery Yard Deeds.
41 *An Act for amending the laws relating to the settlement, imployment, and relief of the poor*, Geo II, c7, 1722.
42 Parliamentary Papers, *Abstract of the returns made by the overseers of the poor, in pursuance of an act, passed in the twenty-sixth year of his present Majesty's reign, intitled, "An act for obliging overseers of the poor to make returns upon oath, to certain questions specified therein, relative to the state of the poor"*, 1777.
43 *St John's Parish Register, Baptisms, Marriages & Burials 1679-1729*, transcription by Barry J. White, http://www.shelwin.com/e/Thanet_Research/pr_marg_x1.pdf.
44 *An Act made and ordained to destroy choughs, crows and rooks*, 24 Hen 8, c10, 1532.
45 *An Act for the preservation of grain*, 8 Eliz I, c15, 1566.
46 Canterbury Cathedral Archives, U3/140/5/1, *St John's Parish Churchwardens accounts 1639-1716*.
47 Canterbury Cathedral Archives, U3/140/11/4, *St John's Parish Churchwardens accounts 1739-1758*.
48 *An Act for Burying in Woollen only*, 18 & 19 Cha II, c4, 1666, and 30 Cha II, c3, 1678.
49 *An Act for granting his Majesty certain rates and duties upon marriages, births, and buriels and upon bachelors and widowers, for the term of five years, for carrying on the war against France with vigour*, 6 & 7 William & Mary, c6, 1695.
50 *Kent Herald*, November 11 1847.

Chapter 5. Managing Margate

1 Norman Landau, *The Justices of the Peace, 1679-1760*, University of California Press, Berkeley, 1984.
2 Bryan Keith-Lucas, *The Unreformed Local Government System*, 1980.
3 Parliamentary Papers, *First report of the commissioners appointed to inquire into the municipal corporations in England and Wales*, 1835
4 K. M. E. Murray, *The constitutional history of the Cinque Ports*, Manchester University Press 1935.
5 Montagu Burrows, *The Cinque Ports*, Longmans, Green and Co., London, 1892.
6 Samuel Jeake, *Charters of the Cinque Ports, Two ancient towns and their members*, London, 1728.
7 Sir Nicholas Harris Nicolas, *A History of the Royal Navy*, Vol 1, London, 1847.
8 John Harris, *The History of Kent*, 1719.
9 John Boys, *A general view of the agriculture of the county of Kent*, 1794.
10 National Archives, SC 8/172/8577, Petition to the King.
11 S. P. H. Statham, *Dover Charters and Other Documents in the Possession of the Corporation of Dover*, London, 1902.
12 *Letters and Papers, Foreign and Domestic, Henry VIII*. Vol 4, Part 3, 1529-30; British Library, Egerton MS. 2,092, f. 303, 1530.
13 *Calendar of State Papers, Domestic, Charles II, 1667-8*, February 26 1682.
14 John Lewis, *The History and antiquities ecclesiastical and civil, of the Isle of Tenet, in Kent*, 1st ed., London, 1723.
15 Stephen Dowell, *History of taxes and taxation in England*, Vol 3, pp 93-102, Longmans, Green and Co., London, 1884.
16 John Lyon, *The History of the Town and Port of Dover*, Dover, 1813.
17 William Batcheller, *A new history of Dover*, 1828.
18 T. A. Critchley, *A history of police in England and Wales 900-1966*, Constable, London, 1967.
19 Joan Kent, *The English village constable 1580-1642*, Oxford, 1986.
20 *The bloody husband and cruell neighbour, or, a true history of two murthers lately committed in Laurence Parish, in the Isle of Thanet*, London, 1653.
21 D. Hay and F. Snyder, *Policing and Prosecution in England 1750-1850*, Oxford University Press, 1989.
22 J. M. Beattie, *Crime and the Courts in England 1600-1800*, Princeton University Press, 1986.
23 *The Times*, December 5 1785.
24 S. P. H. Stratham, *The history of the town and port of Dover*, Longmans, Green and Co., London, 1899.

25 *Kentish Post*, April 18 1733.
26 *Kentish Post*, May 16 1733.
27 Arthur Rowe, *Accounts of the Poor House 1666 to 1716*, Margate Public Library, manuscript, Y060.755.
28 Arthur Rowe, *Accounts of the Poor House 1716 to 1738*, Margate Public Library, manuscript, Y060.755.
29 Alfred T. Walker, *The Ville of Birchington*, Ramsgate, 3rd ed., 1991.
30 *The New Margate and Ramsgate Guide in letters to a friend*, Letter IX, ca 1789.
31 *Kentish Post*, July 16 1729.
32 *Calendar of the Patent Rolls, Edward I, 1292-1301*, June 7 1298.
33 *Calendar of Close Rolls, Edward III, 1343-1346*, June 4, 12 1345.
34 *Acts of the Privy Council of England*, Vol 11, 1578-1580, July 26 1579.
35 *Acts of the Privy Council of England*, Vol 11, 1578-1580, November 1579.
36 *Calendar of State Papers, Domestic, Elizabeth, 1601-1603 with addenda 1547-1565*, August 10 1602.
37 James Neild, *An account of the rise, progress, and present state of the Society for the discharge and relief of persons imprisoned for small debts throughout England and Wales . . .* , John Nichols and Son, London, 3rd ed., 1808.
38 *Calendar of Treasury books and papers, 1735-1738*, March 30 1738.
39 Susan Wright, (Ed.), *Parish Church and People*, Hutchinson, London, 1988.
40 John Lewis, *The History and antiquities as well ecclesiastical as civil, of the Isle of Tenet, in Kent*, 2nd ed., London, 1736.
41 *Calendar of the Patent Rolls, Philip and Mary*, Vol 1, 1553-1554, November 6 1553.
42 Arthur Hussey, *Visitations of the Archdeacon of Canterbury: St John's and St Peter's in Thanet*, Archaeologia Cantiana, 26, 17-50, 1904.
43 Peter Marshall, *Mother Leakey and the Bishop*, Oxford University Press, 2007.
44 Charles Cotton, *The Church of St John the Baptist, Margate*, Archaeologica Cantiana, 25, 64-74, 1902.
45 John Lawson, *Mediaeval education and the Reformation*, Routledge, 2007.
46 *Calendar of State Papers, Domestic, Charles II, 1667-8*, February 12 1675.
47 W. Benham, *A study of an old parish register*, Macmillan's magazine, 43, 190-200, Nov 1880-April 1881.
48 Thomas Staveley, *The history of Churches in England*, London, 1773.
49 *St John's Parish Register, Marriages 1679-1729*, transcription by Barry J. White, http://www.shelwin.com/e/Thanet_Research/pr_marg_x1.pdf.
50 *Calendar of state papers, Domestic, Interregnum, 1651*, August 27 1651.
51 Stephen Palmer, *The nonconformists's memorial; being an account of the ministers who were ejected or silenced after the restoration, particularly by the Act of Uniformity*, Vol 2, London, 1775.
52 John Frederick Archibold and James Paterson, *Archibold's parish officer and Shaw's parish law*, Shaw and Son, 4th ed., 1864.

53 *Calendar of State Papers, Domestic, Charles II, 1664-5*, February 5 1665.
54 Edward Hasted, *The history and topographical survey of the county of Kent*, Vol 10, 1800.
55 John Shirley, *John Lewis of Margate*, Archaeologia Cantiana, 64, 39-56, 1951.
56 Arthur J. Willis, *Church Life in Kent, being church court records of the Canterbury diocese, 1559-1565*, Phillimore, London, 1975.
57 Joseph Strutt, *The sports and pastimes of the people of England*, Methuen and Co., London, 1801.
58 Marjorie Keniston McIntosh, *Controlling Misbehaviour in England, 1370-1600*, Cambridge University Press, 1998.
59 *Letters of Momus from Margate*, 1777.
60 *St James's Chronicle or the British Evening Post*, September 27 1777.
61 *Morning Herald and Daily Advertiser*, September 25 1784.
62 Robin Craig and John Whyman, *Kent and the Sea*, in Alan Armstrong, (Ed.), *The Economy of Kent 1640-1914*, Boydell Press, Woodbridge, 1995.
63 Roy Philp, *The Coast Blockade*, Compton Press, 1999.
64 Norman Scott Brien Gras, *The early English customs system*, Oxford University Press, 1918.
65 Elizabeth Evelynola Hoon, *The organization of the English Customs system 1696-1786*, David and Charles, 1968.
66 Roger Knight, *Britain against Napoleon*, Allen Lane, 2013.
67 *Calendar of the Patent rolls, Edward II, 1324-1327*, January 3 1327
68 *Calendar of Close Rolls, Edward III, 1343-1346*, October 13 1345.
69 *Calendar of Close Rolls, Edward III, 1354-1360*, November 6, 1354.
70 *Calendar of Close Rolls, Edward III, 1354-1360*, November 20, 1358.
71 *Historical Manuscripts Commission, Thirteenth Report*, Appendix, Part IV, The Manuscripts of Rye and Hereford Corporations, February 9 1606.
72 *Historical Manuscripts Commission, Thirteenth Report*, Appendix, Part IV, The Manuscripts of Rye and Hereford Corporations, May 23 1606.
73 B. J. Cigrand, *History of the Crispe family*, Chicago, 1901.
74 *Historical Manuscripts Commission, Thirteenth Report*, Appendix, Part IV, The Manuscripts of Rye and Hereford Corporations, February 5, 1636.
75 *Calendar of State Papers, Domestic, William III*, Vol 6, 1695, December 16 1695.
76 *Calendar of State Papers, Domestic, William III*, Vol 7, 1696, October 17 1696.
77 *Calendar of State Papers, Domestic, William III*, Vol 8, 1697, March 4 1697.
78 William Cambell, (Ed.), *Materials for a history of the region of Henry VII*, Vol 1, Cambridge University Press, 1873.
79 *Calendar of State Papers, Domestic, Interregnum*, Vol 13, 1659-60, January 28 1660.
80 *Calendar of Treasury Books*, Vol 3, 1669-1672, Entry Book, January 9 1672.

81 *Calendar of Treasury Books*, Vol 4, 1672-1675, Entry Book, January 13 1675.
82 *Calendar of Treasury Books*, Vol 5, 1676-1679, Entry Book, June 15 1676.
83 *Calendar of Treasury Books*, Vol 7, 1681-1685, Entry Book, April 10 1682
84 *Calendar of Treasury Books*, Vol 7, 1681-1685, Entry Book, December 22 1683, January 10 1684.
85 *Calendar of Treasury Books*, Vol 8, 1685-1689, Entry Book, March 31, May 30 1685.
86 *Calendar of Treasury Books*, Vol 8, 1685-1689, Entry Book, August 4 1687.
87 *Calendar of Treasury Books*, Vol 8, 1685-1689, Entry Book, October 22 1687.
88 *Calendar of Treasury Books*, Vol 9, 1689-1692, Entry Book, April 9 1690.
89 *Calendar of Treasury Books*, Vol 28, Warrant Books, Sandwich Port, January 28 1714.
90 National Archives, C11/9/29, Spooner v Glover.
91 *Calendar of Treasury Books*, Vol 32, 1718, March 10 1718.
92 *Calendar of Treasury Books and Papers*, Vol 1, 1729-1730, March 5 1729.
93 Rachel Weil, *A plague of informers*, Yale University Press, 2013.
94 *Calendar of State Papers, Domestic, William and Mary, 1690-1691*, October 7 1691; National Archives T1/15/46.
95 *Historical Manuscripts Commission*, Vol 71, Report on the manuscripts of the late Allan George Finch, Vol III, 1691, May 7, 14, 27 1691.
96 *Calendar of Treasury Papers*, Vol 8, 1675-1689, November 20 1685.
97 *Calendar of Treasury Books*, Vol 9, 1689-1692, April 6 1690.
98 *Historical Manuscripts Commission*, Vol 71, Report on the manuscripts of the late Allan George Finch, Vol III, 1691, June 3 1691.
99 *Historical Manuscripts Commission*, Vol 71, Report on the manuscripts of the late Allan George Finch, Vol III, 1691, July 4, 11 1691.
100 *Historical Manuscripts Commission*, Vol 71, Report on the manuscripts of the late Allan George Finch, Vol III, 1691, July 17 1691.
101 *Historical Manuscripts Commission*, Vol 71, Report on the manuscripts of the late Allan George Finch, Vol III, 1691, July 25 1691.
102 *Calendar of Treasury papers*, Vol 1 1556-1696, October 5 1691; National Archives T1/15/41.
103 *Calendar of Treasury Books*, Vol 9, 1689-1692, Out Letters, October 23 1691.
104 *Calendar of State Papers, Domestic, William and Mary*, June 6 1698.
105 *Calendar of Treasury Papers*, Vol 54, 1698, June 12 1698; National Archives T54/51.
106 *Calendar of Treasury Books*, Vol 9, 1689-1692, April 6 1690.
107 National Archives ADM 106/487/315, Complaint of Mr Child 1696.
108 *Calendar of Treasury Papers*, Vol 2, 1697-1702, October 30 1697.
109 *Calendar of State Papers, Domestic, William III*, Vol 8, 1697, March 4 1697.
110 *Calendar of Treasury Books*, Vol 11, 1660-1667, January 30 1697.

111 *Journal of the House of Commons*, Vol 12, 1697-1699, April 16 1698.
112 *British Journal*, December 19 1724.
113 *Calendar of Treasury Books*, Vol 8, 1685-1689, Entry Book, March 13 1688.
114 *Calendar of Treasury Books*, Vol 8, 1685-1689. Entry Book, April 7 1686.
115 *London Journal*, April 27 1723.
116 *Kentish Post*, October 19 1726.
117 *Kentish Post*, August 2 1729.
118 *Old England's Journal*, March 10 1753.
119 J. H. Andrews, *The Thanet Seaports 1650-1750*, in *Essays in Kentish History*, Margaret Roake and John Whyman (Eds.), Frank Cass, London, 1973.
120 *Calendar of Treasury Books and Papers, 1731-1734*, January 12 1732; National Archives T1/278.
121 *Calendar of Treasury Books and Papers, 1731-1734*, March 20 1731.
122 *Calendar of Treasury Books and Papers, 1731-1734*, September 16 1732; National Archives T1/279.
123 *Calendar of Treasury Books and Papers, 1729-1745*, August 16 1733.
124 J. D. Hume, *The Law of the Customs*, 1825.
125 Kent Archives, R/U45 Item No 14, *Pier Accounts 1732 to 1749*.
126 National Archives, CUST 51/25, Customs Books, Letters from Sandwich 1743-1750, January 11 1744.
127 National Archives, CUST 51/25, Customs Books, Letters from Sandwich 1743-1750, January 6 1749.
128 National Archives, CUST 51/25, Customs Books, Letters from Sandwich 1743-1750, December 24, 1743.
129 National Archives, CUST 51/25, Customs Books, Letters from Sandwich 1743-1750, January 6 1749.
130 *Calendar of Treasury Papers*, Vol 48, October 1 1697-November 12 1697, November 9 1697.
131 National Archives, CUST 148/13, Papers of John Collier, Surveyor General of Riding Officers in Kent, 1734-1741 and 1743.
132 National Archives, CUST 51/25, Customs Books, Letters from Sandwich 1743-1750, October 4 1744.
133 National Archives, CUST 51/25, Customs Books, Letters from Sandwich 1743-1750, July 3 1745.
134 United Service Journal, *Coast Blockade Service*, Part 3, pp 26-35, 194-203, and 477-490, 1839.
135 National Archives, CUST 51/25, Customs Books, Letters from Sandwich 1743-1750, December 29 1743.
136 National Archives, CUST 51/25, Customs Books, Letters from Sandwich 1743-1750, April 9 1745.
137 National Archives, CUST 51/25, Customs Books, Letters from Sandwich 1743-1750, April 4 1747

138 National Archives, CUST 51/25, Customs Books, Letters from Sandwich 1743-1750, June 14 1748.

Chapter 6. Riots and Wars

1 Alastair Dunn, *The Great Rising of 1381: the Peasant's Revolt and England's failed revolution*, Tempus, Stroud, 2002.
2 Juliet Barker, *England, arise: the people, the King and the Great Revolt of 1381*, Little, Brown, 2014.
3 W. E. Flaherty, *The Great Rebellion in Kent of 1381, illustrated from the public records*, Archaeologica Cantiana, 3, 65-96, 1860.
4 R. K. I. Quested, *The Isle of Thanet Farming Community*, 2nd ed., 2001.
5 K. M. E. Murray, *The constitutional history of the Cinque Ports*, Manchester University Press, 1935.
6 P. R. Cavill, *The problem of labour and the parliament of 1495*, in Linda Clark, (Ed.), *Of mice and men: image, belief and regulation in late medieval England*, Boydell Press, 2005.
7 Samuel Jeake, *Charters of the Cinque Ports, Two ancient towns and their members*, London, 1728.
8 Sir Nicholas Harris Nicolas, *A History of the Royal Navy*, Vol 1, London, 1847.
9 Craig Lambert, *The contribution of the Cinque Ports to the wars of Edward II and Edward III*, in Richard Gorski, (Ed.), *Roles of the sea in medieval England*, Boydell Press, 2012.
10 *Calendar of Close Rolls, Edward II, 1323-1327*, September 12 1326.
11 Sir Nicholas Harris Nicolas, *A History of the Royal Navy*, Vol 2, London, 1847.
12 *Calendar of Close Rolls, Edward III, 1343-1356*, June 8 1343.
13 *Letters and Papers, Foreign and Domestic, Henry VIII*, Vol 19, Part I, 1544, May 10 1544.
14 David Potter, (Ed.), *Henry VIII and Francis I; the final conflict 1540-47*, Brill, 2011.
15 *Margate Ships 1584*, Margate Public Library, manuscript, 060.198.L 3392.
16 John Lewis, *The History and antiquities ecclesiastical and civil, of the Isle of Tenet, in Kent*, 1st ed., London, 1723.
17 *Acts of the Privy Council of England*, Vol 43, 1627-1628, July 17 1628.
18 *Calendar of Close Rolls, Edward III, 1337-1339*, April 6 1338.
19 *Calendar of Close Rolls, Edward III, 1337-1339*, May 15 1338.
20 *Calendar of Close Rolls, Edward III, 1339-1341*, July 10 1339.
21 *Calendar of the Patent Rolls, Richard II, 1381-1385*, January 18 1385.
22 *Calendar of the Patent Rolls, Richard II, 1381-1385*, January 24 1385.
23 *Calendar of the Patent Rolls, Richard II, 1381-1385*, April 11 1385.

24 *Calendar of Patent Rolls, Richard II, 1385-1389*, April 31, June 18 1386.
25 *Calendar of Close Rolls, Richard II, 1385-1389*, May 14 1386.
26 *Calendar of Patent Rolls, Richard II, 1391-1396*, February 12 1392.
27 *Calendar of the Patent Rolls, Henry IV, 1408-1413*, March 14 1410.
28 *Calendar of the Patent Rolls, Henry VI, 1446-1452*, April 4 1451.
29 *Calendar of the Close Rolls, Edward III, 1360-1364*, June 1 1363.
30 Mike Loades, *The Longbow*, Osprey Publishing, Oxford, 2013.
31 Lindsay Boynton, *The Elizabethan Militia 1558-1638*, Routledge and Kegan Paul, 1967.
32 James Anthony Froude, *History of England, Vol 1, Henry the Eighth*, Longmans, Green, London, new ed., 1893.
33 *Letters and Papers, Foreign and Domestic, Henry VIII*, Vol 20, Part 1, January-July 1545, February 21 1545.
34 *Letters and Papers, Foreign and Domestic, Henry VIII*, Vol 20, Part 1, January-July 1545, May 7 1545.
35 *An Act for the having of horse, armour and weapon*, 4 and 5 Philip and Mary, c2, 1557.
36 *An Act for the taking of musters*, 4 and 5 Philip and Mary, c3, 1557.
37 John S. Nolan, *The militarization of the Elizabethan state*, The Journal of Military History, 58, 391-420, 1994.
38 J. Brigstocke Sheppard, *The Canterbury Marching Watch with the pageant of St Thomas*, Archaeologica Cantiana, 12, 27-47, 1878.
39 Arthur Rowe, *Accounts of the Poor House 1666 to 1716*, Margate Public Library, manuscript, Y060.755.
40 *An Act for the better ordering of the Militia Forces in the several counties of that part of Great Britain called England*, 30 Geo. II, c25, 1757.
41 *Calendar of State Papers, Domestic, Charles II*, Vol 19 March 1677 - February 1678; National Archives SP 44/29 f. 221.
42 *Archaeological notes on Thanet*, Archaeologica Cantiana, 12, 329-419, 1878.
43 Margaret Bolton, *The Isle of Thanet*, Lulu.com, 2006.
44 Paul E. J. Hammer, *Elizabeth's Wars*, Palgrave Macmillan, 2003.
45 Duncan Harrington, *Lost Sandwich muster records and other records*, Kent Archaeological Society, Kent Records, www.kentarchaeology.ac/Records/KRNS4-4.pdf.
46 *Muster Role, St John's, St Peter's, Thanet and Birchington, 11 August 1599*, Kent Family History Society, Fiche No 1114.
47 *Calendar of State Paper Domestic, James I*, Vol 3, 1619-1623, April 1 1619; National Archives SP 14/108 f.14 and SP 14/108 f.15.
48 Viscount Dillon, *Armour Notes*, Archaelogical Journal, 60, 95-136, 1903.
49 *Calendar of State Papers, Domestic, Charles II*, Vol 26, October 1683-April 1684, April 14 1684; National Archives SP 44/69 f.113.

50 John R. Hutchinson, *The Press-gang afloat and ashore*, 1913.
51 J. D. Davies, *Pepy's Navy: ships, men and warfare 1649-89*, Seaforth, 2008.
52 R. G. Marsden, *The Vice-Admirals of the coast*, The English Historical Review, 23, 736-757, 1908.
53 C. S. Knighton and David Loades, *The Navy Treasurer's Quarter Books for 1562-1563*, Ashgate, 2013.
54 J. J. N. McGurk, *A levy of the seamen in the Cinque Ports, 1602*, The Mariner's Mirror, 66, 137-140, 1980.
55 *Calendar of State Papers Domestic, James I, 1619-1623*, April 19 1621.
56 *The life and works of Sir Henry Mainwaring*, Vol 1, p 88, Publications of the Naval Records Society, London, 1920.
57 *Calendar of State Papers, Domestic, James I, 1619-1623*, March 25 1623.
58 *Cobbett's Parliamentary history of England*, Vol 2, p 172, London, 1807.
59 Roger Lockyer, *Buckingham: The life and political career of George Villiers, first Duke of Buckingham*, Longman, 1981.
60 *Calendar of State papers, Domestic, Charles I, 1625-1626*, June 20 1626.
61 *Historical Manuscripts Commission, Thirteenth Report*, Appendix Part IV, The corporation of Rye: 1621-30, April 26, 28 1627.
62 *Calendar of State Papers, Domestic, Charles I*, Vol 2, 1627-1628, June 8 1627.
63 *Acts of the Privy Council of England*, Vol 43, 1627-1628, March 14 1628.
64 Felix Hull (Ed.), *A calendar of the White and Black books of the Cinque Ports, 1432-1955*, p 521, Her Majesty's Stationary Office, 1966.
65 Stephen Pritchard, *The history of Deal, and its neighbourhood*, Deal, 1864.
66 Henry Stephen Chapman, *Deal past and present*, p 52, Reeves and Turner, London, 1890.
67 *Kentish Chronicle*, November 18 1803.
68 Anthony Lee, *Margate Crime and Margate Punishment*, www.margatelocalhistory.co.uk.
69 A. W. Ward, G. W. Prothero and Stanley Leathes, (Eds.), *The Cambridge Modern History, Vol 3, The Wars of Religion*, Cambridge University Press, 1907.
70 *Calendar of Letters and State Papers relating to English Affairs, in the Archives of Simancas*, Vol IV, Elizabeth 1587-1603, September 4 1587.
71 J. N. McGurk, *Armada preparations made in Kent and arrangements made after the defeat*, Archaeologia Cantiana, 85, 71-93, 1977.
72 J. Brigstocke Sheppard, *The Canterbury Marching Watch with the pageant of St Thomas*, Archaeologia Cantiana, 12, 27-47, 1878.
73 Duncan Harrington, *Lost Sandwich muster records and other records*, Kent Archaeological Society, Kent Records, www.kentarchaeology.ac/Records/KRNs4-4.pdf.
74 *Acts of the Privy Council of England*, Vol 15, 1587-1588, August 28 1587.

75 *Acts of the Privy Council of England*, Vol 16, 1588, July 1 1588.
76 *Calendar of State Papers, Domestic, Elizabeth, 1581-1590*, August 9 1588.
77 John Knox Laughton, *State papers relating to the defeat of the Spanish Armada, 1588*, Navy Records Society, 1895.
78 *Calendar of State Papers, Domestic, Elizabeth, 1581-1590*, August 10 1588.
79 *Calendar of State Papers, Domestic, Elizabeth, 1581-1590*, August 22 1588.
80 *Calendar of State Papers, Domestic, Elizabeth, 1595-1597*, June 7 1596.
81 *Acts of the Privy Council of England*, Vol 25, 1595-1596, June 6 1596.
82 *Acts of the Privy Council of England*, Vol 29, 1598-1599, January 14 1599.
83 *Historical Manuscripts Commission, Fifteenth Report*, Appendix, Part V, The manuscripts of F. J. Savile Foljambe, London, 1897.
84 *Calendar of State Papers, Domestic, Charles I*, Vol 3, March 1628-June 1629, August 23 1628; National Archives, SP 16/113 f. 101.
85 W. D. Belcher, *Kentish Brasses collected by W. D. Belcher*, Vol 1, Sprague & Co., London, 1888.
86 *Archaeologia Or Miscellaneous Tracts Relating to Antiquity*, Vol 12, p 268, 1796.
87 *Calendar of Letters and State Papers relating to English Affairs, in the Archives of Simancas*, Vol 2, Elizabeth 1568-1579, November 8 1569.
88 *Calendar of Letters and State Papers relating to English Affairs, in the Archives of Simancas*, Vol 2, Elizabeth 1568-1579, September 3 1570.
89 *Calendar of State Papers Relating To English Affairs in the Archives of Venice*, Vol 8, 1581-1591, September 23 1588.
90 *Acts of the Privy Council of England*, Vol 6, 1556-1558, March 16 1558.
91 David Childs, *Tudor sea power*, Seaforth Publishing, 2009
92 *Calendar of State Papers, Domestic, Charles I*, Vol 1, March 1625-December 1626, September 10 1625; National Archives SP 16/6 f.69.
93 *Acts of the Privy Council of England*, Vol 40, 1625-1626, October 30 1625.
94 *Acts of the Privy Council of England*, Vol 42, 1627, March 12 1627.
95 *Calendar of State Papers, Domestic, Charles I*, Vol 2, 1627-1628, February, March 1627.
96 *Acts of the Privy Council of England*, Vol 42, 1627, November 4 1627.
97 *Calendar of State Papers, Domestic, Charles I*, Vol 14, April-September 1639, September 26 1639.
98 John Evelyn, *Diary and Correspondence of John Evelyn*, Henry Colburn, London, 1854.
99 National Archives, PC 1/1/153 and PC 1/1/221, *Fort petition and reply*, 5 August 1702 and 3 November 1702.
100 *Calendar of State Papers, Domestic, William and Mary*, Vol 1, March 24 1690.
101 *Calendar of State Papers, Domestic, William and Mary*, Vol 1, June 23 1693.
102 *Observator*, March 25 1704.
103 D. M. Loades, *The making of the Elizabethan navy*, 1540-1590, Boydell Press, 2009.

104 Gary M. Anderson and Adam Gifford, *Privateering and the private production of naval power*, Cato Journal, 11, 99-122, 1991.

105 Kenneth R. Andrews, *The economic aspects of Elizabethan privateering*, Bulletin of the Institute of Historical Research, 25, 84, 1952.

106 *Calendar of the Patent Rolls, Edward II, 1313-1317*, November 2 1315, September 30 1316

107 N. G. Brett-James, *Pirates off Margate in 1315*, Transactions of the London and Middlesex Archaeological Society, Vol 90 (new series), 35- 41, 1948.

108 *Calendar of the Patent Rolls, Edward II, 1313-1317*, September 30 1316.

109 *Calendar of Close Rolls, Edward II, 1313-1318*, June 11, August 13, September 10 1318, January 16 1319, August 28 1320.

110 *Calendar of Close Rolls, Edward II, 1313-1318*, November 2 1315.

111 T. H. Lloyd, *The English Wool Trade in the Middle Ages*, Cambridge University Press, 1977.

112 Bryan D. Dick, *Framing Piracy: restitution at sea in the later Middle Ages*, PhD thesis, University of Glasgow, 2010.

113 *Calendar of Inquisitions Miscellaneous (Chancery)*, Vol 2, 26 March 1317.

114 *Calendar of Close Rolls, Edward II*, 1313-1318, February 1 1318

115 *Calendar of Close Rolls, Edward II*, 1318-1323, December 7 1319.

116 *Calendar of Close Rolls, Edward II*, 1315-1318, November 15 1317.

117 *Calendar of Inquisitions Miscellaneous (Chancery)*, Vol 2, 8 June 1319.

118 *Calendar of Close Rolls, Edward II, 1318-1323*, August 21 1320.

119 *Calendar of Close Rolls, Edward II, 1313-1318*, September 13 1317.

120 *Letters and Papers, Foreign and Domestic, Henry VIII*, Vol 12, Part 1, 1537, March 24 1537.

121 *Calendar of State Papers, Domestic, Interregnum, 1649-1650*, August 20, 1649.

122 *Calendar of State Papers, Domestic, Interregnum, 1649-1650*, August 22, 1649.

123 *Calendar of State Papers, Domestic, Interregnum, 1649-1650*, November 5, 1649.

124 *St John the Baptist, Margate, Parish Registers*, Kent Family History Society, CD27.

125 *Calendar of State papers, Domestic, Interregnum, 1649-1650*, 9 and 19 November, 18 December 1649.

126 *Calendar of State papers, Domestic, Interregnum, 1649-1650*, November 13, 1649.

127 Granville Pen, *Memorials of the professional life and times of Sir William Penn, Knt. Admiral and General of the Fleet during the Interregnum*, James Duncan, London, 1833.

128 *Journal of the House of Commons*, Vol 7, 1651-1660, 30 October 1651.

129 *Calendar of State Papers, Domestic, Interregnum*, Vol 4, November 1651- November 1652, March 12, October 20 1652.

130 *Calendar of the Patent Rolls, Edward II, 1321-1324*, March 1 1323.
131 *Calendar of the Patent Rolls, Henry IV*, Vol 2, 1401-1405, July 10 1404.
132 *Calendar of Close Rolls, Edward III*, 1339-1341, February 3, April 28 1340.
133 *Calendar of State Papers, Spain*, Vol 10, 1550-1552, January 21 1551, January 14 1552.
134 *Acts of the Privy Council of England*, Vol 3, 1550-1552, December 28 1551, February 1, 11, 1552.
135 Robyn Adams, *All at sea; an accusation of piracy against William Herle in 1565*, http://discovery.ucl.ac.uk/1367031/1/Adams.pdf.
136 *Acts of the Privy Council of England*, Vol 7, 1558-1570, 1565.
137 National Archives, HCA 1/36/393, Examination of Pirates.
138 National Archives, SP 15/12/76, *William Herle's Diary*; www.livesandletters.ac.uk, transcript HRL/002/PDF/219.
139 *Acts of the Privy Council of England*, Vol 7, 1558-1570, June 11 1570.
140 *Acts of the Privy Council of England*, Vol 10, 1577-1578, November 10 1578.
141 *Acts of the Privy Council of England*, Vol 11, 1578-1580, September 14 1579.
142 *Acts of the Privy Council of England*, Vol 11, 1578-1580, 1579.
143 J. R. Jones, *The Anglo-Dutch Wars of the Seventeenth Century*, Longman, London, 1996.
144 Samuel Rawson Gardiner and C. T. Atkinson, *Letters and papers relating to the first Dutch War 1652-1654*, Navy Records Society, 1906.
145 *Calendar of State Papers, Domestic, Charles II*, Vol 6, August 1666-March 1667, November 6 1666.
146 *Calendar of State Papers, Domestic, Charles II*, Vol 7, April-October 1667, May 10 1667.
147 *Calendar of State Papers, Domestic, Charles II*, Vol 13, May-September 1672, July 24 1672.
148 *The diary of Samuel Pepys*, http://www.pepysdiary.com/diary/1665/10.
149 *Calendar of State Papers, Domestic, Charles II*, Vol 5, October 1665-July 1666, October 15 1665.
150 *Calendar of State Papers, Domestic, Charles II*, Vol 5, October 1665-July 1666, July 1 1666.
151 *Calendar of State Papers, Domestic, Charles II*, Vol 5, October 1665-July 1666, July 10 1666.
152 *Calendar of State Papers, Domestic, Charles II*, Vol 5, October 1665-July 1666, July 27 1666.
153 *Calendar of State Papers, Domestic, Charles II*, Vol 5, October 1665-July 1666, August 31 1666.
154 *Calendar of State Papers, Domestic, Charles II*, Vol 6, August 1666-March 1667, August 29 1666.

155 *Calendar of State Papers, Domestic, Charles II*, Vol 7, April-October 1667, April 8 1667.
156 *Calendar of State Papers, Domestic, Charles II*, Vol 7, April-October 1667, May 17 1667.
157 *Calendar of State Papers, Domestic, Charles II*, Vol 7, April-October 1667, May 21 1667.
158 *Calendar of State Papers, Domestic, Charles II*, Vol 7, April-October 1667, May 31 1667.
159 *Calendar of State Papers, Domestic, Charles II*, Vol 7, April 1667-October 1667, June 25 1667.
160 *Calendar of State Papers, Domestic, Charles II*, Vol 7, April 1667-October 1667, July 5 1667.
161 *Calendar of State Papers, Domestic, Charles II*, Vol 7, April-October 1667, September 3 1667.
162 *Calendar of State Papers, Domestic, Charles II*, Vol 7, April-October 1667, September 3 1667.
163 *Calendar of State Papers, Domestic, Charles II*, Vol 12, December 1671-May 1672, May 11 1672.
164 *Calendar of State Papers, Domestic, Charles II*, Vol 12, December 1671-May 1672, May 13 1672.
165 *Calendar of State Papers, Domestic, Charles II*, Vol 12, December 1671-May 1672, May 14 1672.
166 *Calendar of State Papers, Domestic, Charles II*, Vol 12, December 1671-May 1672, May 16 1672.
167 *Calendar of State Papers, Domestic, Charles II*, Vol 13, May-September 1672, June 10 1672.
168 *Calendar of State Papers, Domestic, Charles II*, Vol 6, August 1666-March 1667, October 1666.
169 J. J. Keevil, *Medicine and the Navy*, Vol 2, E & S Livingstone, 1958
170 *Calendar of State Papers, Domestic, Charles II*, Vol 12, December 1671-May 1672, March 18 1672.
171 *Calendar of State Papers, Domestic, Charles II*, Vol 12, December 1671-May 1672, March 18 1672,
172 *Calendar of State Papers, Domestic, Charles II*, Vol 13, May-September 1672, September 2 1672.
173 Edward White, *Miscellaneous extracts relating to the Isle of Thanet*, Margate Public Library, manuscript.
174 *Calendar of Treasury Papers*, Vol 1, June 28 1693.
175 *Calendar of Treasury Papers*, Vol 1, September 8 1693.

176 *Calendar of Treasury Papers*, Vol 2, October 16 1700; National Archives T1/70/55.
177 http://en.wikipedia.org/wiki/Edmund_Dummer_(naval_engineer).
178 *Calendar of the Manuscripts of the Marquis of Salisbury*, Part 9, p 259.
179 John A. Lynn, *The Wars of Louis XIV 1667-1714*, Routledge, 2013.
180 National Archives, HCA 1/38/18, *Examination of Pirates*.

The Future

1 William Camden, *Britain, or, a Chorographicall Description of the most flourishing Kingdomes, England, Scotland, and Ireland Brittania*, 1st ed., tr. by Philemon Holland, London, 1610.
2 A. L. Beier and R. Finlay, *The Making of the Metropolis, London 1500-1700*, London, 1986.
3 *A Description of the Isle of Thanet and particularly of the Town of Margate*, Printed for J. Newbery and W. Bristow, London, 1763.
4 John Lewis, *The History and antiquities ecclesiastical and civil, of the Isle of Tenet, in Kent*, 1st ed., London, 1723.
5 Mr Senex, *A new general atlas containing a geographical and historical account of all the empires, kingdoms, and other dominions of the world*, 1721.
6 James Joel Cartwright (Ed.), *The travels through England of Dr Richard Pococke*, Cambden Society, Vol 2, p 86, 1889.
7 Daniel Defoe, *The complete English tradesman. In familiar letters: Directing him in the several parts and progressions of trade*, 2nd ed., London, 1732.
8 Arthur Rowe, *Notes on the History of Margate*, Margate Public Library, manuscript.
9 Z. Cozens, *A Tour through the Isle of Thanet*, J. Nichols, London, 1793.
10 A. B. Granville, *The Spas of England and Principal Sea-Bathing Places*, 1841.
11 Celia Fiennes, *Through England on a Side Saddle in the Time of William and Mary*, Ed. Mrs Griffiths, 1888.
12 James Walvin, *Beside the Seaside*, Allen Lane, 1978.
13 Philomaris, *Some peculiar advantages which Margate pre-eminently enjoys, for the benefit of bathing in the sea*, The Gentleman's Magazine, 41, 166-168, 1777.
14 Edward Hasted, *The history and topographical survey of the County of Kent*, Vol 10, 2nd ed., Canterbury, 1800.

Index

Admiralty and Cinque-Ports Committee, 83, 86
Admiralty Committee, 86, 87, 88, 313
Alkali Row, 15, 140
almshouses, 173, 178, 181–82
amputation, 195
anchors, 113, 115, 256
Anglo-Dutch war, 42, 149, 321–26
apothecaries, 146, 147, 152, 159, 196
apprenticeships, 167, 168, 197, 198
Archdeacon, 155, 156, 171, 221–26, 238
Archdeacon's Court, 156, 171, 221, 231, 236-40
archers, 278, 280, 282
Armada, 297
Armstrong, William, 27, 54, 55
Assizes, Kent, 207
attorney, 38, 39, 53, 144, 145, 198

Bailiff of Margate, 315, 317
Baker, Elizabeth, 36–39
Baker, John, 36–39, 152, 179, 233, 258
Baker, Stephen, 36, 39, 114, 190, 196, 202
bands, trained, 285–88, 323
Banks, John, 229, 232, 234
Bankside, 15, 46
Baptists, 45
Barber, John, 269
Barber, Thomas, 11, 46, 197
barbers, 144, 145, 196, 198
bathing, 10, 11, 50
Baylif of Margate, 17, 317
beer, 110, 132, 135, 173, 183, 191, 197
  at funerals, 191

bellman. *See* town crier
Bennet, Stephen, 162
Bing, Edward, 186, 231–32
Birch, William, 70
Birchington, 8, 123, 205, 209, 270
  customs, 268
  lock-up, 215
  mill, 19
  muster, 285, 287
  parish, 1, 5
  road, 4, 64
  workhouse, 182
Black Horse Inn, 11, 46
blacksmiths, 144, 145, 151, 215
Boreman, Thomas, 136
Bowling Green, 31–32, 52, 55
brewers, 23, 27, 35, 135, 136, 143, 144, 151
brewhouse, 23, 27–28, 34, 36–39, 136
Broadstairs, 107, 116, 140, 268, 269, 291
Broad Street, 3, 53
Brooke, Capt., 99, 102, 121
Brooks, The, 4, 5, 64
Brooman, John, 95, 154, 163, 189
Buckingham, First Duke of, 291–93, 302
Buller's Charity, 179–81
Buller's Court, 24, 25, 173
Buller's square, 179
Buller's yard, 172–73, 179, 181
Bull's Head Inn, 52, 53, 127
burials, 9, 155, 191-94, 220, 221, 226, 233, 238
Bushell, John, 55, 89
Butler, Daniel, 145, 198

Cade, Jack, 274
cage, 215
Calais, 108–10, 255, 262, 309–10
  siege of, 276
Canterbury, 27, 65, 182, 241, 246, 278, 282, 285
  comedians, 55
  Flying-Stage Coach, 58
  inns and stables, 45, 50, 58
  postal service, 57, 68
  road, 15–16, 56, 57, 58, 282
  Wat Tyler, 271–74
Carpenter, Francis, 146, 241
carriages, 60, 61, 65, 66
Carter, William, 253–55
Chambers, George, 151, 152
charity-houses, 178, 181
Checoney, Dr, 152–53
Cherchedowne, 20
Chewney, Nicholas, 151, 152–53, 194
Child, Thomas, 252-62
children
  bastard, 198–99
  poor, 156, 184
chirurgeons, 22, 143, 144-54, 194
Church hill, 6, 20, 21, 23, 25, 142, 143
church vestry, 96, 219
churchwardens, 186, 222, 234, 235
  licensing, 146, 156, 241
  literate, 127, 155
  parish cess, 220, 221
  poor relief, 174, 176, 182, 187, 329
  sequestration, 236, 238
  visitation reports, 155, 156, 170–72, 226, 231, 238–41
Cinque Ports, 203-10, 274, 275
Clarendon Code, 224, 225
Claybrook, Paul, 74, 139, 287
Claybrooke, family, 124, 125, 287
coach, 50, 57-60, 65, 120, 121
coach houses, 29, 40, 41, 53
coal, 70, 93, 94, 266, 324
  import of, 105, 116
  for the poor, 172, 184, 190
coast waiters, 243, 245

Cobb, Francis, 27–29, 34, 38-41, 51, 52, 136, 195
Cobb, William, 189
Cobb's Brewery, 23, 26, 27, 30
Cobham, Lord, 217, 291, 297-300, 318, 320, 321, 329
Cock, William, 304, 305
cocquet, 244, 245, 264, 265
Cold Harbour, 288
Coleman, Roger, 239
Collector, 45, 115, 121, 243, 257, 264, 266
Collier, John, 268, 269
Comptroller, 243, 257, 264, 266
Constable, High, 210
constables, petty. *See* parish constables
Constant, Edward, 36, 47, 183
Constant, Ralph, 27, 98, 140
conventicle house, 44, 225
Coppin, James, 313, 314
Coppin, William, 83
Coppyn, John, 217, 218
coquet. *See* cocquet
corn, 107–8, 110, 113, 114, 265, 266
  factors, 132, 133
  to London, 102, 105, 141, 293
Court, Nash, 19, 287
Court House, 18
Covells Row, 26
Cowell, Benjamin, 22–23, 186
Cowper, Gervase, 267, 268, 269–70
Crampe, John, 236
Creed, Thomas, 231, 240
creek, 3, 5, 6, 71-74, 110, 242, 244, 264, 266, 299
Crispe, Henry, 79-83, 86, 156, 249
Culmer, Henry, 45
Culmer, Mary, 151, 152
Customer, 42, 243, 244, 251
Customs, 110, 112, 148, 242–45, 251–53, 266
  Commissioners of, 42, 214, 251, 256, 259, 263–66
  officers, 243–46, 262, 264, 266, 270, 320
  smack, 42, 251–52

INDEX

Dandelyon, 6, 142, 143
Dane, Palmer, 6
Dane Court, 17, 18
Defoe, Daniel, 1, 132, 133, 157
Dene, manor of, 17, 18, 19, 20
Deputy, Margate, 96, 210–12, 301, 303
Deputy Pier Wardens, 96, 97, 105
Diggs, Francis, 255, 256, 258
diocesan licentiate, 147–48, 151–54
Dixon, Francis, 196–98
Dixon's Court, 25
Doctors. *See* chirurgeon
Doncaster, Benjamin, 28
dove-house, 20, 227
Dover
   Castle, 108, 116, 214, 280, 281
   lieutenant of, 248, 299
   corporate members of, 205
   freemen of, 210, 212
   gaol, 212–14
   harbour, 99, 100
   limb of, 8
   port of, 205, 206, 208, 247, 293
   Road, 56–68
   town of, 209, 214
drapers, 144, 145, 159–63, 172, 173, 189
Duke of Buckingham, 292, 302
Duke's Head, 52
Dunkirk, 111, 253–56, 259, 313, 314
Dutch men-of-war, 68, 321–25

Evelyn, John, 130, 134, 149, 304, 326
Expenditor, 80–88

farmers, 101, 124, 127–36, 144, 173, 184, 200
fisherman, 17, 117, 118, 128, 137, 141, 313, 323
fishing, 4, 107, 118, 130
   decline of, 118, 137, 138, 141
Five Bells, 13, 25, 143
Flanders, 56, 109, 251, 277, 310–15, 329–30
Flanders, Count of, 310, 312, 313
Fleet, Thomas, 262–63

Foley House, 29
Fort, The, 12, 13, 301–6, 321, 324–25
Fort Green, 33, 35, 38, 39
Fort Hill, 3, 12
fortifications, 301, 302, 329
Fort Road, 26, 34
Fountain Inn, 26, 34, 40, 52-54
Fountain Lane, 26–27, 33, 34, 41
foying, 115, 140
Friend, George, 27, 37–39, 158
Frog house, 178, 179
funerals, 162, 191–93

Garlinge, 5, 6, 142, 143
George Inn, 53
Glasshouse, 15
glebe land, 20, 220, 236, 237
Glover, John, 27, 33–36, 41–44, 225, 251–52, 324
Glover, Susannah, 35, 36, 122
Goatham, Edward, 37, 38, 39
Goatham, William, 35
Goldsmith, Franklin, 189
Goody, meaning of, 177
Gore, John, 33, 162
Gore, Robert, 189
Grant, Martha, 126, 127
Grant, Thomas, 30, 89, 97, 126
Gravesend, 42, 47, 57–58, 60, 68, 118, 253, 326, 328
Greedier, Stephen, 158
grocers, 126, 144, 158–60
gunner, 93, 304, 305–6

Hammond, George, 143, 153, 154, 194
Hannaker, James, 83
harbour
   dues, 98, 103, 104
   old, 5, 12, 71, 88
   regulations, 93-5
   trade of, 105-122
Harman, Martha, 35
Hart, Paul, 48, 49, 69, 99, 190, 253, 256, 262
Hartsdown, 56, 126

head ports, 203–5, 242–45
hedgehogs, 186–87
Hemmings, John, 199
herrings, 114, 116, 128, 137, 265
  red, 114, 116
High Street, 15, 17, 22–26, 136, 137
Hodges, John, 26
Hogbin, Valentine, 96, 113
Hough, Abraham, 252, 254–59
hoymen, 144, 173, 260
hoys, 67, 69, 105–7, 112, 140, 141, 265, 277
Huffam, Thomas, 138, 143
Humber's Mill, 19

inns, 25, 45–55, 57, 66, 133, 255

Jarvis, Edward, 65, 143, 152–53, 194, 195
Jarvis, William, 23, 136, 183
Jenkinson, Robert, 155, 156, 226
jetties, 15, 72, 74, 99, 104
Jewell, Joseph, 126, 158
Jewell, Valentine, 49, 95, 126, 158
  junior, 46, 47, 49, 50, 126, 159, 258
Jolly Sailor, 52, 54
Jurats of Dover, 86, 173, 175, 209–10, 216, 294
Justices of the Peace, 8, 173, 203, 209–10

kelp ash, 15, 140
Kentish Post, 9, 66, 201
King George's Stairs, 13
King's Head, 50, 54
King's highway, 15–16, 20, 27
King Street, 3, 15, 27, 29, 33, 34, 136
King's warehouse, 13, 263, 266
King's watch house, 266
Knatchbull, Sir Edward, 101, 102

Ladd, William, 52, 115
Laming, Elizabeth, 51, 126, 198
Laming, John, 30, 74, 102, 113, 125, 188
Laming, Richard, 33, 114, 174, 185, 197, 253
Laming, Roger, 52, 113, 125–27, 143, 170, 259–61

Laming, William, 161, 162, 198
Land Guard, 245–46
land waiters, 243, 245, 252
Langley, Richard, 44, 69, 147, 158, 211
Leese, Ludovic, 151, 152
Lethered, John, 253–62
Lewis, John, 4, 12, 237, 238
lime kilns, 2, 21–23
Lister, John, 140, 190, 193
Lithered. *See* Lethered, John
lock up. *See* cage
Lombard Street, 32–33
Lord High Admiral, 208, 289, 291, 292, 294
Lord Warden of the Cinque Ports, 48, 72, 138, 207, 208, 216, 218, 248, 289–94
Love Lane, 32, 52, 54
Lucas Dane, 5, 6, 18, 29, 31, 129

malt houses, 17, 23, 27, 133, 136–37
malting, 132, 133, 144
maltsters, 25, 27, 132, 136, 143, 173, 181
Mansion House, 33–41, 122, 252
Margate
  ale, 134, 135
    See also Northdown ale
  excise division, 45–46
  geography, 1
  name, 6
  population, 8–10
Market Place, 3, 31–32, 55, 215
Market Street, 3, 15, 52, 53
masons, 124, 144, 145, 197, 201, 280
Medmenham, William, 272, 273
mercers, 159–61, 163
midwife, 194, 229
Mill Lane, 19, 22, 158
Mill Lane Mill, 19, 22, 127, 143
Minster, 1, 64, 125, 158
Morris, Roger, 288
muskets, 286–87, 304
muster, 284-88
  master, 285
  role, 9, 286, 287

Nayland Rock, 308
Northdown ale, 1, 134–35, 149
North Foreland, 12, 43, 47, 68, 102, 116, 319, 323–25
Norwood, Alexander, 17–19, 21, 26, 125, 317
Norwood, John, 196–97
Norwood, Joseph, 220, 238
Norwood, Manasses, 18, 19, 287
Norwood, Nicholas, 179, 185
Norwood, Richard, 17, 19, 21, 22
Norwood, William, 17, 95, 97, 125, 147, 154
Norwood family, 17–21
Nottingham, Earl of, 253–57

Old Crown, 32, 52, 54
Old Kings Arms, 32, 52
Old White Hart, 50, 51
One Bell, 25
Omer, James, 126–27
Omer, Roger, 95–97, 126–27, 304, 305
ordnance, for Margate, 299, 301, 305, 306, 323
Overing, John, 235–37
overseers of the poor, 66, 67, 152, 156, 165–76
  beer, 53, 55, 191
  offices, 25
  payments by, 142, 165, 173–215
Oxenden, Sir James, 78, 79

Pain, Matthew, 213
Pamflett, Daniel, 114, 126, 184, 199
Pannell, Martha, 51
Pannell, Roger, 22
Parade, The, 3, 15, 46, 51
parish
  clerk, 67, 162, 191, 199, 229, 234, 240
  constables, 201, 210, 211
  house, 178, 182, 185
  land, 166
  meetings, 13, 182
Parker, Francis, 220, 235
Parker, William, 27, 239, 287

paultring, 215-18
paupers, 8, 166, 167, 169, 182, 189
Payne, William, 96, 130
Peasants' Revolt, 271-74
pensions, 167, 177, 197
Petken, Henry, 23, 28, 121, 183, 191, 196, 266
Petken, William, 23, 25, 27, 28, 182
Petkin, Henry, 143, 154, 266
Petkin, William, 156
Pettit, Valentine, 74, 75, 139, 207, 221, 229, 287
Pier, 12, 13, 71–122
  accounts, 66, 89, 90, 95, 114, 115, 133, 266
  droits, 72, 101, 102–4
  Green, 32
  rebuilding, 72, 74, 77, 89–92, 127
  Wardens, 17, 72, 75, 82, 90, 94-97, 101-4
    accounts of, 113, 127
    election of, 96, 97
piracy, 307–21
Pish houses, 178, 181
playhouse, 40
Pond, Abraham, 70
Poole, Ann, 199–200
poor house, 156, 178, 180–85, 189, 190
Poor Laws, 164–66, 174, 184
poor rate, 137, 142, 143, 165, 168, 219
Posthouse, 47, 48, 49, 50, 66, 162
postmasters, 42, 44, 47, 67–69, 251, 252, 256
post office, 67–69
press gangs, 289, 296
Prince, John, 22, 135, 184
prison. See Dover, gaol
Pritchard, John, 300
privateers, 305, 307–22
public houses. See inns
Puddle Dock, 32, 37
Pudner, Humphrey, 211
Pump Lane, 33, 34, 41, 46

Queen's Arms, 32, 52–53

Quex, 19, 79, 82, 119, 156

Ramsgate, 158, 182, 205, 244, 269, 291, 313, 329
 inns, 45, 46
 population of, 10
 riding officers, 268
 ships exempted, 100
 vessels, 106, 107, 116
 Wat Tyler, 272
Ricards, William, 47, 48, 49
riding officers, 243, 245, 261, 267–68
roads, 4, 6, 15–17, 56–65, 68, 219
Rose, Daniel, 33, 37, 38, 39
Rose and Crown, 55
Rowe, Arthur, 3, 22, 143
Royal Charter, 203, 204–5

Sacket's Boarding House, 40
salt duties, 116
Sandford, Henry, 74, 172
Sandwich
 collector of, 115, 256, 264
 port of, 279
Sarre, 4, 15, 62–64, 71–72, 279
Saunders, Joseph, 261–62
Savage, Arnald, 280, 281
Savage, John, 30, 46, 69, 160, 239
Savage, Mary, 46, 69
Savage, William, 30, 158, 160
schooling, 155, 156, 184, 224, 239
scot (tax), 75–85, 283
sea defences, 72–76, 84
seamen, 140, 255, 292, 294, 328
searcher, 42, 148, 151, 243-45, 251–54, 260, 263, 267, 269, 319
Select Company, 285, 287
sequestration, 236–38
Sewers, Commissioners of, 63, 73–76, 80, 87, 88
shoemakers, 124, 144, 145, 185, 186, 189, 196, 198
shops, 94, 136, 144, 153, 157–62, 189
Silk, Matthew, 21–22
Slater, George, 154, 194, 195

slaughter house, 158
Smith, John, doctor, 22, 134, 148–52, 323, 325
Smith, John, Expenditor, 76–134
Smith, Robert, 98, 138, 143, 156
Smith, Thomas, 40, 147–48, 189
smuggling, 140, 141, 205, 215, 242, 245, 253–70
Southampton, 275, 278, 309, 312
sparrows heads, 186
spectacles, 194
Sprackling, Adam, 211–12
Sprackling, Henry, 138
Sprackling, Luke, 319, 320
stabling, 40, 45, 46, 50, 66
Stephens, Thomas, 235–36
St John's church, 2, 3, 5, 6, 12, 13, 172, 219, 220–32
Stoacks, John, 114, 116
stocks, 214, 215
Stone, James, 183, 196
Stone, William, 228, 229
St Peter's, 1, 5, 8, 101, 209, 285, 287, 290, 302
surgeon, 146–54, 241, 270
Swinford, Stephen, 33, 114, 115, 127

Taddy, James, 31
Thornden, John, 198, 199
tide surveyor, 245, 253, 267, 269
tokens, trade, 158
Tomlin, Cornelius, 173, 174
Tomlin, Jeffrey, 34, 35
town crier, 69, 70, 94, 193
Trapham's Lane, 27, 30
Trapps, Michael, 50, 161, 162, 192, 199-201
Tudor House, 30, 160
Turner, Capt. David, 29
Turner, David, 19, 153
Turner, John, 46, 96, 98, 181
turnpikes, 57, 61, 65
Tyler, Wat, 271–74

Underdown, Thomas, 92, 181

undertakers, 92–93, 95

Venetian ships, 110
vestry, 13, 96–97, 173, 190, 199, 219, 229
vicarage, 13, 20, 220, 225–27
Vicarage Green, 235
Violett, Alexander, 174, 221, 240, 241

waggons, 58–60, 286, 287
waiter and searcher, 151, 252, 260, 263, 267, 269
Wallis, Henry, 154, 194, 195
Ward, Richard, 37, 38
warehouses, 13, 15, 98, 269
Warwick, Earl of, 76, 77, 82
watch-houses, 12, 215, 303
water guard, 245, 267
Watkins, John, 253–59

Watts, John, 151, 152, 154
wax-houses, 13, 223
wenches, 214–15
Westbrook, 4, 5, 6, 142
Westbrook Mill, 4, 64
wheat, 108–10, 114, 131, 132, 133, 239
Wheatley, Thomas, 86, 154, 194, 195
Wheatsheaf Inn, 54, 55
White Hart, 46–51, 56, 122, 143, 202
White Hart and Star, 50, 51
Whitehead, Roger, 99, 138
Williamson, Sir Joseph, 43, 44, 116, 134, 149, 150, 225, 237, 322, 324
windmill, 2, 3, 18, 19, 23, 127, 239
workhouse, 178–85, 189
Wren, Sir Christopher, 92

Zouch, Lord, 139, 292

Printed in Great Britain
by Amazon.co.uk, Ltd.,
Marston Gate.